Linguine with Sautéed Shrimp and
Coconut-Lime Sauce, page 129

Lemon-Poppy Seed Cake,
page 108

Tabbouleh Cobb Salad,
page 193

Peppered Flank Steak with Chive-
Buttermilk Mashers, page 152

food lovers
weight loss
COOKBOOK

compiled and edited by
Carolyn Land, M.S., R.D.

from the editors of health

Be sure to check with your health-care provider
before making any changes in your diet.

Oxmoor House, Inc.
Editor-in-Chief: Nancy Fitzpatrick Wyatt
Executive Editor: Katherine M. Eakin
Art Director: Cynthia R. Cooper
Copy Chief: Catherine Ritter Scholl

Food Lovers Weight Loss Cookbook
Editor: Carolyn Land, M.S., R.D, L.D.
Copy Editor: Jacqueline B. Giovanelli
Editorial Assistant: McCharen Pratt
Director, Test Kitchens: Elizabeth Tyler Luckett
Assistant Director, Test Kitchens: Julie Christopher
Recipe Editor: Gayle Hays Sadler
Test Kitchens Staff: Kristi Carter, Nicole Faber,
    Jan A. Smith, Elise Weis, Kelly Wilton
Publishing Systems Administrator: Rick Tucker
Director, Production and Distribution: Phillip Lee
Books Production Manager: Greg Amason
Production Coordinator: Leslie Johnson
Production Assistant: Faye Porter Bonner

Contributors:
Designer: Rita Yerby
Indexer: Mary Ann Laurens
Editorial Intern: Terri Laschober
Test Kitchens Intern: Mary Beth Brookby

Health
Vice President/ Editor: Doug Crichton
Executive Editor: Lisa Delaney
Design Director: Paul Carstensen
Managing Editor: Candace H. Schlosser
Senior Editors: Nichele Hoskins (*Fitness*), Susie Quick
    (*Food/Nutrition*), Abigail M. Walch
Beauty and Fashion Editor: Colleen Sullivan
Associate Editors: Laurie Herr, Leah Wyar (*Beauty/
    Fashion*)
Editorial Coordinator: Christine O'Connell
Assistant Editors: Molly Campbell (*Beauty/ Fashion*),
    Su Reid, Sara Jane Weeks (*Food/ Nutrition*)
Art Director: Amy Heise
Graphic Designers: Christen Colvert, Soo Yeon Hong
Photo Coordinator: Angie Wilson Kelly
Assistant Photo Coordinator: Jeanne Dozier Clayton
Copy Chief: John R. Halphen
Production Manager: Faustina S. Williams
Research Editors: Martha Yielding Scribner,
    Eric Steinmehl
Production Editor: Julie Fricke Collins
Assistant Copy Editor: Julie H. Bosché
Office Manager: Stephanie Wolford
Editorial Assistant: Amanda Storey
Health.com Editor: Jerry Gulley II
Health.com Managing Editor: Vanessa Rush
Test Kitchens Director: Vanessa Taylor Johnson
Test Kitchens Staff: Sam Brannock, Kathryn Conrad,
    M. Kathleen Kanen, Kellie Gerber Kelley, John
    Kirkpatrick, Tiffany Vickers, Mike Wilson

To order additional publications, call
1-800-765-6400.

For more books to enrich your life, visit
oxmoorhouse.com

Cover: Grilled Chicken and Wheat Berry Salad
(page 196)

contents

page **148**

page **210**

page **112**

welcome

Dear Friend,

I don't need to scare you into losing weight with statistics about how overweight Americans are, or how bad that extra weight is for you. By picking up this book you've taken an important step toward achieving a healthy weight. And for that I congratulate you.

It's an incredibly smart step, too, because here you'll find more than just healthy (and delicious) recipes and menus. This is a lifestyle plan whose easy-to-follow advice will help you make healthy living a habit, and that will resonate with you long after you've reached your ideal weight.

Reaching a healthy weight has never been more important than it is today. The U.S. Surgeon General now attributes more than 300,000 deaths per year to overweight and obesity, and estimates that the public-health costs are nearly $117 billion a year. He warns, in fact, that excess weight may soon cause as much preventable disease and death as smoking.

There's plenty of hope, however, and you'll find it here in these pages. And if you need any extra impetus, consider new research indicating that losing weight and exercising may help reprogram your brain such that keeping off lost pounds gets easier over time, says Arthur Campfield, a Colorado State University researcher.

So again, congratulations. I hope you find this book as inspirational as it is helpful, and that it motivates you to seek a a happier, healthier life.

Warmly,

Doug Crichton

Vice President/Editor, *Health* magazine

the inside scoop

I always knew there had to be a better way to lose weight. Simply living on tasteless rice cakes and water just wasn't a practical way to eat for the rest of my life. When I became a registered dietitian, I gained a very good scientific understanding of how the body gains and loses weight. However, I loved good food and often found my brain and appetite in conflict. Not until *Health* magazine asked me to create a healthy and practical weight-loss program did I begin to realize how easy enjoying delicious food and looking good can be.

My challenge was to develop a weight-loss program that would complement the magazine's overall food philosophy. And here is the result—a combination weight-loss guide and cookbook that will help you balance weight loss, good health, and the enjoyment of delicious food. Inside, you'll discover:

- 6 Secret Keys to Weight Loss

- How women just like you found inner strength to make healthy lifestyle changes

- Why you shouldn't weigh yourself

- How you can look and feel better in just 6 weeks

- Ways to outwit cravings so you'll be ready anytime they strike

- Real-life techniques to keep you on the path to a healthier you

- Personal weight-loss strategies from *Health* readers...plus a few of my own tried-and-true tricks.

To make weight loss even simpler, you'll find 4 weeks of healthy menu plans (starting on page 241) plus over 350 delicious, kitchen-tested recipes. Here are my personal favorites:

- **Mu Shu Pork Wraps** (page 69)—Thin slices of pork, garlic, chile paste, and Asian veggies are stir-fried together and then wrapped tight in a warm tortilla. Great as an appetizer, but hard to resist as your main meal!

- **Grilled Mexican Pizzas** (page 153)—Pizza crusts warmed by hot coals make the perfect topping for filet mignon, fresh chiles, salsa, and bubbly Monterey Jack.

- **Sticky Caramel-Pecan Rolls** (page 82)—Refrigerated roll dough and caramel sundae syrup make these gooey, sweet rolls a snap to throw together.

- **Warm Bittersweet Chocolate-Rum Torte in Vanilla-Rum Custard Sauce** (page 111)—Bittersweet chocolate and Dutch process cocoa impart a double shot of chocolate in this dense torte. Served with the smooth, creamy vanilla sauce, fresh raspberries, or a dusting of powdered sugar, this dessert is impossible not to love.

- **Orange-Ginger Salmon with Sautéed Greens** (page 116)—A tangy mixture of ginger, soy sauce, and brown sugar serves as both a marinade and a glaze on fresh salmon. When served over a bed of spinach sautéed with fresh basil and garlic, the end result is magnificent.

Mu Shu Pork Wraps, page 69

- **Microwave Risotto with Ham and Corn** (page 165)—With two different cheeses, ham, and red bell pepper, this irresistible risotto is the ultimate comfort food.

- **Turkey Enchilada Suizas** (page 184)—Tender chunks of turkey seasoned with sautéed onion, garlic, and cumin are wrapped in corn tortillas and drenched in a cilantro cream sauce.

- **Oven-Roasted Sweet Potato Fries** (page 210)—You'll never settle for fast-food fries again after tasting these! Wedges of sweet potato are baked until crisp and tossed with olive oil, rosemary, and salt.

Food Lovers Weight Loss Cookbook is your all-in-one guide to balancing weight loss, good health, and your enjoyment of good food. May it inspire you to embrace the power of living well.

Happy eating!

Carolyn Land

Carolyn Land, M.S., R.D.
Editor, *Food Lovers Weight Loss Cookbook*

part 1

a winning strategy for weight loss

a healthy diet without sacrifice

Is it possible...

to love food and be thin at the same time? As a dietitian and as the editor of the *Food Lovers Weight Loss Cookbook,* I've decided it is. — *written by Carolyn Land, M.S., R.D.*

I LOVE TO EAT DELICIOUS FOOD—FROM THE THIN caramelized sugar crust on top of crème brûlée to a juicy slice of beef tenderloin braised in wine and fresh herbs. As a matter of fact, eating is one of my favorite activities. Don't get me wrong, though—I also love being able to slip into my favorite "thin" jeans. So what's the solution to being able to maintain my ideal weight while enjoying the foods I love?

At *Health* magazine, we've found that to lose weight and be healthy you don't have to deprive yourself of delicious food or even spend time counting calories and fat grams. These strategies usually don't work anyway, at least not for people who want to lose weight and keep it off. What *does* work is learning how to make smart, healthy choices every day from the foods you enjoy.

So how do you make these smart choices if you're simply eating the foods you love? (See me on the right day, and this could entail a menu of all-I-can-eat brownies and diet Cokes!) The secret is balance—learning how to incorporate nutritious, good-for-you foods into your diet by making wiser, more educated food choices and by enhancing flavor and taste with some simple cooking techniques.

But, if you're like me, you've got to have a little more direction in an eating plan before you trust it as the answer to your health and weight-loss challenges. That's why I recommend our **6 Keys to Weight Loss.** Based on the most current research and on the opinions of weight-loss experts across the country, these keys form the foundation of *Health's* weight-loss philosophy.

Our 6 keys to weight loss

- A Diet Is Not the Answer
- Carbohydrates and Fats Are NOT Bad
- Stop Counting Calories— Think Portion Size
- Fruits, Veggies, and Water Are Your Best Friends
- Celebrate the Good Foods
- Make the Commitment

In the next few pages, you'll find each key clearly defined. I think you'll begin to see that it's easy to embrace our philosophy on weight loss.

To make the process even simpler, we've included over 350 delicious, healthy recipes you can enjoy with friends and family. And starting on page 241, you get four weeks of menu plans. Get ready to feel and look better, because this book is your all-in-one guide to balancing weight loss and good health.

Key #1:
A Diet Is Not the Answer

I'll admit it—I've tried them all! From diets that had me eating cabbage soup to steak and eggs at every meal to nothing but grapefruit. You name it, I've eaten it—all in the pursuit of losing pounds and becoming healthier. The funny thing is that when I was on these diets, even if the numbers on the scale appeared to be dropping, I often felt the least healthy. So what if I could wear a size 6 if it meant never again eating a crusty piece of French bread slathered with creamy Brie or sipping on a cool margarita after work on Fridays? Yet advertising in magazines and on TV makes it seem that the only way a person can lose weight is to go on one of those life-altering, rigid diets comprised of odd food combinations.

Fad diet facts

"Fad diets get all the publicity," says Rena Wing, Ph.D., creator of the National Weight Control Registry. The Registry compiles stories and strategies from successful "losers"—people around the country who have been successful at losing weight. Success means not only that they've lost pounds, but that they've kept them off. "We've found," Professor Wing says, "that very few people who succeed in losing weight do so with approaches such as high-protein regimens or very low-calorie diets." In fact, studies have shown that nearly 95% of the people who lose

To lose weight...you have to throw the word "diet" out of your vocabulary.

weight on any kind of diet gain the pounds back, and often more, within a year.

Break barriers with baby steps

It's not rocket science: To lose weight, you have to eat less or move more. But to actually do this and keep the weight off, you have to throw the word "diet" out of your vocabulary, and then make some realistic changes that will last your entire life. This doesn't mean making a complete overhaul today. It means making small changes—taking baby steps—towards a healthier lifestyle by changing the way you eat and increasing your activity level. Below are a few suggestions.

Small steps that lead to big changes

- Pack a nutritious snack before heading out the door to go to work or to run errands.

- Expand your taste buds by trying a new fruit or vegetable each week.

- Take your friend up on that offer to work out at the new gym or to take a walk after work.

- Enjoy your daily latte from Starbucks. Order it with 2% milk for a few days. Then, slowly wean yourself down to a latte with 1% or fat-free milk.

> What *does* work is learning how to make smart, healthy choices every day from the foods you enjoy.

Key #2: Carbohydrates and Fats Are NOT Bad

Carbohydrates and fats have gotten quite a bad rap lately. But actually, these nutrients are essential for a healthy diet and body.

The truth about carbs

First, your body *needs* carbohydrates (fruits, vegetables, grains, pasta) for proper functioning. Your brain relies on carbohydrates (broken down into simpler sugars) to fuel basic body functions such as breathing. Second, eating pasta and bread is not the sole cause of your weight troubles, but your serving size may be. Any food—no matter how healthy it is—can make you gain weight if you eat too much of it.

You can still eat foods rich in carbohydrates and lose weight; you just have to watch serving sizes and learn some ways to make wiser choices about which carbohydrates you eat. Carbohydrates are in starchy foods (such as bread

and potatoes), but also in all fruits and vegetables. What research has shown is that not only are carbohydrates from fruits, vegetables, and whole grain products more nutrient rich, but they also keep you full because they're naturally good sources of fiber. Consequently, you feel more satisfied with one serving so it's easier to eat less of them.

The skinny on fat

The same principle is true for fats. "For years the official message was to cut back on all fat," says Penny Kris-Etherton, Ph.D., R.D. "But in all our studies we've helped to show that diets very low in total fat may not be as healthy as diets that include some good fat." In fact, a moderate amount of fat is essential for hormone production and healthy skin, hair, and nails. The key is to incorporate healthier (good) fats, such as olive oil, peanut oil, canola oil, corn oil, and the fats in fish and nuts, into your diet and to reduce fat from fried foods and meat.

how much is a serving? a 21st-century guide

STANDARD FOOD SERVING guidelines—like figuring out the size of a serving of meat by comparing it to the size of a cassette tape—are *so* last century. Since debit cards and personal digital assistants (PDAS) have replaced checkbooks and date books in your purse, here's a modern way to spot serving sizes.

FOOD ITEM	MODERN EQUIVALENT
1 medium (6-ounce) potato	a mini (6-ounce) soda can
3 ounces of cooked meat	a floppy disk
1 scoop ($1/2$ cup) of ice cream	a round iMac mouse
6 ounces of grilled fish	a PDA (personal digital assistant)
1 ounce of cheese	a pager
1 tablespoon of oil, salad dressing, or mayonnaise	an individual eye-shadow compact or tip of the thumb
1 serving of pretzels (1 ounce or about 18 small) or other snack food	a coffee mug full

Key #3: Stop Counting Calories—Think Portion Size

The tedious task of counting calories may not be the healthiest way to control what you eat. In fact, research has shown that counting calories has little effect on how much we eat since most people who count calories routinely take in 20 percent more than they think they do.

To begin losing weight while still enjoying the foods you love, you need to learn what reasonable portions really are and how they look on your plate. So how do you do this?

First, you need to start reading food labels, looking particularly at what the manufacturer calls "one serving" and how many servings are in a package. Next, get an idea of what a typical serving of meat, cheese, or salad dressing looks like. The chart above will help. By learning to compare a serving of food to a familiar, everyday object, such as the mouse for a computer, you can instantly tell if you're eating too much. With a little forethought and planning, you will reduce the amount of food (and consequently calories) you consume and lose weight while still enjoying your favorite foods.

For more help on learning and controlling portion sizes turn to the **Top 10 Secrets to Portion Control** on the next page.

Key #4: Fruits, Veggies, and Water Are Your Best Friends

Fruits and vegetables are key parts of any healthy eating plan because they're low in calories yet high in water and fiber. To cut to the chase, they fill you up for very few calories. But perhaps more importantly, they're some of the most nutrient-dense foods available to us in our diet and offer health benefits galore.

The power of produce

Fruits and vegetables contain antioxidants, compounds that protect normal, healthy cells in your body from damage. Vitamins A, C, and E and selenium are antioxidants. Research has shown that

top 10 secrets to portion control

1. Go One by One
Start by revamping just one meal at a time—breakfast one week, lunch the next, dinner the third. That way, you won't feel overwhelmed by making too many changes at once.

2. Measure First, Eat Later
Buy a kitchen scale you can adjust to zero after you put a bowl or plate on it. Keep measuring cups and spoons handy. Weigh out pasta before you cook it. Make a mental note of what a 4-ounce serving of meat looks like. Before long, you'll be able to tell just by looking when you've got the right amount.

3. Get Friendly with the Butcher, Baker, and Produce Man
Get to know the people behind the meat counter at your supermarket and ask them to cut your meat into 4-ounce portions before you bring it home. Ask which breads are made with whole grains; don't just guess—color can be deceiving. And weigh items like potatoes individually before you buy them.

4. Serve in the Kitchen
Decide how much you're going to eat before you sit down at the table, and then measure it out in the kitchen. Don't bring serving dishes to the table where you'll be tempted to help yourself to seconds.

5. Trick Yourself
If you use a slightly smaller plate than usual and arrange the food attractively, the plate will look full and you won't feel as if you're depriving yourself.

6. Think Ahead
On nights when you aren't as busy, make batches of pasta sauce or soup, or casseroles such as lasagna, for future meals. Then freeze them in individual portion-sized containers.

7. Half It
When you order a sandwich out at lunch, ask for half the amount of meat and cheese. An appropriate portion is a total of 4 ounces of meat and cheese on your sandwich. Or, order half of a sandwich or split one with a friend. You can also remove the top half of a bun and eat a sandwich open-faced.

8. Hold It
Keep in mind that the low, flat clear plastic deli containers in which you get food to go usually hold one cup. An appropriate serving is half a cup, so save the rest for tomorrow's lunch.

9. Snack All Day
Eat a low-calorie snack between each meal. Eating at even intervals throughout the day will help you avoid feeling overly hungry and will make it easier to control portions at meals.

10. Pack It to Go
Rather than getting snacks from vending machines or convenience stores, buy pretzels, animal crackers, or baked chips when you shop for your other groceries. When you get home, divide them into single serving portions, and store the servings in plastic bags. That way, you won't absent-mindedly eat more than you should.

antioxidants may be key in preventing various forms of cancer, heart disease, and other diseases.

Fresh, frozen, or canned?
You're probably assuming that to reap all these benefits, you can eat only fresh produce, right? The fact is, it doesn't matter if the fruits and vegetables you eat are fresh, frozen, or canned. The health benefits are basically the same. I like to buy fresh produce because of the control it gives me. For example, I get to decide how the produce is cut, what it's cooked in, and how it's cooked, crisp-tender or well-done. But I also like the convenience of frozen corn and canned tomatoes. The important issue is that you eat at least 5 servings of fruits and veggies a day. Deciding whether to eat fresh, frozen, or canned produce is truly a personal preference and a convenience issue.

Simple pleasures
Let's face it: Fruits and vegetables aren't typically considered the most exciting foods to eat. But if you think about it, meals would be quite boring without the fruits, vegetables, and herbs that add color, flavor, crunch, and texture to our meals. They can turn a simple fish dinner into a delectable meal such as **Salmon with Moroccan**

get more bang for your buck from fruits & veggies

Buy only what you need. The longer fresh vegetables and fruit sit on your counter or in your refrigerator, the more nutritional value they lose. So only buy as much as you'll use within a few days.

Check out your local farmer's market. Fresh foods can be as cheap as or cheaper than processed foods when they don't have to travel far to reach the market. And they'll be fresher, too. In addition, most farmers are eager to talk about their crops, so you may learn something in the process.

Eat them raw. Cooking causes a breakdown of fiber and some loss of nutrients. When you do cook fresh produce, microwave or blanch it to preserve nutrients and fiber as well as appearance and flavor.

Leave the skin on. You'll get the most fiber and nutrients by leaving the skin on. In a potato, for instance, fiber, B vitamins, calcium, iron, and potassium are all concentrated in the skin. When you peel an apple or remove the skin from a peach, you're cutting away a large portion of what's good for you.

Sneak them in. Be on the lookout for opportunities to add fruits and vegetables to your recipes. Toss fresh spinach leaves into salads or use them in place of iceberg lettuce in tacos or on sandwiches. You can also put fresh spinach or other vegetables into dishes like lasagna to increase the amount of vegetables your family eats. Enhance a muffin's nutrition by adding a variety of fresh or dried fruits to the batter.

Substitute for ice. Freeze banana or other fruits like strawberries or blueberries for an icy and nutritious addition to your favorite smoothie.

Decorate your plate. Cut up an apple, and put it in your oatmeal. Or garnish your supper plate with raw or poached pear halves. Your family will appreciate them a lot more than a sprig of parsley.

Stock up. To help keep hunger at bay before dinner, have medium-sized apples, oranges, grapes, carrots or celery sticks on hand.

Ahh...Water

Water is another natural ally when you're trying to control your weight. For one thing, it can help tame that hungry feeling. Some researchers think that the body doesn't make a clear distinction between hunger and thirst. So your mind may get the idea that you want something to eat when all your body wants is a glass of water. Taking a drink of water before you open the refrigerator to look for a snack may save you some unnecessary calories.

Need to take a baby step to slowly increase your water consumption? So did I, and here's how I did it: I started carrying a water bottle with me everywhere I went. Whether I was in a business meeting or in the car running errands, I always kept a full bottle of water within arm's reach.

Tomato Relish (page 116) with a side of **Lemony Spring Vegetables** (page 206).

Key #5: Celebrate the Good Foods

There's great news! Researchers are now telling us that we need small amounts of nuts, chocolate, and wine in our diet. So, lose the guilt and enjoy these foods—in moderation, of course.

Nuts (and peanut butter)

In one recent weight-loss study, half the participants were asked to eat only low-calorie, low-fat foods. The other half, while restricted to the same number of calories, were allowed to snack on items with monounsaturated fats. Those snack items included one ounce of mixed nuts or peanuts (about ¼ cup) or peanut butter (about 2 tablespoons) on whole wheat crackers every day. After a year and a half, the nut bunch had lost weight, kept it off, and continued with their new regimen long after the study ended. The group that didn't snack on nuts had twice as many dropouts, and its members had gained an average of five pounds.

The researchers are quick to point out that it's wrong to say that nuts or any other single item by itself was responsible for making the diet work. Eating nuts and peanut butter probably contributed to helping the participants control hunger. A study at Purdue University found that snacking on nuts or peanut butter staved off hunger in some people for two hours or longer. Other snacks only curbed appetite for an average of 30 minutes.

Chocolate

Good news for chocolate lovers everywhere: a number of studies have shown that dieters who indulge in a chocolate chip cookie between meals control both their hunger and, more importantly, their urge to binge on forbidden foods. Plus, chocolate may play a role in preventing heart disease. Studies have shown that chocolate contains a compound that may reduce the risk of heart disease, and one study even indicated that those who eat candy one to three times a month live longer than those who never eat candy.

Wine

An important factor in successful weight loss is the enjoyment of mealtime! So if you like to have a glass of wine with your dinner, go ahead.

Moderate drinkers (for women, that's the equivalent of one 4-ounce glass of wine a day) have a 30 to 40 percent lower risk of heart disease than do teetotalers. A Danish study found that moderate wine drinkers also

had about half the risk of cancer than nondrinkers did. And while heavy drinking can weaken bones, a French study of women 75 and older showed that those who drank modestly actually added bone mass. A glass of wine also adds elegance for food lovers who feel that wine is "part of a well-set table."

If you don't already drink wine, don't feel pressured to start; there are other ways to reduce your risk of heart disease and cancer.

The lowdown on the good foods

As you can see, we don't consider any foods "bad." Some are just better for you than others. We think this positive approach towards food is especially effective for weight-loss for a couple of reasons. First, when you focus on the good qualities in food, it's much easier to make healthy changes and to succeed at maintaining them over a long period of time. Second, depriving yourself of a particular food can set you up for failure. In the past, when you've gone on one of those crazy fad diets that wouldn't let you eat any carbohydrates, didn't you crave gooey cinnamon rolls or big bowls of pasta even more? Denying yourself particular foods eventually leads to that late night binge in the kitchen.

> Making the commitment to alter your lifestyle, to eat and live healthier, and to increase your activity is actually the master key to the whole weight-loss process.

KEY #6: Make the Commitment

Making the commitment to alter your lifestyle, to eat and live healthier, and to increase your activity is actually the master key to the whole weight-loss process. The other five keys give you the information you need to keep this commitment. Most importantly, you've got to be realistic about working towards a healthier lifestyle—it's not a change you're going to see overnight. Here are three techniques that can help you keep your commitment.

1. Write it down.

Keep a food and activity log. Record what you eat at every meal and in between meals. Write down the portion size, and note how you feel about the food you eat.

Also, write down how much exercise you get. And when you think of ways to increase your activity level (like parking further from the store entrance or taking the stairs rather than the elevator) write those things down, too. When you record what you eat and what you do, you'll become aware of patterns—patterns you want to change and healthy patterns you want to emphasize more. You'll also have a record of your progress.

2. Go public.

You can help yourself succeed by making your plan public. Let family and friends know that you're trying to eat healthy and to lose weight. It will hold you more accountable and give you more motivation to stick with it. It's much easier to succeed when your family and friends are there helping you.

3. Have a crisis plan.

You need to devise what I like to call a crisis-management strategy. Picture yourself two weeks into the future, hassled by piles of paper at work or screaming toddlers at home or whatever your stress trigger is, and think about how this stress might make you want to run through the fast-food drive-through for dinner instead of making healthy choices. Now, create your plan. Think about how you're going to handle these stressful situations. Maybe you need to plan meals and grocery shop on Saturday or Sunday so that during the week you're always ready to prepare a quick, healthy meal. Or maybe all you need is a few minutes of time alone to gather your thoughts and remember the motivation that initiated this change.

A change that lasts for a lifetime isn't going to happen all at once. But as you stick with your plan, you'll begin to see and feel the results.

> **It's much easier to succeed when your family and friends are there helping you.**

it's your turn

healthy inspirations

In the past...

I've always used the way my clothes fit—particularly the tightness of them—as a signal that I needed to get control over my eating habits.

WHENEVER THIS HAPPENED, I'D JUMP INTO MY WELL-rehearsed plan of action: After getting myself out of my depressed funk by eating a pint of Häagen Dazs, I'd seek out the newest diet plan on the market and totally revamp my entire life based upon it. I'd usually lose some weight, maybe even reach my goal weight, and then head back to my usual haphazard diet only to repeat this whole process four months later.

But when I finally committed to a healthy lifestyle, the action wasn't spurred on by a tight waistband. In fact, I made the commitment at a rather sane moment when I was actually pleased with my physical appearance. One morning, I was suddenly overcome with the realization that I wasn't getting any younger and that I had a pretty scary family history of heart disease and breast cancer. I knew that I had to get my act together and start taking care of myself. It was time to adopt some healthy lifestyle habits— habits that I could maintain for the rest of my life, not just those

Realizing what truly motivates you...will help you succeed at adopting healthy changes for life.

that I could pick up whenever my pants got too tight.

An "awakening" like the one I just described comes when we realize that health—emotional and physical—must become a priority. It's brought about by a motivating force (in my case, the fear of future disease). Realizing what truly motivates you and believing that it is the reason for much-needed change will help you succeed at adopting healthy changes for life. Making temporary changes so that you can fit into a certain dress or just look better isn't going to keep you going. Don't get me wrong—I love the way the new me looks. But changing to reduce the risk of developing a serious disease, to lower your blood pressure, or to increase your quality of life and have more years to spend with your kids will keep you going for the long haul. The difficult part is putting your finger on that deeper source of inspiration.

To help you find your inspiration, we interviewed different women to learn what motivated them to make a commitment to a healthier lifestyle. We lead with a personal story from our executive editor, Lisa Delaney. As you read through these stories, I hope that you'll find some spark of inspiration that will motivate you to make a positive lifestyle change.

the "aha" moment

MINE WAS A HALF-GALLON OF mint-chocolate-chip ice cream. I polished off the last third of the container left from the previous day's pig-out straight from the carton (yes, I used a spoon). This was nothing new for me: I had no self-control when it came to food—never had, never thought I would. But something happened that day. It was as if I had been in a pitch-black room, and someone had suddenly switched on the light. For the first time, I saw how out of control I was. And I had to do something about it.

That was my turning point, the "aha" moment that got me moving toward a healthier life. I started to exercise. It was Jazzercise at first. Then I graduated to running, then cycling, then swimming, eventually competing in triathlons. I began to see food as fuel—never losing the pleasure I got from it, but learning how to find pleasure in the fresh flavors of vegetables, fruits, and meats, and weaning myself off junk food.

It isn't enough to say that I lost weight. It isn't important, even, how much. What I did was embark on an adventure that helped me discover who I am: a confident, powerful woman who believes she can do just about anything, including pass up (or indulge in, if I feel like it) a dish of mint-chocolate-chip ice cream.

Lisa Delaney
executive editor
Health *magazine*

the trip of a lifetime

TWO YEARS AGO I DECIDED TO TAKE MY SONS SKIING FOR SPRING break. I went to the gym and told the trainers they had six weeks to make me strong enough to keep up with two teenagers on the slopes. The trip was a success: I kept up all four days. I still go to the gym three times a week and work with a personal trainer. I also re-evaluated my eating habits. I limit desserts and try to fill up on fruits and vegetables. I'm more fit than ever, with lots of energy and focus.

Sharon Keys Seal, 47
business coach

a healthy legacy

THREE YEARS AGO, MY healthy 60-year-old father had an emergency triple bypass. His doctors told us his clean lifestyle was the only thing that helped him survive: If my dad had been overweight, smoked, or drank, he would have died instantly.

This made me dig up my family medical history. Turns out, both sides of my dad's family have histories of chronic heart and artery problems. I had to face the reality that I might suffer the same fate. So I began a huge lifestyle overhaul. Prior to my dad's operation, my diet consisted entirely of fast food, sweets, and soda. These days, I eat cereal and fruit for breakfast every morning, and a healthy lunch and dinner. I did this all in stages—I did not change my life all at once. Each month, too, I tack on some new exercise. I get annual stress tests to monitor my heart, and I'm confident that while I may not be able to avoid a heart attack completely, I've increased my chances of surviving one.

Christina Miranda, 31
public relations executive

Jeannie

you betcha

A FEW YEARS AGO, I TOLD MY SISTERS I was planning to run the Chicago marathon. They didn't believe I could, so I said, "Wanna bet?" Michelle bet five bucks, Linda said she'd make my wedding cake, and Sandy bet $2,000 and said, "No walking."

So I started training. At first, I couldn't go a mile without stopping. I called my sisters when I got up to five miles, and then 18, and they still said I'd never make it. None of them made good on their bets, but they did send me a pre-race care package. I finished Chicago in about four and a half hours, have run the Honolulu marathon, and hope to run New York this fall. Now, Michelle and Linda are marathon runners.

Jeannie Wong-Lin, 29
optometrist

moved by the spirit

MY BROTHER WAS DIAGNOSED WITH HIGH BLOOD pressure when he was 20, but because he didn't take his medication, he required a kidney transplant about five years ago. That was a real wake-up call for me. I went to the doctor and found out that I also have high blood pressure, as well as high cholesterol, and I decided to make some changes. I started eliminating salty foods from my diet and cut back on sweets. I eat a lot more vegetables these days—salads, spinach, broccoli—stuff I never used to look twice at! I try to walk each day at lunch for about half an hour; it really helps clear my head. I smile a lot, because it's important to have a good sense of humor about things. And I haven't lost my sense of faith: I pray every day. Ninety percent of good health is keeping a positive attitude. I look at everything my brother is going through. He still has such strong spirits, and he's getting along fine.

Stefanie Bryant, 37
administrative assistant

Christina

sweatin' to the oldies

I DIDN'T KNOW IT AT THE TIME, but I started making my health a priority back in the '60s, when I was just 3 years old. I would exercise with my mom to an exercise album—an old 33 LP. I loved it so much that I just kept doing it, even after she stopped. I still work out almost every day, even now—38 years later. In addition to running about 25 miles a week, I also lift weights and practice Ashtanga yoga. And just for fun, I stand on my head every day. I figure that one day I might not be able to do it, and I want to know the exact day when that happens!

Nita Hughes, 41
graphic designer

mother nature, therapist

IN JANUARY 1994, I LOST all my possessions in the Los Angeles earthquake, dumped my boyfriend, and realized the only thing between me and the job of my dreams was a nightmare boss. I was anxious, couldn't eat or sleep, and was basically a mess. A friend suggested we go for a hike in the Santa Monica Mountains. I was amazed: The trails scale dry mountain ridges and dip into green valleys, and are home to deer, mountain lions, and other wildlife. I was hooked. Soon I began trekking into the mountains on weekends and summer evenings. I began to sleep better, eat more, and care less about my ex-boyfriend and boss. The trails became the place I could lose myself, exercise, and reflect. Today I live in New York City, but I found an apartment near the park, because I still need a brisk walk every day.

Andrea Scharff
landscape designer

putting stock in exercise

IN 1994, MY JOB AS A STOCKBROKER HAD BECOME ENTIRELY TOO STRESSFUL. I was never at home, always focused on work, and completely burned out. No matter how many successes I had under my belt, there was always someone who was opening a bigger account or getting more accounts than I was.

That's when I decided to put myself first. So I left my job, went back to school to get my MBA, and started running again, which I had done only sporadically since 1985. Running makes me feel as if I've accomplished something worthwhile. So, first thing in the morning, I 'pay myself first' by getting out to exercise. It's a great way to start the day. I have a new job that I love, feel better about myself than I have in years, and have more energy to spend on doing fun things with my husband!

Claire Cooney, 38
financial consultant

off the meds and in control

BACK IN 1995, ONE OF MY DOCTORS PRESCRIBED A VERY POTENT DRUG TO HELP ME battle insomnia. Although I didn't realize how strong the drug was at the time, I soon found out. After eight months, I looked like a walking skeleton (at 5 feet 8 inches tall, I had dropped to just 107 pounds). I was weak and terribly out of shape. Although I had been a runner, I had to give it up while I was taking this medication because physically I just couldn't handle it—I had absolutely no energy or stamina.

That's when I realized that I had to retake control of my health. First, I changed doctors and got off the medication. Then, by eating a healthy diet, starting to run again, and weight training, I was able to regain the weight I had lost and get back into shape.

That scary experience made me realize that we can't take our bodies or our health for granted. We are in control of how we feel by how we take care of ourselves. Life is short enough as it is, and I want to do my part to be able to enjoy every minute of it!

Kim Fisher, 41
insurance company vice president

inspired by friends

LAST HALLOWEEN WEEKend, I had a reunion with four friends from college who live all over the country. Even though we rarely see each other, they're some of my best friends—things I could never say to other people I can openly say to them. We had a great time: All five of us crashed in the same room, and we went for walks and ate long dinners. Before we went out one night, we had an epic discussion about everything from politics to men. As we were talking, I was thinking, "Here I am, surrounded by these women who are all so amazing. Why don't I feel that way about myself?" So when I got home, I decided to treat myself like I was amazing, too. I gave up self-deprecating remarks and started on an exercise regimen: I now run or walk five days a week, crank out 250 sit-ups and 30 push-ups daily, and go to yoga twice a week. The next time I saw my college friends, they couldn't believe what great shape I was in! That felt good, but the best thing is that I've created a healthy pattern for a lifetime.

Alicia Brabazon, 29
first-grade teacher

the unexpected gift

I WAS DIAGNOSED WITH MULTIPLE SCLEROSIS IN 1992: THE diagnosis devastated me. I was working full time and caring for a young child while my husband was on the road. I wasn't eating right or exercising regularly.

It wasn't until a relapse in 1998 that I started taking better care of myself. One day I woke up in excruciating pain and could barely move; the symptoms were related to MS. That was the defining moment for me. I had to make some changes in my life, and I had to start making my health a priority.

Because stress can trigger MS symptoms, I cut back on my work hours. My part-time job allows me time to take care of my family. Before my relapse, I thought that taking care of myself was selfish. Now I realize that it's actually a very giving thing to do because I need to be healthy to be a good wife and mother. In many ways, getting this disease has been a gift—it is a constant reminder of my priorities: my health and my family.

Sandi Salera Lloyd, 38
book researcher

no more quick fix

I WAS A PRODUCT OF THE '80S—AND YOU can read whatever you want into that—and I spent a lot of time lost and consuming everything in my path. About six years ago, though, I began taking some yoga classes, which pushed me both physically and mentally. Although I continued to eat Crunch Berries for dinner and drink six cups of coffee for breakfast, a four-month spiritual retreat to an ashram made me re-examine my attitude toward wellness.

I came from a quick-fix approach: lose 10 pounds in a week, go to the gym for four hours every day for a month, put 18 carrots in the juicer and drink it all. But I learned through meditation and yoga the level of commitment necessary to effect change, and that's what really made a difference in my life.

Anastasia Levinson, 35
yoga instructor

find your healthy weight

No matter how fit...

I am or how healthy and strong I feel, there's one thing that I always dread—stepping onto a scale.

MY HANDS GET CLAMMY, MY HEART RACES, AND MY day (and my diet) is determined by the number I see between my toes. Let's face it: We've all been trained to believe that how much we weigh is the utmost assessment of our health. And why shouldn't we think that? Every time we go to the doctor, we get weighed. The doctor's advice is often based on how our weight compares with a chart of ideal weights or how much we weighed at our last visit. When we join a commercial diet program, our progress is measured by how many pounds we shed in a week. However, I'm happy to tell you that the scale might not be the best indicator of the progress you're making or your level of health.

If you're trying to lose weight, you step onto a scale to see if you've lost any body fat, right? But if you lead an active, healthy lifestyle you may not be getting the real truth from the scale because it can't differentiate between fat mass and muscle mass.

To further explain, not all pounds are equal; muscle, in fact, weighs more than fat.

> ...the scale might not be the best indicator of the progress you're making or your level of health.

Ellen

Tracy

Kim

Pauline

Joyce

See how the same weight, *140 pounds,* looks on these women.

Can you tell who is the healthiest? Who eats the most or who exercises regularly? You may be surprised at the answers, but you shouldn't be surprised that <u>the number on the scale isn't the key.</u> See their stories on the next page.

And while you want to lose fat, you don't want to lose muscle. Muscle gives you strength to exercise, protects you from injury, and helps your body burn more calories, even when you're at rest. So even though muscle weighs more than fat, by increasing your muscle mass you decrease fat mass, boost your metabolism, and make your body appear more compact.

To illustrate how the number on the scale can be deceiving, we found five women who all weigh 140 pounds. However, they have different body types and shapes, are at different fitness levels, and have different eating habits. As you read each story and look at the pictures above, you'll begin to understand how body type and shape, level of fitness, and eating habits affect how 140 pounds can look so different on different women.

"When I look in the mirror, I see a normal American woman."

Ellen Wilson is 5 feet, 1 inch tall.

Ellen is 41 years old and a stay-at-home mom. Five years ago, after the birth of her daughter, she was diagnosed with a thyroid condition that made it hard for her to get back to her pre-baby weight. But while she still struggles with her disease, she's developed new eating habits that keep her feeling healthy, including getting at least 4 cups of vegetables a day. Her workouts consist of four or five indoor and outdoor cycling sessions each week. "Before the baby," she says, "I weighed 117 pounds. I know that's not realistic now. You really can't go by weight. And, for exercise, you have to do what you love." Then she adds, "When I look in the mirror, I see a normal American woman."

She's weighed less than 140, but people asked her if she was sick and that made her uncomfortable.

Pauline Millard is 5 feet, 7 inches tall.

Pauline, a 24-year-old writer and grad student, weighs 140 pounds. "It's the weight I feel best at," she says. Pauline exercises four or five times a week, running outdoors in the summer and on a treadmill or taking dance classes in the winter. She says exercise helps her control her stress, and she makes sure to get a lot of fruit in her diet because it gives her energy. She's weighed less than 140, but people asked her if she was sick and that made her feel uncomfortable.

"My main goal is to focus on nutrition and exercise so I can participate in the activities that I enjoy..."

Joyce Hundley

 is 5 feet, 7 inches tall.

Joyce works as an antitrust attorney for the U.S. Department of Justice. Although she feels her diet has always been reasonably nutritious, she recently made the decision to become a little more knowledgeable about how to eat healthfully. As a esult, she now chooses fat-free milk and whole grains, cuts out red meat and fills her plate with more vegetables. One of her favorite pastimes is walking or jogging along the trails of a nearby city park. "My main goal is to focus on nutrition and exercise so I can participate in the activities that I enjoy with my friends and family."

"I feel fit, lean, and strong at 140."

Tracy Ducan is 5 feet, 7 inches tall.

Tracy is 28 years old, and a professional soccer player for the Boston Breakers. She tries to get protein at every meal to build up her strength, but other than that, she simply makes healthy choices without obsessing about fat or calories. "I feel fit, lean, and strong at 140," she says. In addition to training on the field two hours a day and working out with weights two or three times a week, she also runs regularly to make sure she gets enough cardiovascular exercise.

"140 pounds sounds like a lot, but for me it's an ideal weight. I'm in the best shape of my life."

Kim Clark is 6 feet tall.

Kim, age 32, works as a fitness model. She eats less than 18 grams of fat a day and also tries to limit the amount of carbohydrates she eats. *Clark, who is a second-degree black belt, trains in Tae Kwon Do three to four times a week for two hours a session and also plays a weekly game of pick-up basketball. "140 pounds sounds like a lot," she says, "but for me it's an ideal weight. I'm in the best shape of my life." She says her main motivation for working out is to look good and feel good.*

so how do you measure your progress?

IF YOU CAN'T BEAR TO GET rid of your bathroom scales, try to use them less and less. In place of scales, here are three alternate ways to measure your progress and assess your health.

> ## 3 Alternate Ways to Measure Your Progress
> - Measure Your Percent (%) Body Fat or BMI
> - Measure How Your Clothes Fit
> - Measure How You Feel

At *Health*, we've found that the most accurate way to assess your health and keep track of your progress towards a healthier you is to use all three of these methods.

Method #1: Measure Your Body Fat

Women should have between 20 to 25 percent body fat (men 15 to 18 percent). And women over 30 percent are considered "obese." In years past, finding out your percent body fat was difficult and expensive. Fortunately, today there are much easier, more convenient, and more accurate methods available.

How to Measure % Body Fat
First, there are body fat scales that estimate your percent body fat by sending a small electric current—so weak you can't feel it—through your body to measure the resistance. You can also make an appointment at your local health club or with a dietitian to have your body fat measured using skinfold calipers, a quick and painless tool. Finally, find a place in your town that has a Bod Pod. The Bod Pod is a small chamber that uses air displacement to calculate your percent body fat.

How to Figure Out Your BMI
Because it may not be possible for you to easily obtain your percent body fat, you can calculate your Body Mass Index instead. **Body Mass Index** (or BMI) is a number based on a ratio between your weight and height, and it approximates your percentage of body fat. For example, if you calculate your BMI to be 20, you can assume that about 20 percent of your body weight is fat. You can do the calculation, but it's easier to look it up on a chart (see the chart on page 34) or to use one of the BMI

calculators available on the Internet on sites such as the National Heart Lung and Blood Institute (www.nhlbi.nih.gov).

Method #2: Measure How Your Clothes Fit

Let's go ahead and be honest—you know when your clothes are fitting tighter than they used to. I'm not talking about your jeans being slightly snug one day and not the next. I'm talking about when your clothes just don't fit right anymore or when you slowly start going up a size every so often. Though this method may appear the least scientific, it can be one of the most telling methods—if you're honest with yourself!

Method #3: Measure How You Feel

Finally, what the scale or any other measurement says isn't nearly as important as how you feel. If you feel good about yourself, if you continue to make healthy choices, and if you stay committed to being physically active, your body is probably pretty healthy, too.

body mass index (BMI)

HOW TO USE THE BMI TABLE BELOW:

1. Find your height (in inches) on the left side of the table.
2. Find your current weight on the row corresponding to your height.
3. Look at the number at the very top of the column to find your BMI.

using your BMI to assess your weight and health

BMI	19	21	23	25	27	30	32	34	36	38
Height					Weight (pounds)					
58"	91	100	110	119	129	143	152	162	172	181
59"	94	104	114	124	134	149	159	169	179	188
60"	97	107	117	127	138	153	163	173	183	194
61"	101	111	122	132	143	159	169	180	191	201
62"	103	114	125	136	147	163	174	185	196	206
63"	107	119	130	141	152	169	181	192	203	214
64"	111	123	135	146	158	176	187	199	211	223
65"	114	126	138	150	162	180	192	204	216	228
66"	118	131	143	156	168	187	199	212	224	236
67"	121	134	147	159	172	191	204	217	229	242
68"	125	139	152	165	178	198	211	224	238	251
69"	128	142	155	169	182	203	216	230	243	257
70"	133	147	161	175	189	210	224	237	251	265
71"	136	150	164	179	193	214	229	243	257	271
72"	140	155	170	185	199	221	236	251	266	281
73"	143	158	174	189	204	226	241	257	272	287
74"	148	164	179	195	210	234	249	265	281	296

Below 18.5 = Underweight

18.5 to 24.9 = Healthy Weight

25.0 to 29.9 = Overweight

30+ = Obese

For example, if you're 5 feet 7 inches (67") and weigh 147 pounds, your BMI is 23. This means that you're in the healthy weight range and have a reduced risk of developing a weight-related disease, such as heart disease or type 2 diabetes. If you're in the overweight weight range, you're at moderate risk, and if you're in the obese range, you're at high risk.

make workouts work for you

Exercise is....

absolutely essential to a healthy lifestyle and a healthier you.

YOU'VE HEARD THAT ADVICE TIME AND TIME AGAIN. And like me, in response, you may have started and stopped many a workout routine, joined and rejoined countless fitness clubs, and finally concluded that you're not an "exerciser." Take it from me, now a dedicated workout queen, getting fit (or more fit) is easier than you think.

Don't flip to the next chapter—turn to page 39, and you'll find a six-week program to help you get started. The program, called **Get Fit in Six**, was designed by *Health* contributing editor and Reebok University master trainer Petra Kolber to meet a wide range of fitness goals, from weight loss and strengthening to endurance and better flexibility.

Take a look at your calendar, count out six weeks from today, and circle the date. After following **Get Fit in Six**, you'll notice that you have more energy, feel stronger, and sleep more soundly. Your clothes will fit better. And you'll have made exercise a habit—one you can vary to keep it interesting.

But how do you get yourself to keep even a six-week commitment to exercise? The editors at *Health* are here to help. On the next page are our four simple steps to making exercise a permanent part of your life.

> **Take a look at your calendar, count out six weeks from today, and circle the date.**

Step #1: Make The Case To Yourself

• *Envision a new you.*
Imagine the clothes you'll be able to wear, the energy you'll have, the confidence that you'll gain, and how good you'll look and feel.

• *Add up all the pluses.*
Working out has more than 50 proven benefits, from the long-term (warding off disease), to the immediately motivating (weight loss, stress release).

• *Rethink the timing.*
Ask yourself this: If you weren't walking or lifting weights, what would you be doing? Be honest. Watching the TV? Reading the paper?

• *See the possibilities.*
You'll happily join your friends for a bike ride. You'll have enough stamina to climb the trail to the peak. Most importantly, you'll be taking part in life rather than watching it pass by.

Step #2: Check Yourself Out

Before you lace up those running shoes, it's important to take a snapshot of your health and fitness history to determine your current fitness level. To create that snapshot, take the self-check quiz (on page 40) that's based on insights from Kolber and Liz Neporent, a New York-based personal trainer and coauthor of the book *Fitness for Dummies*. Also, before you start any new fitness program, you should check with your doctor, especially if you have any health concerns or are over the age of 35.

Step #3: Plot Your Future

• *Pick a date.*
Choose a definite date within the next month. Don't put off that date for anything—weather, social obligations, work.

• *Set three goals.*
How often and how long will you exercise the first month, in six months, and a year from now? Start with times that you can easily manage, even as little as two ten-minute sessions a day.

• *Write it all down.*
Go through the details: What kind of workout most appeals to you? Where and when will you do it? How will it fit into your schedule? What are the potential road-blocks (foul weather, vacations), and how will you deal with them (buy a treadmill or join a gym; stay in a hotel that has workout facilities)?

• *Go public.*
Let everyone know that you're starting an exercise program, and don't be afraid to tell them how they can help.

> **Exercise boosts confidence, fights depression, and speeds healing.**

Step #4: Outwit Your Weaknesses

• *Take charge of your environment.*
If you plan to work out in the morning, lay out your gym clothes the night before. Should television's siren call

prove too strong, move an exercise machine into the TV room.

• *Reward yourself.*
"If I stick to my plan for a week, I can treat myself to a manicure. After two weeks, I can get a massage."

• *Find a workout partner.*
The more support and accountability you have, the better.

• *Stay focused:*
If calamity threatens to derail you, remember that your workouts can help you cope. Exercise boosts confidence, fights depression, and speeds healing. Repeat: "I am an exerciser." Researchers are finding that giving yourself an "exercise identity" is key to making your habit stick. Forever.

Ready, Set, Exercise!

What are you waiting for? Use the **Get Fit in Six** program as your personal guide to fitness. As you get more accustomed to your new workout routine, you may want to hire a personal trainer. In just a single one-hour session, a trainer can give you new ideas and tips to keep your workout interesting and effective.

a basic exercise dictionary

CARDIO WORK Cardiovascular work is any kind of exercise that speeds up your heart rate for more than 10 minutes. Examples of cardio work include walking (at a 4.0 mph pace or greater), running, aerobics, swimming, and biking. In **Get Fit in Six**, you will see that cardio work is called for two ways, beginning after Week 3 either as interval training or as distance training.

- **Interval training-**This cardio training involves alternating between short, intense periods of exercise and longer recovery periods. For example, after a 5- to 10-minute warmup, go all out—whether you're walking, jogging, cycling, etc.— for 1 minute, then slow to an easier pace for 2 minutes. Alternate between the 1- and 2-minute cycles for about 15 minutes, then cool down.
- **Distance training-**This cardio work increases the speed and efficiency with which you can cover a certain distance. Choose a goal—say, 2 miles or a specific number of steps on a stair climber—and chart how long it takes you to cover that distance. With each workout, shave a little time (5 to 10 seconds) off your overall time.

STRENGTH TRAINING Strength training builds muscle and helps ward off osteoporosis, and more muscle means a higher calorie-burning metabolism. Simple strength-training moves you can do include push-ups and sit-ups. As you gain more strength, you might want to try hand weights or weight machines.

FLEXIBILITY WORK Flexibility work makes exercise and daily living safer and more comfortable while improving your posture and range of motion. Remember to hold each stretch at least 15 seconds. Simple flexibility work includes slow leg lunges, toe touches, pulling your knees into your chest, and slow head turns.

get fit in six

<table>
<tr>
<td></td>
<td>Week 1: The Big 3</td>
<td>Week 2: Adding On</td>
<td>Week 3: Building the Base</td>
</tr>
<tr>
<td>LEVEL 1</td>
<td>• 3 times a week: 20 to 30 minutes of cardio exercise, each in one continuous workout or two or three 10-minute sessions per day
• 2 times a week: 20 minutes of strength training
• 3 times a week: 10 minutes of flexibility work</td>
<td>• 3 times a week: 20 to 30 minutes of cardio exercise (20 minutes continuously, then try for an additional 10 minutes; or do 10 more minutes later in the day)
• 2 times a week: 25 minutes of strength training
• 3 times a week: 15 minutes of flexibility work</td>
<td>• 3 times a week: 30 minutes of continuous cardio exercise
• 2 times a week: 25 minutes of strength training
• 3 times a week: 15 minutes of flexibility work</td>
</tr>
<tr>
<td>LEVEL 2</td>
<td>• 3 times a week: 30 minutes of continuous cardio exercise
• 2 times a week: 20 minutes of strength training
• 3 times a week: 10 minutes of flexibility work</td>
<td>• 3 times a week: 35 minutes of continuous cardio exercise
• 2 times a week: 30 minutes of strength training
• 3 times a week: 15 minutes of flexibility work</td>
<td>• 4 times a week: 35 minutes of continuous cardio exercise
• 3 times a week: 30 minutes of strength training
• 4 times a week: 15 minutes of flexibility work</td>
</tr>
<tr>
<td>LEVEL 3</td>
<td>• 4 times a week: 30 minutes of continuous cardio exercise
• 2 times a week: 20 minutes of strength training
• 3 times a week: 15 minutes of flexibility work</td>
<td>• 4 times a week: 35 minutes of continuous cardio exercise
• 2 times a week: 30 minutes of strength training
• 3 times a week: 15 minutes of flexibility work</td>
<td>• 4 times a week: 40 minutes of continuous cardio exercise
• 3 times a week: 30 minutes of strength training
• 4 times a week: 15 minutes of flexibility work</td>
</tr>
<tr>
<td></td>
<td>Week 4: Adding Intervals</td>
<td>Week 5: Going the Distance</td>
<td>Week 6: Going Strong</td>
</tr>
<tr>
<td>LEVEL 1</td>
<td>• 3 times a week: 30 minutes of continuous cardio exercise, including two interval workouts
• 2 times a week: 25 minutes of strength training
• 3 times a week: 15 minutes of flexibility work</td>
<td>• 4 times a week: 30 minutes of continuous cardio exercise, including two distance workouts
• 3 times a week: 25 minutes of strength training
• 4 times a week: 15 minutes of flexibility work</td>
<td>• 4 times a week: 35 minutes of continuous cardio exercise
• 3 times a week: 30 minutes of strength training
• 4 times a week: 15 minutes of flexibility work</td>
</tr>
<tr>
<td>LEVEL 2</td>
<td>• 4 times a week: 35 minutes of continuous cardio exercise, including two interval workouts
• 3 times a week: 30 minutes of strength training
• 4 times a week: 15 minutes of flexibility work</td>
<td>• 4 times a week: 40 minutes of continuous cardio exercise, including two distance workouts
• 3 times a week: 30 minutes of strength training
• 4 times a week: 15 minutes of flexibility work</td>
<td>• 4 times a week: 45 minutes of continuous cardio exercise
• 4 times a week: 30 minutes of strength training (to allow adequate rest between workouts, devote two sessions to legs, hips, buttocks, and back; and two to chest and arms)
• 4 times a week: 15 minutes of flexibility work</td>
</tr>
<tr>
<td>LEVEL 3</td>
<td>• 4 times a week: 40 minutes of continuous cardio exercise, including two interval workouts
• 3 times a week: 30 minutes of strength training
• 4 times a week: 15 minutes of flexibility work</td>
<td>• 4 times a week: 45 minutes of continuous cardio exercise, including two distance workouts
• 3 times a week: 40 minutes of strength training
• 4 times a week: 15 minutes of flexibility work</td>
<td>• 4 times a week: 50 minutes of continuous cardio exercise
• 4 times a week: 40 minutes of strength training (to allow adequate rest between workouts, devote two sessions to legs, hips, buttocks, and back; and two workouts to chest and arms)
• 4 times a week: 15 minutes of flexibility work</td>
</tr>
</table>

After six weeks, you can switch to a maintenance program, working out at least three times a week with 30 to 45 minutes of cardio, plus weight training and flexibility work.
Get Fit in Six *designed by Petra Kolber, Health contributing editor and Reebok University master trainer.*

big fat fitness myths

1. **For a flat stomach, do crunches.**
   Crunches will tone the muscles in your belly, but they won't put a dent in the fat obscuring those muscles. The only way to shed fat is to expend more fuel than you eat.

2. **Exercise cranks up your appetite.**
   Not true. Studies show that working out doesn't spur an automatic increase in appetite. What's more, intense exercise can actually blunt your appetite over the short term.

3. **You don't need as much exercise if you're thin.**
   Exercise offers protection against ailments that strike the slim and the stocky alike, such as cancer, depression, and arthritis. But it's especially key in warding off osteoporosis, a disease that disproportionately strikes slim women. The bottom line: No one can afford to skip exercise.

4. **If you stop lifting weights, your muscles will turn to fat.**
   This myth can be traced to football players who stop working out and suddenly get plump. What happens is that the players' muscle fibers begin to shrink, they burn fewer calories. If they don't eat less, they gain fat.

5. **The stair machine will give you a big butt.**
   This myth, popularized by fitness infomercials, posits that you shouldn't exercise the body parts you want to shrink. Infomercials maintain that stair climbing and bicycling only increase the size of your hips and derriere. While these regimens don't add much muscle, they're excellent for burning calories, which *will* reduce the size of your hips and rear.

what about you?

1. When was the last time you exercised regularly—that is, at least three times a week?
   a. More than a year ago (or never)
   b. 6 months ago
   c. Within the past 2-4 weeks

2. Do you have a personal or family history of heart disease?
   a. Yes.
   b. I don't know; I haven't had a physical exam in a while.
   c. No, and I've had a physical in the last year.

3. Do you have high blood pressure, either now or in the past?
   a. Yes.
   b. I don't know; I haven't had a physical exam in a while.
   c. No, and I've had a physical in the last year.

4. Do you have a personal or family history of diabetes or high blood sugar?
   a. Yes.
   b. I don't know; I haven't had a physical in a while.
   c. No, and I've had a physical in the last year.

5. Do you smoke?
   a. Yes.
   b. I used to, but quit in the last 2 years.
   c. No.

6. How long does it take you to walk one mile?
   a. 18+ minutes
   b. 14-17 minutes
   c. 13 or fewer minutes

7. How long can you sustain physical activity?
   a. A few minutes (I don't do any regular physical activity.)
   b. At least 20 minutes (I do something active about 3 times a week.)
   c. At least 30 minutes (I do something active 3-4 times a week.)

ANSWER ASSESSMENT

QUESTIONS 1-5: If you answered A or B to one or more of these, see a doctor before starting any fitness program. Because you have some health risks and haven't been exercising regularly, it's best to have a checkup first.

QUESTIONS 6 & 7: If you answered A or B to one or more of these, you're a Level 1 exerciser. Start at Level 1 in our **Get Fit in Six** program on page 39. If you answered C to these questions, begin at Level 2 (also on page 39).

make peace with your cravings

You know it...

when it happens. You can't concentrate. You try to block it out of your mind but that just makes it worse.

YOU START TO SALIVATE. ALL YOU CAN DO IS THINK about it—that creamy bowl of macaroni and cheese, that dense slice of chocolate-praline cheesecake, or that cheesy piece of pepperoni pizza.

We've all had cravings, and they're completely normal. How normal? In one Canadian study, nearly 97 percent of the women surveyed said they had had food cravings during the previous week. But what may perplex you is why they're almost always for sugary or higher-fat foods.

Some experts have suggested that cravings are the body's way to signal that it's lacking a particular nutrient. But that may not be the case. Most researchers believe that cravings are more psychological in nature—a desire for pleasure, an attempt to escape from stress, or a coping mechanism. Think about your cravings and when you have them. When I start craving my

Most researchers believe that cravings are more psychological in nature—a desire for pleasure, an attempt to escape from stress, or a coping mechanism.

dad's famous grilled pork tenderloin, drenched in his own tangy soy sauce-fresh rosemary marinade, I know it's time for me to go home for a visit. But am I really craving the tenderloin or am I simply missing the family talks that we'd be having around the grill?

The best way I've found to keep cravings from wreaking havoc on my waistline is to learn how to respond to them. Totally ignoring a craving rarely works for two reasons: 1.) You eat a lot of other things you don't want in an attempt to satisfy the craving (such as fat-free chocolate chip cookies), or 2.) You feel deprived until you can't stand it, and then binge and eat a whole large meat-lovers pizza. What *does* work is being prepared for action when cravings creep in on you.

Check out the information on healthy snacking below, the **8 Ways to Curb Cravings** at right, and our list of favorite low-fat snacks on page 46. These ideas will help you keep cravings from sabotaging your best efforts at making healthy food choices.

Putting Snacks to Work for You

While cravings and hunger are not the same thing, hunger can make your

8 ways to curb cravings

1. Identify Triggers
Keep a diary to note what was going on when cravings hit. Were you lonely? Depressed? Alone or with others? By learning when you're the most vulnerable, you may begin to understand your longings and be able to address their root cause.

2. Give It Time
Cravings ebb and flow. Wait a few minutes before you indulge, and the urge may subside.

3. Give In
If the craving doesn't pass and you know you've got to have chocolate, go ahead. Denial could lead to overeating, while a small indulgence could reduce the intensity of the craving.

4. Don't Try Flimsy Substitutes
If you really want a square of dark chocolate, chances are nothing else will do. Don't suck on hard candy or sip sugar-free hot chocolate instead. You'll probably end up eating the chocolate anyway, and you'll spare yourself some calories by skipping the substitutes.

5. Don't Buy In Bulk
If overindulgence is a problem, buy single-serving packages: one candy bar instead of a bag, or a scoop of ice cream at the corner shop instead of a pint.

6. Don't Skip Meals
Part of your craving may be hunger. To feel full longer and keep your blood sugar on an even keel, balance your intake of carbohydrates and protein by eating regular meals and snacks.

7. Try Non-Food Solutions
Sometimes cravings signal a need for pampering or a break in routine. So treat yourself to a massage, a movie, or a long, hot bath instead.

8. Get Help
"If your craving is troubling, speak to a dietitian or psychologist," says Marion Hetherington, Ph.D., editor of the book *Food Cravings and Addictions*. "If cravings are learned, as some studies suggest, cravings can be unlearned."

craving seem worse. One of the easiest ways to control hunger is with a snack. In fact, including snacks in your daily routine can actually be an important part of your plan for healthy eating. When you plan for snacks, it's easier to keep hunger away and binges under control.

So what are some of the best snacks to pack? Here are some of my favorites.

Sip on soup.

I love soup because it tricks your mind and stomach: Your eyes see a big portion, your nose is stimulated by the steamy aroma, and your stomach gets very full from a large volume of liquid. Plus, an ingredient-rich soup takes time to digest, keeping you satisfied longer. In a study conducted at Penn State, people who consumed a bowl of soup before a meal took in an average of 100 fewer calories per meal. Just watch out for cream-based soups, which are loaded with fat and calories. Try a cup of **Caribbean Chicken Chili** (page 224) for a light lunch, or whip up **Santa**

Fe Ravioli Soup (page 226) as a last-minute dinner.

Pour a bowl of cereal.

When I need a quick comfort food and an escape back to childhood, I reach for a bowl of cereal and milk. There's just something very satisfying about the combination of crisp flakes and cool milk. Pick a cereal low in fat and calories (watch out for those sugary ones!), and keep it on hand for breakfasts and snacks. You'll get a nutrition boost, too, since all cereals are now fortified with vitamins and minerals.

Pick berries.

With their appealing sweetness and juiciness, berries may be the smartest snack of all. Berries have a high water content along with lots of fiber, so they're filling with few calories. Picture these 100-calorie snacks: 10 jelly beans, 18 fat-free pretzels, or 2 cups of fresh strawberries. That's not enough jelly beans or pretzels to put a dent in your appetite, but the berries will—and that satisfaction can make a big difference.

Whip up a smoothie.

A smoothie is a cool, refreshing drink made from a blend of fruits and fruit juices, ice, and other natural ingredients. It's a quick and easy snack to make. Using frozen fruit will make an extra cold, thick drink. Two of my favorites are the **Blackberry Smoothie** and **Mango-Strawberry Smoothie** (page 72).

Making your own smoothie gives you control over the ingredients. But if you want to treat yourself at a smoothie cafe, beware—all smoothies aren't low in fat and calories. Extra ingredients such as ice cream and peanut butter can add calories quickly. So check the ingredient list before you order.

Pack a peanut butter sandwich.

When I'm extremely hungry, this is the snack I reach for. One tablespoon of peanut butter has only about 7 grams of fat and also offers a small dose of protein to keep me full and satisfied. Plus, eating a peanut butter sandwich just seems so decadent to me (maybe I was on those low-fat diets too long).

Crunch on baked chips and salsa.

Did you know that the hot stuff in red pepper (capsaicin) slightly increases the calories you burn (a physiological process called thermogenesis),

particularly after high-fat meals? Might as well put that trick to work. Keep baked tortilla chips and salsa on hand for times when you need something salty and crunchy to munch on. For recipes and nutritional information on salsa, turn to pages 82 through 84.

Quench your thirst with low-fat chocolate milk.

When's the last time you drank a big glass of cold chocolate milk? If it's been a while, you need to treat yourself. Satisfy your sweet tooth and your craving for something chocolate, plus get filled up quickly and get an extra serving of calcium!

Chow down on some cheese.

Eat just a 1-ounce serving of cheese (about the size of a pair of dice or your thumb), and I guarantee you won't be hungry for hours. Why? Cheese is a great source of protein, and that combined with a few grams of fat will keep you satisfied. I like to take a mozzarella cheese stick to work each day. It gets me through that afternoon lull and keeps me away from the fat-filled, sugary items in the vending machines.

Indulge in some low-fat frozen desserts

Frozen desserts are one of the best ways to satisfy a sweet tooth without piling on the calories. A Creamsicle weighs in at just 100 calories; a Tofutti Cutie vanilla or wild berry sandwich, 120 calories. A half-cup of chocolate frozen yogurt adds a modest 115 calories to your dinner. Be sure to try **Passionfruit Sorbet** (page 96) and **Peach Ice Cream** (page 101).

our favorite low-fat snacks

IT DOESN'T HURT HAVING AN INSIDER'S TIPS ON THE best low-fat and healthy snacks out there to get you started, so I've compiled this quick list. Here are some of the healthy goodies you'll find in the pantries, freezers, and refrigerators of *Health's* editorial team.

OUR FAVORITES

- Eggo Waffles: Special K, Nutri-Grain varieties
- Peter Pan Peanut Butter
- Lean Cuisine Pepperoni French Bread Pizza
- Cabot 50%-reduced-fat jalapeño Cheddar cheese
- Breakstone reduced-fat sour cream (terrific for making dips)
- Skim Plus Milk
- Baked Ruffles: Cheddar & Sour Cream
- Robert's American Gourmet Veggie Booty
- Pringles reduced-fat Crisps
- Reduced-fat Oreos
- York Peppermint Patties
- Nilla Wafers
- Entenmann's low-fat crumb cake
- Sorbet: Ben & Jerry's, Sharon's
- Edy's Grand Light: Vanilla, French Silk
- Skinny Cow ice cream sandwiches
- Philadelphia Light Chive and Onion cream cheese with wheat crackers
- Minute Maid light lemonade
- Mission 98%-fat-free flour tortillas
- Yoplait Whips! yogurt
- Crystal Light Peach tea
- Entenmann's fat-free oatmeal-raisin cookies
- Edy's Light Peanut Butter Cup ice cream
- Reduced-fat Wheat-Thins
- Low-fat Sargento part-skim mozzarella string cheese
- 94%-fat-free Smart-Pop! popcorn
- Newman's Own pretzels with Hellman's Dijonnaise

celebrate your love of food

I am a food lover...

who struggles daily to find that balance between trying to eat what's good for me, exercising regularly, and maintaining a healthy body.

BUT I ALSO LOVE TO EAT DELICIOUS FOOD. IN THE past, I felt like I had to choose one or the other—delicious food or a lean, healthy body. But by using *Health*'s philosophy and recipes, I've learned that I can have both.

Health's philosophy focuses on what you *can* eat to be healthy. In fact, I like to think of the philosophy as a way to celebrate both good food and good health. We've focused on good food in the recipe section of this book and have given you over 350 recipes to prove it. You'll see that we've tried to incorporate this philosophy into all our recipes.

But if you're saying "Whoa! 350 recipes is a bit intimidating," an easy way to get started is by using **8 Ways to Celebrate Good Food and Good Health.** These are 8 techniques that we use to bring out the maximum amount of flavor in food. These 8 techniques are also simple guidelines that you can apply when cooking and eating. In addition, I've also highlighted some of my favorite recipes that use the techniques.

> *Health's* philosophy focuses on what you *can* eat to be healthy.

8 Ways to Celebrate Good Food and Good Health

- Buy the Best
- Don't Fear Fat
- Add Fire
- Gradually Go for Lower-Fat Foods
- Choose Cooked Over Raw—Sometimes
- Banish Bitterness
- Sweeten the Pot
- Wait It Out

#1: Buy the Best

There can be a big difference in the flavor of a supermarket tomato and one that's grown by a local farmer who concentrates on only a few small crops. Foods purchased at a roadside stand, a local farmer's market, or a specialty market such as Wild Oats or Whole Foods are often tastier and fresher than those in the grocery store. You may spend a bit more to get quality items, but chances are you'll end up saving both money and calories because you'll eat them instead of letting them spoil in the fridge while you call the pizza guy.

Try this:

• Conduct your own search for the best-tasting tomato, peach, and green beans: Case the farmers' markets and natural-food stores. Compare what you buy at each place until you find the best purveyor.

• Experiment in the kitchen with this high-quality produce. Try **Vegetable-Steamed Orange Roughy** (page 115); you'll be amazed at how fresh vegetables, thyme, and lemon juice can punch up the flavor of fish. My favorite in the summer is **Sweet Onion, Tomato, and Corn Salad with Basil** (page 189). Or try **Campanelle with Summer Vegetables** (page 134) where broccoli, zucchini, and asparagus contribute crunch, flavor, and a nutrition punch to pasta.

Campanelle with Summer Vegetables, page 134

Dried Cherry Scones, page 86

#2: Don't Fear Fat

You may have noticed that many of the fat-free foods that were so popular in the 90's are no longer available. Let's face it—fat makes foods taste good. Without the fat, breads, cookies, cakes, and salad dressings are often dry or flavorless. Plus, they're often packed with extra calories used to replace the fat. Today, we know that fat in moderation is okay. So don't be afraid to add a little oil or butter. But think small drops of olive oil, a trickle of butter; a little fat can go a long way. Not only will this little bit of fat make food more flavorful and moist, but it will also make you feel more satisfied.

Try this:

• Don't be afraid of butter! Both the **Dried Cherry Scones** (page 86) and the **Sour Cream-Fudge Cake with Mocha Glaze** (page 112) recipes include a few

Tabbouleh Cobb Salad, page 193

tablespoons of butter. This butter is essential for making these treats tender, moist, and flavorful, but they're still low in fat.

• Dress your greens. What fun is a salad if you have to eat it without dressing? Roasted red bell peppers and olive oil combine to make a delicious, but still healthy, dressing for **Tabbouleh Cobb Salad** (page 193). In **Asian-Style Slaw** (page 186) shredded veggies are tossed with a sesame oil mixture and then sprinkled with peanuts.

#3: Add Fire

Spicy sauces and salsas not only change the flavor of a food, they can change the way you feel. In fact, hot foods are believed to trigger secretion of a neuropeptide, which is similar to endorphins, those feel-good brain chemicals. Researchers are also studying the idea that spicy foods slightly boost your resting metabolism. Be on the lookout for more information about hot foods and their benefits.

Try this:

• Spoon a piquant tomatillo salsa on top of grilled chicken breasts and fish fillets. (See pages 44 and 63 for more information on salsa, plus delicious recipes.)

• Season foods with a pungent curry to add spicy heat and flavor. Curry powder and jalapeño peppers give a double punch of spice to **Curried Chickpeas in Coconut-Cilantro Broth** (page 145).

• Think outside the Tabasco bottle. **Mu Shu Pork Wraps** (page 69) feature Asian veggies and pork sautéed in a spicy chile paste, which is available in the ethnic section of most large supermarkets.

Mu Shu Pork Wraps, page 69

> You've got to slowly decrease the amount of fat you consume in order for your taste buds and stomach to not feel deprived.

#4: Gradually Go for Lower-Fat Foods

As a food lover and a dietitian, I definitely encourage adding a little fat here and there to make foods more tantalizing and tasty. But keeping your overall fat intake low is still important. So what do you do if fat-free milk doesn't go down quite as easily as whole, and premium ice cream is just too hard to resist? As with any other habit you're trying to break, going cold turkey probably isn't going to create long-lasting results. You've got to slowly decrease the amount of fat you consume in order for your taste buds and stomach to not feel deprived.

Science supports this idea. Evidence suggests that if you

make the change gradually, you probably won't miss the fat—and you may even grow to dislike it. Participants in the Women's Health Trial, a long-term study for the prevention of breast cancer at Fred Hutchinson Cancer Center in Seattle, Washington, reported that after reducing fat in their diets, they actually felt physically uncomfortable after eating high-fat foods. One explanation may be that the body loses some of its ability to break down fat, making it more difficult to digest.

Try this:

• Switch from whole milk to 2 percent first, then try 1 percent, then fat-free.

• In both **Curried Deviled Eggs** (page 70) and **Vegetable-Cheddar Frittata** (page 32), the total fat and cholesterol is lowered by using more egg whites than egg yolks.

• In **Raspberry-Corn Muffins** (page 88), half the fat is replaced with low-fat yogurt so that you still get a tender muffin.

#5: Choose Cooked Over Raw—Sometimes

Most people can only eat so many raw vegetables, and some vegetables aren't palatable unless they're cooked. Cooking mellows the flavor and softens the texture of vegetables, but the trick is to not overcook them. A quick steam or stir-fry is all many vegetables require. Plus, cooking condenses them: One serving of raw spinach leaves is a full cup, but steam or stir-fry the spinach, and a serving shrinks to half a cup. Think how much easier it will be to get your five a day!

Try this:

• Be adventurous! Rather than boiling, baking, or steaming veggies, give roasting or grilling a shot. Roasted in a hot oven (400°), just about any veggie, even asparagus and squash, takes on a sweet, caramelized flavor.

> The next time you fire up the grill, don't just cook fish, meat, or chicken... throw on slices of eggplant, summer squash, and sliced onions.

Oven-Roasted Sweet Potato Fries, page 210

A favorite roasted veggie of mine is sweet potatoes. Turn to page 210 for **Oven-Roasted Sweet Potato Fries.**

• The next time you fire up the grill, don't just cook fish, meat, or chicken. Instead, throw on slices of eggplant, summer squash, sliced onions, or one of my favorites, **Grilled Rosemary Plum Tomatoes** (page 214).

#6: Banish Bitterness

Do you typically turn up your nose at Brussels sprouts, beet greens, and other bitter veggies, many of which happen to have cancer-fighting properties? Many people (women more often than men) are born with taste buds that can't tolerate bitter foods. But bitterness can be blunted with just a shake of the hand. Sprinkle a little salt on the offending food or toss it with a salty condiment such as anchovies, salad dressing, or an Asian condiment like hoisin or oyster sauce. One caveat: Skip this strategy if you have any health problems that require you to watch your sodium intake.

Try this:

• Keep a jar of capers or olives on hand and stir a few of them in with bitter foods. The briny taste of these bite-sized additions will do the trick. Give **Baked Catfish with Tomato-Kalamata Salsa** (page 114) a try.

Warm Bittersweet Chocolate-Rum Torte, page 111

• This concept even works in sweet treats! When bittersweet chocolate and rum are combined with sugar and a creamy vanilla custard sauce, the result is a too-good-to-be-true dessert, **Warm Bittersweet Chocolate-Rum Torte with Vanilla-Rum Custard Sauce** (page 111).

• Sometimes you can combine several bitter foods to get a surprisingly delicious

Chicken with Lemon Caper Sauce, page 171

result. Vermouth, lemon juice, capers, and parsley combine to create a flavorful sauce in **Chicken with Lemon-Caper Sauce** (page 171). We use this technique again in **Panzanella with Tuna** (page 194), where tuna is tossed with basil, mint, and red wine vinegar to make a refreshing salad.

#7: Sweeten the Pot

It may come as a surprise that many savory recipes include a sweet ingredient like sugar, honey, molasses, hoisin sauce, fruit jam or jelly, or even wine. A little sweetness helps to balance the tart and tangy flavors of many dishes.

Try this:

• Hoisin sauce, a sweet Asian condiment, is used in **Hoisin Snow Peas and Peppers** (page 211) to add a touch of sweetness to the fresh veggies.

• **Honey-Glazed Salmon** (page 116) is irresistible when topped with its sweet glaze, and **Kung Pao Scallops with Snap Peas** (page 127) are better than any take-out version with their sweet sauce of soy sauce, sugar, and wine.

Honey-Glazed Salmon, page 116

#8: Wait It Out

Your tastes won't change overnight, but remain positive and be patient. It can be a slow process, but over time you'll notice that your taste preferences have changed. Your taste buds need time to adapt and evolve just like you do when you're trying to take on a new habit.

Try this:

• Introduce one of these strategies every week instead of adopting them all at once.

• Prepare one new recipe each week.

• Try a new vegetable or fruit.

• Allow yourself to enjoy good food!

Toasted Oat Scones,
page 87

Tortilla Chicken Soup,
page 230

White Sangría Fizz,
page 71

Spicy Chicken Couscous,
page 169

part 2

delicious light & healthy recipes

about our recipes

We take great pride in ensuring that each of our recipes is the healthiest and tastiest it can be. With registered dietitians, chefs, and test kitchen professionals on staff, and a computer system that analyzes every recipe, *Health* gives you up-to-date, authoritative nutrition and cooking information. At the end of each recipe you'll see a nutritional analysis. Not only have we included the calories and fat, but we've also included sodium, cholesterol, and saturated fat for those of you who might be following special diets. And because women often don't get enough iron or calcium, we list those values, too. Finally, there's a fiber analysis for those of us who need more roughage.

Nutritional analysis numbers are based on these assumptions:

- Unless otherwise indicated, meat, poultry, and fish refer to skinned, boned, and cooked servings.

- When we give a range for an ingredient (3 to 3½ cups flour, for instance), we calculate using the lesser amount.

- Some alcohol calories evaporate during heating; the analysis reflects that.

- Only the amount of marinade absorbed by the food is used in calculation.

- Garnishes and optional ingredients are *not* included in an analysis.

- When we give a product name or brand, it is what we tested with and what we were successful with in our test kitchens. You may substitute another brand.

Nutritional values used in our calculations either come from The Food Processor, Version 7.5 (ESHA Research), or are provided by food manufacturers.

satisfying appetizers & beverages

Roasted Asparagus and Goat
Cheese Crostini, page 65

crispy asian chips

Prep: *9 minutes* **Cook:** *7 minutes*
Serves 4

*These gingery chips pair nicely with
Curried Nectarine Salsa, page 62.*

    18 fresh or frozen won ton
        wrappers, thawed
     1 tablespoon low-sodium soy
        sauce
    1/2 teaspoon sugar
    1/2 teaspoon minced peeled fresh
        ginger
    1/2 teaspoon dark sesame oil
     1 garlic clove, minced
Dash of hot sauce
Cooking spray

1. Preheat oven to 375°.
2. Cut won ton wrappers in half
diagonally.
3. Combine soy sauce and next
5 ingredients (soy sauce through
hot sauce) in a small bowl.
Brush both sides of won ton
wrappers lightly with soy sauce
mixture.
4. Arrange won ton wrappers in
a single layer on a baking sheet
coated with cooking spray. Bake
at 375° for 7 minutes or until
won ton wrappers are lightly
browned and crisp; let cool
completely. Store in an airtight
container for up to a week.

PER SERVING (9 chips): Calories 116 (9% from fat);
Protein 4g; Fat 1g (sat 0g, mono 0g, poly 0g);
Carbohydrate 22g; Fiber 1g; Cholesterol 3mg;
Iron 1mg; Sodium 359mg; Calcium 18mg

artichoke spread with melba toast

Prep: *5 minutes*
Serves 6

*Creamy herbed cheese and crunchy
water chestnuts accent chopped
artichokes in this spread. Look for
Alouette cheese in the specialty
cheese case at your market.*

    1/2 cup spreadable cheese with
        garlic and herbs (such as
        Alouette)
     1 (14-ounce) can quartered
        artichoke hearts, drained and
        chopped
     1 (8-ounce) can sliced water
        chestnuts, drained and
        chopped
Dash of black pepper
    30 Melba toast slices

1. Combine all ingredients
except Melba toast in a bowl; stir
well. Serve with Melba toast slices.

PER SERVING (1/4 cup spread and 5 Melba toast slices):
Calories 164 (26% from fat); Protein 6g; Fat 5g (sat 3g,
mono 0g, poly 0g); Carbohydrate 27g; Fiber 2g;
Cholesterol 20mg; Iron 2mg; Sodium 281mg;
Calcium 33mg

smoked trout spread

Prep: *5 minutes*
Serves 12

     4 ounces skinned, boned smoked
        trout, flaked
     1 tablespoon finely chopped red
        bell pepper
     2 tablespoons fat-free
        mayonnaise
     2 teaspoons finely chopped red
        onion
     2 teaspoons minced capers
     2 teaspoons fresh lemon juice
    1 1/2 teaspoons prepared horseradish
Paprika (optional)

1. Combine first 7 ingredients
(trout through horseradish) in a
medium bowl, stirring well.
Cover and chill. Sprinkle with
paprika just before serving, if
desired. Serve with Melba toast,
unsalted crackers, or toasted
French baguette slices.

PER SERVING (1 tablespoon): Calories 15 (60% from
fat); Protein 2g; Fat 1g (sat 0g, mono 0g, poly 0g);
Carbohydrate 1g; Fiber 0g; Cholesterol 0mg; Iron 0mg;
Sodium 164mg; Calcium 1mg

hot parmesan cheese dip

Prep: *11 minutes* **Cook:** *30 minutes*
Serves 32

*There's no need to give up cheesy
dips just because you're trying to
lose weight. Enjoy this one slathered
on toasted French bread slices.*

     1 cup light mayonnaise
    1/2 cup thinly sliced green onions
    1/3 cup (about 1 1/2 ounces) grated
        Parmesan cheese
    1/4 cup sliced mushrooms
    1/4 cup sun-dried tomato sprinkles
     1 (8-ounce) carton low-fat sour
        cream
Cooking spray
     1 tablespoon grated Parmesan
        cheese

1. Preheat oven to 350°.
2. Combine first 6 ingredients
(mayonnaise through sour
cream) in a bowl; spoon into a
1-quart casserole coated with
cooking spray. Sprinkle with 1
tablespoon cheese. Bake at 350°
for 30 minutes or until bubbly.
Serve with toasted bread.

PER SERVING (1 tablespoon): Calories 44 (69% from fat);
Protein 1g; Fat 3g (sat 1g, mono 0g, poly 0g);
Carbohydrate 3g; Fiber 0g; Cholesterol 6mg; Iron 0mg;
Sodium 130mg; Calcium 30mg

light guacamole

pictured on page 75

Prep: *5 minutes*
Serves 8

You may think avocados are a "no-no" when watching your waistline because of their high fat content. However, this creamy fruit is packed full of potassium, niacin, vitamins A and C, and heart-healthy, cholesterol-lowering fat. Tomatillo salsa also may be labeled salsa verde. (We tested with the Herdez brand.)

- 1 large Anaheim chile (about 3 ounces)
- 2 green onions, cut into 2-inch pieces
- 2 garlic cloves, peeled and halved
- 2 large plum tomatoes (about 6 ounces), quartered
- 3/4 cup diced peeled avocado (about 1 small)
- 1/2 cup tomatillo salsa
- 1/4 cup cilantro sprigs
- 2 tablespoons fresh lemon or lime juice
- 1/2 teaspoon ground cumin
- 1/4 teaspoon salt
- Lime slices (optional)

1. Cut chile in half lengthwise; discard stem, seeds, and membranes. Place chile, green onions, and garlic in a food processor; pulse 5 times or until coarsely chopped. Add tomato and next 6 ingredients (tomato through salt); pulse 10 times until blended (mixture should be chunky). Spoon into a bowl; garnish with lime slices, if desired.

PER SERVING (1/4 cup): Calories 40 (52% from fat); Protein 1g; Fat 2g (sat 0g, mono 1g, poly 0g); Carbohydrate 4g; Fiber 1g; Cholesterol 0mg; Iron 1mg; Sodium 79mg; Calcium 12mg

chili-bean dip

Prep: *3 minutes*
Serves 7

If you love chili, then this smooth Tex-Mex dip will become a favorite. Serve it with a tray of assorted raw vegetables, such as carrots, broccoli, and cucumbers.

- 1 (19-ounce) can cannellini beans or other white beans, drained
- 2 tablespoons lime juice
- 2 teaspoons chili powder
- 1 teaspoon ground cumin
- 1/8 teaspoon garlic powder

1. Place all ingredients in a food processor, and process until smooth.

PER SERVING (1/4 cup): Calories 69 (5% from fat); Protein 5g; Fat 0g; Carbohydrate 13g; Fiber 2g; Cholesterol 0mg; Iron 1mg; Sodium 156mg; Calcium 42mg

roasted eggplant dip

Prep: *23 minutes* **Cook:** *45 minutes*
Chill: *2 hours*
Serves 12

Serve on warm focaccia or pita bread or with pita chips.

- 1 (1-pound) eggplant
- 2 tablespoons olive oil
- 2 tablespoons sherry vinegar
- 1/2 teaspoon salt
- 1/2 teaspoon dried marjoram
- 1/8 teaspoon pepper
- 2 garlic cloves, minced
- 1 cup finely chopped onion
- 1 cup finely chopped tomato
- 2 tablespoons chopped fresh parsley

1. Preheat oven to 425°.
2. Place eggplant on a baking sheet; bake at 425° for 45 minutes or until tender. Cool. Peel; finely chop to measure 1 cup.
3. Combine oil and next 5 ingredients (oil through garlic) in a medium bowl. Add eggplant, onion, tomato, and parsley. Cover and chill at least 2 hours.

PER SERVING (1/4 cup): Calories 31 (69% from fat); Protein 0g; Fat 2g (sat 0g, mono 2g, poly 0g); Carbohydrate 2g; Fiber 1g; Cholesterol 0mg; Iron 0mg; Sodium 99mg; Calcium 0mg

sun-dried tomato dip

Prep: *6 minutes* **Stand:** *15 minutes*
Serves 20

- 1 (3-ounce) package sun-dried tomatoes, packed without oil
- 1 cup boiling water
- 1/3 cup fresh basil leaves
- 2 tablespoons balsamic vinegar
- 2 tablespoons Italian-style tomato paste
- 1 tablespoon olive oil
- 1/8 teaspoon salt
- 1/8 teaspoon pepper
- 1 (15-ounce) can white beans, drained
- 1 garlic clove, minced

1. Combine tomatoes and 1 cup boiling water in a bowl; let stand 15 minutes or until soft. Drain tomatoes in a sieve over a bowl, reserving 1/2 cup soaking liquid.
2. Place tomatoes, reserved liquid, basil, and remaining ingredients in a food processor; process until smooth. Serve with baked tortilla or pita chips.

PER SERVING (2 tablespoons): Calories 42 (26% from fat); Protein 2g; Fat 1g (sat 0g, mono 1g, poly 0g); Carbohydrate 7g; Fiber 1g; Cholesterol 0mg; Iron 0mg; Sodium 134mg; Calcium 14mg

hummus with raspberry vinegar

Prep: *12 minutes* **Cook:** *8 minutes*
Serves 8

Raspberry vinegar gives this hummus a touch of sweetness, but you can substitute cider or any other fruit-flavored vinegar you have on hand. Serve it with pita bread.

    1   tablespoon olive oil
1 1/2   cups chopped onion
    2   tablespoons raspberry vinegar
    1   (15 1/2-ounce) can chickpeas
        (garbanzo beans), undrained
    1   tablespoon chopped fresh
        cilantro
  1/2   teaspoon ground cumin
  1/2   teaspoon coarsely ground
        black pepper
  1/4   teaspoon salt
Cilantro sprigs (optional)

1. Heat oil in a nonstick skillet over medium-high heat. Add onion, and sauté 5 minutes or until onion begins to brown. Add vinegar, bring to a boil, and cook 2 minutes or until vinegar evaporates. Cool to room temperature.
2. Drain chickpeas through a sieve over a bowl, reserving 1/4 cup liquid. Place chickpeas and chopped cilantro in a food processor, and process until mixture resembles coarse meal. Add onion mixture, 1/4 cup reserved liquid, cumin, pepper, and salt, and process until smooth. Garnish with cilantro sprigs, if desired.

PER SERVING (1/4 cup): Calories 88 (27% from fat); Protein 4g; Fat 3g (sat 0g, mono 2g, poly 1g); Carbohydrate 13g; Fiber 2g; Cholesterol 0mg; Iron 1mg; Sodium 150mg; Calcium 28mg

beef and spinach dip

Prep: *10 minutes* **Cook:** *20 minutes*
Serves 32

Adding cream cheese to creamed spinach gives the dip a rich, smooth base. Serve it with baked tortilla chips.

  3/4   pound lean ground beef
    1   small onion, chopped
    1   (8-ounce) tub light cream
        cheese, softened
    2   (10-ounce) packages frozen
        creamed spinach, thawed
    1   to 1 1/2 teaspoons hot sauce
  1/4   teaspoon ground nutmeg
  1/3   cup (1 1/2 ounces) grated fresh
        Parmesan cheese

1. Cook beef and onion in a skillet, stirring until beef crumbles and is no longer pink; drain. Stir in cream cheese and next 3 ingredients, and cook over low heat, stirring often, until cream cheese melts. Sprinkle with Parmesan.

PER SERVING (2 tablespoons): Calories 52 (50% from fat); Protein 4g; Fat 3g (sat 2g, mono 1g, poly 0g); Carbohydrate 2g; Fiber 0g; Cholesterol 8mg; Iron 0mg; Sodium 149mg; Calcium 41mg

curried nectarine salsa

Prep: *8 minutes* **Cook:** *1 minute*
Serves 10

Serve this sweet and tangy salsa over a block of reduced-fat cream cheese with crackers.

    1   teaspoon curry powder
    2   cups chopped nectarines
  1/2   cup chopped red bell pepper
  1/4   cup chopped red onion
  1/4   teaspoon salt

1. Place curry in a large skillet; cook over high heat 30 seconds or until fragrant, stirring occasionally. Remove pan from heat; add nectarine and remaining ingredients, stirring until well blended. Serve warm or at room temperature.

PER SERVING (1/4 cup): Calories 19 (10% from fat); Protein 0g; Fat 0g; Carbohydrate 4g; Fiber 1g; Cholesterol 0mg; Iron 0mg; Sodium 59mg; Calcium 4mg

plum salsa

Prep: *6 minutes*
Serves 12

The sweetness of the plums and the pungency of the onions complement the spicy flavors in Moroccan Chicken Thighs, page 173.

1 1/4   pounds ripe red plums
        (about 7), quartered and pitted
    1   small red onion (about
        4 ounces), quartered
    1   cup cilantro sprigs
  3/4   cup mint leaves
    1   tablespoon white wine vinegar
  1/2   teaspoon salt
  1/4   teaspoon black pepper
  1/8   teaspoon ground red pepper

1. Place plums and onion in a food processor; pulse 10 times, scraping sides of processor bowl occasionally. Add cilantro and remaining ingredients; pulse 5 times or until mixture is chopped (do not overprocess or salsa will be mushy). Serve at room temperature.

PER SERVING (1/4 cup): Calories 57 (10% from fat); Protein 1g; Fat 1g (sat 0g, mono 0g, poly 0g); Carbohydrate 13g; Fiber 2g; Cholesterol 0mg; Iron 0mg; Sodium 198mg; Calcium 16mg

Salsa – A Tasty Low-Calorie Nutrient Boost

Traditional salsas rely on tomatoes, but today, salsas include ingredients such as fruit, corn, and beans. And the flavor can range from mild to fiery. Salsa is Spanish for "sauce" and can be any kind of fresh or cooked, hot or cold chunky food mixture. At first, it may appear as if we've gone salsa-crazy in this chapter. We included a wide assortment of salsa recipes for two reasons: First, we love their versatility. From a fresh dip for chips to a zesty topping on fish, chicken, burritos, and egg dishes, salsas are a healthy way to liven up almost any dish and transform it from something plain to something extraordinary.

More important though, salsas are one of the most nutrient-rich foods around. Packed full of fresh vegetables, fruit, herbs, and possibly a little olive oil, salsas are rich in antioxidants—cancer-fighting compounds, fiber, and energy-boosting B-Vitamins. Plus, a 1/4-cup serving of salsa typically has less than 50 calories and little, if any, fat. So treat your taste buds and try our salsas made with grilled vegetables, nectarines, or asparagus. We guarantee you'll have fun adding a flavor zip to your dishes while also giving yourself a low-calorie nutrient boost!

asparagus-raspberry salsa

pictured on page 75

Prep: *9 minutes* **Cook:** *3 minutes*
Chill: *1 hour*
Serves 8

- 1 pound asparagus spears
- 1 cup fresh raspberries, halved
- 1/4 cup finely chopped shallot
- 1 tablespoon raspberry vinegar
- 1 to 3 teaspoons minced seeded jalapeño pepper
- 1/4 teaspoon salt
- 1/4 teaspoon black pepper

1. Snap off tough ends of asparagus; remove scales with a knife or vegetable peeler, if desired. Cut asparagus into ½-inch pieces.
2. Steam asparagus, covered, 3 minutes or until crisp-tender; drain. Rinse asparagus under cold water, and drain.
3. Combine asparagus and remaining ingredients in a bowl. Cover and chill at least 1 hour.

PER SERVING (¹/₄ cup): Calories 23 (8% from fat); Protein 1g; Fat 0g; Carbohydrate 5g; Fiber 2g; Cholesterol 0mg; Iron 1mg; Sodium 75mg; Calcium 15mg

mango-black bean salsa

Prep: *8 minutes* **Chill:** *1 hour*
Serves 8

Pack baked tortilla chips to eat with this salsa, and you have a great portable snack to boost your energy before or after a workout.

- 1 (15-ounce) can black beans, drained
- 1 cup chopped peeled fresh mango
- 2 tablespoons chopped fresh cilantro
- 3 tablespoons lime juice
- 1/4 teaspoon salt
- Dash of ground red pepper

1. Combine all ingredients in a bowl; toss well. Cover and chill at least 1 hour.

PER SERVING (¹/₄ cup): Calories 40 (1% from fat); Protein 2g; Fat 0g; Carbohydrate 10g; Fiber 3g; Cholesterol 0mg; Iron 1mg; Sodium 211mg; Calcium 17mg

piccalilli-flavored salsa

Prep: *5 minutes* **Cook:** *10 minutes*
Serves 10

Serve this sweet-and-sour relish with Carolina-Style Barbecued Pork Sandwiches, page 162.

- 3 cups coarsely chopped green bell pepper (about 1¹/₄ pounds)
- 1 cup chopped onion
- 2¹/₂ tablespoons sugar
- 2 tablespoons cider vinegar
- 1 tablespoon water
- 1/2 teaspoon salt
- 1/4 teaspoon black pepper
- 1/8 teaspoon ground cloves

1. Place a large nonstick skillet over medium heat until hot. Add all ingredients; sauté 10 minutes or until most of liquid evaporates. Serve warm or at room temperature.

PER SERVING (¹/₄ cup): Calories 27 (7% from fat); Protein 1g; Fat 0g; Carbohydrate 7g; Fiber 1g; Cholesterol 0mg; Iron 1mg; Sodium 119mg; Calcium 6mg

grilled vegetable salsa

Prep: *15 minutes* Cook: *20 minutes*
Stand: *15 minutes*
Serves 12

 1 pound red bell peppers
 1 pound yellow bell peppers
 1 pound green bell peppers
Cooking spray
 2 portobello mushroom caps
    (about 8 ounces)
 1 red onion, cut into $1/2$-inch-
    thick slices
 1 tablespoon chopped fresh
    thyme
 1 tablespoon balsamic vinegar
$1/2$ teaspoon salt
$1/4$ teaspoon black pepper

1. Cut each bell pepper in half; discard stems, seeds, and membranes.
2. Prepare grill.
3. Place bell pepper halves, skin side down, on grill rack coated with cooking spray. Add mushroom caps and onion slices to rack; cover and grill 20 minutes or until vegetables are tender, turning mushroom caps and onions after 10 minutes (do not turn bell pepper halves). Remove vegetables from grill rack. Set mushroom caps and onions aside. Place bell pepper halves in a large zip-top plastic bag immediately; seal bag, and let stand 15 minutes.
4. Peel bell pepper halves, and coarsely chop. Coarsely chop mushroom caps and onion slices. Combine chopped vegetables, thyme, and remaining ingredients in a bowl; stir well. Serve warm or at room temperature.

PER SERVING ($1/4$ cup): Calories 29 (13% from fat);
Protein 1g; Fat 0g; Carbohydrate 6g; Fiber 2g;
Cholesterol 0mg; Iron 1mg; Sodium 101mg;
Calcium 11mg

pan-roasted corn salsa

pictured on page 74

Prep: *11 minutes* Cook: *18 minutes*
Serves 16

Serve this succotash-like salsa as a side to any seafood or chicken dish for a delicious dinner.

 1 (10-ounce) package frozen
    baby lima beans
$1^{3}/4$ cups fresh corn kernels (about
    3 ears)
Cooking spray
 2 cups chopped tomato
 1 cup thinly sliced fresh basil
    leaves
 1 teaspoon grated lemon rind
 1 tablespoon fresh lemon juice
$1/2$ teaspoon salt
$1/4$ teaspoon pepper

1. Bring 1 cup water to a boil in a large saucepan; add baby lima beans, and return to a boil. Cover, reduce heat, and simmer 12 minutes. Add corn; cover and simmer an additional 2 minutes. Drain well.
2. Coat a large nonstick skillet with cooking spray, and place over high heat until hot. Add bean mixture, and sauté 4 minutes or until lightly browned. Remove pan from heat; stir in tomato and remaining ingredients. Serve warm or at room temperature with baked tortilla chips or as a side dish.

PER SERVING ($1/4$ cup): Calories 42 (7% from fat);
Protein 2g; Fat 0g; Carbohydrate 9g; Fiber 1g;
Cholesterol 0mg; Iron 1mg; Sodium 104mg;
Calcium 10mg

bruschetta pomodoro

Prep: *16 minutes* Stand: *30 minutes*
Makes 10

Pomodoro is Italian for "tomato," and in this recipe tomatoes, capers, olives, and onion top toasted baguette slices for a truly Italian appetizer. To keep the bread slices crisp, add the vegetable mixture just before serving.

 2 cups minced plum tomato
    (about $3/4$ pound)
$1^{1}/2$ teaspoons capers
 2 tablespoons chopped kalamata
    olives
 1 tablespoon chopped red onion
 1 tablespoon chopped fresh basil
 1 tablespoon extra-virgin olive oil
$1/4$ teaspoon salt
$1/4$ teaspoon balsamic vinegar
$1/8$ teaspoon pepper
 10 ($1/2$-inch-thick) slices diagonally
    cut French bread baguette,
    toasted

1. Combine all ingredients except French bread; cover and let stand 30 minutes. Drain tomato mixture. Top each bread slice with 1 tablespoon tomato mixture.

PER SERVING (1 slice): Calories 95 (20% from fat);
Protein 2g; Fat 3g (sat 0g, mono 1g, poly 1g);
Carbohydrate 16g; Fiber 1g; Cholesterol 1mg;
Iron 1mg; Sodium 255mg; Calcium 15mg

roasted asparagus and goat cheese crostini

pictured on page 59 and 75

Prep: *18 minutes* **Cook:** *15 minutes*
Serves 4

 20 thin asparagus spears (about
      $^1/_2$ pound)
Garlic-flavored cooking spray
 $^1/_4$ teaspoon kosher or regular salt
  4 ($^1/_2$-inch-thick) slices French or
      Italian bread
 $^1/_4$ cup goat cheese, softened
  4 teaspoons chopped fresh chives
  2 tablespoons drained bottled
      roasted red bell peppers, cut
      into strips

1. Preheat oven to 400°.
2. Snap off tough ends of spears, and remove scales with a knife or vegetable peeler, if desired. Trim asparagus spears to length of bread slices, and reserve trimmings for another use.
3. Place asparagus in a 9-inch square baking pan; coat asparagus with cooking spray, and sprinkle with salt. Coat one side of bread slices with cooking spray, and set aside. Bake asparagus at 400° for 5 minutes. Turn asparagus spears over, and place bread, coated side up, directly on oven rack next to asparagus. Bake asparagus and bread an additional 10 minutes or until bread is toasted.
4. Combine goat cheese and chives in a small bowl; stir well. Spread cheese mixture evenly over bread slices. Top each slice with 5 asparagus spears. Arrange pepper strips over asparagus.

PER SERVING (1 crostini): Calories 103 (25% from fat); Protein 5g; Fat 3g (sat 2g, mono 1g, poly 0g); Carbohydrate 15g; Fiber 2g; Cholesterol 6mg; Iron 1mg; Sodium 426mg; Calcium 52mg

Using Fresh Herbs

One of the quickest ways to enhance and balance the flavors of any dish—even in the middle of winter—is with fresh herbs. Mince or chop them as close to serving time as possible to help retain flavor and prevent discoloring.

1. If stored correctly, fresh herbs can last a week or more in the refrigerator. Loosely wrap stems in a damp paper towel, place in plastic bags, and refrigerate. Or trim stems, and place herbs in a jar or glass of water; cover leaves loosely.

2. To mince small herbs such as cilantro, use a large, sharp chef's knife. Place your hand over the tip and rock the knife back and forth over the leaves. The small, tender stems can also be chopped.

3. Remove the leaves from thyme (or rosemary) by holding the top of the woody stem with one hand, and then running the fingers of your other hand over the stem from the top to the bottom.

4. To make quick work of larger-leafed herbs like basil, roll up a stack of several leaves lengthwise, and then cut across the stack. The herb can be used in strips or chopped finer, as in step 2.

crostini with roasted pepper spread

Prep: *7 minutes* **Chill:** *4 hours*
Makes 18

Melba toast, pita chips, and bagel chips have a crispy texture and serve as good substitutes for French bread.

- 1/2 cup drained bottled roasted red bell peppers (about 4 ounces)
- 2 tablespoons chopped walnuts
- 2 tablespoons fresh parsley
- 1/4 teaspoon salt
- 1/4 teaspoon freshly ground black pepper
- 18 (1/2-inch-thick) slices thin French bread baguette, toasted

1. Press bell peppers gently between paper towels until barely moist, and set aside.
2. Place walnuts and parsley in a food processor; pulse until coarsely ground, scraping sides of processor bowl once. Add bell peppers; process until smooth. Spoon into a bowl; stir in salt and pepper. Cover and chill at least 4 hours.
3. Spread about 1 teaspoon bell pepper mixture over each bread slice. Serve immediately.

PER SERVING (1 crostino): Calories 25 (29% from fat); Protein 1g; Fat 1g (sat 0g, mono 0g, poly 1g); Carbohydrate 4g; Fiber 0g; Cholesterol 0mg; Iron 0mg; Sodium 157mg; Calcium 9mg

crostini with roasted vegetables and pine nuts

Prep: *32 minutes* **Cook:** *38 minutes*
Stand/Marinate: *2 1/2 hours*
Makes 36

- 1 (1 1/4-pound) eggplant
- 1 large green bell pepper (about 1/2 pound)
- 1 large red bell pepper (about 1/2 pound)
- 1 large yellow bell pepper (about 1/2 pound)
- 1/4 cup pine nuts, toasted
- 1 teaspoon olive oil
- 1/4 teaspoon ground red pepper
- 1 large garlic clove, minced
- 2 tablespoons balsamic vinegar
- 1 tablespoon capers
- 1/2 teaspoon sugar
- 1/4 teaspoon salt
- 36 (3/4-inch-thick) slices French bread (about 1 pound), toasted

1. Preheat oven to 500°.
2. Pierce eggplant several times with a fork; place on a foil-lined baking sheet. Bake at 500° for 20 minutes or until tender. Cut eggplant in half lengthwise. Place in a colander; let stand 15 minutes. Peel eggplant. Cut into 1/2-inch cubes, and place in a medium bowl.
3. Cut bell peppers in half lengthwise; discard stems, seeds, and membranes. Place halves, skin sides up, on a foil-lined baking sheet; flatten with hand. Broil 15 minutes or until blackened. Place in a heavy-duty zip-top plastic bag; seal. Let stand 15 minutes. Peel; cut into 1/2-inch pieces. Add bell peppers and pine nuts to eggplant in bowl; toss well.
4. Heat oil in a nonstick skillet over medium-high heat. Add red pepper and garlic, and sauté 30 seconds. Add vinegar, capers, sugar, and salt. Bring to a boil; cook 30 seconds. Pour over eggplant mixture; toss. Marinate at room temperature 2 hours.
5. Spoon 1 tablespoon eggplant mixture onto each bread slice. Serve immediately.

PER SERVING (1 crostino): Calories 56 (19% from fat); Protein 2g; Fat 1g (sat 0g, mono 1g, poly 0g); Carbohydrate 1g; Fiber 1g; Cholesterol 1mg; Iron 1mg; Sodium 121mg; Calcium 13mg

smoked salmon quesadillas

Prep: *5 minutes* **Cook:** *16 minutes*
Serves 8

The richness of herbed cream cheese and smoked salmon unite in tortillas to create flavorful mini-sandwiches.

- 3/4 cup tub-style light cream cheese with chives and onions (about 6 ounces)
- 8 (7-inch) flour tortillas
- 8 ounces smoked salmon, coarsely chopped
- 1/4 teaspoon freshly ground black pepper

1. Spread cream cheese evenly over 4 tortillas.
2. Divide salmon among tortillas. Sprinkle with pepper. Top each portion with 1 tortilla, pressing gently. Heat a nonstick skillet over medium-high heat. Cook each quesadilla 2 minutes on each side. Cut each quesadilla into 6 wedges.

PER SERVING (3 wedges): Calories 238 (31% from fat); Protein 12g; Fat 8g (sat 3g, mono 2g, poly 1g); Carbohydrate 29g; Fiber 2g; Cholesterol 18mg; Iron 2mg; Sodium 929mg; Calcium 52mg

crab purses

Prep: *30 minutes* **Cook:** *17 minutes*
Serves 24

These elegant appetizers can be steamed up to an hour ahead and then resteamed to heat them just before serving.

- 24 (3-inch) green onion strips
- 6 ounces lump crabmeat, shell pieces removed
- 1 (4-ounce) block $1/3$-less-fat cream cheese
- $1/4$ cup minced green onions
- 2 teaspoons fresh lemon juice
- $1/2$ teaspoon hot sauce
- $1/4$ teaspoon salt
- $1/8$ teaspoon pepper
- 24 won ton wrappers
- 1 large egg white, lightly beaten
- Cooking spray
- 2 tablespoons low-sodium soy sauce
- 1 tablespoon water
- 1 tablespoon fresh lemon juice

1. Drop green onion strips in boiling water, and cook 10 seconds or until limp. Drain onion strips; set aside.
2. Combine crabmeat and next 6 ingredients (crabmeat through pepper) in a medium bowl, and stir well.
3. Working with 1 won ton wrapper at a time (cover remaining wrappers with a damp towel to keep them from drying out), spoon 2 teaspoons crabmeat mixture into center of wrapper. Moisten edges of wrapper with egg white; gather 4 corners of wrapper, and crimp to seal, forming a purse. Tie 1 green onion strip around crimped top of purse. Repeat procedure with remaining won ton wrappers, crabmeat mixture, egg white, and green onion strips.
4. Arrange half of won ton purses in a single layer in a vegetable steamer coated with cooking spray. Steam purses, covered, 8 minutes or until tender. Carefully remove purses from steamer; set aside, and keep warm. Repeat procedure with remaining half of purses.
5. Combine soy sauce, water, and 1 tablespoon lemon juice in a small bowl; stir well. Serve with purses.

PER SERVING (1 purse and $1/2$ teaspoon sauce): Calories 42 (21% from fat); Protein 3g; Fat 1g (sat 1g, mono 0g, poly 0g); Carbohydrate 5g; Fiber 0g; Cholesterol 7mg; Iron 0mg; Sodium 186mg; Calcium 12mg

crab-stuffed portobellos

Prep: *22 minutes* **Cook:** *15 minutes*
Serves 8

Creamy crab stuffing fills the large mushrooms for a fabulous buffet appetizer.

- 8 (4-inch) portobello mushrooms
- 1 (8-ounce) block fat-free cream cheese, softened
- $1/2$ cup finely chopped green onions
- $1/4$ cup light mayonnaise
- 1 teaspoon lemon juice
- $1/2$ teaspoon Old Bay seasoning
- Dash of ground red pepper
- 1 pound lump crabmeat, shell pieces removed
- 1 cup quartered cherry tomatoes (about 12)
- $1/2$ cup (2 ounces) shredded reduced-fat, reduced-sodium Swiss cheese (such as Alpine Lace)
- $1/2$ cup dry breadcrumbs

1. Preheat oven to 425°.
2. Remove brown gills from the undersides of mushrooms using a spoon; discard gills. Remove and discard stems. Set mushroom caps aside.
3. Beat cream cheese with a mixer at medium speed until smooth. Add green onions and next 4 ingredients (green onions through pepper); beat well. Stir in crabmeat, tomatoes, and cheese. Spoon mixture evenly into mushroom caps; sprinkle each cap with 1 tablespoon breadcrumbs, and place on a baking sheet. Bake at 425° for 15 minutes or until tops are lightly browned.

PER SERVING (1 stuffed mushroom): Calories 175 (27% from fat); Protein 21g; Fat 5g (sat 1g, mono 0g, poly 2g); Carbohydrate 11g; Fiber 2g; Cholesterol 69mg; Iron 2mg; Sodium 593mg; Calcium 249mg

Control Those Grazing Cravings

One bite of this, a nibble of that—surely those small bites off the buffet can't ruin one's diet, right? Well, think again because those bites can add up quickly. To keep from overeating, try these tips.

1. Eat an apple or other healthy snack before you go. Don't meet your friends for dinner or go to a party where you know there's food until you've had a small snack. You'll be amazed at how easy it is to by-pass more of those high-fat foods on a full stomach.

2. Fix a plate. When you do eat, fix a plate rather than nibbling on the buffet line as you mingle. When you nibble, you don't realize how much you eat, and it's easy to overeat, so fix a small plate, find a seat, and enjoy your food.

roasted red potatoes filled with corn and shrimp

Prep: 16 minutes **Cook:** 19 minutes
Serves 12

These bite-sized spuds can be cooked ahead of time and filled just before serving.

- 12 small red potatoes (about 1¹/₂ pounds)
- ¹/₄ teaspoon salt
- ¹/₄ teaspoon pepper
- Cooking spray
- 1 tablespoon olive oil
- 1¹/₂ cups frozen whole-kernel corn, thawed and drained
- 3 tablespoons minced green onions
- 2 tablespoons cider vinegar
- 1 teaspoon chopped fresh or ¹/₄ teaspoon dried tarragon
- 24 small shrimp, cooked and peeled
- Tarragon leaves (optional)

1. Preheat oven to 450°.
2. Cut each potato in half crosswise; scoop out pulp, leaving a ¹/₄-inch-thick shell; reserve pulp for another use. Sprinkle insides of potato shells with salt and pepper. Place potato shells upside down on a baking sheet coated with cooking spray. Bake at 450° for 15 minutes; set aside.
3. Heat oil in a medium skillet over medium-high heat. Add corn and green onions; sauté 2 minutes. Add vinegar and chopped tarragon; cook 1 minute. Divide corn mixture evenly among potato shells; top each with 1 shrimp. Garnish with tarragon leaves, if desired.

PER SERVING (2 halves): Calories 90 (16% from fat); Fat 2g (sat 0g, mono 1g, poly 0g); Protein 6g; Carbohydrate 14g; Fiber 2g; Cholesterol 34mg; Iron 1mg; Sodium 94mg; Calcium 18mg

shrimp and black bean nachos

Prep: 14 minutes **Chill:** 30 minutes
Serves 15

Fresh flavors in this shrimp salsa make it a great topping for any grilled fish. You can store the salsa in an airtight container in the refrigerator for up to 2 days.

- ³/₄ cup chopped fresh cilantro
- ¹/₂ cup chopped red onion
- 2 tablespoons fresh lime juice
- 1 tablespoon minced seeded serrano chile
- 1 tablespoon extra-virgin olive oil
- 1 teaspoon Worcestershire sauce
- ¹/₂ teaspoon salt
- ¹/₄ teaspoon black pepper
- ³/₄ pound medium shrimp, cooked, peeled, and chopped
- 2 cups diced tomato
- ¹/₂ cup diced peeled avocado
- 1 cup drained canned black beans
- ¹/₂ teaspoon ground cumin
- 30 baked tortilla chips

1. Combine first 9 ingredients (cilantro through shrimp) in a large bowl; toss well. Cover and refrigerate 30 minutes. Add tomato and avocado; stir well.
2. Place beans and cumin in a food processor or blender, and process 30 seconds or until smooth. Spread each chip with 1 teaspoon black bean mixture. Top with 1 tablespoon shrimp salsa. Serve immediately.

PER SERVING (2 nachos): Calories 83 (26% from fat); Protein 5g; Fat 2g (sat 0g, mono 1g, poly 0g); Carbohydrate 11g; Fiber 2g; Cholesterol 26mg; Iron 1mg; Sodium 187mg; Calcium 29mg

scallops in shiitakes

Prep: 15 minutes **Cook:** 10 minutes
Serves 8

The scallops can be cut in half horizontally or crosswise to fit into the mushroom caps. Double the serving size, and you also have an entrée.

- 24 medium shiitake mushroom caps (about 1¹/₂-inch diameter)
- ¹/₄ teaspoon freshly ground black pepper
- 12 medium sea scallops, cut in half (about 1 pound)
- 2 tablespoons commercial pesto

1. Preheat oven to 450°.
2. Arrange shiitake mushroom caps in a shallow baking dish. Sprinkle pepper into mushroom caps. Place 1 scallop half into each mushroom cap. Spoon ¹/₄ teaspoon pesto onto each scallop half. Bake mushrooms at 450° for 10 minutes or until scallops are done. Serve warm.

PER SERVING (3 stuffed mushrooms): Calories 99 (27% from fat); Protein 12g; Fat 3g (sat 1g, mono 1g, poly 1g); Carbohydrate 8g; Fiber 2g; Cholesterol 18mg; Iron 2mg; Sodium 138mg; Calcium 48mg

Even More Snack Suggestions

We gave you our list of favorite snacks in Chapter 5, but we also have a few favorite snacks in this chapter. Pick a recipe below and keep the ingredients on hand for when hunger strikes.

- Barbecue Pizza Bites (page 69)
- Banana-Nut Energy Bars (page 70)
- Peanut Butter-Granola Trail Mix (page 70)
- Blackberry Smoothie (page 72)
- Peanut Butter-Chocolate Shake (page 72)

barbecue pizza bites

pictured on page 74

Prep: *8 minutes* **Cook:** *24 minutes*
Serves 16

These kid-friendly treats are a perfect after-school snack. But, they're also a favorite with grown-ups. Serve them at your next football party in place of chips and dip.

- 1/2 pound ground round
- 1/2 cup chopped onion
- 1/2 cup chopped carrot
- 1/3 cup barbecue sauce
- 3 tablespoons brown sugar
- 1/4 teaspoon salt
- Dash of black pepper
- 4 (4-ounce) Italian pizza crusts (such as Boboli)
- 1/4 cup (1 ounce) finely shredded provolone or part-skim mozzarella cheese
- 2 tablespoons chopped fresh cilantro

1. Preheat oven to 450°.
2. Cook beef, onion, and carrot in a large nonstick skillet over medium-high heat until browned, stirring to crumble. Drain well; return meat mixture to pan. Stir in barbecue sauce, sugar, salt, and pepper; reduce heat, and simmer 5 minutes.
3. Place pizza crusts on a baking sheet. Divide beef mixture evenly among crusts, and sprinkle with cheese. Bake pizzas at 450° for 12 minutes or until cheese melts. Sprinkle pizzas with cilantro. Cut each pizza into 4 wedges.

PER SERVING (1 wedge): Calories 116 (23% from fat); Protein 7g; Fat 3g (sat 1g, mono 1g, poly 1g); Carbohydrate 15g; Fiber 1g; Cholesterol 10mg; Iron 1mg; Sodium 253mg; Calcium 94mg

mu shu pork wraps

pictured on page 76

Prep: *20 minutes* **Cook:** *7 minutes*
Serves 8

If you like more spice, add extra chile paste when cooking the pork.

- 1/4 cup fat-free, less-sodium chicken broth
- 2 tablespoons low-sodium soy sauce
- 1 tablespoon grated peeled fresh ginger
- 1 tablespoon hoisin sauce
- 1 teaspoon cornstarch
- 1 teaspoon vegetable oil
- 1/2 pound pork tenderloin, trimmed, halved lengthwise, and thinly sliced (1/2 inch)
- 1 teaspoon chile paste with garlic
- 2 garlic cloves, minced
- 4 cups packaged coleslaw mix
- 1 cup red bell pepper, cut into 1/2-inch strips
- 1 cup vertically sliced onion
- 8 (7-inch) flour tortillas

1. Combine first 5 ingredients (broth through cornstarch) in a bowl; set aside.
2. Heat oil in a nonstick skillet over medium-high heat. Add pork, chile paste, and minced garlic; sauté 2 minutes or until pork is lightly browned. Add coleslaw, bell pepper, and onion; sauté 2 minutes or until tender. Stir in broth mixture, and cook 1 minute or until slightly thick.
3. Warm tortillas according to package directions. Spoon 1/2 cup pork mixture into each tortilla; roll up.

PER SERVING (1 wrap): Calories 199 (24% from fat); Protein 10g; Fat 5g (sat 1g, mono 2g, poly 2g); Carbohydrate 27g; Fiber 2g; Cholesterol 19mg; Iron 2mg; Sodium 476mg; Calcium 86mg

curried chicken kebabs

Prep: *14 minutes* **Cook:** *8 minutes*
Marinate: *1 hour*
Serves 12

- 1 pound skinless, boneless chicken breast halves, cut into 1-inch pieces
- 1/4 cup commercial mango chutney
- 1 tablespoon spicy brown mustard
- 1/2 teaspoon curry powder
- 1/8 teaspoon ground red pepper
- 1 red bell pepper, seeded and cut into 1-inch pieces
- 4 green onions, sliced diagonally into 1-inch pieces
- Cooking spray
- Lime wedges
- Chopped fresh cilantro (optional)

1. Place chicken in a shallow dish. Combine chutney and next 3 ingredients, stirring well. Spoon chutney mixture over chicken, stirring to coat. Cover and marinate chicken in refrigerator 1 hour, stirring once.
2. While chicken marinates, soak 12 (6-inch) wooden skewers in water for at least 30 minutes. Remove chicken from marinade, reserving marinade. Thread chicken, red pepper, and green onions alternately onto skewers. Brush kebabs with marinade.
3. Prepare grill.
4. Place kebabs on grill rack coated with cooking spray; grill, covered, 4 minutes on each side or until chicken is done and vegetables are tender. Serve with lime wedges. Garnish with cilantro, if desired.

PER SERVING (1 kebab): Calories 72 (13% from fat); Protein 9g; Fat 1g (sat 0g, mono 0g, poly 0g); Carbohydrate 6g; Fiber 0g; Cholesterol 24mg; Iron 1mg; Sodium 95mg; Calcium 10mg

curried deviled eggs

Prep: *8 minutes* **Chill:** *1 hour*
Serves 16

When eaten in moderation, eggs can be a part of any healthy diet. In this recipe, we've discarded a few of the egg yolks, the yellow part of the egg that's full of fat and cholesterol. The final product is lower in fat while still having a creamy deviled egg filling.

8	hard-boiled large eggs, shells removed
1/4	cup plain fat-free yogurt
2	tablespoons low-fat mayonnaise
2/3	cup cooked cubed peeled baking potato
1	teaspoon curry powder
1/2	teaspoon salt
1/2	teaspoon grated peeled fresh ginger
1/8	teaspoon hot pepper sauce
2	tablespoons chopped green onions (optional)

1. Slice eggs in half lengthwise; remove yolks, and reserve 4 whole yolks for another use.
2. Combine yogurt and next 6 ingredients (yogurt through hot pepper sauce) in a medium bowl; mash with a fork. Add remaining yolks; beat with a mixer at high speed until smooth. Spoon about 1 tablespoon yolk mixture into each egg-white half. Cover and chill 1 hour. Garnish with green onions, if desired.

PER SERVING (1 egg half): Calories 34 (38% from fat); Protein 3g; Fat 1g (sat 0g, mono 1g, poly 0g); Carbohydrate 3g; Fiber 0g; Cholesterol 53mg; Iron 0g; Sodium 123mg; Calcium 13mg

banana-nut energy bars

Prep: *14 minutes* **Cook:** *25 minutes*
Serves 12

Multigrain hot cereal makes these bars a snap to throw together. Keep them on hand in an airtight container for when you need a quick energy boost.

1/2	cup mashed ripe banana
1/3	cup packed brown sugar
1/4	cup honey
1	tablespoon vegetable oil
1/2	teaspoon vanilla extract
1	large egg
1/2	cup all-purpose flour
1 1/4	cups multigrain hot cereal (such as Quaker) or quick-cooking oats
1/4	cup chopped pecans
1/2	teaspoon salt
Cooking spray	

1. Preheat oven to 350°.
2. Beat first 6 ingredients (banana through egg) with a mixer at medium speed until blended. Lightly spoon flour into a dry measuring cup, and level with a knife. Gradually add flour, cereal, pecans, and salt to banana mixture, stirring until well blended.
3. Spoon mixture into an 8-inch square baking pan coated with cooking spray. Bake at 350° for 25 minutes. Cool completely on a wire rack. Cut into bars.

PER SERVING (1 bar): Calories 133 (24% from fat); Protein 2g; Fat 4g (sat 1g, mono 2g, poly 1g); Carbohydrate 24g; Fiber 2g; Cholesterol 18mg; Iron 1mg; Sodium 106mg; Calcium 10mg

peanut butter-granola trail mix

pictured on page 74

Prep: *2 minutes* **Cook:** *25 minutes*
Cool: *30 minutes*
Serves 7

For a quick, on-the-go snack, store this crunchy trail mix in small, plastic zip-top bags.

1/4	cup creamy peanut butter
1/4	cup maple-flavored syrup
1	cup low-fat granola with raisins (such as Kellogg's Low-fat Granola with Raisins)
32	tiny fat-free pretzels, broken into small pieces
Cooking spray	
1/2	cup golden raisins
1/2	cup sweetened dried cranberries (such as Craisins)

1. Preheat oven to 300°.
2. Combine peanut butter and syrup in a small microwave-safe bowl. Microwave at high 30 seconds or until hot; stir well. Place granola and pretzels in a large bowl; pour peanut butter mixture over granola mixture, stirring to coat. Spread mixture on a jelly-roll pan coated with cooking spray.
3. Bake at 300° for 25 minutes, stirring twice. Stir in raisins and cranberries; return pan to oven. Turn oven off; cool mixture in closed oven 30 minutes. Remove from oven; cool completely.

PER SERVING (1/2 cup): Calories 225 (23% from fat); Protein 5g; Fat 6g (sat 1g, mono 3g, poly 2g); Carbohydrate 42g; Fiber 3g; Cholesterol 0mg; Iron 2mg; Sodium 180mg; Calcium 22mg

trail blazin' mix

Prep: *4 minutes* **Cook:** *20 minutes*
Stand: *30 minutes*
Serves 18

- 1 (18-ounce) box low-fat granola with raisins
- 1/2 cup honey
- 1 (6-ounce) package dried chopped tropical fruit medley
- 1 cup tropical-flavored gourmet jelly beans
- 1/4 cup semisweet chocolate minichips

1. Preheat oven to 325°.
2. Spread granola in a jelly-roll pan; drizzle with honey, and toss well. Bake at 325° for 20 minutes, stirring every 7 minutes. Remove from oven, and stir in dried fruit; return to oven. Turn oven off, and let mixture stand in closed oven 30 minutes. Remove from oven, and let cool completely. Combine granola mixture, jelly beans, and minichips in a bowl; toss well.

PER SERVING (1/2 cup): Calories 215 (10% from fat); Protein 3g; Fat 2g (sat 1g, mono 0g, poly 0g); Carbohydrate 49g; Fiber 2g; Cholesterol 0mg; Iron 1mg; Sodium 78mg; Calcium 11mg

moroccan mint tea

Prep: *9 minutes*
Serves 8

Fresh mint offers an invigorating taste and aroma to ordinary tea.

- 8 cups boiling water
- 2 regular-sized tea bags
- 2 cups mint sprigs
- 1/3 cup sugar

1. Pour boiling water over tea bags. Cover and let stand 5 minutes. Remove tea bags; discard.

Add mint and sugar; stir well. Discard mint. Serve hot or cold.

PER SERVING (1 cup): Calories 32 (0% from fat); Protein 0g; Fat 0g; Carbohydrate 8g; Fiber 0g; Cholesterol 0mg; Iron 0mg; Sodium 0mg; Calcium 0mg

cranberry-apple limeade

Prep: *3 minutes* **Chill:** *30 minutes*
Serves 12

- 1/4 cup fresh lime juice
- 2 (6-ounce) cans thawed limeade concentrate, undiluted
- 1 (48-ounce) bottle cranberry juice cocktail, chilled
- 1 (32-ounce) bottle apple juice, chilled

1. Combine all ingredients in a pitcher; stir well, and chill. Serve over ice.

PER SERVING (1 cup): Calories 156 (1% from fat); Protein 0g; Fat 0g; Carbohydrate 40g; Fiber 0g; Cholesterol 0mg; Iron 1mg; Sodium 7mg; Calcium 10mg

white sangría fizz

pictured on page 56

Prep: *6 minutes* **Chill:** *8 hours*
Serves 7

This refreshing drink is perfect for a Mexican fiesta or as an after-work treat.

- 1 medium navel orange, sliced
- 1 lemon, sliced
- 1 lime, sliced
- 1/3 cup fresh orange juice
- 1/4 cup sugar
- 1 (750-milliliter) bottle dry white wine
- 1 1/2 cups seltzer, chilled

1. Combine first 5 ingredients in a pitcher; stir until sugar is nearly dissolved. Stir in wine. Chill 8 hours.
2. Add seltzer just before serving. Divide fruit evenly among glasses; pour wine mixture into glasses.

PER SERVING (1 cup): Calories 121 (0% from fat); Protein 1g; Fat 0g; Carbohydrate 14g; Fiber 1g; Cholesterol 0mg; Iron 1mg; Sodium 20mg; Calcium 25mg

watermelon margaritas

Prep: *7 minutes*
Serves 6

- 2 teaspoons sugar
- 1 lime wedge
- 3 1/2 cups cubed seeded watermelon
- 1/2 cup tequila
- 3 tablespoons sugar
- 3 tablespoons fresh lime juice
- 1 tablespoon triple sec (orange-flavored liqueur)
- 3 cups crushed ice

1. Place 2 teaspoons sugar in a saucer. Rub rims of 6 glasses with 1 lime wedge; spin rim of each glass in sugar to coat. Set prepared glasses aside.
2. Combine watermelon and next 4 ingredients (watermelon through triple sec) in a blender; process until smooth. Fill each prepared glass with 1/2 cup crushed ice. Add 1/2 cup watermelon mixture to each glass. Serve immediately.

NOTE: Add 2 to 3 drops of red food coloring to blender for a deeper red coloring, if desired.

PER SERVING (1 prepared glass): Calories 115 (3% from fat); Protein 1g; Fat 0g; Carbohydrate 16g; Fiber 1g; Cholesterol 0mg; Iron 0mg; Sodium 2mg; Calcium 8mg

blackberry smoothie

Prep: *3 minutes*
Serves 3

You can substitute any fresh or frozen berry for the blackberries in this shake.

- 2 cups fresh or frozen blackberries
- 1 cup plain fat-free yogurt
- 1 cup apple juice
- 1/4 cup honey
- 1 large ripe banana

1. Combine all ingredients in a blender; process until smooth. Strain blackberry mixture through a sieve; discard seeds.

PER SERVING (1 1/2 cups): Calories 265 (3% from fat); Protein 6g; Fat 1g (sat 0g, mono 0g, poly 0g); Carbohydrate 63g; Fiber 9g; Cholesterol 2mg; Iron 1mg; Sodium 62mg; Calcium 192mg

orange-banana shake

Prep: *2 minutes*
Serves 4

Ideal for breakfast or dessert, this shake is a delicious way to get extra calcium and vitamin C.

- 2 cups vanilla low-fat ice cream
- 1 1/2 cups orange juice
- 1 (6-ounce) can pineapple juice
- 1 ripe banana, cut into 4 pieces
Fresh fruit (optional)

1. Place first 4 ingredients in a blender, and process until smooth. Garnish with a skewer of fresh fruit, if desired. Serve immediately.

PER SERVING (1 cup): Calories 185 (15% from fat); Protein 4g; Fat 3g (sat 2g, mono 1g, poly 0g); Carbohydrate 38g; Fiber 1g; Cholesterol 9mg; Iron 0mg; Sodium 58mg; Calcium 109mg

mango-strawberry smoothie

Prep: *5 minutes*
Serves 2

- 1 cup chopped peeled mango
- 1 cup hulled strawberries
- 3/4 cup crushed ice
- 1/2 cup vanilla low-fat yogurt
- 1/4 cup cold water
- 2 teaspoons minced crystallized ginger
- 2 teaspoons honey

1. Combine all ingredients in a blender, and purée until well blended.

PER SERVING (1 1/2 cups): Calories 133 (7% from fat); Fiber 3g; Fat 1g (sat 1g, mono 0g, poly 0g); Protein 4g; Carbohydrate 29g; Cholesterol 3mg; Iron 1mg; Sodium 49mg; Calcium 139mg

peanut butter-chocolate shake

Prep: *3 minutes* **Freeze:** *45 minutes*
Serves 3

- 2 cups sliced banana
- 3/4 cup 1% low-fat milk
- 1/2 cup vanilla low-fat ice cream
- 1/2 cup crushed ice
- 3 tablespoons chocolate-flavored syrup
- 2 tablespoons peanut butter

1. Freeze banana slices in a single layer on a baking sheet 45 minutes or until firm.
2. Place frozen banana slices, milk, and remaining ingredients in a blender; process until smooth. Serve immediately.

PER SERVING (1 cup): Calories 265 (20% from fat); Protein 7g; Fat 7g (sat 2g, mono 3g, poly 2g); Carbohydrate 48g; Fiber 4g; Cholesterol 4mg; Iron 1mg; Sodium 110mg; Calcium 117mg

mocha mudslide

pictured on page 73

Prep: *2 minutes* **Freeze:** *1 hour*
Serves 2

Refuel with this creamy shake. The potassium from the banana helps to restore your energy after a workout.

- 1 cup fat-free milk
- 2/3 cup sliced ripe banana
- 2 tablespoons sugar
- 1 teaspoon instant coffee granules
- 1/4 cup chocolate low-fat yogurt
Banana slices (optional)

1. Place first 4 ingredients in a blender; process until smooth. Place blender container in freezer; freeze 1 hour or until slightly frozen. Loosen frozen mixture from sides of blender container; add yogurt. Process until smooth, and garnish with sliced banana, if desired. Serve immediately.

NOTE: For an extra-chocolatey shake, use reduced-fat chocolate milk instead of plain fat-free milk, and reduce the sugar to 1 tablespoon.

PER SERVING (1 cup): Calories 164 (4% from fat); Protein 6g; Fat 1g (sat 1g, mono 0g, poly 0g); Carbohydrate 34g; Fiber 2g; Cholesterol 4mg; Iron 0mg; Sodium 83mg; Calcium 204mg

Mocha Mudslide,
page 72

Barbecue Pizza Bites,
page 69

Peanut Butter-Granola
Trail Mix, page 70

Pan-Roasted Corn
Salsa, page 64

satisfying appetizers & beverages

Roasted Asparagus and Goat Cheese Crostini, page 65

Light Guacamole, page 61

Asparagus-Raspberry Salsa, page 63

Mu Shu Pork Wraps,
page 69

mouthwatering breads

Parmesan Onion Rolls, page 90

Spinach-Feta Bread, page 85

Lemon-Glazed Cranberry Rolls, page 83

mouthwatering breads

Honey-Wheat Bread,
page 92

Cornmeal-Pecan Pancakes, page 86

Sticky Caramel-Pecan Rolls, page 82

Four-Grain Flapjacks, page 85

Hot Chocolate Muffins,
page 88

mouthwatering breads

Four Grain Flapjacks,
page 85

crisp-and-spicy cheese twists

Prep: *8 minutes* **Cook:** *8 minutes*
Makes 16 breadsticks

With cheese and spice in every twist and turn, these breadsticks make a delicious side for a hearty bowl of chili or a crisp green salad.

- 1/4 cup (1 ounce) grated Parmesan cheese
- 1 teaspoon paprika
- 1/8 teaspoon ground red pepper
- 1 (10-ounce) can refrigerated pizza crust dough
- Cooking spray

1. Preheat oven to 425°.
2. Combine first 3 ingredients (cheese through pepper) in a small bowl; stir well, and set aside.
3. Unroll pizza dough, and roll into an 8- x 12-inch rectangle. Lightly coat surface of dough with cooking spray. Sprinkle with 2 tablespoons cheese mixture. Fold dough in half to form a 6 x 8-inch rectangle. Roll dough into a 12 x 8-inch rectangle. Lightly coat surface of dough with cooking spray, and sprinkle with remaining cheese mixture. Using fingertips, press cheese mixture into dough.
4. Cut dough into 16 (8-inch-long) strips. Gently pick up both ends of each strip, and twist dough. Place dough ½ inch apart on a large baking sheet coated with cooking spray.
5. Bake at 425° for 8 minutes or until lightly browned. Remove breadsticks from pan, and let cool on wire racks.

PER SERVING (1 breadstick): Calories 68 (15% from fat); Protein 28g; Fat 1g (sat 1g, mono 0g, poly 0g); Carbohydrate 12g; Fiber 1g; Cholesterol 1mg; Iron 0mg; Sodium 189mg; Calcium 25mg

sweet onion-poppy seed flatbread

Prep: *25 minutes* **Cook:** *25 minutes*
Serves 8

Don't worry that the dough is patted so thin; flatbreads are traditionally thin and crispy.

- 1 pound Vidalia or other sweet onions
- Cooking spray
- 2 tablespoons chopped fresh parsley
- 1 teaspoon poppy seeds
- 1/4 teaspoon salt
- 1/8 teaspoon pepper
- 1 (11-ounce) can refrigerated French bread dough

1. Preheat oven to 350°.
2. Peel onions, and cut in half lengthwise. Cut each half crosswise into thin slices.
3. Coat a large nonstick skillet with cooking spray, and place over medium-high heat until hot. Add onions; sauté 8 minutes or until golden. Remove from heat; stir in parsley, poppy seeds, salt, and pepper.
4. Unroll bread dough, and place on a baking sheet coated with cooking spray; pat into a 16 x 7-inch rectangle. Spread onion mixture over dough, leaving a ½-inch border. Bake at 350° for 25 minutes or until golden brown. Remove from pan; let cool 5 minutes on a wire rack.

PER SERVING (1 [4 x 3½-inch] piece): Calories 140 (10% from fat); Protein 6g; Fat 2g (sat 0g, mono 1g, poly 1g); Carbohydrate 26g; Fiber 1g; Cholesterol 0mg; Iron 2mg; Sodium 344mg; Calcium 28mg

sticky caramel-pecan rolls

pictured on page 79

Prep: *14 minutes* **Cook:** *14 minutes*
Makes 8 rolls

Because these sweet rolls start with a can of refrigerated crescent dinner roll dough, they're ideal for a leisurely Saturday morning breakfast treat.

- 1/4 cup fat-free caramel-flavored sundae syrup
- Cooking spray
- 1 (8-ounce) can refrigerated reduced-fat crescent dinner rolls
- 1/4 cup firmly packed brown sugar
- 2 tablespoons finely chopped pecans
- 1/2 teaspoon ground cinnamon

1. Preheat oven to 375°.
2. Spoon 1½ teaspoons syrup into each of 8 muffin cups coated with cooking spray; set aside.
3. Unroll dough; separate into 4 rectangles. Combine brown sugar, pecans, and cinnamon. Sprinkle sugar mixture evenly over each rectangle; press gently into dough. Beginning at 1 long edge, roll up jelly-roll fashion. Pinch ends of dough to seal. Cut each roll into 6 slices. Place 3 slices, cut sides down, in prepared muffin cups. Bake at 375° for 14 minutes. Run a knife around edges of cups; invert onto a platter.

PER SERVING (1 roll): Calories 172 (30% from fat); Protein 2g; Fat 6g (sat 1g, mono 1g, poly 0g); Carbohydrate 27g; Fiber 0g; Cholesterol 0mg; Iron 1mg; Sodium 260mg; Calcium 13mg

caramel upside-down pull-apart loaf

Prep: *18 minutes* **Cook:** *20 minutes*
Rise: *50 minutes* **Cool:** *10 minutes*
Serves 12

Dripping with caramel, this bread may take a while to make, but it's well worth the effort.

- 1 (1-pound) loaf frozen white bread dough
- ¹/₂ cup firmly packed brown sugar
- ¹/₄ cup evaporated fat-free milk
- 2¹/₂ tablespoons butter
- 1 tablespoon light-colored corn syrup
- ¹/₄ teaspoon ground ginger
- ¹/₄ cup flaked sweetened coconut
- ¹/₄ cup pineapple preserves
- Cooking spray

1. Thaw bread dough in refrigerator 12 hours.
2. Combine brown sugar and next 4 ingredients (brown sugar through ginger) in a saucepan; cook until butter melts, stirring frequently. Bring mixture to a boil over medium-high heat; cover and cook 1 minute. Remove from heat; stir in coconut and preserves. Let cool; cover and chill.
3. Divide dough into 3 equal portions; cut each portion into 16 (1-inch) pieces. Arrange 16 pieces of dough in an 8¹/₂- x 4¹/₂-inch loaf pan coated with cooking spray. Drizzle with ¹/₃ cup sugar mixture. Arrange another 16 pieces in pan, and drizzle with ¹/₃ cup sugar mixture. Add remaining 16 pieces of dough. Set remaining ¹/₃ cup sugar mixture aside. Cover dough, and let rise in a warm place (85°), free from drafts, 50 minutes or until doubled in size.

4. Preheat oven to 375°.
5. Uncover dough, and bake at 375° for 20 minutes or until brown. Let cool 10 minutes. Place a plate, upside down, on top of pan, and invert bread onto plate. Brush remaining ¹/₃ cup sugar mixture over top and sides of bread.

PER SERVING (4 pull-apart pieces): Calories 179 (22% from fat); Protein 4g; Fat 4g (sat 2g, mono 1g, poly 0g); Carbohydrate 32g; Fiber 0g; Cholesterol 7mg; Iron 1mg; Sodium 217mg; Calcium 44mg

VARIATION:
apricot-chocolate upside-down pull-apart loaf

Prepare as for Caramel Upside-Down Pull-Apart Loaf, substituting apricot preserves for pineapple preserves. Omit coconut from sugar mixture, and add ¹/₄ cup semisweet chocolate chips. Stir mixture until chocolate chips melt.

PER SERVING (4 pull-apart pieces): Calories 187 (24% from fat); Protein 4g; Fat 5g (sat 2g, mono 1g, poly 0g); Carbohydrate 33g; Fiber 0g; Cholesterol 7mg; Iron 1mg; Sodium 208mg; Calcium 45mg

lemon-glazed cranberry rolls

pictured on page 77

Prep: *10 minutes* **Cook:** *15 minutes*
Makes 12 rolls

- 1 (10-ounce) can refrigerated pizza crust dough
- ¹/₂ cup orange marmalade
- ²/₃ cup dried cranberries
- Cooking spray
- ¹/₂ cup sifted powdered sugar
- 1¹/₂ teaspoons lemon juice
- 1 teaspoon hot water

1. Preheat oven to 375°.
2. Unroll pizza dough, and pat into a 12 x 9-inch rectangle. Spread marmalade over dough, leaving a ¹/₂-inch border. Sprinkle cranberries over marmalade, pressing gently into dough. Beginning with a long side, roll up jelly-roll fashion; pinch seam to seal (do not seal ends of roll). Cut roll into 12 (1-inch) slices. Place slices, cut sides up, in muffin cups coated with cooking spray.
3. Bake at 375° for 15 minutes or until golden. Remove rolls from pan. Place on a wire rack.
4. Combine powdered sugar, lemon juice, and hot water in a small bowl, stirring until smooth. Drizzle icing over warm rolls.

PER SERVING (1 roll): Calories 155 (6% from fat); Protein 3g; Fat 1g (sat 0g, mono 0g, poly 0g); Carbohydrate 35g; Fiber 3g; Cholesterol 0mg; Iron 0mg; Sodium 229mg; Calcium 15mg

The Secret to Making Quick Homemade Bread

The bread's out of the bag: Frozen bread dough, refrigerated breadsticks, and refrigerated pizza crust dough are the keys to putting freshly baked bread on the table any (or every) night of the week. To give you an easy start, we've included several recipes that use these products. With our quick tips below, you'll have warm, homemade breads in minutes.

- Thaw the bread dough overnight in the refrigerator.
- Set dough up to rise while you're doing something else.
- Make the glaze, filling, or topping ahead and refrigerate.
- Cut refrigerated dough with a pizza cutter.

apricot-almond braid

Prep: *25 minutes* **Cook:** *22 minutes*
Rise: *40 minutes*
Serves 12

Pretty on a platter and festive for the holidays, this braid is versatile, too. It's simple to substitute your favorite flavor of preserves.

 1 (1-pound) loaf frozen white
    bread dough
Cooking spray
 1 (3-ounce) block cream cheese,
    softened
 1/2 cup apricot preserves
 3 tablespoons sliced almonds,
    divided
 1 large egg white, lightly beaten

1. Thaw dough in refrigerator according to package directions.
2. Cover a large baking sheet with heavy-duty foil; coat foil with cooking spray. Press dough into a 12- x 8-inch rectangle on prepared baking sheet. Spread cream cheese lengthwise down center third of dough. Spread preserves over cream cheese; sprinkle with 2 tablespoons almonds.
3. Make diagonal cuts, 1 inch apart, on opposite sides of filling to within 1/2 inch of filling. Fold strips alternately over filling from each side, overlapping at an angle. Cover; let rise in a warm place (85°), free from drafts, 40 minutes or until puffy.
4. Preheat oven to 350°.
5. Brush egg white over loaf; sprinkle with remaining almonds. Bake at 350° for 22 minutes or until lightly browned.

PER SERVING (1/12 of braid): Calories 171 (26% from fat); Protein 5g; Fat 5g (sat 2g, mono 1g, poly 0g); Carbohydrate 28g; Fiber 0g; Cholesterol 8mg; Iron 0mg; Sodium 218mg; Calcium 40mg

cream cheese-filled monkey bread

Prep: *17 minutes* **Cook:** *28 minutes*
Rise: *40 minutes*
Serves 16

Every bite of this sweet bread is filled with cinnamon-sugar cream cheese and dripping with maple syrup.

 1 (2-pound) package frozen
    white bread dough
 1/2 cup (4 ounces) block-style
    cream cheese
 1/3 cup sugar, divided
 1 1/4 teaspoons ground cinnamon,
    divided
Cooking spray
 1/2 cup maple syrup

1. Thaw dough in refrigerator according to package directions.
2. Combine cream cheese, 1 tablespoon sugar, and 1/4 teaspoon cinnamon in a bowl. Stir well; set aside. Combine remaining sugar and cinnamon; stir well, and set aside.
3. Cut each loaf of dough into 24 equal portions. Flatten each portion into a 2 1/2-inch circle. Spoon 1/2 teaspoon cream cheese mixture into center of each circle. Gather dough around cheese mixture, forming a ball; pinch edges of dough together to seal. Roll each dough ball in cinnamon-sugar mixture. Layer balls in a 12-cup Bundt pan coated with cooking spray. Sprinkle any remaining cinnamon-sugar mixture over dough; pour syrup over dough. Cover and let rise in a warm place (85°), free from drafts, 40 minutes or until doubled in size.
4. Preheat oven to 350°.
5. Bake at 350° for 28 minutes or until lightly browned.

Immediately loosen edges of bread with a knife. Place a serving plate, upside down, on top of pan; invert bread onto plate. Remove pan; drizzle any remaining syrup in pan over bread.

PER SERVING (3 balls): Calories 146 (23% from fat); Protein 4g; Fat 4g (sat 2g, mono 1g, poly 0g); Carbohydrate 26g; Fiber 1g; Cholesterol 8mg; Iron 1mg; Sodium 180mg; Calcium 21mg

cranberry-apple breakfast ring

Prep: *28 minutes* **Cook:** *22 minutes*
Rise: *1 hour*
Serves 12

 1 (1-pound) loaf frozen white
    bread dough
Cooking spray
 1/2 cup whole-berry cranberry
    sauce
 1/3 cup light apple pie filling,
    chopped
 1/4 cup chopped pecans, divided
 1/2 cup sifted powdered sugar
 1 tablespoon water

1. Thaw dough in refrigerator according to package directions.
2. Pat dough into a 16- x 8-inch rectangle on a baking sheet coated with cooking spray.
3. Combine cranberry sauce and pie filling; stir well. Spread fruit mixture down 1 long edge of dough, leaving a 1/2-inch margin around edges. Sprinkle 3 tablespoons pecans over fruit mixture. Beginning at edge with fruit mixture, roll up jelly-roll fashion; pinch seam to seal (do not seal ends of roll). Bring ends of roll together to form a ring; pinch ends together to seal. Cut two-thirds through dough from outer edge at 1-inch intervals. Cover; let rise in a

warm place (85°), free from drafts, 1 hour or until doubled in size.

4. Preheat oven to 375°.

5. Bake at 375° for 22 minutes or until golden brown. Combine powdered sugar and water; stir with a whisk until smooth. Drizzle glaze over warm bread. Sprinkle with remaining pecans.

PER SERVING (¹/₁₂ of ring): Calories 182 (12% from fat); Protein 5g; Fat 3g (sat 0g, mono 1g, poly 1g); Carbohydrate 36g; Fiber 0g; Cholesterol 4mg; Iron 2mg; Sodium 351mg; Calcium 30mg

spinach-feta bread

pictured on page 77

Prep: *18 minutes* **Cook:** *45 minutes*
Rise: *1 hour*
Serves 16

 1 (1-pound) loaf frozen white bread dough
 1 cup (4 ounces) crumbled feta cheese
 ¹/₃ cup (3 ounces) ¹/₃-less-fat cream cheese
 ¹/₂ teaspoon dried oregano
 ¹/₄ teaspoon salt
 1 (14-ounce) can artichoke hearts, drained and chopped
 1 (10-ounce) package frozen chopped spinach, thawed, drained, and squeezed dry
 3 garlic cloves, minced
 1 large egg white
Cooking spray
 2 tablespoons (¹/₂ ounce) grated fresh Parmesan cheese

1. Thaw dough in refrigerator 12 hours.

2. Combine feta and next 7 ingredients (feta through egg white) in a bowl.

3. Roll dough into a 16- x 10-inch rectangle on a lightly floured surface. Spread spinach mixture over dough, leaving a ¹/₂-inch border. Beginning with a long side, roll up jelly-roll fashion; pinch seam and ends to seal. Place roll, seam side down, on a baking sheet coated with cooking spray. Cut diagonal slits into top of roll using a sharp knife. Cover and let rise in a warm place (85°), 1 hour or until doubled in size.

4. Preheat oven to 350°.

5. Sprinkle Parmesan cheese over top of roll. Bake at 350° for 45 minutes or until golden.

PER SERVING (¹/₁₆ of loaf): Calories 143 (23% from fat); Protein 6g; Fat 4g (sat 2g, mono 1g, poly 0g); Carbohydrate 22g; Fiber 1g; Cholesterol 14mg; Iron 2mg; Sodium 461mg; Calcium 99mg

quick cornmeal cakes

Prep: *2 minutes* **Cook:** *33 minutes*
Serves 4

Polenta is a soft cornmeal mixture; using polenta rather than pancake batter packs more fiber and nutrients into your morning hotcakes.

 1 tablespoon vegetable oil
 1 (16-ounce) tube plain polenta, cut into 16 slices
 ¹/₄ cup maple syrup
 1 cup fresh raspberries

1. Heat oil in a large nonstick skillet over medium-high heat. Pat polenta slices dry with a paper towel. Cook 4 minutes on each side or until lightly browned and crisp. Serve warm with syrup and raspberries.

PER SERVING (4 polenta slices, 1 tablespoon syrup, ¹/₄ cup raspberries): Calories 166 (11% from fat); Protein 2g; Fat 2g (sat 1g, mono 1g, poly 1g); Carbohydrate 35g; Fiber 4g; Cholesterol 0mg; Iron 0mg; Sodium 234mg; Calcium 21mg

four-grain flapjacks

pictured on pages 79 and 81

Prep: *30 minutes* **Cook:** *10 minutes*
Serves 9

Filled with four-grain goodness and fiber, these flapjacks will become a breakfast favorite.

 1 cup barley flour
 ¹/₂ cup whole wheat flour
 ¹/₂ cup regular oats
 ¹/₂ cup stone-ground yellow cornmeal
 1¹/₂ teaspoons baking soda
 1 teaspoon baking powder
Dash of salt
 2¹/₂ cups low-fat buttermilk
 ¹/₄ cup maple syrup
 ¹/₄ cup butter, melted
 3 large egg yolks
 3 large egg whites
Cooking spray

1. Lightly spoon barley flour and wheat flour into dry measuring cups; level with a knife. Combine barley flour, wheat flour, and next 5 ingredients (flour through salt) in a large bowl; stir with a whisk.

2. Combine buttermilk, maple syrup, butter, and egg yolks in a bowl; stir with a whisk. Add buttermilk mixture to flour mixture, stirring until combined.

3. Beat egg whites with an electric mixer at high speed until stiff peaks form (do not overbeat). Fold egg whites into batter. Spoon ¹/₃ cup batter onto a hot nonstick griddle or skillet coated with cooking spray. Turn flapjacks when tops are covered with bubbles and edges are cooked.

PER SERVING (2 flapjacks): Calories 247 (29% from fat); Fat 8g (sat 4g, mono 3g, poly 1g); Protein 8g; Carbohydrate 36g; Fiber 4g; Cholesterol 87mg; Iron 2mg; Sodium 434mg; Calcium 116mg

cornmeal-pecan pancakes

pictured on page 79

Prep: *6 minutes* **Cook:** *15 minutes*
Serves 8

If you have time, quickly toast the pecans in a skillet or in the oven to bring out their rich, nutty flavor.

    1   cup all-purpose flour
  1/2   cup yellow cornmeal
  1/4   cup finely chopped pecans,
          toasted
    1   tablespoon sugar
    1   tablespoon baking powder
  1/2   teaspoon baking soda
  1/2   teaspoon salt
    2   cups low-fat buttermilk
    1   tablespoon vegetable oil
    1   large egg, lightly beaten
  3/4   cup maple syrup

1. Combine first 7 ingredients (flour through salt) in a bowl; stir well. Combine buttermilk, oil, and egg; stir well. Add to flour mixture, stirring until smooth.
2. Spoon about 1/4 cup batter for each pancake onto a hot non-stick griddle or nonstick skillet. Turn pancakes when tops are covered with bubbles and edges look cooked. Serve hot with maple syrup.

PER SERVING (2 pancakes and 1 1/2 tablespoons syrup): Calories 247 (23% from fat); Protein 6g; Fat 6g (sat 1g, mono 3g, poly 2g); Carbohydrate 43g; Fiber 1g; Cholesterol 27mg; Iron 2mg; Sodium 387mg; Calcium 168mg

dried cherry scones

Prep: *15 minutes* **Cook:** *18 minutes*
Makes 10 scones

These scones get a double shot of cherry flavor from dried cherries and cherry-flavored yogurt.

  1/2   cup sugar, divided
  2 3/4 cups reduced-fat baking mix
  1/4   cup chilled light butter, cut into
          small pieces
  1/2   cup dried sweet cherries
    1   (8-ounce) carton cherry vanilla
          fat-free yogurt (such as
          Dannon Light)
Cooking spray
    1   tablespoon light butter, melted

1. Preheat oven to 400°.
2. Reserve 1 tablespoon sugar to sprinkle over top of scones; set aside. Combine remaining sugar and baking mix in a bowl; stir well. Cut in 1/4 cup butter with a pastry blender or 2 knives until mixture resembles coarse meal. Add cherries; toss well. Add yogurt, stirring just until moist (dough will be sticky).
3. Turn dough out onto a lightly floured surface. Knead dough with floured hands 4 or 5 times. Pat dough into a 9-inch circle on a baking sheet coated with cooking spray. Cut dough into 10 wedges with a lightly floured knife, cutting into, but not through, dough. Sprinkle reserved sugar over dough.
4. Bake at 400° for 18 minutes or until golden. Remove from oven, and brush with melted butter.

PER SERVING (1 scone): Calories 220 (21% from fat); Protein 4g; Fat 5g (sat 2g, mono 0g, poly 0g); Carbohydrate 41g; Fiber 1g; Cholesterol 11mg; Iron 1mg; Sodium 429mg; Calcium 72mg

gingersnap scones with espresso glaze

Prep: *14 minutes* **Cook:** *15 minutes*
Makes 10 scones

  1 3/4 cups all-purpose flour
  1/4   cup gingersnap crumbs (about
          6 cookies, finely crushed)
  1/4   cup granulated sugar
  1 1/2 teaspoons baking powder
  1/2   teaspoon baking soda
  1/4   teaspoon salt
  1/4   cup chilled butter, cut into
          small pieces
  1/2   cup low-fat buttermilk
    1   large egg, lightly beaten
Cooking spray
    1   tablespoon hot water
  1/2   teaspoon instant coffee
          granules
  3/4   cup sifted powdered sugar
   10   walnut halves

1. Preheat oven to 400°.
2. Combine first 6 ingredients (flour through salt) in a bowl; cut in butter with a pastry blender or 2 knives until mixture resembles coarse meal. Add buttermilk and egg, stirring just until moist (dough will be sticky).
3. Turn dough out onto a lightly floured surface; with floured hands, knead lightly 4 times. Pat dough into a 10-inch circle on a baking sheet coated with cooking spray. Cut dough into 10 wedges, cutting into, but not through, dough.
4. Bake at 400° for 15 minutes or until golden. Combine hot water and coffee granules; stir well. Add powdered sugar and stir well. Drizzle over scones. Cut into 10 wedges; top each with 1 walnut half.

PER SERVING (1 scone): Calories 220 (30% from fat); Protein 4g; Fat 7g (sat 1g, mono 3g, poly 3g); Carbohydrate 35g; Fiber 1g; Cholesterol 24mg; Iron 1mg; Sodium 194mg; Calcium 73mg

toasted oat scones

pictured on page 53

Prep: *18 minutes* **Cook:** *15 minutes*
Makes 12 scones

1¼   cups regular oats
1½   cups all-purpose flour
½   cup sugar
2   teaspoons baking powder
¼   teaspoon baking soda
½   teaspoon salt
½   teaspoon ground nutmeg
4   tablespoons chilled butter, cut into small pieces
½   cup chopped dates
¾   cup low-fat buttermilk
1   teaspoon vanilla extract
Cooking spray
1   tablespoon butter, melted

1. Preheat oven to 450°.
2. Spread oats on a baking sheet; bake at 450° for 3 minutes or until lightly toasted, stirring once. Let cool completely.
3. Combine 1 cup toasted oats, flour, and next 5 ingredients (sugar through nutmeg); cut in chilled butter with a pastry blender or 2 knives until mixture resembles coarse meal. Add dates; toss well. Add buttermilk and vanilla; stir just until moist.
4. Turn dough out onto a floured surface; with floured hands, knead lightly 4 times. Pat dough into a 9-inch circle on a baking sheet coated with cooking spray. Brush melted butter over dough; sprinkle with remaining oats. Cut dough into 12 wedges, separating wedges slightly. Bake at 450° for 12 minutes or until golden. Serve warm.

PER SERVING (1 scone): Calories 189 (27% from fat); Protein 4g; Fat 6g (sat 1g, mono 0g, poly 0g); Carbohydrate 31g; Fiber 2g; Cholesterol 0mg; Iron 1mg; Sodium 232mg; Calcium 59mg

nutty sweet potato biscuits

Prep: *20 minutes* **Cook:** *12 minutes*
Makes 22 biscuits

Nutrient-rich sweet potato adds flavor and moistness to these biscuits without adding extra fat.

2¾   cups all-purpose flour
1   tablespoon plus 1 teaspoon baking powder
½   teaspoon salt
⅔   cup sugar
½   teaspoon ground cinnamon
½   teaspoon ground nutmeg
¼   cup chopped walnuts
2   cups cooked mashed sweet potato
3   tablespoons butter, melted
1   teaspoon vanilla extract
2   tablespoons all-purpose flour
Cooking spray

1. Preheat oven to 450°.
2. Combine first 6 ingredients (flour through nutmeg) in a large bowl. Add nuts; stir well.
3. Combine sweet potato, butter, and vanilla in a medium bowl; add to flour mixture, stirring just until dry ingredients are moistened.
4. Sprinkle 2 tablespoons flour evenly over work surface. Turn dough out onto floured surface, and knead 10 to 12 times. Roll dough to ½-inch thickness; cut into rounds with a 2-inch biscuit cutter. Place rounds on a baking sheet coated with cooking spray. Bake at 450° for 12 to 15 minutes or until biscuits are golden.

PER SERVING (1 biscuit): Calories 143 (19% from fat); Protein 3g; Fat 3g (sat 0g, mono 0g, poly 0g); Carbohydrate 27g; Fiber 2g; Cholesterol 0mg; Iron 1mg; Sodium 76mg; Calcium 61mg

peanutty chocolate chip-banana muffins

Prep: *9 minutes* **Cook:** *20 minutes*
Makes 16 muffins

Add a little chocolate and peanut butter to a packaged banana bread mix and in 20 minutes, you'll have "hard to resist" muffins for breakfasts or snacks.

1   (14-ounce) package banana quick bread mix (such as Pillsbury)
¼   cup semisweet chocolate minichips
¾   cup mashed banana
¾   cup water
⅓   cup chunky peanut butter
3   large egg whites
Cooking spray

1. Preheat oven to 400°.
2. Combine bread mix and chips in a medium bowl; make a well in center of mixture. Combine banana and next 3 ingredients (banana through egg whites); stir with a whisk until blended. Add to dry ingredients, stirring just until moist.
3. Divide batter among 16 muffin cups coated with cooking spray.
4. Bake at 400° for 20 minutes or until muffins spring back when touched lightly in center. Remove muffins from pans immediately, and place on a wire rack.

PER SERVING (1 muffin): Calories 155 (27% from fat); Protein 4g; Fat 5g (sat 1g, mono 2g, poly 1g); Carbohydrate 26g; Fiber 1g; Cholesterol 0mg; Iron 1mg; Sodium 190mg; Calcium 2mg

fig, date, banana, and nut muffins

Prep: *7 minutes* **Cook:** *15 minutes*
Makes 6 muffins

These quick and easy muffins are perfect for when you want just a bite of something sweet. The recipe makes only six muffins, so double the recipe if you're feeding a crowd.

- 1 (6.4-ounce) package banana nut muffin mix (such as Betty Crocker)
- 1/3 cup low-fat buttermilk
- 1 large egg, lightly beaten
- Cooking spray
- 1/4 cup fig preserves
- 2 tablespoons chopped dates

1. Preheat oven to 400°.
2. Combine first 3 ingredients (muffin mix through egg) in a bowl; stir just until moist. Spoon 1 tablespoon batter into each of 6 muffin cups coated with cooking spray, spreading to cover bottom of cups. Spoon 2 teaspoons preserves and 1 teaspoon dates into center of each cup; divide remaining batter evenly among cups to cover fruit. Bake at 400° for 15 minutes. Remove muffins from pan immediately, and place on a wire rack.

PER SERVING (1 muffin): Calories 197 (23% from fat); Protein 4g; Fat 5g (sat 1g, mono 0g, poly 0g); Carbohydrate 33g; Fiber 0g; Cholesterol 35mg; Iron 1mg; Sodium 248mg; Calcium 22mg

hot chocolate muffins

pictured on page 80

Prep: *12 minutes* **Cook:** *11 minutes*
Makes 12 muffins

- 2 1/4 cups reduced-fat biscuit and baking mix
- 1/2 cup sugar
- 2 tablespoons cocoa
- 1/2 cup half-and-half
- 1/4 cup chocolate syrup
- 1 1/2 tablespoons vegetable oil
- 2 teaspoons vanilla extract
- 1 large egg, lightly beaten
- 1/2 cup semisweet chocolate mini-morsels
- 1/4 cup powdered sugar

1. Preheat oven to 400°.
2. Combine baking mix, sugar, and cocoa in a large bowl. Make a well in center of mixture. Combine half-and-half and next 4 ingredients (half-and-half through eggs); add to dry ingredients, stirring just until dry ingredients are moistened. Stir in chocolate morsels.
3. Spoon into greased muffin pans, filling two-thirds full. Bake at 400° for 11 to 12 minutes or until a wooden pick inserted into center comes out clean. Remove from pans immediately. Cool on wire racks.
3. Once cool, sift powdered sugar over tops of muffins.

PER SERVING (1 muffin): Calories 219 (29% from fat); Protein 3g; Fat 7g (sat 2g, mono 2g, poly 1g); Carbohydrate 36g; Fiber 1g; Cholesterol 23mg; Iron 1mg; Sodium 283mg; Calcium 37mg

raspberry-corn muffins

Prep: *25 minutes* **Cook:** *20 minutes*
Cool: *5 minutes*
Makes 12 muffins

Moist pockets of raspberries are scattered throughout these sweet cornmeal muffins.

- 1 1/2 cups all-purpose flour
- 1/2 cup yellow cornmeal
- 1/2 cup packed brown sugar
- 1 teaspoon baking powder
- 1 teaspoon baking soda
- 1/4 teaspoon salt
- 1 1/4 cups plain low-fat yogurt
- 3 tablespoons vegetable oil
- 1 teaspoon grated lemon rind
- 2 large eggs, lightly beaten
- Cooking spray
- 1 cup fresh raspberries
- 1/2 teaspoon granulated sugar

1. Preheat oven to 375°.
2. Combine flour and next 5 ingredients (flour through salt) in a medium bowl.
3. Combine yogurt, oil, lemon rind, and eggs, stirring well with a whisk. Add to flour mixture, stirring until just blended. Spoon batter into 12 muffin cups coated with cooking spray. Sprinkle evenly with raspberries and 1/2 teaspoon sugar.
4. Bake at 375° for 20 minutes or until muffins spring back when touched lightly in center. Remove from oven, and cool 5 minutes in pan. Remove muffins from pan; cool on a wire rack.

PER SERVING (1 muffin): Calories 157 (17% from fat); Protein 4g; Fat 3g (sat 1g, mono 1g, poly 1g); Carbohydrate 29g; Fiber 2g; Cholesterol 2mg; Iron 1mg; Sodium 265mg; Calcium 69mg

jamaican banana bread

Prep: *20 minutes* **Cook:** *1 hour*
Cool: *10 minutes*
Serves 16

- 2 tablespoons butter, softened
- 2 tablespoons $^1/_3$-less-fat cream cheese, softened
- 1 cup granulated sugar
- 1 large egg
- 2 cups all-purpose flour
- 2 teaspoons baking powder
- $^1/_2$ teaspoon baking soda
- $^1/_8$ teaspoon salt
- 1 cup mashed ripe banana
- $^1/_2$ cup fat-free milk
- 2 tablespoons dark rum
- $^1/_2$ teaspoon grated lime rind
- 2 teaspoons lime juice
- 1 teaspoon vanilla extract
- $^1/_4$ cup chopped pecans, toasted
- $^1/_4$ cup flaked sweetened coconut
- Cooking spray
- $^1/_4$ cup packed brown sugar
- 2 teaspoons butter
- 2 teaspoons lime juice
- 2 teaspoons dark rum
- 2 tablespoons chopped pecans, toasted
- 2 tablespoons flaked sweetened coconut

1. Preheat oven to 375°.
2. Beat 2 tablespoons butter and cheese at medium speed of a mixer; add 1 cup sugar, beating well. Add egg; beat well.
3. Combine flour, baking powder, baking soda, and salt, stirring well. Combine banana and next 5 ingredients (banana through vanilla), stirring well. Add flour mixture to sugar mixture alternately with banana mixture, ending with flour. Stir in ¼ cup chopped pecans and ¼ cup coconut.
4. Pour batter into an 8 x 4-inch loaf pan coated with cooking spray; bake at 375° for 1 hour. Cool in pan 10 minutes; remove from pan. Cool on a wire rack.
5. Combine brown sugar and 2 teaspoons each butter, lime juice, and rum in a saucepan; bring to a simmer. Cook 1 minute, stirring constantly. Remove from heat. Stir in 2 tablespoons each pecans and coconut; spoon over loaf.

PER SERVING (1 slice): Calories 193 (26% from fat); Protein 3g; Fat 6g (sat 2g, mono 2g, poly 1g); Carbohydrate 32g; Fiber 1g; Cholesterol 20mg; Iron 1mg; Sodium 163mg; Calcium 55mg

pumpkin, raisin, and nut bread

Prep: *8 minutes* **Cook:** *45 minutes*
Cool: *10 minutes*
Serves 12

Get a jump start on this recipe by using a packaged bread mix. Then, add raisins, pumpkin, and spice to give the bread a homemade taste.

- 1 (15.4-ounce) package nut quick bread mix (such as Pillsbury)
- $^1/_2$ cup raisins
- $^3/_4$ cup canned unsweetened pumpkin
- $^1/_2$ cup water
- $^1/_4$ cup egg substitute
- 1 teaspoon pumpkin pie spice
- Cooking spray

1. Preheat oven to 350°.
2. Combine bread mix and raisins; make a well in center of mixture. Combine pumpkin and next 3 ingredients (pumpkin through spice). Add to dry ingredients, stirring just until moist.
3. Spoon batter into an 8½ x 4-inch loaf pan coated with cooking spray. Bake at 350° for 45 minutes or until a wooden pick inserted in center comes out clean. Let cool in pan 10 minutes on a wire rack; remove from pan. Let cool on wire rack.

PER SERVING (¹⁄₁₂ of loaf): Calories 173 (19% from fat); Protein 4g; Fat 4g (sat 1g, mono 0g, poly 0g); Carbohydrate 32g; Fiber 2g; Cholesterol 0mg; Iron 2mg; Sodium 189mg; Calcium 29mg

Spoon, Don't Scoop

Lower-fat baking presents some extra challenges. Less fat means less room for error, particularly when measuring flour. The following technique ensures that you'll measure the right amount of flour.

1. Using a large spoon, stir flour gently before measuring, and spoon into a dry measuring cup.

2. Then, level flour with a knife or small metal spatula. Don't shake the cup—it packs the flour.

sweet rosemary bread

Prep: *15 minutes* **Cook:** *35 minutes*
Cool: *10 minutes*
Serves 12

Cooking spray
1½ teaspoons all-purpose flour
1 cup fat-free milk
½ cup golden raisins
¼ cup unsweetened applesauce
1 tablespoon finely chopped
  fresh rosemary
2 large eggs
⅔ cup sugar
1 tablespoon butter, melted
2 cups all-purpose flour
1½ teaspoons baking powder
½ teaspoon salt

1. Preheat oven to 350°.
2. Coat a 9-inch round cake pan with cooking spray; dust pan with 1½ teaspoons flour.
3. Combine milk, raisins, applesauce, and chopped fresh rosemary in a small saucepan, and bring to a simmer over medium heat. (Do not boil.) Remove from heat; cover and set aside.
4. Beat eggs with a mixer at medium speed until foamy. Add sugar and butter, beating well. Combine 2 cups flour, baking powder, and salt; add to egg mixture, beating until smooth. Add milk mixture; beat until smooth. (Batter will be thin.)
5. Pour batter into prepared pan. Bake at 350° for 35 minutes or until a wooden pick inserted in center comes out clean. Cool in pan on a wire rack 10 minutes. Remove from pan, and cool completely on wire rack.

PER SERVING (¹⁄₁₂ of loaf): Calories 168 (10% from fat); Protein 4g; Fat 2g (sat 0g, mono 0g, poly 0g); Carbohydrate 34g; Fiber 1g; Cholesterol 36mg; Iron 1mg; Sodium 190mg; Calcium 70mg

sour cream coffee cake

Prep: *20 minutes* **Cook:** *35 minutes*
Serves 10

Our test kitchens staff found that light butter works best in this tender cake. Avoid the temptation to substitute margarine; the end result will not be as good.

Cooking spray
¼ cup all-purpose flour
¼ cup firmly packed brown sugar
3 tablespoons chopped pecans
½ teaspoon ground cinnamon
1 tablespoon light butter, melted
1 (8-ounce) carton fat-free sour
  cream, divided
1 teaspoon vanilla extract
1 large egg
1 large egg white
1⅔ cups sifted cake flour
1 cup granulated sugar
1 teaspoon baking soda
½ teaspoon baking powder
¼ teaspoon salt
7 tablespoons light butter,
  softened

1. Preheat oven to 350°.
2. Coat a 9-inch springform pan with cooking spray; line bottom of pan with wax paper. Coat wax paper with cooking spray; set aside.
3. Combine all-purpose flour and next 3 ingredients (flour through cinnamon) in a bowl. Add 1 tablespoon melted butter; toss with a fork (streusel will be crumbly). Set aside.
4. Combine ¼ cup sour cream, vanilla, egg, and egg white in a small bowl; stir well with a whisk.
5. Combine cake flour and next 4 ingredients (cake flour through salt) in a bowl; stir well. Add remaining sour cream and 7 tablespoons butter; beat with a mixer at low speed until moist.

Beat at medium speed 1½ minutes. Add sour cream-egg mixture in thirds, beating 10 seconds after each addition.
6. Pour batter into prepared pan. Sprinkle streusel evenly over batter. Bake at 350° for 35 minutes or until a wooden pick inserted in center comes out clean. Let cool completely on a wire rack. Remove sides of pan before serving.

PER SERVING (¹⁄₁₀ of cake): Calories 248 (25% from fat); Protein 5g; Fat 7g (sat 4g, mono 1g, poly 1g); Carbohydrate 4g; Fiber 0g; Cholesterol 37mg; Iron 2mg; Sodium 243mg; Calcium 21mg

parmesan-onion rolls

pictured on page 77

Prep: *24 minutes* **Cook:** *20 minutes*
Stand: *35 minutes*
Serves 16

Save time by starting with hot roll mix rather than measuring out flour.

Cooking spray
¾ cup finely chopped onion
½ teaspoon dried oregano
½ teaspoon dried basil
1 (16-ounce) box hot roll mix
1 cup warm water (100° to 110°)
2 tablespoons butter, softened
1 large egg white, lightly beaten
1 cup (4 ounces) grated fresh
  Parmesan cheese

1. Coat a nonstick skillet with cooking spray; place over medium-high heat until hot. Add onion, oregano, and basil; sauté until onion is tender. Set aside.
2. Combine contents of roll mix and enclosed yeast packet in a large bowl; stir well. Add warm water, butter, and egg white, stirring until dough pulls away from

sides of bowl. Turn dough out onto a lightly floured surface. Sprinkle with onion mixture; knead until blended. Sprinkle dough with cheese; knead 5 minutes or until dough is smooth and elastic. Cover dough; let rest 10 minutes.

3. Divide dough into 16 equal portions. Shape each portion into a ball. Place 8 balls in each of 2 (8-inch) round cake pans coated with cooking spray. Cover; let rise in a warm place (85°), free from drafts, 25 minutes or until dough doubles in size.

4. Preheat oven to 375°.

5. Bake at 375° for 20 minutes or until lightly browned.

PER SERVING (1 roll): Calories 156 (29% from fat); Protein 6g; Fat 5g (sat 2g, mono 2g, poly 1g); Carbohydrate 22g; Fiber 0g; Cholesterol 10mg; Iron 0mg; Sodium 249mg; Calcium 109mg

cinnamon-raisin bagels

Prep: *35 minutes* **Cook:** *16 minutes*
Stand/Rest/Chill: *12 hours 10 minutes*
Makes 12 bagels

1	package dry yeast
1³/₄	cups warm water (100° to 110°)
2	tablespoons honey
5	to 5¹/₂ cups bread flour, divided
2	teaspoons salt
1	cup raisins
2	teaspoons ground cinnamon
	Cooking spray
3¹/₂	quarts water

1. Combine yeast and warm water in a 2-cup liquid measuring cup; let stand 5 minutes. Add honey, stirring well. Combine yeast mixture, 2 cups flour, and salt in a large mixing bowl; beat with a heavy-duty electric mixer at low speed 4 minutes or until smooth.

2. Gradually stir in enough remaining flour to make a soft dough. Beat at medium-low speed with a dough hook 8 minutes or until smooth and elastic. Stir in raisins and cinnamon.

3. Divide dough into 12 equal pieces. Roll each piece into a smooth ball. Cover balls, and let rest 5 minutes.

4. Shape each ball into an 11-inch rope. Bring ends of ropes together, and pinch to seal. Roll bagel around palm of hand to make a ring. Place on baking sheets coated with cooking spray; cover and chill 12 to 18 hours.

5. Preheat oven to 450°.

6. Bring water to a boil in a Dutch oven. Boil bagels, 4 at a time, 30 seconds, turning once. Remove with a slotted spoon; place on wire racks.

7. Place bagels on baking sheets lightly coated with cooking spray. Bake at 450° for 13 to 14 minutes or until golden.

PER SERVING (1 bagel): Calories 216 (0% from fat); Protein 7g; Fat 0g; Carbohydrate 50g; Fiber 2g; Cholesterol 0mg; Iron 3mg; Sodium 391mg; Calcium 8mg

garlic-rosemary focaccia

Prep: *22 minutes* **Cook:** *25 minutes*
Rest/Rise: *40 minutes*
Serves 8

³/₄	cup plus 2 tablespoons water
2	tablespoons olive oil
2¹/₄	cups bread flour, divided
1	teaspoon salt
1	package rapid-rise yeast
1	tablespoon bread flour
	Olive oil-flavored cooking spray
1	tablespoon cornmeal
1¹/₂	tablespoons minced garlic
2	teaspoons chopped fresh rosemary

1. Combine water and oil in a saucepan; heat to 120° to 130°. Combine 1 cup bread flour, salt, and yeast in a large mixing bowl, stirring well. Gradually add liquid mixture to flour, beating well with an electric mixer at low speed. Beat 2 additional minutes at medium speed. Gradually add ³/₄ cup flour; beat 2 minutes at medium speed. Stir in enough of the remaining ¹/₂ cup flour to make a soft dough.

2. Sprinkle 1 tablespoon flour evenly over work surface. Turn dough out onto floured surface; knead until smooth and elastic (about 10 minutes). Cover dough; let rest 10 minutes.

3. Coat a 14-inch round pizza pan with cooking spray; sprinkle with cornmeal.

4. Punch dough down; turn out onto work surface, and knead lightly 4 or 5 times. Roll dough into a 14-inch circle. Place dough in prepared pan. Poke holes in dough at 1-inch intervals with handle of a wooden spoon. Cover and let rise in a warm place (85°), free from drafts, 30 minutes or until doubled in size.

5. Preheat oven to 375°.

6. Coat top of dough with cooking spray. Sprinkle garlic and rosemary evenly over dough. Bake at 375° for 25 minutes or until golden. Cut into wedges.

PER SERVING (¹/₈ of loaf): Calories 155 (19% from fat); Protein 5g; Fat 3g (sat 0g, mono 3g, poly 0g); Carbohydrate 27g; Fiber 1g; Cholesterol 0mg; Iron 2mg; Sodium 291mg; Calcium 4mg

honey-wheat bread

pictured on page 78

Prep: *32 minutes* **Cook:** *20 minutes*
Rise: *1 hour 15 minutes*
Makes 3 loaves

Everyone loves homemade bread, and this recipe makes three loaves. Keep one loaf for yourself, and give the other two to friends or neighbors as an unexpected treat.

    2 packages dry yeast
  1/3 cup honey
    1 cup warm water (100° to 110°)
    1 cup half-and-half
    4 large eggs, lightly beaten
 1½ cups whole wheat flour
 1½ teaspoons salt
 4¾ cups bread flour
Cooking spray

1. Dissolve yeast and honey in warm water in a mixing bowl; let stand 5 minutes. Add half-and-half and eggs; beat at medium speed of a heavy-duty stand mixer until well blended. Add whole wheat flour and salt, beating well. Stir in bread flour, ½ cup at a time, to form a soft dough.
2. Turn dough out onto a well-floured surface. Knead until smooth and elastic (about 5 minutes).
3. Place dough in a large bowl coated with cooking spray, turning to coat top. Cover and let rise in a warm place (85°), free from drafts, 45 minutes or until doubled in size.
4. Punch dough down; turn dough onto a lightly floured surface, and knead lightly 4 or 5 times. Divide dough into 3 equal portions. Working with one portion at a time (cover remaining dough to keep it from drying out), roll each portion into a 12- x 8-inch rectangle on a lightly floured surface. Roll up each rectangle tightly, starting with a short side. Press firmly to eliminate air pockets; pinch seam and ends to seal. Place each roll of dough, seam side down, in an 8 x 4-inch loaf pan coated with cooking spray.
5. Cover and let rise 30 minutes or until doubled in size.
6. Preheat oven to 375°.
7. Uncover dough. Bake at 375° for 20 minutes or until loaves sound hollow when tapped. Remove bread from pans immediately, and let cool on wire racks.

NOTE: You may use a dough hook and a heavy-duty stand mixer for kneading, if desired.

PER SERVING (1/12 of a loaf): Calories 100 (12% from fat); Protein 4g; Fat 1g (sat 1g, mono 0g, poly 0g); Carbohydrate 18g; Fiber 1g; Cholesterol 27mg; Iron 1mg; Sodium 108mg; Calcium 10mg

red pepper-cheese bread

Prep: *27 minutes* **Cook:** *35 minutes*
Rise: *2 hours*
Serves 16

To get the most cheesy flavor, make sure to use extra-sharp Cheddar.

    1 package dry yeast
    2 teaspoons sugar
    1 cup warm water (100° to 110°)
    3 cups bread flour, divided
    2 teaspoons Dijon mustard
    1 tablespoon vegetable oil
  ½ teaspoon salt
  ¼ to ½ teaspoon ground red pepper
  ¾ cup (3 ounces) shredded extra-sharp Cheddar cheese
Cooking spray

1. Dissolve yeast and sugar in warm water in a large bowl, and let stand 5 minutes. Add 1 cup flour, mustard, oil, salt, and pepper, and stir until smooth. Add 1¾ cups flour and cheese, and stir to form a soft dough. Turn dough out onto a lightly floured surface. Knead until smooth and elastic (about 10 minutes); add enough of remaining flour, 1 tablespoon at a time, to prevent dough from sticking to hands.
2. Place dough in a large bowl coated with cooking spray, turning to coat top. Cover and let rise in a warm place (85°), free from drafts, 1 hour or until doubled in size. Punch dough down; turn out onto a lightly floured surface. Roll dough into a 14- x 7-inch rectangle. Roll up rectangle tightly starting with a short edge, pressing firmly to eliminate air pockets; pinch seam and ends to seal. Place roll, seam side down, in a 9 x 5-inch loaf pan coated with cooking spray. Cover and let rise 1 hour or until doubled in size.
3. Preheat oven to 375°.
4. Uncover dough; bake at 375° for 35 minutes or until loaf sounds hollow when tapped. Remove from pan immediately; cool on a wire rack.

PER SERVING (1/16 of loaf): Calories 126 (22% from fat); Protein 5g; Fat 3g (sat 1g, mono 1g, poly 1g); Carbohydrate 19g; Fiber 0g; Cholesterol 6mg; Iron 1mg; Sodium 125mg; Calcium 42mg

BREAD MACHINE VARIATION: Follow manufacturer's instructions for placing all dough ingredients in bread pan. Select cycle, and start bread machine.

decadent desserts

*Sour Cream-Fudge
Cake with Mocha
Glaze, page 112*

orange, blackberry, and honey dessert sauce over yogurt and sorbet

Prep: *7 minutes*
Serves 4

The combination of fresh fruit and honey makes a colorful sauce for any flavor of frozen yogurt or sorbet.

1	cup navel orange sections
1	cup fresh blackberries
1	tablespoon honey
1	tablespoon fresh orange juice
1/2	pint raspberry sorbet
1/2	pint vanilla low-fat frozen yogurt
4	tablespoons sliced almonds, toasted

1. Combine oranges (and any juices from the cutting board), blackberries, honey, and juice in a medium bowl.
2. Divide sorbet and yogurt among 4 bowls. Top with fruit sauce, and sprinkle with nuts.

PER SERVING (1 scoop sorbet, 1 scoop yogurt, 1/3 cup fruit, and 1 tablespoon almonds): Calories 202 (18% from fat); Fat 4g (sat 1g, mono 2g, poly 1g); Protein 4g; Carbohydrate 40g; Fiber 5g; Cholesterol 3mg; Iron 0mg; Sodium 30mg; Calcium 123mg

vanilla custard sauce over strawberries

Prep: *10 minutes* **Cook:** *15 minutes*
Serves 6

1	large egg
1/3	cup sugar
1	tablespoon cornstarch
2	cups 1% low-fat milk
1	teaspoon vanilla extract
4	cups quartered small strawberries

1. Beat egg in a medium bowl until frothy.
2. Combine sugar and cornstarch in a small, heavy sauce-pan. Stir in milk; heat over medium-high heat to 180° or until tiny bubbles form around edge (do not boil). Gradually add hot milk mixture to eggs, stirring constantly with a whisk. Return mixture to pan. Cook over medium heat until thick, stirring constantly (do not boil). Remove from heat; stir in vanilla. Cover and chill until ready to serve. Serve over strawberries.

PER SERVING (1/3 cup sauce and 2/3 cup strawberries): Calories 132 (14% from fat); Protein 5g; Fat 2g (sat 1g, mono 1g, poly 0g); Carbohydrate 25g; Fiber 3g; Cholesterol 40mg; Iron 1g; Sodium 55mg; Calcium 110mg

very berry summer fruit compote

pictured on page 99

Prep: *5 minutes* **Cook:** *16 minutes*
Stand/Chill: *2 hours 10 minutes*
Serves 4

1	vanilla bean
1 1/2	cups water
1	cup sugar
1	(3-inch) cinnamon stick
2	cups fresh raspberries
2	cups fresh blackberries
2	cups fresh blueberries
	Pineapple-mint sprigs or spearmint sprigs (optional)

1. Split vanilla bean lengthwise, and scrape seeds from bean into a large saucepan. Add vanilla bean to pan. Add water, sugar, and cinnamon stick; stir well. Bring to a boil; reduce heat, and simmer 5 minutes, stirring occasionally. Add berries; cook 1 minute, stirring gently. Remove from heat; let stand 10 minutes.
2. Drain berry mixture, reserving sugar syrup. Place berries, vanilla bean, and cinnamon stick in a medium bowl; set aside. Return sugar syrup to pan; bring to a boil. Cook 10 minutes or until slightly thick. Pour syrup over berry mixture; cover and chill 2 hours. Discard vanilla bean and cinnamon stick just before serving. Garnish with mint sprigs, if desired.

PER SERVING (1 cup): Calories 290 (2% from fat); Protein 1g; Fat 1g (sat 0g, mono 0g, poly 0g); Carbohydrate 74g; Fiber 9g; Cholesterol 0mg; Iron 1mg; Sodium 5mg; Calcium 35mg

summer fruit in vanilla syrup

Prep: *8 minutes* **Cook:** *3 minutes*
Chill: *8 hours*
Serves 6

Chill this low-calorie berry treat overnight for a refreshing breakfast or snack.

1	cup fresh blueberries
1	cup fresh raspberries
1	cup sliced peeled fresh peaches
1/2	cup water
1/4	cup sugar
1	vanilla bean, split lengthwise

1. Combine fruit in a bowl.
2. Combine water and sugar in a saucepan. Scrape seeds from vanilla bean; add seeds and bean to sugar mixture. Bring to a boil. Pour boiling syrup over fruit; let cool. Cover and chill 8 hours. Discard bean before serving.

PER SERVING (1/2 cup): Calories 68 (3% from fat); Protein 1g; Fat 0g; Carbohydrate 17g; Fiber 3g; Cholesterol 0mg; Iron 0mg; Sodium 2mg; Calcium 7mg

How to Poach Pears

Poaching pears in a flavorful liquid enhances its naturally good taste. Instead of draining off the poaching liquid, it is cooked down to make the syrup.

1. Keep the poaching liquid below the boiling point, or barely trembling when cooking. If the liquid boils, the pears toughen and cook too quickly.

2. The pears need to be in a single layer and surrounded by the poaching liquid, but not submerged. Once covered, steam will baste the pears and keep them moist.

3. Check the pears a minute or two before the timer says they're ready. Vegetables and fruits are done when a fork easily pierces the surface.

4. After removing the pears, reduce the poaching liquid by vigorously cooking over high heat until the liquid is thick and syrupy.

port-glazed pears with toasted hazelnuts

pictured on page 97

Prep: *10 minutes* **Cook:** *36 minutes*
Serves 4

Ripe pears will soak up the sweet, cranberry-mint syrup.

   2 large ripe Anjou pears (about 1 pound)
   1 cup port or other sweet red wine
   1 cup cranberry juice cocktail
 ¹/₂ cup water
 ¹/₃ cup fresh mint leaves
   3 tablespoons honey
1¹/₃ cups vanilla low-fat ice cream
   2 tablespoons chopped blanched hazelnuts, toasted

1. Peel and core pears; cut each pear in half lengthwise. Cut a ¼-inch slice from rounded side of each pear half so pears sit flat. Combine wine and next 4 ingredients (wine through honey) in a skillet; bring mixture to a boil. Cover, reduce heat, and simmer 5 minutes. Arrange pears, cut sides down, in pan; cover and simmer 8 minutes (do not boil). Turn pear halves over; cover and simmer an additional 8 minutes or until tender. Remove pears from pan with a slotted spoon; place pears in a shallow dish.
2. Bring poaching liquid to a boil; cook, uncovered, 10 minutes or until reduced to ½ cup. Pour poaching liquid through a sieve over pears in dish; discard mint leaves. Turn pears over to coat; cover and chill until ready to serve.
3. Arrange 1 pear half, cut side up, on each of 4 plates; top each with ⅓ cup ice cream. Drizzle 2 tablespoons poaching liquid over each serving, and sprinkle with 1½ teaspoons hazelnuts.

PER SERVING: Calories 232 (16% from fat); Protein 3g; Fat 4g (sat 1g, mono 2g, poly 0g); Carbohydrate 50g; Fiber 3g; Cholesterol 3mg; Iron 1mg; Sodium 36mg; Calcium 91mg

cinnamon-spiced peaches

Prep: *4 minutes* **Cook:** *10 minutes*
Serves 5

Serve as a side dish with ham or roast pork or as a sauce on pound cake, angel food cake, or ice cream.

 ¹/₂ (16-ounce) package frozen sliced peaches, thawed (about 2 cups)
 ¹/₄ cup sweetened dried cranberries (such as Craisins)
 ¹/₄ cup peach nectar
   3 tablespoons dark brown sugar
 ¹/₂ teaspoon ground cinnamon

1. Combine all ingredients in a medium nonstick skillet; stir well. Cover and cook over medium heat 10 minutes or until peaches are tender.

PER SERVING (¹/₄ cup): Calories 67 (1% from fat); Protein 0g; Fat 0g; Carbohydrate 17g; Fiber 1g; Cholesterol 0mg; Iron 0mg; Sodium 3mg; Calcium 10mg

passionfruit sorbet

Prep: *5 minutes* **Cook:** *5 minutes*
Freeze: *2 hours 20 minutes*
Serves 3

Lime juice adds a refreshing tartness to this sweet palate cleanser.

    2   cups water
    3/4 cup sugar
    1 1/2 cups passionfruit nectar
    3   tablespoons fresh lemon juice

1. Combine water and sugar in a small saucepan; bring to a boil, and cook 5 minutes. Pour into an 8-inch square baking dish; freeze 20 minutes. Stir in nectar and lemon juice, and freeze 30 minutes. Stir well with a fork; freeze 1 1/2 hours or until solid (do not stir). Let stand at room temperature until slightly softened. Break frozen mixture into chunks. Place frozen chunks in a food processor; pulse 5 times or until smooth. Serve immediately.

PER SERVING (1 cup): Calories 248 (0% from fat); Protein 0g; Fat 0g; Carbohydrate 64g; Fiber 1g; Cholesterol 0mg; Iron 0mg; Sodium 10mg; Calcium 11mg

mangoes and cream

Prep: *6 minutes* **Freeze:** *2 hours*
Serves 8

    2 1/2 cups chopped peeled mango
          (about 2 large)
    3/4 cup evaporated fat-free milk
    1/2 cup sugar
    1/2 cup pear-and-passionfruit
          nectar

1. Place all ingredients in a food processor. Process until smooth.
2. Pour mixture into freezer can of an ice cream freezer; freeze

according to manufacturer's instructions. Spoon into a freezer-safe container; cover and freeze 2 hours or until firm.

NOTE: If you prefer not to use an ice cream freezer, simply pour puréed mango mixture into an 8-inch square baking pan; cover and freeze 4 hours or until firm. Break mixture into small chunks. Place half of frozen chunks in a food processor, and process until smooth. Return mixture to baking pan. Repeat procedure with remaining half of frozen chunks. Cover and freeze puréed mixture an additional 4 hours or until firm.

PER SERVING (1/2 cup): Calories 116 (4% from fat); Protein 2g; Fat 1g (sat 0g, mono 0g, poly 0g); Carbohydrate 27g; Fiber 1g; Cholesterol 4mg; Iron 0mg; Sodium 31mg; Calcium 68mg

mango mousse with raspberry sauce

pictured on page 98

Prep: *25 minutes* **Cook:** *12 minutes*
Chill: *3 hours*
Serves 6

    4   cups cubed peeled mango
          (about 4 large)
    2   tablespoons fresh lime juice
    1   envelope unflavored gelatin
    1/3 cup water
    3   large egg whites
    1/2 cup sugar
    Raspberry Sauce
    3/4 cup frozen reduced-calorie
          whipped topping, thawed
    Fresh raspberries (optional)

1. Place mango and lime juice in a food processor; process until smooth, scraping sides of bowl occasionally. Set aside.

2. Sprinkle gelatin over 1/3 cup water in a 1-cup heatproof glass measure; let stand 10 minutes. Fill a 1-quart saucepan half-full with water; place over medium heat until very hot. Place glass measure in saucepan; stir until gelatin dissolves. Stir gelatin mixture into mango mixture; set aside.
3. Combine egg whites and sugar in top of a double boiler, and place over gently simmering water. Stir egg white mixture with a rubber spatula, scraping sides and bottom of pan frequently; cook 9 minutes or until mixture is 140°, stirring constantly. Remove from heat. Beat egg white mixture with a mixer at high speed until stiff peaks form (do not overbeat). Gently fold half of egg white mixture into mango mixture. Fold mango mixture into remaining egg white mixture. Divide mixture evenly among 6 (8-ounce) dessert glasses. Cover and chill 3 hours or until set.
4. Serve with Raspberry Sauce and whipped topping. Garnish with fresh raspberries, if desired.

raspberry sauce:

    4   cups fresh raspberries
    6   tablespoons sugar
    2   tablespoons fresh lime juice

1. Place raspberries in a blender or food processor; process until smooth. Press raspberry purée through a fine sieve into a medium bowl; discard seeds. Add sugar and lime juice to raspberry purée; stir well. Cover and chill. Yield: 1 1/3 cups.

PER SERVING (1/6 of mousse, 3 tablespoons Raspberry Sauce, and 2 tablespoons whipped topping): Calories 235 (3% from fat); Protein 4g; Fat 1g (sat 0g, mono 0g, poly 0g); Carbohydrate 58g; Fiber 5g; Cholesterol 0mg; Iron 1mg; Sodium 32mg; Calcium 33mg

Rustic Red Plum Tart, page 106

Port-Glazed Pears with Toasted Hazelnuts, page 95

Sour Cream-Fudge Cake with Mocha Glaze, page 112

*Mango Mousse with Raspberry
Sauce , page 96*

decadent desserts

*Brown Sugar-Rum
Pound Cake with
Strawberries, page 110*

*Pineapple-Banana
Tart, page 105*

*Basic Layer Cake with Rich
Chocolate Frosting, page 109*

*Very Berry Summer Compote,
page 94*

Warm Bittersweet Chocolate Rum Torte with Vanilla-Rum Custard Sauce, page 111

tropical sorbet sandwiches

Prep: *20 minutes* **Cook:** *10 minutes*
Chill: *15 minutes* **Cool:** *10 minutes*
Freeze: *30 minutes*
Serves 6

Make these sandwiches, and store them in the freezer for those times when you need a bit of something cold, creamy, and sweet.

- 1/2 (18-ounce) package refrigerated sugar cookie dough
- 1 tablespoon unsweetened cocoa
- 1/3 cup flaked sweetened coconut
- 2 cups mango or other flavored sorbet, slightly softened

1. Combine cookie dough and cocoa in a bowl; knead dough until well blended. Cover and chill 15 minutes.
2. Preheat oven to 350°.
3. Turn dough out onto a lightly floured surface; roll dough to 1/8-inch thickness. Cut 6 cookies with a 3-inch-round cookie cutter; place cookies on a baking sheet. Reroll dough, and cut 6 more cookies; place on baking sheet. Sprinkle coconut evenly over cookies; lightly press coconut into dough. Bake at 350° for 10 minutes; let cool on pan 10 minutes. Remove cookies from pan; cool completely on wire racks.
4. Spread 1/3 cup sorbet onto each of 6 cookies, and top with remaining cookies, pressing gently. Wrap sandwiches; freeze at least 30 minutes.

NOTE: If you prefer plain sugar cookies, simply omit the cocoa, and proceed with the recipe.

PER SERVING (1 sandwich): Calories 280 (29% from fat); Protein 2g; Fat 9g (sat 4g, mono 3g, poly 1g); Carbohydrate 49g; Fiber 1g; Cholesterol 5mg; Iron 0mg; Sodium 198mg; Calcium 2mg

peach ice cream

Prep: *24 minutes* **Cook:** *25 minutes*
Freeze: *2 hours*
Serves 8

For the best flavor, use peaches that are fragrant and fully ripe in this ice cream. The soft flesh will be much easier to mash, and the peachy aroma will be so inviting.

- 2 cups peeled, coarsely chopped fresh peaches (about 2 large)
- 1/4 cup sugar
- 1/4 teaspoon almond extract
- 1 1/3 cups 1% low-fat milk, divided
- 1/4 cup nonfat dry milk
- 2 large egg yolks
- 1 (14-ounce) can fat-free sweetened condensed milk
- 1 tablespoon lemon juice
- 1 tablespoon vanilla extract
Mint sprigs (optional)

1. Combine peaches and sugar in a 1-quart saucepan; partially mash peaches with a fork or potato masher. Place over medium heat, and cook 20 minutes or until thick and bubbly, stirring frequently. Pour into a bowl, and stir in almond extract. Cover surface of peach mixture with plastic wrap; let cool to room temperature. Chill.
2. Combine 2/3 cup 1% low-fat milk, dry milk, and yolks in a saucepan. Heat over medium-low heat to 180° or until tiny bubbles form around edge of pan, stirring frequently (do not boil). Remove from heat; add remaining 2/3 cup milk, sweetened condensed fat-free milk, lemon juice, and vanilla, stirring with a whisk until well blended. Cover and chill until ready to use.
3. Combine milk mixture and peach mixture; stir well. Pour into freezer can of an ice cream freezer. Freeze according to

manufacturer's instructions. Spoon into a freezer-safe container; cover and freeze 2 hours or until firm. Garnish with mint sprigs, if desired.

PER SERVING (1/2 cup): Calories 231 (7% from fat); Protein 8g; Fat 2g (sat 1g, mono 1g, poly 0g); Carbohydrate 45g; Fiber 1g; Cholesterol 63mg; Iron 0mg; Sodium 93mg; Calcium 232mg

creamy coconut rice pudding

Prep: *4 minutes* **Cook:** *25 minutes*
Stand: *5 minutes*
Serves 5

To add more coconut flavor and a surprise crunch to the pudding, sprinkle toasted flaked sweetened coconut on each serving.

- 1 (14-ounce) can light coconut milk
- 3/4 cup water
- 1/4 teaspoon salt
- 3/4 cup uncooked long-grain rice
- 1/2 cup sugar
- 1/4 teaspoon coconut extract

1. Combine coconut milk, water, and salt in a medium saucepan; bring to a boil. Stir in rice. Cover, reduce heat, and simmer 25 minutes or until rice is tender and liquid is absorbed, stirring gently after 10 minutes. Remove from heat; stir in sugar and extract. Let stand, covered, 5 minutes. Stir gently before serving.

PER SERVING (1/2 cup): Calories 229 (17% from fat); Protein 2g; Fat 4g (sat 3g, mono 0g, poly 0g); Carbohydrate 45g; Fiber 0g; Cholesterol 0mg; Iron 2mg; Sodium 150mg; Calcium 8mg

banana-raisin bread pudding

Prep: *9 minutes* **Cook:** *25 minutes*
Stand: *10 minutes*
Serves 8

There's no need to save this dish for dessert; try it for breakfast in place of sweet rolls or muffins.

  1   cup fat-free milk
 1/2 cup sugar
  3   large eggs
 12   (1-ounce) slices cinnamon-raisin bread, cut into 3/4-inch cubes
  3   bananas (about 3/4 pound), cut into 1/4-inch-thick slices
Cooking spray
  1   tablespoon sugar

1. Preheat oven to 350°.
2. Combine milk, 1/2 cup sugar, and eggs in a large bowl; stir mixture well with a whisk. Add bread and banana; toss gently to moisten. Cover and let stand 10 minutes.
3. Spoon mixture into a shallow 1 1/2-quart baking dish coated with cooking spray. Sprinkle 1 tablespoon sugar over bread mixture. Bake at 350° for 25 minutes or until golden and set.

PER SERVING (3/4 cup): Calories 234 (15% from fat); Protein 7g; Fat 4g (sat 1g, mono 2g, poly 0g); Carbohydrate 45g; Fiber 3g; Cholesterol 80mg; Iron 2mg; Sodium 192mg; Calcium 75mg

chocolate bread pudding

Prep: *9 minutes* **Cook:** *25 minutes*
Stand: *10 minutes*
Serves 9

French bread tends to become stale quickly, making it ideal for bread pudding. If it's too hard to cut into cubes, break it into small chunks. Once the milk mixture is added, the bread will soften.

 1 2/3 cups fat-free milk, divided
  3   tablespoons semisweet chocolate chips
  1   (1-ounce) square unsweetened chocolate, chopped
 1/2 cup sugar
 1/2 teaspoon vanilla extract
  2   large eggs, lightly beaten
  4   cups (1-inch) cubed stale French bread (about 4 ounces)
Cooking spray

1. Preheat oven to 350°.
2. Combine 1 cup milk, chocolate chips, and chocolate in a microwave-safe bowl. Microwave at HIGH 3 minutes or until chocolate melts, stirring every minute.
3. Add remaining milk, sugar, vanilla, and eggs; stir well. Add bread cubes; toss well to coat. Let stand 10 minutes. Spoon mixture into an 8-inch square baking dish coated with cooking spray. Bake at 350° for 25 minutes or until set.

PER SERVING (1/9 of pudding): Calories 145 (29% from fat); Protein 5g; Fat 4g (sat 2g, mono 2g, poly 0g); Carbohydrate 23g; Fiber 1g; Cholesterol 48mg; Iron 1mg; Sodium 121mg; Calcium 75mg

light vanilla crème brûlée

Prep: *22 minutes* **Cook:** *47 minutes*
Chill: *3 hours*
Serves 6

The longer the vanilla bean soaks in milk, the more intense the vanilla flavor will be in the dessert.

  1   (12-ounce) can evaporated fat-free milk
 1/2 cup 1% low-fat milk
  1   (2-inch) piece vanilla bean, split lengthwise
 1/3 cup granulated sugar
 1/8 teaspoon salt
  2   large eggs, lightly beaten
  2   large egg whites, lightly beaten
  3   tablespoons brown sugar

1. Preheat oven to 325°.
2. Combine milks in a medium bowl. Scrape seeds from vanilla bean; add seeds and bean to milks. Cover and let milk mixture stand in refrigerator at least 10 minutes. Discard vanilla bean.
3. Add 1/3 cup sugar and next 3 ingredients (sugar through egg whites) to milk mixture; beat at medium speed of a mixer 1 minute. Pour evenly into 6 (6-ounce) ramekins or custard cups. Place ramekins in a 13 x 9-inch baking pan; add hot water to pan to depth of 1 inch.
4. Bake at 325° for 45 minutes or until knife inserted near center comes out clean. Remove cups from pan; let cool on a wire rack. Cover and chill at least 3 hours.
5. Sprinkle 1 1/2 teaspoons brown sugar over each serving. Place ramekins on a baking sheet; broil 2 minutes or until brown sugar melts. Serve immediately.

NOTE: You may substitute 1 1/2 teaspoons vanilla extract for vanilla bean, if desired. Simply add extract to milk mixture and proceed to Step 3 of recipe.

PER SERVING (1 brûlée): Calories 145 (12% from fat); Protein 8g; Fat 2g (sat 1g, mono 1g, poly 0g); Carbohydrate 24g; Fiber 0g; Cholesterol 74mg; Iron 1mg; Sodium 168mg; Calcium 210mg

lime flan

Prep: *28 minutes* **Cook:** *47 minutes*
Chill: *4 hours*
Serves 8

Look for sweetened lime juice with cocktail beverage mixes in most grocery stores.

$^1/_2$ cup sweetened lime juice (such as Rose's)
1 lime
1$^1/_2$ cups water
1 (14-ounce) can fat-free sweetened condensed milk
1 vanilla bean, split lengthwise
1 (8-ounce) carton egg substitute
$^1/_4$ teaspoon salt
3 large egg yolks
Fresh lime zest (optional)

1. Preheat oven to 325°.
2. Place lime juice in a heavy saucepan over medium heat; cook 6 minutes or until golden, stirring constantly. Immediately pour into 8 (6-ounce) custard cups, tipping quickly until caramelized juice coats bottoms of cups; set aside.
3. Remove rind from lime in large strips, using a vegetable peeler or paring knife (do not remove the bitter white pith). Reserve lime for another use.
4. Combine lime rind strips, water, condensed milk, and vanilla bean in a saucepan; bring to a boil, stirring frequently. Reduce heat, and simmer 5 minutes, stirring occasionally.

Discard rind and vanilla bean.
5. Combine egg substitute, salt, and egg yolks; stir well. Gradually add 1 cup hot milk mixture to egg mixture, stirring constantly with a whisk. Return mixture to pan, stirring constantly. Divide mixture evenly among prepared custard cups. Place cups in 2 (8-inch) square baking pans; add hot water to pans to a depth of 1 inch. Bake at 325° for 35 minutes or until a knife inserted in center comes out clean. Remove cups from pans. Let custards cool completely on a wire rack. Cover and chill at least 4 hours.
6. Loosen edges of custards with a knife or rubber spatula. Place a dessert plate, upside down, on top of each cup; invert custards onto plates. Drizzle any remaining caramelized syrup over custard. Garnish with lime zest, if desired.

PER SERVING (1 flan): Calories 205 (9% from fat); Protein 8g; Fat 2g (sat 1g, mono 1g, poly 0g); Carbohydrate 37g; Fiber 0g; Cholesterol 86mg; Iron 1mg; Sodium 98mg; Calcium 144mg

chocolate-topped butternut squash flan

Prep: *34 minutes* **Cook:** *1 hour 35 minutes*
Chill: *8 hours*
Serves 8

1 butternut squash (about 1 pound)
$^3/_4$ cup granulated sugar
3 large eggs
$^1/_2$ cup firmly packed dark brown sugar
2 cups evaporated fat-free milk
$^1/_2$ teaspoon vanilla extract
$^1/_8$ teaspoon salt
$^1/_4$ cup (1 ounce) grated sweet dark chocolate (such as Ghirardelli)

1. Preheat oven to 350°.
2. Cut squash in half lengthwise, and discard seeds and membrane. Place squash halves, cut sides down, in a baking dish. Bake at 350° for 45 minutes or until tender. Use a spoon to scoop 1$^1/_3$ cups squash pulp from halves. Place 1$^1/_3$ cups squash in a food processor; process until puréed. Set aside. Reserve remaining squash for another use. Discard shells.
3. Place granulated sugar in a small heavy saucepan over medium-high heat; cook until sugar dissolves, stirring constantly. Reduce heat to medium; continue cooking until golden, stirring frequently. Immediately pour into an 8-inch round cake pan, tipping quickly until caramelized sugar coats bottom of cake pan.
4. Place eggs in a bowl; stir with a whisk. Stir in brown sugar, milk, vanilla, and salt; stir well. Add $^3/_4$ cup puréed squash; stir until well blended.
5. Pour squash mixture into prepared pan. Place pan in a shallow roasting pan; add hot water to roasting pan to a depth of 1 inch. Bake at 350° for 50 minutes or until a knife inserted in center comes out clean. Remove cake pan from water; let cool completely on a wire rack. Cover surface of flan with plastic wrap; chill 8 hours.
6. Loosen edges of flan with a knife or rubber spatula. Place a large plate, upside down, on top of cake pan; invert flan onto plate. Drizzle any remaining syrup over flan. Cut into wedges. Sprinkle with grated chocolate.

PER SERVING (1 wedge): Calories 230 (13% from fat); Protein 8g; Fat 3g (sat 1g, mono 1g, poly 0g); Carbohydrate 44g; Fiber 0g; Cholesterol 85mg; Iron 1mg; Sodium 142mg; Calcium 217mg

spiced rum flan

Prep: *12 minutes* **Cook:** *1 hour 10 minutes*
Chill: *3 hours*
Serves 8

When caramelizing the sugar in Step 2, be sure to use a heavy skillet rather than a nonstick skillet. After the sugar dissolves, watch it carefully because it caramelizes quickly. If it gets too brown, it will be bitter.

- 1¼ cups sugar, divided
- 5 large eggs
- 2½ cups 1% low-fat milk
- ¼ cup spiced rum or dark rum
- 1 teaspoon vanilla extract

1. Preheat oven to 325°.
2. Place ¾ cup sugar in a small heavy skillet over medium heat; cook 3 minutes or until sugar dissolves (do not stir). Cook an additional 3 minutes or until golden, stirring constantly. Immediately pour into a 9-inch round cake pan, tipping quickly until caramelized sugar coats bottom of cake pan.
3. Place eggs in a medium bowl; stir with a whisk until well blended. Set aside. Combine remaining sugar, milk, rum, and vanilla in a large heavy saucepan; stir well. Place over medium heat; cook 5 minutes or just until mixture comes to a simmer. Gradually add hot milk mixture to eggs, stirring constantly with a whisk.
4. Pour milk mixture into prepared pan; place cake pan in a large shallow baking pan. Add hot water to baking pan to a depth of 1 inch. Bake at 325° for 55 minutes or until a knife inserted near center comes out clean. Remove cake pan from water; let cool completely on a wire rack. Cover and chill at least 3 hours.

5. Loosen edge of flan with a knife or rubber spatula. Place a serving plate, upside down, on top of pan; invert flan onto serving plate. Drizzle any remaining caramelized syrup over flan.

PER SERVING (⅛ of flan): Calories 203 (18% from fat); Protein 7g; Fat 4g (sat 2g, mono 1g, poly 1g); Carbohydrate 35g; Fiber 0g; Cholesterol 141mg; Iron 1mg; Sodium 79mg; Calcium 110mg

apple crumble

Prep: *8 minutes* **Cook:** *51 minutes*
Serves 8

- ⅔ cup quick-cooking oats
- ⅓ cup packed brown sugar, divided
- ¼ cup all-purpose flour
- 3 tablespoons chilled butter or stick margarine, cut into small pieces
- 3 (12-ounce) packages frozen escalloped apples

1. Preheat oven to 375°.
2. Combine oats, 4 tablespoons sugar, and flour; cut in chilled butter with a pastry blender or 2 knives until mixture resembles coarse meal.
3. Remove plastic film from apples. Place 3 packages of apples in microwave oven; microwave at HIGH 11 minutes or until partially thawed. Spoon apples into an 8-inch square baking dish. Add remaining sugar; stir well. Sprinkle oat mixture over apples. Bake at 375° for 40 minutes or until apple mixture is bubbly and topping is golden.

PER SERVING (⅛ of crumble): Calories 254 (21% from fat); Protein 1g; Fat 7g (sat 2g, mono 0g, poly 0g); Carbohydrate 46g; Fiber 4g; Cholesterol 0mg; Iron 1mg; Sodium 72mg; Calcium 14mg

mango crisp

Prep: *8 minutes* **Cook:** *35 minutes*
Serves 8

Packets of flavored oatmeal add spice and keep this ingredient list extra-short.

- 4 cups cubed peeled ripe mango (about 5 mangoes)
- 5 tablespoons brown sugar, divided
- ¼ cup butter, melted and divided
- 2 (1.62-ounce) packets instant cinnamon and spice oatmeal (such as Quaker)
- 4 cups vanilla fat-free ice cream

1. Preheat oven to 375°.
2. Combine mango cubes, 3 tablespoons brown sugar, and 1 tablespoon melted butter in a large bowl; stir well. Spoon mango mixture into an 8-inch square baking dish.
3. Combine remaining brown sugar, remaining melted butter, and oatmeal in a bowl; toss with a fork until well blended. Sprinkle over mango mixture. Bake at 375° for 35 minutes or until bubbly. Serve warm with ice cream.

PER SERVING (⅛ of crisp and ½ cup ice cream): Calories 288 (20% from fat); Protein 5g; Fat 6g (sat 4g, mono 2g, poly 0g); Carbohydrate 55g; Fiber 2g; Cholesterol 3mg; Iron 1mg; Sodium 196mg; Calcium 142mg

plum cobbler

Prep: *17 minutes* **Cook:** *35 minutes*
Serves 12

To ripen plums, place them in a paper bag and store at room temperature until slightly soft.

    1³/₄ cups sugar, divided
       2 tablespoons all-purpose flour
       8 cups sliced ripe red plums
          (about 3 pounds)
Cooking spray
       2 cups all-purpose flour
       2 teaspoons baking powder
     ¹/₂ teaspoon baking soda
     ¹/₂ teaspoon salt
     ³/₄ cup low-fat buttermilk
     ¹/₄ cup vegetable oil
       1 teaspoon vanilla extract
       1 large egg, lightly beaten
       1 large egg white, lightly beaten
    1¹/₂ teaspoons sugar

1. Preheat oven to 350°.
2. Combine 1 cup sugar and 2 tablespoons flour in a bowl; stir well. Add plums; toss well to coat. Spoon into a 13 x 9-inch baking dish coated with cooking spray.
3. Combine 2 cups flour, baking powder, baking soda, and salt in a bowl; make a well in center of mixture. Combine ³/₄ cup sugar, buttermilk, and next 4 ingredients (oil through egg white) in a bowl; stir well. Add to flour mixture, stirring just until moist. Spoon batter over plum mixture, spreading gently to edges of dish. Sprinkle 1¹/₂ teaspoons sugar over batter.
4. Bake at 350° for 35 minutes or until golden. Cool on a wire rack. Serve cobbler warm or at room temperature.

PER SERVING (¹/₁₂ of cobbler): Calories 307 (18% from fat); Protein 4g; Fat 6g (sat 1g, mono 3g, poly 2g); Carbohydrate 61g; Fiber 3g; Cholesterol 18mg; Iron 1mg; Sodium 203mg; Calcium 58mg

raspberry cobbler

Prep: *14 minutes* **Cook:** *30 minutes*
Serves 8

       1 cup firmly packed dark brown
          sugar
     ¹/₂ cup water
       4 teaspoons cornstarch
       2 teaspoons vanilla extract
     ¹/₂ teaspoon ground cinnamon
     ¹/₄ teaspoon ground nutmeg
       6 cups fresh raspberries
Cooking spray
       1 cup all-purpose flour
     ¹/₄ cup granulated sugar
       1 teaspoon baking powder
     ¹/₄ teaspoon baking soda
     ¹/₄ teaspoon salt
       5 tablespoons chilled unsalted
          butter, cut into small pieces
     ¹/₂ cup low-fat buttermilk

1. Preheat oven to 400°.
2. Combine first 6 ingredients (brown sugar through nutmeg) in a large bowl. Add raspberries, and toss gently to coat. Spoon raspberry mixture into a shallow 2-quart baking dish coated with cooking spray.
3. Combine 1 cup flour, granulated sugar, baking powder, baking soda, and salt in a bowl; cut in butter with a pastry blender or 2 knives until mixture resembles coarse meal. Add low-fat buttermilk, tossing with a fork just until mixture forms a soft dough. Spoon dough into 8 mounds on top of raspberry mixture. Bake at 400° for 30 minutes or until topping is lightly browned and filling is bubbly. Serve warm or at room temperature.

PER SERVING (¹/₈ of cobbler): Calories 248 (29% from fat); Protein 3g; Fat 8g (sat 5g, mono 2g, poly 1g); Carbohydrate 43g; Fiber 6g; Cholesterol 19mg; Iron 2mg; Sodium 189mg; Calcium 87mg

pineapple-banana tart

pictured on page 99

Prep: *16 minutes* **Cook:** *40 minutes*
Cool: *10 minutes*
Serves 8

       1 (12-ounce) peeled and cored
          fresh pineapple
       1 (9-inch) refrigerated piecrust
          (such as Pillsbury)
       2 bananas, sliced
       2 teaspoons cinnamon-sugar,
          divided
    1¹/₂ to 2 teaspoons water
       1 (12-ounce) jar guava jelly

1. Preheat oven to 425°.
2. Cut pineapple crosswise into ¹/₄-inch-thick slices; cut each slice in half. Set aside.
3. Roll piecrust into a 13-inch circle on a lightly floured surface. Place piecrust on a baking sheet lined with parchment paper. Arrange banana slices over crust, leaving a 2-inch border. Sprinkle 1 teaspoon cinnamon-sugar over banana slices. Arrange pineapple slices over banana. Fold 2-inch border of dough over fruit, pressing firmly (dough will cover only outside edge of fruit). Brush border of dough with water; sprinkle with remaining cinnamon-sugar.
4. Bake at 425° for 30 minutes or until crust is golden. Let cool slightly. Carefully slide tart onto a serving platter, using a spatula. Cut tart into 8 wedges.
5. Place jelly in a small saucepan, and cook over medium heat 10 minutes or until jelly melts, stirring occasionally. Remove from heat; let cool 10 minutes. Drizzle jelly over each serving.

PER SERVING (1 wedge and 2 tablespoons jelly): Calories 299 (22% from fat); Protein 1g; Fat 7g (sat 3g, mono 0g, poly 0g); Carbohydrate 56g; Fiber 1g; Cholesterol 5mg; Iron 0mg; Sodium 101mg; Calcium 5mg

rustic red plum tart

pictured on page 97

Prep: *35 minutes* **Cook:** *48 minutes*
Chill: *15 minutes*
Serves 10

This free-form fruit tart is reminiscent of simpler times. It makes an impressive addition to a holiday buffet.

1¼   cups all-purpose flour
   1   tablespoon sugar
   ¼   teaspoon salt
   4   tablespoons chilled butter
   ¼   cup ice water
   ½   teaspoon cider vinegar
   ¼   cup chopped walnuts
   ¼   cup all-purpose flour
   1   teaspoon ground cinnamon,
        divided
1½   pounds ripe red plums
        (about 9), each cut into 12
        wedges
   ⅓   cup sugar
   ¼   teaspoon ground nutmeg
1½   tablespoons water, divided
   ¼   cup apricot preserves

1. Preheat oven to 400°.
2. Place first 3 ingredients (flour through salt) in a food processor; pulse until blended. Add butter; pulse 4 times or until mixture resembles coarse meal. Combine ice water and vinegar. With processor on, add mixture through food chute, processing just until blended (do not form a ball). Press mixture gently into a 4-inch circle on heavy-duty plastic wrap; cover with additional plastic wrap. Roll dough, still covered, into a 14-inch circle. Chill dough 15 minutes.
3. Remove plastic wrap. Fit dough into a 12- or 13-inch round pizza pan, allowing edges of dough to extend over edges of pan. Set aside.

4. Place walnuts, ¼ cup flour, and ½ teaspoon cinnamon in a food processor; process 20 seconds or until walnuts are finely ground (do not overprocess to a paste).
5. Sprinkle walnut mixture evenly over pastry, leaving a 1- to 2-inch border. Working from the outside edge of pan to the center, arrange plum wedges in a spiral pattern, overlapping slightly.
6. Combine ⅓ cup sugar, remaining ½ teaspoon cinnamon, and nutmeg. Reserve 1 tablespoon sugar mixture. Sprinkle remaining sugar mixture over plum wedges. Fold edges of pastry over plums (pastry will cover only outside edges of fruit). Brush edge of pastry with 1½ teaspoons water, and sprinkle with reserved 1 tablespoon sugar mixture.
7. Bake at 400° for 45 minutes or until pastry is lightly browned. Let cool in pan on a wire rack.
8. Combine remaining 1 tablespoon water and preserves in a small saucepan; bring to a boil over medium heat. Reduce heat; simmer 1 minute, stirring constantly. Gently brush mixture over plums. Let cool completely.

PER SERVING (¹⁄₁₀ of tart): Calories 207 (30% from fat); Protein 3g; Fat 7g (sat 3g, mono 2g, poly 2g); Carbohydrate 35g; Fiber 2g; Cholesterol 12mg; Iron 1mg; Sodium 63mg; Calcium 13mg

graham cracker cream pie

Prep: *20 minutes* **Cook:** *40 minutes*
Chill: *2 hours*
Serves 8

   1   cup plus 1 tablespoon graham
        cracker crumbs, divided
   1   tablespoon sugar
   2   teaspoons all-purpose flour
   1   teaspoon ground cinnamon
   3   tablespoons butter, melted
Cooking spray
   ⅔   cup sugar
   ¼   cup cornstarch
   ¼   teaspoon salt
   2   cups 1% low-fat milk
   2   large egg yolks, lightly beaten
   1   teaspoon butter
   1   teaspoon vanilla extract
   3   large egg whites
   ½   teaspoon cream of tartar
   ⅓   cup sugar
   ½   teaspoon vanilla extract

1. Preheat oven to 350°.
2. Combine 1 cup crumbs, sugar, flour, and cinnamon; stir well. Add butter; toss until moist. Press in bottom and up sides of a 9-inch pie plate coated with cooking spray; lightly coat crust with cooking spray. Bake at 350° for 8 minutes; let cool. Reduce oven temperature to 325°.
3. Combine ⅔ cup sugar, cornstarch, and salt in a saucepan; stir in milk. Bring to a boil over medium heat. Cook 1 minute, stirring constantly.
4. Gradually add hot milk mixture to egg yolks, stirring constantly with a whisk. Return mixture to pan. Cook over medium heat 2 minutes or until thick, stirring constantly. Remove from heat; stir in 1 teaspoon butter and 1 teaspoon vanilla. Pour hot filling into crust.
5. Beat egg whites and cream of tartar with clean, dry beaters at

high speed with a mixer until foamy. Gradually add ⅓ cup sugar, 1 tablespoon at a time, beating until stiff peaks form. Add ½ teaspoon vanilla; beat well. Spread over hot filling, sealing to edge of crust. Sprinkle with 1 tablespoon cracker crumbs. Bake at 325° for 25 minutes or until meringue is golden. Let cool. Chill at least 2 hours.

PER SERVING (⅛ of pie): Calories 262 (27% from fat); Protein 5g; Fat 8g (sat 2g, mono 2g, poly 1g); Carbohydrate 43g; Fiber 0g; Cholesterol 57mg; Iron 1mg; Sodium 257mg; Calcium 90mg

lemon meringue pie

Prep: *23 minutes* **Cook:** *39 minutes*
Chill: *5 minutes*
Serves 8

Don't let the lengthy ingredient list and method keep you from making this luscious pie. Just pick a day when you have extra time.

  1 cup all-purpose flour
  ¼ teaspoon salt
  3 tablespoons vegetable shortening
  6 tablespoons ice water
Cooking spray
  1 large egg yolk
1¼ cups sugar
  6 tablespoons cornstarch
  1 cup water
  ⅓ cup fresh lemon juice
  2 tablespoons butter
  ¼ teaspoon grated lemon rind
  4 large egg whites
  ½ teaspoon cream of tartar
  ¼ cup sugar

1. Preheat oven to 450°.
2. Combine flour and salt in a bowl; cut in shortening with a pastry blender or 2 knives until mixture resembles coarse meal. Add ice water, 1 tablespoon at a time, tossing with a fork until moist. Press mixture gently into a 4-inch circle on heavy-duty plastic wrap; cover with additional plastic wrap. Roll dough, still covered, into an 11-inch circle. Chill 5 minutes.
3. Remove plastic wrap; fit dough into a 9-inch pie plate coated with cooking spray. Fold edges of dough under, and flute. Pierce bottom and sides of dough with a fork. Bake at 450° for 10 minutes or until lightly browned. Let cool completely on a wire rack. Reduce oven temperature to 325°.
4. Place egg yolk in a bowl; stir well, and set aside. Combine 1¼ cups sugar and cornstarch in a nonaluminum saucepan; stir well. Stir in 1 cup water and lemon juice; bring to a boil. Cook 1 minute or until thick, stirring constantly with a whisk. Gradually add hot cornstarch mixture to egg yolk, stirring constantly with whisk. Return mixture to pan. Cook over medium heat 2 minutes, stirring constantly. Remove from heat; stir in butter and lemon rind. Spoon into crust. Cover surface of filling with plastic wrap; set aside.
5. Beat egg whites and cream of tartar with clean, dry beaters with a mixer at high speed until foamy. Gradually add ¼ cup sugar, 1 tablespoon at a time, beating until stiff peaks form. Uncover pie. Spread meringue evenly over hot filling, sealing to edge of crust. Bake at 325° for 25 minutes or until meringue is golden. Let cool completely on a wire rack. Store loosely covered in refrigerator.

PER SERVING (⅛ of pie): Calories 304 (23% from fat); Protein 4g; Fat 7g (sat 1g, mono 2g, poly 1g); Carbohydrate 56g; Fiber 1g; Cholesterol 27mg; Iron 1mg; Sodium 135mg; Calcium 9mg

How to Make Meringue for a Pie

Making a meringue can be tricky if you've never done it before. For a fool-proof pie, follow the instructions in the method at left and use the step-by-step photos below as a guide.

1. Beat egg whites and cream of tartar in a metal bowl until foamy. Add sugar, 1 tablespoon at a time, beating until stiff peaks form and sugar is dissolved.

2. Dollop meringue onto the hot filling, using a spatula or large spoon.

3. Spread meringue with a spatula or the back of a spoon until it covers the filling and forms a seal around the edges of the crust.

fudgy pie with ice cream

Prep: *25 minutes* **Cook:** *35 minutes*
Stand: *5 minutes*
Serves 8

Cooking spray
2 tablespoons dry breadcrumbs
3 tablespoons unsalted butter
1 (1-ounce) square unsweetened chocolate
1/2 cup Dutch process cocoa
1 1/3 cups sugar
1/4 cup all-purpose flour
1/4 cup finely chopped walnuts
1/4 cup warm water
2 teaspoons vanilla extract
1/4 teaspoon salt
2 large egg yolks, lightly beaten
3 large egg whites
2 tablespoons sugar
1/2 cup fat-free hot fudge topping (such as Hershey's)
1/2 cup vanilla low-fat ice cream or frozen yogurt
Fresh strawberries (optional)

1. Preheat oven to 350°.
2. Coat a 9-inch pie plate with cooking spray; dust with breadcrumbs. Turn pie plate upside down to remove excess breadcrumbs; discard. Set prepared pie plate aside.
3. Melt butter and chocolate over low heat in a medium heavy saucepan, stirring with a whisk until smooth. Stir in cocoa, and cook over medium heat 1 minute, stirring constantly. Stir in 1 1/3 cups sugar (mixture will be very thick), and cook 1 minute, stirring constantly. Remove from heat; add flour and next 5 ingredients (flour through egg yolks), stirring until mixture is well blended. Set aside.
4. Beat egg whites with clean, dry beaters with a mixer at high speed until foamy. Gradually add 2 tablespoons sugar, 1 table-spoon at a time, beating until stiff peaks form. Gently stir one-third of egg white mixture into chocolate mixture; gently fold in remaining egg white mixture. Pour into prepared pie plate, spreading evenly.
5. Bake at 350° for 30 minutes. Turn off oven; let pie stand in closed oven 5 minutes. Remove from oven; let cool completely on a wire rack. Serve with hot fudge topping and ice cream. Garnish with strawberries, if desired.

PER SERVING (1/8 of pie, 1 tablespoon each of hot fudge topping and ice cream): Calories 339 (28% from fat); Protein 6g; Fat 11g (sat 5g, mono 3g, poly 2g); Carbohydrate 56g; Fiber 1g; Cholesterol 68mg; Iron 2mg; Sodium 185mg; Calcium 50mg

lemon-poppy seed cake

pictured on page 2

Prep: *17 minutes* **Cook:** *54 minutes*
Cool: *10 minutes*
Serves 18

The sugary glaze enhances the cake's tart lemon flavor.

Cooking spray
1 1/2 tablespoons all-purpose flour
1 1/2 cups fat-free milk
2/3 cup vegetable oil
2 tablespoons grated lemon rind
1 1/2 teaspoons vanilla extract
1/2 teaspoon almond extract
2 large eggs
1 large egg white
3 cups all-purpose flour
2 1/4 cups sugar
2 1/2 tablespoons poppy seeds
1 1/2 teaspoons baking powder
3/4 teaspoon salt
Lemon Glaze

1. Preheat oven to 350°.
2. Coat a 10-inch Bundt pan with cooking spray; dust with 1 1/2 tablespoons flour.
3. Combine milk and next 6 ingredients (milk through egg white) in a bowl. Combine 3 cups flour and next 4 ingredients (flour through salt); add to milk mixture, beating with a mixer at medium speed 2 minutes.
4. Pour batter into prepared pan. Bake at 350° for 54 minutes or until a wooden pick inserted in center comes out clean. Let cool in pan 10 minutes on a wire rack. Remove from pan; and place on wire rack. Brush Lemon Glaze evenly over warm cake; let cool completely.

lemon glaze:

1/4 cup sugar
1/4 cup fresh lemon juice

1. Combine sugar and lemon juice in a small saucepan. Place over medium heat; cook 3 minutes or until sugar dissolves, stirring occasionally.

PER SERVING (1/18 of cake with glaze): Calories 281 (30% from fat); Protein 4g; Fat 9g (sat 2g, mono 5g, poly 3g); Carbohydrate 46g; Fiber 1g; Cholesterol 25mg; Iron 1mg; Sodium 160mg; Calcium 73mg

Butter is Back

You may wonder why we've included recipes that call for butter in a weight-loss cookbook. There's a good reason: Butter is essential in baked goods. It gives cookies their crunch, cakes their tenderness, and pie crusts their flakiness. Don't worry, though—we kept the amount of butter to the bare minimum without sacrificing the quality of the finished product.

hot milk cake with lemon sauce

Prep: *14 minutes* **Cook:** *39 minutes*
Cool: *45 minutes*
Serves 15

- $3/4$ cup 1% low-fat milk
- $1/3$ cup butter
- $1 3/4$ cups all-purpose flour
- $1 3/4$ cups sugar
- 2 teaspoons baking powder
- $1/4$ teaspoon salt
- 2 teaspoons vanilla extract
- 2 large eggs, lightly beaten
- 2 large egg whites, lightly beaten
- Cooking spray
- Lemon Sauce
- Fresh strawberries (optional)

1. Preheat oven to 325°.
2. Combine milk and butter in a small saucepan. Place over medium-low heat, and cook until butter melts, stirring occasionally.
3. Combine flour and next 3 ingredients (flour through salt) in a large bowl; stir well. Add milk mixture, stirring well. Add vanilla, eggs, and egg whites; stir until well blended. Pour into a 13 x 9-inch baking pan coated with cooking spray.
4. Bake at 325° for 35 minutes or until a wooden pick inserted in center comes out clean. Let cool in pan at least 45 minutes on a wire rack. Serve warm or at room temperature with Lemon Sauce. Garnish with strawberries, if desired.

lemon sauce:

- 1 cup water
- $1/3$ cup sugar
- 1 tablespoon cornstarch
- $1/8$ teaspoon salt
- $2 1/2$ tablespoons fresh lemon juice
- $1 1/2$ teaspoons butter

1. Combine first 4 ingredients (water through salt) in a saucepan; stir with a whisk until well blended. Bring to a boil; cook 2 minutes, stirring constantly. Pour into a bowl. Add lemon juice and butter, stirring until butter melts.

PER SERVING (1 slice cake and 4 teaspoons Lemon Sauce): Calories 222 (22% from fat); Protein 3g; Fat 5g (sat 3g, mono 2g, poly 0g); Carbohydrate 41g; Fiber 0g; Cholesterol 42mg; Iron 1mg; Sodium 191mg; Calcium 59mg

basic layer cake with rich chocolate frosting

pictured on page 99

Prep: *34 minutes* **Cook:** *23 minutes*
Cool: *10 minutes*
Serves 16

- Cooking spray
- $1 1/3$ cups 1% low-fat milk, divided
- 2 teaspoons vanilla extract
- 1 large egg
- 1 large egg yolk
- $2 1/3$ cups sifted cake flour
- $1 1/4$ cups sugar
- 1 tablespoon baking powder
- $1/2$ teaspoon salt
- 6 tablespoons butter, softened
- Rich Chocolate Frosting

1. Preheat oven to 350°.
2. Coat 2 (9-inch) round cake pans with cooking spray; line bottoms of pans with wax paper. Coat wax paper with cooking spray.
3. Combine $1/3$ cup milk, vanilla, egg, and egg yolk in a bowl; stir with a whisk until well blended.
4. Combine flour and next 3 ingredients (flour through salt). Add 1 cup milk and butter; beat with a mixer at low speed until blended. Beat at medium speed $1 1/2$ minutes. Add egg mixture in thirds, beating 20 seconds after each addition or until blended.
5. Pour batter into prepared pans. Bake at 350° for 23 minutes or until a wooden pick inserted in center comes out clean. Let cool in pans 10 minutes on wire racks; remove from pans. Let cool completely on racks.
6. Place 1 cake layer on a plate; spread with $1/4$ cup Rich Chocolate Frosting. Top with second cake layer; spread $1/3$ cup frosting over top. Spread remaining $3/4$ cup frosting around sides of cake.

rich chocolate frosting:

- $2 3/4$ cups sifted powdered sugar
- 3 tablespoons unsweetened cocoa
- $1/4$ teaspoon salt
- 1 (1-ounce) square unsweetened chocolate
- $5 1/2$ tablespoons evaporated fat-free milk
- 1 teaspoon vanilla extract

1. Combine first 3 ingredients (sugar through salt) in a small bowl; stir well.
2. Place chocolate square in a microwave-safe bowl. Microwave at HIGH 1 minute or until very soft, stirring until smooth. Immediately add 3 tablespoons milk to chocolate, stirring with a whisk until blended. Gradually add sugar mixture to chocolate, beating with a mixer at low speed. Add remaining milk, beating until smooth. (If frosting is too stiff, add an additional 1 to 2 tablespoons milk.) Stir in vanilla. Let frosting stand 5 minutes. Yield: about $1 1/3$ cups.

PER SERVING ($1/16$ of cake with frosting): Calories 267 (22% from fat); Protein 3g; Fat 6g (sat 4g, mono 2g; poly 0g); Carbohydrate 50g; Fiber 0g; Cholesterol 40mg; Iron 2mg; Sodium 236 mg; Calcium 84mg

traditional marble cake

Prep: *21 minutes* **Cook:** *45 minutes*
Cool: *10 minutes*
Serves 12

The marble cake you're used to is most likely a mixture of vanilla and chocolate cake. But originally, the vanilla cake batter was swirled with ribbons of spiced batter. One taste will make you wonder why the recipe was ever changed.

Cooking spray
  1 tablespoon cake flour
  2 cups sugar
 $1/2$ cup butter, softened
  2 large eggs
  2 large egg whites
 $2^3/4$ cups sifted cake flour
 $2^3/4$ teaspoons baking powder
 $1/2$ teaspoon salt
  1 cup 1% low-fat milk
 $1^1/2$ teaspoons vanilla extract
  2 teaspoons ground cinnamon
 $1/2$ teaspoon ground cloves
 $1/2$ teaspoon ground nutmeg

1. Preheat oven to 350°.
2. Coat a 10-inch tube pan with cooking spray, and dust with 1 tablespoon flour; set aside.
3. Combine sugar and butter in a bowl; beat with a mixer at low speed 2 minutes or until well blended. Add eggs and egg whites, one at a time, beating just until blended after each addition. Combine $2^3/4$ cups flour, baking powder, and salt; stir well. Add flour mixture to sugar mixture, alternately with milk, beginning and ending with flour mixture. Add vanilla, beating until blended.
4. Remove 1 cup batter to a small bowl; stir in cinnamon, cloves, and nutmeg. Spoon remaining vanilla batter into prepared tube pan. Dollop spice batter over vanilla batter, and swirl batters together with a knife.
5. Bake at 350° for 45 minutes or until a wooden pick inserted in center comes out clean. Let cool in pan 10 minutes on a wire rack; remove from pan. Let cool completely on wire rack.

PER SERVING ($1/12$ of cake): Calories 317 (26% from fat); Protein 5g; Fat 9g (sat 5g, mono 3g, poly 1g); Carbohydrate 55g; Fiber 0g; Cholesterol 58mg; Iron 2mg; Sodium 319mg; Calcium 103mg

coconut-lime-brushed pound cake with frozen yogurt

Prep: *10 minutes* **Cook:** *10 minutes*
Serves 8

 $1/3$ cup cream of coconut (such as Coco Lopez)
  1 tablespoon grated lime rind
 $2^1/2$ tablespoons fresh lime juice
  1 teaspoon rum flavoring
  1 (13.6-ounce) fat-free golden loaf cake (such as Entenmann's)
  2 cups strawberry fat-free frozen yogurt or pineapple sherbet

1. Preheat oven to 350°.
2. Combine first 4 ingredients (cream of coconut through rum flavoring) in a small bowl; stir well, and set aside.
3. Cut cake into 8 (1-inch-thick) slices; place on a large baking sheet. Brush cream of coconut mixture evenly over tops of cake slices. Bake at 350° for 10 minutes. Let cool. Place cake slices on individual plates; top with frozen yogurt.

PER SERVING (1 slice cake and $1/4$ cup frozen yogurt): Calories 227 (14% from fat); Protein 4g; Fat 4g (sat 3g, mono 0g, poly 0g); Carbohydrate 42g; Fiber 1g; Cholesterol 0mg; Iron 0mg; Sodium 200mg; Calcium 78mg

brown sugar-rum pound cake with strawberries

pictured on page 99

Prep: *16 minutes* **Cook:** *1 hour 20 minutes*
Cool/Stand: *40 minutes*
Serves 24

Rum-flavored sugared strawberries top slices of this cake. Be sure to spoon the syrup over the cake, too.

Cooking spray
 $2/3$ cup butter, softened
 $1^1/2$ cups firmly packed dark brown sugar
 $1^1/2$ cups granulated sugar
  1 cup egg substitute
 $4^1/2$ cups sifted cake flour
 $1^1/2$ teaspoons baking soda
 $1/4$ teaspoon salt
  1 cup low-fat buttermilk
  2 tablespoons white rum
 $1^1/2$ teaspoons vanilla extract
 $4^1/2$ cups sliced fresh strawberries
  2 tablespoons granulated sugar
  1 tablespoon white rum

1. Preheat oven to 325°.
2. Coat a 10-inch tube pan with cooking spray; set aside.
3. Cream butter. Gradually add brown sugar and $1^1/2$ cups granulated sugar; beat with a mixer at medium speed until well blended. Add egg substitute; beat until blended.
4. Combine flour, baking soda, and salt. Add flour mixture to creamed mixture alternately with buttermilk, beginning and ending with flour mixture. Beat in 2 tablespoons rum and vanilla.
5. Pour into prepared pan. Bake at 325° for 1 hour and 20 minutes or until a wooden pick inserted in center comes out clean. Let cool in pan 10 minutes on a wire rack; remove from pan. Let cool completely on wire rack.

6. Combine strawberries, 2 tablespoons granulated sugar, and 1 tablespoon rum in a large bowl, and stir well. Let stand 30 minutes, stirring occasionally. Spoon strawberries and liquid over pound cake slices.

PER SERVING ($^1/_{24}$ of cake and 2 tablespoons strawberry mixture): Calories 237 (21% from fat); Protein 3g; Fat 6g (sat 3g, mono 2g, poly 0g); Carbohydrate 44g; Fiber 1g; Cholesterol 14mg; Iron 2mg; Sodium 154mg; Calcium 36mg

warm bittersweet chocolate-rum torte with vanilla-rum custard sauce

pictured on page 100

Prep: *25 minutes* **Cook:** *49 minutes*
Serves 8

Melt-in-your-mouth chocolate cake rests on top of rich, rum-flavored sauce.

Cooking spray
1 (3-ounce) bar premium bittersweet chocolate (such as Lindt Swiss)
$^1/_2$ cup granulated sugar
$3^1/_2$ tablespoons butter, softened
1 teaspoon vanilla extract
1 large egg
$^1/_4$ cup fat-free milk
2 tablespoons dark rum
$^1/_4$ cup Dutch process cocoa
2 tablespoons all-purpose flour
4 large egg whites
$^1/_4$ teaspoon cream of tartar
$^1/_4$ cup granulated sugar
Vanilla-Rum Custard Sauce
2 tablespoons powdered sugar
24 fresh raspberries

1. Preheat oven to 300°.
2. Coat bottom and sides of an 8-inch springform pan with cooking spray. Set aside.

3. Break chocolate into small pieces; place in a microwave-safe bowl. Microwave at MEDIUM (50% power) 2 minutes or until softened, stirring until smooth.
4. Combine $^1/_2$ cup sugar and butter; beat with a mixer at medium speed until well blended (about 3 minutes). Add vanilla and egg; beat 1 minute. Add milk and rum; beat well (mixture will appear curdled). Add melted chocolate; beat just until blended. Add cocoa and flour; beat at low speed just until blended.
5. Using clean, dry beaters, beat egg whites and cream of tartar at high speed until foamy. Add $^1/_4$ cup sugar, 1 tablespoon at a time, beating until stiff peaks form. Stir $^1/_4$ of egg white mixture into batter; gently fold in remaining egg white mixture. Spoon batter into prepared pan.
6. Bake at 300° for 45 minutes or until a wooden pick inserted in center comes out slightly wet and with a few crumbs on it. Remove torte from oven; immediately run tip of a small knife around edge of torte. Let cool (torte will rise to top of pan while baking, but will sink while it cools). Remove sides of springform pan; cut torte with a sharp knife rinsed in hot water.
7. Spoon $^1/_4$ cup Vanilla-Rum Custard Sauce onto each of 8 dessert plates; top each with a slice of torte. Sift powdered sugar over each serving; garnish with raspberries.

NOTE: This torte is excellent served warm, at room temperature, or chilled.

PER SERVING ($^1/_8$ torte, $^1/_4$ cup sauce, and 3 raspberries): Calories 296 (30% from fat); Protein 8g; Fat 10g (sat 6g, mono 2g, poly 0g); Carbohydrates 44g; Fiber 1g; Cholesterol 70mg; Iron 1mg; Sodium 133mg; Calcium 159mg

vanilla-rum custard sauce:

1 cup fat-free milk
1 cup evaporated fat-free milk
$^1/_4$ cup sugar
1 large egg yolk
4 teaspoons cornstarch
$^1/_8$ teaspoon salt
2 tablespoons dark rum
2 teaspoons vanilla extract

1. Combine milks in a medium saucepan; cook over medium heat until hot (do not boil).
2. Combine sugar and egg yolk in a bowl; stir well. Add cornstarch and salt; stir until well blended (mixture will be thick). Gradually add hot milk to egg yolk mixture, stirring constantly with a whisk. Return mixture to pan. Cook over medium heat 4 minutes or until thick, stirring constantly. Remove from heat; stir in rum and vanilla. Pour into a bowl; cover surface of custard with plastic wrap. Chill. Stir well with a whisk before serving.

VARIATION:
warm bittersweet chocolate-kahlúa torte

Prepare as directed for Warm Bittersweet Chocolate-Rum Torte, using 2 tablespoons Kahlúa instead of rum. Dissolve 1 tablespoon instant espresso granules or 2 tablespoons instant coffee granules in $^1/_4$ cup fat-free milk before adding to torte batter. Substitute 2 tablespoons Kahlúa for rum in custard sauce.

PER SERVING: Calories 299 (30% from fat); Protein 8g; Fat 10g (sat 6g, mono 2g, poly 0g); Carbohydrate 45g; Fiber 1g; Cholesterol 70mg; Iron 1mg; Sodium 133mg; Calcium 159mg

sour cream-fudge cake with mocha glaze

pictured on pages 93 and 97

Prep: *32 minutes* **Cook:** *30 minutes*
Serves 15

The stronger the coffee, the more intense the flavor is in this cake. If you don't want to brew a pot of coffee, you can dissolve 1½ teaspoons instant coffee granules in ¼ cup hot water.

Cooking spray
- 1 teaspoon all-purpose flour
- 2 (1-ounce) squares unsweetened chocolate, coarsely chopped
- 1½ cups sifted cake flour
- 1½ cups sugar
- 3 tablespoons unsweetened cocoa
- 1 teaspoon baking soda
- ¼ teaspoon salt
- ¼ cup butter, softened
- 1 (8-ounce) carton 30%-less-fat sour cream (such as Breakstone)
- ¼ cup hot brewed coffee
- 1 teaspoon vanilla extract
- 1 large egg
Mocha Glaze

1. Preheat oven to 350°.
2. Coat a 13 x 9-inch baking pan with cooking spray, and dust with 1 teaspoon all-purpose flour; set aside.
3. Place chocolate in the top of a double boiler. Cook over simmering water 5 minutes or until melted, stirring until smooth. Remove from heat; set aside.
4. Combine cake flour and next 4 ingredients (flour through salt) in a large bowl. Add butter and sour cream; beat with a mixer at low speed 30 seconds or until blended. Beat at high speed 2 minutes. Add melted chocolate, coffee, vanilla, and egg; beat at low speed until blended. Beat at high speed 2 minutes.
5. Pour batter into prepared pan. Bake at 350° for 30 minutes or until a wooden pick inserted in center of cake comes out clean.
6. Cool completely in pan on a wire rack. Spread Mocha Glaze over cooled cake.

mocha glaze:

- 1½ cups sifted powdered sugar
- 3 tablespoons unsweetened cocoa
- 3 tablespoons hot brewed coffee

1. Combine all ingredients in a small bowl; stir until smooth. Yield: about ⅔ cup.

PER SERVING (¹/₁₅ of cake with glaze): Calories 245 (28% from fat); Protein 3g; Fat 8g (sat 5g, mono 2g, poly 0g); Carbohydrate 43g; Fiber 0g; Cholesterol 29mg; Iron 2mg; Sodium 166mg; Calcium 27mg

mocha brownie torte

Prep: *12 minutes* **Cook:** *20 minutes*
Cool: *5 minutes*
Serves 12

Serve a wedge of this rich chocolate torte with a cup of coffee for an elegant dessert.

- ⅔ cup hot water
- 2 tablespoons instant coffee granules
- 1 (20.5-ounce) box low-fat brownie mix (such as Sweet Rewards)
- 2 teaspoons vanilla extract
- 4 large egg whites, lightly beaten
Cooking spray
Coffee Whipped Frosting

1. Preheat oven to 325°.
2. Combine hot water and coffee granules; stir well. Add brownie mix, vanilla, and egg whites; stir until well blended. Pour mixture evenly into 2 (9-inch) cake pans coated with cooking spray. Bake at 325° for 20 minutes. Let cool in pans 5 minutes on a wire rack. Spray wire racks with cooking spray. Loosen brownie layers from sides of pans, using a narrow metal spatula, and turn out onto greased wire racks. Let cool completely.
3. Spread Coffee Whipped Frosting between layers and over top and sides of torte. Serve immediately or store, loosely covered, in refrigerator.

NOTE: To loosely cover torte, use a cake dome or place 6 toothpicks in top of torte, spacing evenly to prevent plastic wrap from sticking to whipped topping. Cover with plastic wrap.

coffee whipped frosting:

- 3 cups frozen reduced-calorie whipped topping, thawed
- 1 tablespoon instant coffee granules

1. Place whipped topping in a bowl; sprinkle with coffee granules. Gently fold coffee into whipped topping (fold only until coffee granules disperse and whipped topping has a speckled look).

PER SERVING (¹/₁₂ of torte with frosting): Calories 246 (23% from fat); Protein 5g; Fat 6g (sat 1g, mono 0g, poly 0g); Carbohydrate 46g; Fiber 2g; Cholesterol 0mg; Iron 2mg; Sodium 210mg; Calcium 14mg

fresh fish & shellfish

*Herb-Marinated Shrimp
Kebabs, page 128*

seafood grill with fresh tomato sauce

Prep: *19 minutes* **Cook:** *8 minutes*
Chill: *30 minutes*
Serves 4

This grilled dish, served with a chunky vegetable sauce, is perfect for a summer evening meal.

³/₄	pound mahimahi or other firm white fish fillet
3	tablespoons fresh lime juice
1	tablespoon olive oil
¹/₂	teaspoon black pepper
¹/₄	teaspoon salt
¹/₈	teaspoon chili powder
¹/₈	teaspoon garlic powder
18	large shrimp (about 9 ounces), peeled and deveined
3	cups peeled, seeded, and coarsely chopped tomato
¹/₂	cup chopped yellow squash
¹/₄	cup chopped fresh banana peppers or pepperoncini peppers
¹/₄	cup chopped onion
¹/₄	cup chopped fresh cilantro
1	tablespoon fresh lime juice
¹/₂	teaspoon sugar
¹/₂	teaspoon chili powder
¹/₄	teaspoon salt
¹/₄	teaspoon black pepper
¹/₈	teaspoon ground red pepper

Cooking spray

1. Cut fish into 4 portions. Combine lime juice and next 5 ingredients (lime juice through garlic powder) in a zip-top plastic bag. Add fish and shrimp; seal bag. Refrigerate 30 minutes to 2 hours.
2. Combine tomato and next 10 ingredients (tomato through red pepper); toss gently. Set aside.
3. Remove fish and shrimp from bag; discard marinade. Place on grill rack coated with cooking spray; grill 4 minutes on each side or until shrimp is done and fish flakes easily when tested with a fork. Serve with tomato mixture.

PER SERVING (3 ounces fish, 2 ounces shrimp, and ³/₄ cup tomato mixture): Calories 187 (24% from fat); Protein 26g; Fat 5g (sat 1g, mono 3g, poly 1g); Carbohydrate 11g; Fiber 3g; Cholesterol 138mg; Iron 3mg; Sodium 471mg; Calcium 46mg

baked catfish with tomato-kalamata salsa

Prep: *5 minutes* **Cook:** *25 minutes*
Serves 4

Tomatoes, olives, and cilantro prove that three simple ingredients can create a super-flavorful dish.

2¹/₄	cups chopped seeded plum tomato
¹/₂	cup chopped pitted kalamata olives
¹/₃	cup chopped fresh cilantro
4	(6-ounce) farm-raised catfish fillets

1. Preheat oven to 375°.
2. Combine first 3 ingredients (tomato through cilantro) in a bowl; stir well.
3. Place catfish fillets in a 13 x 9-inch baking dish; top with tomato mixture. Bake fillets at 375° for 25 minutes or until fish flakes easily when tested with a fork.

PER SERVING (1 fillet and about ³/₄ cup tomato topping): Calories 232 (36% from fat); Protein 31g; Fat 9g (sat 2g, mono 3g, poly 2g); Carbohydrate 5g; Fiber 2g; Cholesterol 97mg; Iron 3mg; Sodium 268mg; Calcium 89mg

orange-teriyaki grouper kebabs

pictured on page 117

Prep: *15 minutes* **Cook:** *19 minutes*
Marinate: *15 minutes*
Serves 4

3	tablespoons low-sodium soy sauce
1	tablespoon rice vinegar
1	tablespoon honey
1	teaspoon minced peeled fresh ginger
1¹/₂	pounds skinless grouper fillets, cut into 1-inch pieces
1	(8-ounce) package fresh mushrooms
1	medium-sized green bell pepper, cut into 1¹/₂-inch pieces
1	medium-sized red bell pepper, cut into 1¹/₂-inch pieces

Cooking spray
| 6 | tablespoons orange juice |

1. Combine first 4 ingredients (soy sauce through ginger) in a shallow dish; stir well. Add fish, stirring to coat. Cover; marinate in refrigerator 15 minutes. Remove fish from dish, reserving marinade. Thread fish, mushrooms, and bell pepper alternately onto 8 (10-inch) skewers. Place kebabs on a broiler pan coated with cooking spray; broil 6 minutes. Turn kebabs over; broil 6 minutes or until vegetables are tender and fish flakes easily when tested with a fork.
2. Combine marinade and orange juice in a saucepan; bring to a boil. Reduce heat; simmer 5 minutes or until reduced to ¹/₂ cup. Drizzle over kebabs.

PER SERVING (2 kebabs and 2 tablespoons sauce): Calories 284 (26% from fat); Protein 38g; Fat 8g (sat 2g, mono 2g, poly 1g); Carbohydrate 13g; Fiber 2g; Cholesterol 87mg; Iron 3mg; Sodium 432mg; Calcium 67mg

grouper veracruz

Prep: *20 minutes* **Cook:** *26 minutes*
Marinate: *1 hour*
Serves 6

A refreshing tomato sauce full of olives and onions tops delicate fish seared in butter in this south-of-the-border dish.

6	(6-ounce) grouper fillets
4	garlic cloves, crushed
1/2	teaspoon salt
3	tablespoons grated lime rind
1/4	cup fresh lime juice
2	teaspoons extra-virgin olive oil
3	cups thinly sliced onion (about 1 large)
1/3	cup chopped pitted green olives
1 1/2	teaspoons minced jalapeño pepper
1/4	teaspoon dried oregano
1/4	teaspoon dried thyme
1/4	teaspoon sugar
2	bay leaves
1	(28-ounce) can whole tomatoes, undrained
1	tablespoon capers
2	teaspoons butter
1/2	cup fresh cilantro leaves

1. Rub both sides of fillets with garlic; sprinkle with salt. Arrange fillets in a single layer in a large shallow dish. Add lime rind and juice, turning to coat. Cover and marinate in refrigerator 1 hour.
2. Heat oil in a large nonstick skillet over medium-high heat. Add onion; sauté 5 minutes or until golden. Stir in olives and next 6 ingredients (olives through tomatoes). Reduce heat and simmer, uncovered, 10 minutes, stirring occasionally. Stir in capers. Remove from pan.
3. Melt butter in pan over medium-high heat. Add fillets; cook 3 minutes on each side or until fish flakes easily when tested with a fork. Pour tomato mixture over fillets; cook 5 minutes or until thoroughly heated. Sprinkle with cilantro.

PER SERVING (1 fillet and 1/2 cup tomato sauce): Calories 249 (21% from fat); Protein 35g; Fat 6g (sat 2g, mono 3g, poly 1g); Carbohydrate 14g; Fiber 3g; Cholesterol 66mg; Iron 3mg; Sodium 727mg; Calcium 123mg

vegetable-steamed orange roughy

Prep: *10 minutes* **Cook:** *16 minutes*
Serves 4

Fresh vegetables, thyme, and lemon juice infuse the fish with fabulous flavor without adding any extra fat.

1	tablespoon olive oil
1	cup green bell pepper strips
1	cup red bell pepper strips
1	cup chopped onion
3	garlic cloves, minced
1	large yellow squash, cut in half lengthwise and sliced (about 2 cups)
1/3	cup water
2	tablespoons fresh lemon juice
1	tablespoon chopped fresh thyme, divided
3/4	teaspoon salt, divided
1/4	teaspoon hot sauce
4	(6-ounce) orange roughy fillets
1/4	teaspoon black pepper

1. Heat olive oil in a 2-inch-deep, straight-sided skillet or Dutch oven over medium-high heat. Add bell pepper strips, onion, and garlic; sauté 2 minutes. Add squash, and sauté 2 minutes. Reduce heat to medium, and add water, lemon juice, 2 teaspoons thyme, 1/2 teaspoon salt, and hot sauce. Arrange fish fillets in a single layer over vegetable mixture, and sprinkle fillets with remaining 1 teaspoon thyme, 1/4 teaspoon salt, and pepper. Cover, reduce heat, and simmer 12 minutes or until fish flakes easily when tested with a fork.

PER SERVING (1 fillet and 1 cup vegetables): Calories 161 (26% from fat); Protein 19g; Fat 5g (sat 1g, mono 3g, poly 0g); Carbohydrate 12g; Fiber 3g; Cholesterol 23mg; Iron 2mg; Sodium 518mg; Calcium 40mg

greek-style cod

Prep: *9 minutes* **Cook:** *24 minutes*
Serves 4

Cooking the cod in the sautéed leek mixture imparts a pleasing garlic aroma to the fish.

1	tablespoon olive oil
2	cups chopped leek
2	garlic cloves, minced
1 1/2	teaspoons paprika
1/4	teaspoon ground red pepper
1	cup dry red wine
1	tablespoon tomato paste
1	teaspoon salt
4	(6-ounce) cod fillets

1. Heat oil in a large nonstick skillet over medium-high heat until hot. Add leek and garlic; sauté 3 minutes. Add paprika and red pepper; sauté 1 minute. Add wine and tomato paste; reduce heat, and simmer 4 minutes.
2. Sprinkle salt evenly over both sides of fillets. Add to skillet, nestling fillets into leek mixture. Cover, reduce heat, and simmer 15 minutes or until fish flakes easily when tested with a fork.

PER SERVING (1 fillet and 1/3 cup sauce): Calories 204 (21% from fat); Protein 31g; Fat 5g (sat 1g, mono 3g, poly 1g); Carbohydrate 8g; Fiber 1g; Cholesterol 73mg; Iron 2mg; Sodium 689mg; Calcium 59mg

salmon with moroccan tomato relish

Prep: *16 minutes* **Cook:** *16 minutes*
Serves 4

Citrus rind, cinnamon, and fresh mint give this salmon dish its Moroccan flair.

- 1/2 teaspoon salt, divided
- 4 (6-ounce) skinless salmon fillets
- 2 teaspoons olive oil, divided
- 1 3/4 cups chopped red onion
- 1 tablespoon minced peeled fresh ginger
- 4 1/2 cups coarsely chopped tomato
- 1 teaspoon grated orange rind
- 2 tablespoons fresh orange juice
- 1 teaspoon grated lemon rind
- 1 tablespoon fresh lemon juice
- 1 tablespoon capers
- 1/4 teaspoon ground cinnamon
- 1/4 cup chopped fresh mint
- 3 tablespoons chopped fresh cilantro
- Mint sprigs (optional)

1. Sprinkle 1/4 teaspoon salt evenly over salmon. Heat 1 teaspoon oil in a large nonstick skillet over medium-high heat until hot. Add salmon; cook 3 minutes on each side or until lightly browned. Remove from pan; set aside, and keep warm.
2. Add remaining oil to pan; place over medium-high heat until hot. Add onion and ginger; sauté 2 minutes. Add remaining 1/4 teaspoon salt, tomato, and next 6 ingredients (orange rind through cinnamon); cook 5 minutes, stirring occasionally.
3. Return salmon to pan, nestling fillets into tomato mixture; cook 3 minutes until salmon is medium-rare or desired degree of doneness. Remove from heat; place salmon on individual plates. Stir chopped mint and cilantro into tomato mixture; spoon mixture around each fillet. Garnish with mint sprigs, if desired.

PER SERVING (1 fillet and 3/4 cup tomato relish): Calories 334 (35% from fat); Protein 39g; Fat 13g (sat 2g, mono 5g, poly 5g); Carbohydrate 15g; Fiber 3g; Cholesterol 66mg; Iron 2mg; Sodium 559mg; Calcium 28mg

orange-ginger salmon with sautéed greens

Prep: *30 minutes* **Cook:** *14 minutes*
Marinate: *20 minutes*
Serves 4

- 3 tablespoons low-sodium soy sauce
- 2 teaspoons grated peeled fresh ginger
- 1 1/2 teaspoons brown sugar
- 1 teaspoon finely grated fresh orange zest
- 4 (4-ounce) skinless salmon fillets (about 1 inch thick)
- 2 teaspoons vegetable oil
- 3 cups chopped fresh basil
- 1/4 teaspoon salt
- 1/8 teaspoon pepper
- 2 garlic cloves, minced
- 1 pound fresh spinach, stems trimmed (about 16 cups)
- 6 tablespoons water
- 1 teaspoon dark sesame oil

1. Combine soy sauce, ginger, sugar, and orange zest in a zip-top plastic bag. Add fish, and marinate 20 minutes in refrigerator. Remove fish; reserve marinade.
2. Heat vegetable oil in a large nonstick skillet over medium-high heat. Add fish, and cook 3 minutes, without turning. Reduce heat to medium, turn fish, and cover. Cook 3 minutes or until just cooked through. Transfer fish to a plate, cover with foil, and keep warm.
3. Return pan to heat. Pour marinade into pan, and bring to a boil. Simmer 1 minute. Transfer to a bowl, and cover with foil. Wipe out pan with a paper towel.
4. Return pan to medium-high heat. Add half of basil, salt, pepper, garlic, spinach, and 3 tablespoons water. Cover and cook 2 minutes, or until spinach is wilted. Transfer to a bowl, and repeat with remaining basil, salt, pepper, garlic, spinach, and water. Combine with other spinach mixture, and toss with sesame oil.
5. Top greens with salmon, and drizzle with glaze.

PER SERVING (1 fillet, 2/3 cup spinach mixture, and 1 1/2 teaspoons glaze): Calories 287 (50% from fat); Protein 27g; Fat 16g (sat 3g, mono 5g, poly 7g); Carbohydrate 9g; Fiber 5g; Cholesterol 67mg; Iron 5mg; Sodium 705mg; Calcium 182mg

honey-glazed salmon

pictured on page 120

Prep: *4 minutes* **Cook:** *12 minutes*
Serves 4

- 3 tablespoons honey
- 1 tablespoon Dijon mustard
- 1/4 teaspoon cayenne pepper
- 4 (6-ounce) salmon fillets (about 1 inch thick)

1. Whisk together honey, mustard, and pepper.
2. Brush salmon with honey mixture. Broil 6 minutes on each side or until fish flakes easily when tested with a fork.

PER SERVING (1 fillet): Calories 295 (34% from fat); Protein 34g; Fat 11g (sat 2g, mono 4g, poly 4g); Carbohydrate 14g; Fiber 0g; Cholesterol 94mg; Iron 2mg; Sodium 170mg; Calcium 27mg

Orange-Teriyaki Grouper Kebabs, page 114

Tuna with Coriander Mayonnaise, page 123

Pan-Seared Tilapia with Mojo, page 123

Sicilian Tuna with
Fettuccine, page 124

Chicken and Shellfish
Paella, page 130

Herb-Marinated Shrimp
Kebabs, page 128

fresh fish & shellfish

Honey-Glazed Salmon,
page 116

How to Blacken Fish

In blackening, fish, beef, pork, or vegetables are coated with an herb or a spice mixture, and then seared in an intensely hot cast-iron skillet. In just minutes, a flavorful crust develops that locks in the food's natural juices. Blackening produces a lot of smoke, so we recommend cooking outside on a grill. But it can be done inside on a cooktop with a commercial hood vent. For best blackening results in the recipe at right, choose salmon fillets with even thickness and a flat surface area.

1. Place spices for salmon in a zip-top plastic bag, and crush with a meat mallet.

2. Press crushed spices onto one side of salmon fillets.

3. Place a cast-iron skillet on grill rack over hot coals. The skillet should preheat at least 10 minutes. Add salmon fillets, seasoned side down, and cook 3 minutes or until slightly charred.

4. Turn fillets over, and cook until desired degree of doneness.

spiced salmon fillets with fennel mayonnaise

Prep: *12 minutes* **Cook:** *6 minutes*
Serves 4

- 2 teaspoons fennel seeds
- 1 1/2 teaspoons black peppercorns
- 1/4 teaspoon salt
- 1 garlic clove, minced
- 2 tablespoons light mayonnaise
- 1 tablespoon honey
- 1 teaspoon lemon juice
- 4 (4-ounce) skinless salmon fillets
Cooking spray
Fresh fennel fronds (optional)

1. Prepare grill.
2. Place a 10-inch cast-iron skillet on grill rack over hot coals; let skillet heat at least 10 minutes.
3. Combine fennel seeds and peppercorns in a zip-top plastic bag; seal bag. Crush spices, using a meat mallet or rolling pin. Combine crushed spices, salt, and garlic.
4. Combine 1 teaspoon garlic-spice mixture, mayonnaise, honey, and lemon juice; stir well, and set aside.
5. Press remaining garlic-spice mixture onto one side of salmon fillets, and coat with cooking spray.
6. Place fillets, spice side down, in preheated skillet, and cook 3 minutes on each side or until fish flakes easily when tested with a fork.
7. Place a fillet, spice side up, on each of 4 plates; serve with mayonnaise mixture. Garnish with fennel fronds, if desired.

PER SERVING (1 fillet and about 2 teaspoons mayonnaise mixture): Calories 228 (46% from fat); Protein 24g; Fat 12g (sat 2g, mono 3g, poly 3g); Carbohydrate 6g; Fiber 0g; Cholesterol 76mg; Iron 1mg; Sodium 260mg; Calcium 23mg

teriyaki-glazed salmon with noodles

Prep: *5 minutes* **Cook:** *15 minutes*
Serves 4

Cooking spray
2 tablespoons water
1/4 cup packed light brown sugar
2 tablespoons rice vinegar
2 tablespoons reduced-sodium soy sauce
1/2 teaspoon ground dried ginger
1/2 teaspoon garlic powder
4 (5-ounce) salmon fillets
8 ounces uncooked vermicelli or somen noodles
2 teaspoons dark sesame oil
1/4 cup chopped fresh scallions

1. Preheat oven to 400°.
2. Coat a shallow roasting pan with cooking spray. Set aside.
3. To prepare teriyaki glaze, whisk together water, brown sugar, vinegar, soy sauce, ginger, and garlic in a shallow dish.
4. Add fillets, and turn to coat.
5. Transfer fillets to prepared roasting pan, and pour teriyaki mixture over it. Bake at 400° for 15 minutes or until fish flakes easily when tested with a fork.
6. Meanwhile, cook noodles in a medium-sized pot of rapidly boiling water according to package directions. Drain and transfer to a large bowl. Add sesame oil, and toss to coat.
7. Transfer noodles to 4 individual plates, and top each portion with a salmon fillet. Spoon any teriyaki glaze remaining in pan over salmon, and sprinkle chopped scallions on top.

PER SERVING (1 fillet and 1 cup noodle mixture):
Calories 451 (20% from fat); Protein 28g; Fat 10g
(sat 1g, mono 4g, poly 5g); Carbohydrate 62g; Fiber 2g;
Cholesterol 61mg; Iron 3mg; Sodium 325mg;
Calcium 30mg

southwestern snapper

Prep: *13 minutes* **Cook:** *32 minutes*
Serves 4

4 (6-ounce) red snapper fillets
Olive oil-flavored cooking spray
1/2 cup fresh orange juice, divided
2 teaspoons olive oil, divided
1/2 teaspoon salt
1 (10-ounce) can diced tomatoes and green chiles, undrained
1 large green bell pepper, cut into thin strips
1 small red onion, cut into strips
2 teaspoons minced garlic
1/4 cup sliced pitted green olives
1 tablespoon minced fresh cilantro
1 tablespoon capers
1 tablespoon caper juice

1. Preheat oven to 350°.
2. Place fillets in a 13 x 9-inch baking dish coated with cooking spray. Combine 2 tablespoons orange juice and 1 teaspoon olive oil; pour over fillets, and sprinkle with salt. Bake at 350° for 20 minutes or until fish flakes easily when tested with a fork.
3. Drain tomatoes, reserving 1/4 cup juice; set both aside. Coat a large nonstick skillet with cooking spray; add remaining 1 teaspoon oil, and place over medium-high heat until hot. Add bell pepper, onion, and garlic; sauté 7 minutes. Add remaining 6 tablespoons orange juice, tomatoes, reserved 1/4 cup tomato juice, olives, and next 3 ingredients (cilantro through caper juice); cook until thoroughly heated. Spoon vegetable mixture over fillets.

PER SERVING (1 fillet and 1/2 cup vegetable mixture):
Calories 247 (20% from fat); Protein 4g; Fat 6g (sat 1g,
mono 3g, poly 1g); Carbohydrate 13g; Fiber 2g;
Cholesterol 60mg; Iron 2mg; Sodium 994mg;
Calcium 125mg

braised red snapper

Prep: *30 minutes* **Cook:** *25 minutes*
Serves 6

Braising allows time for the flavors to develop without a loss of moisture. In Step 4 be sure to use a tight-fitting lid or secure the foil snugly to prevent liquid from evaporating.

1/4 cup all-purpose flour
2 teaspoons Old Bay seasoning
1 whole red snapper or striped bass (3 to 4 pounds), scaled, head and tail removed
1/4 cup olive oil
3/4 cup chopped shallots or sweet onion
3 garlic cloves, minced
2 cups dry white wine or vermouth
2 sprigs tarragon or Italian parsley
2 sprigs thyme
1 teaspoon coriander seeds
1 teaspoon whole peppercorns
1/2 teaspoon salt
1 tablespoon butter
2 tablespoons chopped fresh tarragon or parsley

1. Preheat oven to 350°.
2. Combine flour and Old Bay seasoning in a shallow dish or pie plate. Dredge both sides of fish in flour mixture, patting to coat. Discard excess flour mixture.
3. Over medium heat, heat oil in large, deep ovenproof skillet or roasting pan; add fish. Cook 5 minutes per side or until deep golden brown. Carefully transfer fish to a platter; set aside.
4. Pour off oil. Add shallots and garlic to pan; cook 30 seconds. Add wine, herb sprigs, coriander, peppercorns, and salt; bring to a simmer, scraping browned bits from bottom of pan.
5. Return fish to pan. Cover with lid or heavy-duty foil; cook at

350° for 25 minutes or until fish is opaque throughout.

6. Carefully transfer fish to a serving platter. Strain pan juices; return to pan. Bring to a boil; remove from heat. Stir in butter until melted; spoon juices over fish. Garnish with chopped tarragon or parsley.

PER SERVING (about 5 ounces fish): Calories 236 (27% from fat); Protein 21g; Fat 7g (sat 2g, mono 4g poly 1g); Carbohydrate 8g, Fiber 0g; Cholesterol 96mg; Iron 2mg; Sodium 421mg; Calcium 40mg

pan-seared tilapia with mojo

pictured on page 118

Prep: *10 minutes* **Cook:** *12 minutes*
Serves 4

A quick sear on the stovetop gives this white fish a crusty, browned outside while finishing it off in the oven seals in moisture.

  1 tablespoon olive oil, divided
  4 garlic cloves, thinly sliced
 ¼ cup water
  3 tablespoons fresh lime juice
1½ teaspoons ground cumin, divided
 ¾ teaspoon salt, divided
  3 tablespoons all-purpose flour
 ¼ teaspoon ground red pepper
Olive oil-flavored cooking spray
  4 (6-ounce) tilapia or other mild white fish fillets

1. Preheat oven to 400°.
2. Heat 2 teaspoons oil in a saucepan over medium-high heat. Add garlic; sauté 2 minutes. Stir in water, lime juice, ½ teaspoon cumin, and ¼ teaspoon salt; simmer 1 minute. Remove from heat.
3. Combine 1 teaspoon cumin, ½ teaspoon salt, flour, and red pepper in a shallow dish. Lightly coat

fillets with cooking spray; dredge in flour mixture.
4. Heat 1 teaspoon oil in a large ovenproof skillet coated with cooking spray over medium-high heat. Add fillets; cook 2 minutes on each side or until lightly browned. Remove from heat. Spoon lime mixture evenly over fillets; transfer skillet to oven, and bake 5 minutes or until fish flakes easily when tested with a fork.

PER SERVING (1 fillet): Calories 204 (25% from fat); Protein 30g; Fat 6g (sat 1g, mono 3g, poly 1g); Carbohydrate 7g; Fiber 1g; Cholesterol 52mg; Iron 1mg; Sodium 533mg; Calcium 60mg

tuna with coriander mayonnaise

pictured on page 117

Prep: *12 minutes* **Cook:** *8 minutes*
Serves 4

  2 tablespoons light mayonnaise
  4 teaspoons fat-free milk
  1 tablespoon plain fat-free yogurt
 ⅛ teaspoon ground coriander
 ⅛ teaspoon pepper
 ¼ cup coriander seeds
 ½ teaspoon salt
 ¼ teaspoon pepper
  4 (6-ounce) tuna steaks (about ¾ inch thick)
Cooking spray

1. Combine first 5 ingredients (mayonnaise through ⅛ teaspoon pepper). Chill. Place seeds in a heavy-duty, zip-top plastic bag; seal. Crush seeds with a rolling pin. Sprinkle salt and ¼ teaspoon pepper over tuna; press crushed coriander into both sides of steaks.
2. Coat a large nonstick skillet with cooking spray; place over medium-high heat until hot. Add tuna; cook 4 minutes on each

side until medium-rare or desired degree of doneness. Serve tuna with mayonnaise mixture.

PER SERVING (1 tuna steak and about 1 tablespoon mayonnaise mixture): Calories 286 (36% from fat); Protein 41g; Fat 11g (sat 2g, mono 3g, poly 3g); Carbohydrate 4g; Fiber 2g; Cholesterol 67mg; Iron 3mg; Sodium 422mg; Calcium 50mg

citrus-teriyaki tuna

Prep: *10 minutes* **Cook:** *14 minutes*
Marinate: *30 minutes*
Serves 4

  1 cup orange juice
 ¼ cup minced peeled fresh ginger
 ¼ cup chopped green onions
 ¼ cup low-sodium teriyaki sauce
  3 tablespoons fresh lemon juice
  2 garlic cloves, minced
  3 drops hot sauce
  4 (6-ounce) tuna steaks (about ¾ inch thick)
Cooking spray

1. Combine first 7 ingredients (orange juice through hot sauce) in a shallow dish. Add tuna, turning to coat. Cover. Marinate in refrigerator 30 minutes, turning tuna occasionally. Remove tuna from dish; reserve marinade.
2. Strain marinade through a sieve into a saucepan, discarding solids. Bring marinade to a boil over high heat; cook 6 minutes or until slightly thick. Keep warm.
3. Prepare grill.
4. Place tuna steaks on grill rack coated with cooking spray, and grill 4 minutes on each side until tuna is medium-rare or until desired degree of doneness. Top tuna evenly with prepared sauce.

PER SERVING (1 tuna steak): Calories 285 (26% from fat); Protein 40g; Fat 8g (sat 2g, mono 3g, poly 3g); Carbohydrate 12g; Fiber 0g; Cholesterol 63mg; Iron 2mg; Sodium 323mg; Calcium 15mg

sicilian tuna with fettuccine

pictured on page 119

Prep: *9 minutes* **Cook:** *18 minutes*
Serves 4

   1   tablespoon olive oil, divided
   4   (4-ounce) tuna steaks (about
       $^1/_2$ inch thick)
 $^1/_2$ teaspoon coarsely ground
       black pepper
$1^1/_2$ cups slivered Vidalia or other
       sweet onion
$2^1/_2$ cups chopped plum tomato
       (about 1 pound)
   3   garlic cloves, minced
 $^1/_4$ cup sliced green olives
$1^1/_2$ tablespoons capers
   1   tablespoon balsamic vinegar
   1   tablespoon fresh lemon juice
   1   teaspoon dried oregano
   3   cups hot cooked fettuccine
       (about 6 ounces uncooked)

1. Brush $1^1/_2$ teaspoons olive oil evenly over tuna steaks; sprinkle with pepper. Place a nonstick skillet over medium-high heat until hot. Add tuna steaks. Cook 4 minutes on each side until medium-rare or desired degree of doneness. Remove tuna from pan; set aside, and keep warm.
2. Add remaining olive oil to pan. Add onion, and sauté 5 minutes. Add tomato and garlic, and sauté 2 minutes or until tender. Add olives and next 4 ingredients (olives through oregano); cook 2 minutes or until thoroughly heated.
3. Place hot fettuccine on individual plates; top with tuna. Spoon tomato mixture over tuna steaks and fettuccine.

PER SERVING ($^3/_4$ cup pasta, 1 tuna steak, and $^1/_2$ cup tomato mixture): Calories 382 (25% from fat); Protein 33g; Fat 11g (sat 2g, mono 5g, poly 2g); Carbohydrate 38g; Fiber 4g; Cholesterol 43mg; Iron 4mg; Sodium 384mg; Calcium 39mg

grilled tuna with honey-mustard dressing

Prep: *15 minutes* **Cook:** *15 minutes*
Stand: *5 minutes*
Serves 4

We made our own low-fat honey-mustard dressing for this dish. Serve any leftover dressing over greens or with grilled chicken.

   4   (5-ounce) tuna steaks ($^1/_2$-inch
       thick)
 $^1/_2$ teaspoon salt
 $^1/_4$ teaspoon freshly ground black
       pepper
   1   cup quick-cooking barley
 $^1/_2$ cup apple cider vinegar
   3   tablespoons honey
   1   tablespoon Dijon mustard
   1   shallot, minced
   1   teaspoon poppy seeds
   2   teaspoons olive oil
  10   ounces fresh spinach, rinsed
       well and stems trimmed

1. Prepare grill.
2. Sprinkle both sides of tuna with salt and pepper to taste, and set aside.
3. To prepare barley, bring 2 cups water to a boil in a medium-sized saucepan over medium-high heat. Add barley, reduce heat to low, cover, and cook 10 minutes, or until barley is tender and liquid is absorbed. Let stand 5 minutes.
4. While barley is cooking, whisk together vinegar, honey, and mustard in a small bowl. Transfer $^1/_3$ cup of mixture to a shallow dish (reserve remainder), add tuna steaks one at a time, and turn to coat. Discard marinade.
5. Grill tuna 3 minutes per side, or until fork-tender.
6. To prepare dressing, add shallot and poppy seeds to

remaining honey mixture. Mix well, and set aside.
7. To prepare spinach, heat olive oil in a large skillet over medium-high heat. Add spinach, cover, and cook 1 minute, until wilted.
8. To serve, spoon barley and spinach evenly onto serving plates. Place tuna steaks alongside, and spoon honey-poppy seed mixture evenly over top.

NOTE: Tuna may also be broiled, 5 inches from heat source, 5 minutes per side.

PER SERVING (1 entrée): Calories 467 (21% from fat); Protein 41g; Fat 11g (sat 2g, mono 2g, poly 2g); Carbohydrate 51g; Fiber 10g; Cholesterol 56mg; Iron 6mg; Sodium 497mg; Calcium 116mg

Quick Fish Substitutions

Can't find a particular fish? Use this substitution list to select another fish that has a texture and flavor similar to the one called for in the recipe.

Flounder: ocean perch, orange roughy, sole

Grouper: halibut, sea bass, snapper

Orange roughy: flounder, sole, snapper, grouper

Perch: orange roughy, sole, flounder

Salmon: swordfish, halibut, trout, yellowtail tuna

Sea bass: grouper, halibut, snapper

Snapper: sea bass, grouper, redfish, pompano

crab quesadillas with poblano cream

Prep: *22 minutes* **Cook:** *12 minutes*
Stand: *5 minutes*
Serves 6

*For Shrimp Quesadillas, substitute
1 pound cooked peeled shrimp,
coarsely chopped, for the crab.*

- 2 fresh poblano chiles
- 1/3 cup (2.6 ounces) light cream cheese, softened
- 1/4 cup low-fat sour cream
- 1 tablespoon fresh lime juice
- 1 teaspoon bottled minced roasted garlic
- 1 pound lump crabmeat, shell pieces removed
- 1 1/4 cups (5 ounces) shredded reduced-fat Monterey Jack cheese
- 1/2 cup sliced green onions
- 1 teaspoon ground coriander
- 1/4 teaspoon salt
- 6 (8-inch) low-fat flour tortillas
- Butter-flavored cooking spray
- 1 1/2 cups chopped tomato

1. Preheat broiler.
2. Cut chiles in half lengthwise, and discard stems, seeds, and membranes. Place chile halves, skin side up, on a foil-lined baking sheet, and flatten with hand. Broil 15 minutes or until chiles are blackened. Place in a zip-top plastic bag; seal bag, and let stand 5 minutes. Peel chiles.
3. Place roasted chiles, cream cheese, and next 3 ingredients (sour cream through garlic) in a food processor; process until smooth, scraping sides of processor bowl twice. Reserve 6 tablespoons poblano cream to top quesadillas.
4. Combine remaining poblano cream, crabmeat, and next 4 ingredients (cheese through salt) in a bowl; stir until blended.

Spread about 1/2 cup crab mixture over half of 1 tortilla; fold tortilla in half to cover filling. Repeat procedure with remaining crab mixture and tortillas. Cover quesadillas with a slightly damp towel to keep them from drying out.
5. Coat a large nonstick skillet with cooking spray, and place over medium heat until hot. Add 2 quesadillas, and cook 2 minutes on each side or until browned. Remove quesadillas from pan; set aside, and keep warm. Repeat procedure with remaining quesadillas.
6. Cut each quesadilla in half. Top each serving with 1/4 cup chopped tomato and 1 tablespoon reserved poblano cream.

PER SERVING: Calories 337 (29% from fat); Protein 28g; Fat 11g (sat 6g, mono 0g, poly 1g); Carbohydrate 32g; Fiber 2g; Cholesterol 106mg; Iron 3mg; Sodium 770mg; Calcium 306mg

thai crab cakes with cilantro-peanut sauce

Prep: *20 minutes* **Cook:** *12 minutes*
Chill: *1 hour*
Serves 4

- 1 1/4 cups fresh breadcrumbs
- 1 cup fresh bean sprouts, chopped
- 1/4 cup finely chopped green onions
- 1/4 cup chopped fresh cilantro
- 2 tablespoons fresh lime juice
- 1/8 teaspoon ground red pepper
- 1 large egg
- 1 large egg white, lightly beaten
- 1 pound lump crabmeat, shell pieces removed
- 2 teaspoons olive oil, divided
- Cooking spray
- Cilantro-Peanut Sauce

1. Combine first 9 ingredients (breadcrumbs through crabmeat) in a medium bowl; cover and chill 1 hour. Divide mixture into 8 equal portions, shaping each into a 1/2-inch-thick patty.
2. Heat 1 teaspoon oil in a large nonstick skillet coated with cooking spray over medium heat until hot. Add 4 patties; cook 3 minutes on each side or until lightly browned. Remove patties from pan, and keep warm. Wipe pan clean with paper towels; recoat with cooking spray. Repeat procedure with 1 teaspoon oil and 4 patties. Serve with Cilantro-Peanut Sauce.

cilantro-peanut sauce:

- 1/4 cup balsamic vinegar
- 2 1/2 tablespoons granulated sugar
- 2 tablespoons brown sugar
- 2 tablespoons low-sodium soy sauce
- 1/2 teaspoon crushed red pepper
- 1/8 teaspoon salt
- 1 garlic clove, minced
- 2 tablespoons creamy peanut butter
- 1/2 cup chopped fresh cilantro
- 2 tablespoons chopped fresh mint

1. Combine first 7 ingredients (vinegar through garlic) in a small saucepan, and bring to a boil, stirring frequently. Remove from heat. Add peanut butter, and stir with a whisk until smooth. Cool, and stir in cilantro and mint. Yield: 3/4 cup.

PER SERVING (2 patties and 3 tablespoons sauce): Calories 315 (30% from fat); Protein 31g; Fat 11g (sat 2g, mono 5g, poly 3g); Carbohydrate 25g; Fiber 2g; Cholesterol 169mg; Iron 3mg; Sodium 784mg; Calcium 169mg

louisiana crab jambalaya

Prep: *13 minutes* **Cook:** *28 minutes*
Serves 6

This spicy seafood stew has only 135 calories per 1-cup serving. Serve over hot cooked rice or with French bread, if desired.

- 1 tablespoon olive oil
- 1¹/₂ cups chopped onion
- 1 cup frozen whole-kernel corn
- ¹/₂ cup chopped green bell pepper
- 1 (14¹/₂-ounce) can diced tomatoes with green bell pepper and onion, undrained
- 1 (10-ounce) package frozen cut okra
- 2 (6-ounce) cans lump crabmeat, drained
- 1 (8-ounce) bottle clam juice
- 1 tablespoon seafood seasoning blend (such as Chef Paul Prudhomme's Seafood Magic)
- 1 tablespoon bottled minced garlic
- 1 teaspoon dried fines herbes
- ¹/₄ teaspoon salt

1. Heat oil in a saucepan over medium-high heat. Add onion, corn, and bell pepper; sauté 5 minutes. Add tomatoes and remaining ingredients; bring to a boil. Reduce heat; simmer, uncovered, 20 minutes, stirring occasionally.

PER SERVING (1 cup): Calories 135 (19% from fat); Protein 10g; Fat 3g (sat 0g, mono 2g, poly 1g); Carbohydrate 19g; Fiber 3g; Cholesterol 38mg; Iron 2mg; Sodium 946mg; Calcium 124mg

mussels en brodo

Prep: *15 minutes* **Cook:** *40 minutes*
Serves 4

Brodo is the Italian word for broth. Olive oil, garlic, and fennel help create the fragrant simmering broth that's used to cook the mussels.

- 2 tablespoons extra-virgin olive oil
- 4 garlic cloves, minced
- 1 cup chopped fennel bulb
- 1 teaspoon fennel seeds
- 2 (14.5-ounce) cans diced tomatoes, undrained
- ³/₄ cup dry white wine
- ¹/₂ cup water
- 2 tablespoons lemon juice
- 1 tablespoon tomato paste
- ¹/₂ teaspoon salt
- ¹/₄ teaspoon crushed red pepper
- 4 dozen mussels (about 4¹/₂ pounds), scrubbed and debearded
- 1 garlic clove, halved
- 4 (1-inch-thick) slices stale sourdough bread (about 5 ounces)

1. Heat oil in a large Dutch oven over medium-high heat until hot. Add minced garlic, and sauté 3 minutes. Add fennel and seeds; sauté 2 minutes. Add tomatoes and next 6 ingredients (tomatoes through red pepper); bring to a boil. Reduce heat, and simmer 10 minutes. Add mussels, and bring to a boil. Cover, reduce heat, and simmer 10 minutes or until shells open. Remove from heat. Discard any unopened shells.
2. Preheat oven to 375°.
3. Rub garlic on both sides of bread slices; discard garlic. Place bread on a baking sheet; bake at 375° for 5 minutes on each side or until toasted.
4. Place 1 toasted bread slice in each of 4 bowls; top with mussels and tomato mixture.

PER SERVING (1 slice bread, 12 mussels, and 1¹/₄ cups tomato mixture): Calories 424 (28% from fat); Protein 34g; Fat 13g (sat 2g, mono 7g, poly 2g); Carbohydrate 44g; Fiber 2g; Cholesterol 64mg; Iron 11mg; Sodium 1,631mg; Calcium 151mg

How to Clean Mussels

If you've never cooked mussels before, you may be a little unsure as to how to clean and prepare them for cooking. Below are two quick steps to get mussels ready for a recipe.

1. First, scrub the mussels with a stiff brush; then rinse them well.

2. Second, debeard the mussels. The "beard" is the name given to the strands of tissue attached to the shell. To "debeard," simply pull the strands off and then rinse with cold water.

spinach-steamed mussels with thin spaghetti

Prep: *20 minutes* **Cook:** *15 minutes*
Serves 4

Spinach, tomato, and garlic add texture and flavor to this pasta and shellfish dish.

1 1/2 tablespoons butter
  1 cup finely chopped onion
  2 garlic cloves, minced
  1 bay leaf
  2 cups chopped tomato
2/3 teaspoon salt
  1 (10-ounce) package fresh spinach, chopped
1/2 cup dry white wine
  2 pounds mussels (about 36)
  4 cups hot cooked spaghettini (about 1/2 pound uncooked thin pasta)
1/4 teaspoon ground black pepper

1. Melt butter in a large stockpot over medium heat. Add onion, garlic, and bay leaf; sauté 3 minutes. Add tomato, salt, and spinach; cover and cook 4 minutes, stirring once. Add wine and mussels; bring to a boil. Cover and cook 5 minutes or until mussels open; discard any unopened shells. Discard bay leaf. Remove mussels with a slotted spoon. Arrange pasta on each plate; top with mussels. Ladle spinach sauce over each serving; sprinkle with pepper.

PER SERVING (1 cup pasta, about 9 mussels, and 1/2 cup spinach): Calories 367 (18% from fat); Protein 20g; Fat 8g (sat 3g, mono 2g, poly 1g); Carbohydrate 57g; Fiber 6g; Cholesterol 32mg; Iron 8mg; Sodium 621mg; Calcium 120mg

kung pao scallops with snap peas

Prep: *20 minutes* **Cook:** *5 minutes*
Serves 6

Sake is a Japanese wine made from rice. You may also see it referred to as mirin. Substitute a sweet white wine, if desired, or for a nonalcoholic substitute try apple juice.

3/4 cup fat-free, less-sodium chicken broth
1/4 cup low-sodium soy sauce
  2 tablespoons sugar
  1 tablespoon cornstarch
  3 tablespoons sake (rice wine)
  2 tablespoons Chinese black vinegar or Worcestershire sauce
  1 teaspoon dark sesame oil
1 1/2 tablespoons vegetable oil
  3 tablespoons minced green onions
  3 tablespoons minced garlic
  2 tablespoons minced peeled fresh ginger
1 1/2 teaspoons chili paste with garlic
  1 pound large sea scallops, cut in half
  2 (8-ounce) cans sliced water chestnuts, rinsed and drained
  1 pound fresh or 2 (9-ounce) packages frozen sugar snap peas, thawed
3/4 cup dry-roasted peanuts
  3 cups hot cooked long-grain rice

1. Combine first 7 ingredients (chicken broth through sesame oil) in a bowl, stirring with a whisk. Set aside.
2. Heat vegetable oil in a large nonstick skillet or wok over medium-high heat. Add onions, garlic, ginger, and chili paste; sauté 15 seconds. Add scallops and stir-fry 1 minute. Add water chestnuts; stir-fry 1 1/2 minutes. Add sauce mixture and peas. Bring to a boil; cook 1 minute

or until thick. Stir in peanuts. Serve with rice.

PER SERVING (1 1/3 cups stir-fry and 1/2 cup rice): Calories 465 (29% from fat); Protein 24g; Fat 15g (sat 2g, mono 6g, poly 6g); Carbohydrate 57g; Fiber 5g; Cholesterol 25mg; Iron 4mg; Sodium 825mg; Calcium 95mg

balsamic-glazed scallops

Prep: *7 minutes* **Cook:** *37 minutes*
Serves 4

  2 cups water
  1 tablespoon balsamic vinegar
1/4 teaspoon salt
  1 cup uncooked long-grain rice
  1 tablespoon olive oil
1 1/2 pounds sea scallops
1/4 cup balsamic vinegar
  1 tablespoon honey
  1 teaspoon dried marjoram

1. Combine first 3 ingredients (water through salt) in a medium saucepan; bring to a boil. Add rice; cover, reduce heat, and simmer 20 minutes or until rice is tender and liquid is absorbed. Remove from heat; set aside (do not uncover rice).
2. Heat oil in a large nonstick skillet over medium-high heat until hot. Add scallops; sauté 5 minutes. Remove scallops from pan; set aside.
3. Add vinegar, honey, and marjoram to pan; bring to a boil. Reduce heat to medium; cook 3 minutes. Return scallops to pan; cook 2 minutes or until thoroughly heated. Serve scallops and sauce over rice.

PER SERVING (1/4 of scallop mixture and 3/4 cup rice): Calories 365 (12% from fat); Protein 32g; Fat 5g (sat 1g, mono 3g, poly 1g); Carbohydrate 46g; Fiber 1g; Cholesterol 56mg; Iron 3mg; Sodium 423mg; Calcium 57mg

pesto pizza with shrimp, asparagus, and prosciutto

Prep: *16 minutes* **Cook:** *15 minutes*
Serves 6

If you can't find thin asparagus spears, use larger ones, and cut them in half lengthwise. Substitute good-quality smoked ham for the prosciutto.

- 1 (10-ounce) can refrigerated pizza crust dough
- Cooking spray
- 1/4 cup commercial pesto
- 12 thin asparagus spears, cut into 2-inch pieces
- 1/2 pound medium shrimp, peeled and deveined
- 2 ounces very thinly sliced prosciutto, chopped

1. Preheat oven to 425°.
2. Unroll pizza crust dough on a large baking sheet coated with cooking spray; pat dough into a 14 x 9-inch rectangle. Bake at 425° for 5 minutes.
3. Spread pesto over dough, leaving a ½-inch border. Top with asparagus spears, shrimp, and prosciutto. Bake pizza at 425° for 10 minutes or until shrimp are done and crust is lightly browned.

PER SERVING (1/6 of pizza): Calories 235 (32% from fat); Protein 14g; Fat 8g (sat 2g, mono 4g, poly 1g); Carbohydrate 27g; Fiber 3g; Cholesterol 45mg; Iron 4mg; Sodium 555mg; Calcium 105mg

herb-marinated shrimp kebabs

pictured on pages 113 and 119

Prep: *10 minutes* **Cook:** *6 minutes*
Marinate: *30 minutes*
Serves 4

- 1/3 cup fresh basil leaves
- 1/4 cup fresh mint leaves
- 2 tablespoons fresh oregano leaves
- 1/2 teaspoon salt
- 1/4 teaspoon pepper
- 3 garlic cloves, halved
- 2 1/2 teaspoons extra-virgin olive oil
- 1 1/2 pounds large shrimp, peeled and deveined
- Cooking spray

1. Combine first 6 ingredients (basil through garlic) in a food processor, and pulse until mixture is coarsely chopped. Add olive oil, and process until well blended.
2. Combine herb mixture and shrimp in a large bowl; toss to coat. Cover and marinate shrimp in refrigerator 30 minutes.
3. Thread shrimp onto 12 (6-inch) skewers.
4. Prepare grill.
5. Place kebabs on grill rack coated with cooking spray; grill shrimp 3 minutes on each side or until done.

NOTE: To prepare indoors, place a large grill pan over medium-high heat until hot; coat grill pan with cooking spray. Place 6 kebabs on grill pan, and cook 3 minutes on each side or until done. Repeat procedure with remaining kebabs.

PER SERVING (3 kebabs): Calories 153 (26% from fat); Protein 25g; Fat 4g (sat 1g, mono 2g, poly 1g); Carbohydrate 3g; Fiber 0g; Cholesterol 228mg; Iron 5mg; Sodium 556mg; Calcium 94mg

stir-fried shrimp and vegetables

Prep: *5 minutes* **Cook:** *18 minutes*
Serves 6

Ramen noodle soup serves two purposes in this dish: It adds Asian flavor and provides the noodles for the stir-fry.

- 2 (3-ounce) packages Asian-flavored ramen noodle soup
- 1/4 cup hoisin sauce
- 1 tablespoon dark sesame oil
- 2 (16-ounce) packages frozen Peking-style stir-fry vegetables (such as VIP)
- 1 pound medium shrimp, peeled and deveined

1. Remove seasoning packets from noodles; set aside.
2. Cook noodles according to package directions, omitting seasoning packets. Drain noodles, reserving ¼ cup cooking liquid. Set noodles aside. Combine reserved ¼ cup cooking liquid, seasoning packets, and hoisin sauce; stir well. Set aside.
3. Heat oil in a large nonstick skillet over high heat until hot. Add vegetables; stir-fry 6 minutes or until crisp-tender. Add shrimp; stir-fry 3 minutes. Stir in noodles and hoisin sauce mixture; cook until mixture is thoroughly heated.

PER SERVING (1 1/3 cups): Calories 282 (28% from fat); Protein 18g; Fat 9g (sat 3g, mono 1g, poly 1g); Carbohydrate 30g; Fiber 4g; Cholesterol 101mg; Iron 3mg; Sodium 946mg; Calcium 74mg

orange-hoisin shrimp stir-fry

Prep: *6 minutes* **Cook:** *5 minutes*
Serves 4

Hoisin or Peking sauce is a spicy, sweet blend of soybeans, chile peppers, garlic, and spices. Look for it on the ethnic foods aisle at the supermarket.

- $1/3$ cup hoisin sauce
- 2 tablespoons frozen orange juice concentrate
- 1 tablespoon low-sodium soy sauce
- 1 tablespoon bottled minced garlic
- $1/8$ teaspoon crushed red pepper
- 2 teaspoons dark sesame oil
- 1 teaspoon ground ginger
- 1 (16-ounce) package frozen Beijing-style stir-fry vegetables (such as VIP)
- 1 (8-ounce) can sliced water chestnuts, drained
- 1 (16-ounce) package frozen cooked and peeled large shrimp, thawed
- 4 cups hot cooked rice

1. Combine first 5 ingredients (hoisin sauce through red pepper) in a bowl; stir well. Place a wok or a large nonstick skillet over high heat until hot. Add sesame oil, ginger, vegetables, and water chestnuts; stir-fry 3 minutes. Add hoisin sauce mixture and shrimp; stir-fry 2 minutes or until shrimp are warm and vegetables are crisp-tender. Serve over rice.

PER SERVING ($1^1/4$ cups stir-fry and 1 cup rice): Calories 465 (7% from fat); Protein 32g; Fat 4g (sat 1g, mono 1g, poly 2g); Carbohydrate 75g; Fiber 6g; Cholesterol 221mg; Iron 6mg; Sodium 803mg; Calcium 96mg

linguine with sautéed shrimp and coconut-lime sauce

pictured on page 1

Prep: *15 minutes* **Cook:** *10 minutes*
Serves 4

Sweet coconut milk, tart lime juice, and fresh shellfish give this noodle stir-fry a Caribbean flair.

- 8 ounces uncooked linguine
- 2 cups sugar snap peas, trimmed
- $1^1/2$ cups red bell pepper strips
- 1 tablespoon dark sesame oil
- 1 tablespoon grated peeled fresh ginger
- 2 garlic cloves, minced
- 1 pound peeled and deveined large shrimp
- $1/2$ cup fat-free, low-sodium chicken broth
- 1 cup light coconut milk, well stirred
- $1/4$ cup low-sodium soy sauce
- 1 teaspoon grated lime rind (bright green part only)
- 1 tablespoon fresh lime juice
- $1/2$ cup (1-inch) diagonally cut scallions

1. Cook pasta according to package directions, omitting salt and fat. Place sugar snap peas and red bell pepper in a colander. Drain pasta over pea mixture.
2. Heat oil in a large nonstick skillet over medium-high heat. Add ginger, garlic, and shrimp; sauté 3 minutes or until shrimp is bright pink. Remove shrimp from pan. Add broth to pan, scraping pan to loosen browned bits. Add coconut milk, soy sauce, lime rind, and lime juice; bring to a boil. Reduce heat, and simmer 5 minutes or until slightly thick.

3. Add pasta mixture and shrimp; toss to coat. Sprinkle each serving evenly with scallions.

PER SERVING (2 cups): Calories 467 (22% from fat); Protein 35g; Fat 11g (sat 4g, mono 2g, poly 3g); Carbohydrate 55g; Fiber 5g; Cholesterol 173mg; Iron 5mg; Sodium 862mg; Calcium 120mg

shrimp with cilantro and lime

Prep: *7 minutes* **Cook:** *4 minutes*
Serves 4

All you need from the market is shrimp and a lime, and you'll have dinner on the table in almost 10 minutes.

- $1^3/4$ pounds large shrimp, peeled and deveined
- 2 tablespoons fresh lime juice
- $1/2$ teaspoon ground cumin
- $1/4$ teaspoon ground ginger
- 2 garlic cloves, minced
- 1 tablespoon olive oil
- $1/4$ cup chopped fresh cilantro
- 1 teaspoon grated lime rind
- $1/2$ teaspoon salt
- $1/4$ teaspoon pepper

1. Combine first 5 ingredients (shrimp through garlic) in a large bowl; toss well. Heat oil in a large nonstick skillet over medium-high heat. Add shrimp mixture, and sauté 4 minutes or until shrimp is done. Remove from heat; stir in cilantro and remaining ingredients.

PER SERVING (about $1^1/2$ cups): Calories 217 (27% from fat); Protein 35g; Fat 6g (sat 1g, mono 3g, poly 1g); Carbohydrate 3g; Fiber 0g; Cholesterol 259mg; Iron 5mg; Sodium 546mg; Calcium 98mg

rainbow fried rice

Prep: *18 minutes* **Cook:** *5 minutes*
Serves 5

Leftover cold rice works best in fried rice dishes, so always keep some in the fridge for a quick throw-together meal.

3¹⁄₂ tablespoons low-sodium soy sauce
2¹⁄₂ tablespoons sake (rice wine)
2 tablespoons water
1¹⁄₂ teaspoons dark sesame oil
¹⁄₄ teaspoon salt
¹⁄₄ teaspoon freshly ground black pepper
2 tablespoons vegetable oil
1 large egg, lightly beaten
1 cup finely chopped green onions
2 teaspoons minced peeled fresh ginger
1¹⁄₃ cups chopped cooked shrimp (about 8 ounces)
1 (10-ounce) package frozen green peas, thawed
4¹⁄₂ cups chilled cooked basmati rice

1. Combine first 6 ingredients (soy sauce through pepper) in a small bowl, stirring with a whisk.
2. Heat vegetable oil in a wok over high heat. Add egg; stir-fry 30 seconds or until scrambled. Add onions and ginger; stir-fry 1 minute. Add shrimp, peas, and rice; stir-fry 3 minutes or until thoroughly heated. Stir in soy sauce mixture. Serve immediately.

PER SERVING (1¹⁄₃ cups): Calories 385 (24% from fat); Protein 19g; Fat 11g (sat 2g, mono 3g, poly 5g); Carbohydrate 54g; Fiber 6g; Cholesterol 131mg; Iron 4mg; Sodium 690mg; Calcium 58mg

chicken and shellfish paella

pictured on page 119

Prep: *21 minutes* **Cook:** *33 minutes*
Stand: *15 minutes*
Serves 8

If you don't have a paella pan, use a 12-inch nonstick ovenproof skillet.

3 cups fat-free, less-sodium chicken broth
¹⁄₄ teaspoon saffron threads, crushed
3 tablespoons olive oil
1 link Spanish chorizo sausage (3 ounces), thinly sliced
4 (4-ounce) skinless, boneless chicken breast halves, cut into bite-sized pieces
2 cups thinly sliced fennel bulb (about 2 bulbs)
1 cup chopped yellow bell pepper
1 cup chopped red onion
¹⁄₄ teaspoon salt
¹⁄₄ teaspoon pepper
2 garlic cloves, minced
1¹⁄₂ cups chopped tomato, divided
¹⁄₄ cup minced fresh flat-leaf parsley, divided
1 tablespoon sweet Spanish or Hungarian paprika
1¹⁄₂ cups uncooked Valencia or Arborio rice (or other short-grain rice)
12 large shrimp, peeled and deveined
12 mussels (about ¹⁄₂ pound), scrubbed and debearded

1. Preheat oven to 425°.
2. Bring broth and crushed saffron to a simmer in a small saucepan, but don't boil. Cover and keep broth warm.
3. Heat oil in a skillet (or paella pan) over medium heat, until hot but not smoking. Add sausage, and brown; transfer to a plate. Add chicken to pan, and cook, stirring 4 minutes or until browned. Transfer to plate with sausage.
4. Add fennel, bell pepper, onion, salt, pepper, and garlic to pan, and sauté 3 to 5 minutes until vegetables are tender. Add 1 cup tomatoes and 2 tablespoons parsley, and cook 1 minute.
5. Stir in paprika and rice (be sure to stir well so the rice absorbs the olive oil). Return sausage and chicken to pan, and add warm broth. Bring paella to a boil, stirring occasionally, and continue to cook about 3 minutes until it is no longer soupy (but there is still some broth in the bottom of the pan).
6. Remove pan from heat, and arrange shrimp and mussels on top, nestling mussels into rice. Sprinkle with remaining ¹⁄₂ cup tomatoes.
7. Bake at 425° for 15 minutes, or until mussel shells open. Discard any unopened shells. Remove from oven, and cover tightly with aluminum foil. Let stand 15 minutes to allow rice to steam until tender. Sprinkle with remaining 2 tablespoons parsley, and serve immediately.

PER SERVING (about 1¹⁄₄ cups): Calories 381 (26% from fat); Protein 26g; Fat 11g (sat 2g, mono 6g, poly 2g); Fiber 3g; Carbohydrate 45g; Cholesterol 65mg; Iron 3mg; Sodium 509mg; Calcium 57mg

hearty meatless dishes

*Couscous-Stuffed
Portobellos, page 146*

western egg casserole

Prep: *15 minutes* **Cook:** *1 hour 20 minutes*
Chill: *8 hours* **Cool:** *5 minutes*
Serves 8

- 12 (6-inch) corn tortillas
- 8 large eggs
- 4 large egg whites
- 2 1/2 cups fat-free milk
- 1 cup 1% low-fat cottage cheese
- 3/4 teaspoon salt
- 3/4 teaspoon pepper
- 1 1/2 cups (6 ounces) crumbled feta cheese
- 1 cup thinly sliced green onions
- Cooking spray
- 1 1/2 cups salsa
- 1/4 cup diagonally sliced green onion tops (optional)

1. Cut tortillas in half; slice tortilla halves crosswise into 1-inch strips. Set aside.
2. Combine eggs and egg whites in a large bowl; stir well with a whisk. Add milk, cottage cheese, salt, and pepper; stir well. Add tortilla strips, feta cheese, and 1 cup green onions; stir well. Pour into a 13 x 9-inch baking dish coated with cooking spray. Cover with foil, and chill 8 hours.
3. Preheat oven to 325°.
4. Bake, covered, at 325° for 1 hour. Uncover and bake an additional 20 minutes or just until set (casserole will continue to firm as it cools). Let cool 5 minutes, and cut into 8 squares. Spoon 2 tablespoons salsa over each serving, and top each with 1 teaspoon sliced green onion tops, if desired.

PER SERVING: Calories 293 (34% from fat); Protein 20g; Fat 11g (sat 5g, mono 3g, poly 1g); Carbohydrate 29g; Fiber 3g; Cholesterol 234mg; Iron 2mg; Sodium 977mg; Calcium 324mg

south-of-the-border breakfast wrap

Prep: *10 minutes* **Cook:** *2 minutes*
Serves 4

Chock-full of fresh veggies, eggs, and cheese, this hearty, hand-held wrap is good any time of the day.

- 3/4 cup fresh white corn kernels (about 2 ears)
- 2 tablespoons finely chopped green bell pepper
- 2 tablespoons finely chopped seeded plum tomato
- 1 teaspoon minced seeded jalapeño pepper
- 1 tablespoon minced fresh cilantro
- 1 tablespoon fresh lime juice
- 1/2 teaspoon salt, divided
- 4 large eggs, lightly beaten
- 1/4 teaspoon ground cumin
- Cooking spray
- 2 tablespoons finely shredded Monterey Jack cheese
- 4 (8-inch) flour tortillas
- 4 lettuce leaves

1. Combine first 6 ingredients (corn through lime juice) in a small bowl, and stir in 1/4 teaspoon salt.
2. Combine remaining 1/4 teaspoon salt, eggs, and cumin. Heat a medium nonstick skillet coated with cooking spray over medium heat. Add egg mixture; cook 2 minutes, stirring gently until set. Remove from heat; sprinkle with cheese.
3. Warm tortillas according to package directions. Top each tortilla with a lettuce leaf and 1/4 cup corn mixture. Divide egg mixture evenly among tortillas; roll up. Serve immediately.

PER SERVING (1 wrap): Calories 300 (28% from fat); Protein 14g; Fat 10g (sat 3g, mono 4g, poly 2g); Carbohydrate 41g; Fiber 2g; Cholesterol 215mg; Iron 2g; Sodium 646mg; Calcium 165mg

vegetable and cheddar frittata

Prep: *20 minutes* **Cook:** *10 minutes*
Serves 4

Extra egg whites stretch how far the eggs go without adding fat and cholesterol.

- 2 tablespoons chopped fresh cilantro or parsley
- 1/2 teaspoon salt, divided
- 1/4 teaspoon pepper
- 4 large egg whites
- 3 large eggs
- 12 green onions, trimmed
- Cooking spray
- 1 cup frozen corn, thawed
- 16 grape or cherry tomatoes, halved (about 3/4 cup)
- 1/2 cup (2 ounces) shredded reduced-fat Cheddar cheese, divided

1. Preheat broiler.
2. Combine cilantro or parsley, 1/4 teaspoon salt, and next 3 ingredients (pepper through eggs) in a bowl, stirring with a whisk.
3. Cut 8 green onions in half crosswise, and set aside. Thinly slice remaining onions to measure 1/2 cup.
4. Heat a medium nonstick skillet coated with cooking spray over medium heat. Add onion halves; cook 3 minutes. Add corn; cook 1 minute. Add sliced onions and tomatoes; cook 1 minute. Sprinkle with 1/4 teaspoon salt and 6 tablespoons cheese. Pour in egg mixture; cook 3 minutes or until egg mixture is almost set. Tilt pan, and carefully loosen edges of cooked portion with a spatula; allow uncooked portion to flow underneath cooked portion. Wrap handle of pan with foil; broil 2 minutes or until egg

mixture is set. Sprinkle with 2 tablespoons cheese. Cut into 4 wedges.

PER SERVING (1 wedge): Calories 185 (30% from fat); Protein 18g; Fat 6g (sat 3g, mono 2g, poly 1g); Carbohydrate 16g; Fiber 3g; Cholesterol 165mg; Iron 2mg; Sodium 581mg; Calcium 162mg

southwestern omelet

Prep: *10 minutes* **Cook:** *6 minutes*
Serves 2

  2 tablespoons chopped fresh cilantro
$^1/_4$ teaspoon salt
  4 large egg whites
  1 large egg
$^1/_2$ cup canned black beans, rinsed and drained
$^1/_4$ cup chopped green onions
$^1/_4$ cup (1 ounce) reduced-fat shredded cheddar cheese
$^1/_4$ cup bottled salsa
Cooking spray

1. Combine first 4 ingredients (cilantro through egg) in a medium bowl, stirring with a whisk. Combine beans, onions, cheese, and salsa in a medium bowl.
2. Heat a medium nonstick skillet coated with cooking spray over medium heat. Pour egg mixture into pan; let egg mixture set slightly. Tilt pan and carefully lift edges of omelet with a spatula; allow uncooked portion to flow underneath cooked portion. Cook 3 minutes; flip omelet. Spoon bean mixture onto half of omelet. Carefully loosen omelet with a spatula; fold in half. Cook 1 minute or until cheese melts.

PER SERVING ($^1/_2$ omelet): Calories 181 (27% from fat); Protein 20g; Fat 6g (sat 2g, mono 1g, poly 1g); Carbohydrate 14g; Fiber 6g; Cholesterol 116mg; Iron 2mg; Sodium 822mg; Calcium 184mg

mediterranean garlic pizza

Prep: *6 minutes* **Cook:** *17 minutes*
Serves 4

This pizza is loaded with heart-healthy garlic. To avoid burning the garlic, stir it constantly while it cooks.

  1 (10-ounce) can refrigerated pizza crust dough
Cooking spray
  6 tablespoons sun-dried tomato spread or sun-dried tomato paste
  4 garlic cloves, thinly sliced
$^3/_4$ cup (3 ounces) crumbled feta cheese with garlic and herbs
$^1/_4$ cup chopped ripe olives

1. Preheat oven to 450°.
2. Unroll dough on a baking sheet coated with cooking spray; pat dough into a 10 x 8-inch rectangle. Spread sun-dried tomato spread over dough, leaving a ½-inch border.
3. Coat a small nonstick skillet with cooking spray, and place over medium heat until hot. Add garlic, and sauté 5 minutes or until browned. Sprinkle garlic, crumbled feta, and chopped olives evenly over tomato spread. Bake pizza at 450° for 12 minutes or until crust is lightly browned.

PER SERVING ($^1/_4$ of pizza): Calories 297 (32% from fat); Protein 10g; Fat 10g (sat 3g, mono 2g, poly 0g); Carbohydrate 40g; Fiber 1g; Cholesterol 19mg; Iron 8mg; Sodium 967mg; Calcium 133mg

pesto-bean pizza with fresh tomatoes

Prep: *8 minutes* **Cook:** *8 minutes*
Serves 6

Cannellini beans and garlic make a creamy hummus-like sauce for this pizza layered with tomatoes, bell peppers, and feta cheese.

$^1/_2$ cup drained canned cannellini beans or other white beans
$^1/_3$ cup fresh basil leaves
  2 tablespoons water
  2 garlic cloves, minced
  1 (10-ounce) package thin Italian cheese-flavored pizza crust (such as Boboli)
$^1/_2$ cup (2 ounces) grated Romano cheese, divided
  1 large tomato, cut into thin wedges
  1 small yellow bell pepper, cut into rings
$^1/_2$ cup (2 ounces) crumbled feta cheese with garlic and herbs
$^1/_2$ teaspoon freshly ground black pepper

1. Preheat oven to 425°.
2. Place first 4 ingredients (beans through garlic) in a food processor; process until smooth. Spread over pizza crust; sprinkle with 3 tablespoons Romano cheese. Top with tomato, bell pepper, remaining Romano cheese, feta cheese, and pepper.
3. Place pizza on oven rack or baking sheet; bake at 425° for 8 minutes or until cheese melts.

PER SERVING ($^1/_6$ of pizza): Calories 225 (29% from fat); Protein 12g; Fat 7g (sat 4g, mono 1g, poly 0g); Carbohydrate 28g; Fiber 2g; Cholesterol 22mg; Iron 2mg; Sodium 511mg; Calcium 215mg

spinach and caramelized onion pizza

pictured on page 137

Prep: *8 minutes* **Cook:** *24 minutes*
Serves 5

Cooking spray
- 1 large onion, thinly sliced and separated into rings
- 2 tablespoons water
- 1 tablespoon balsamic vinegar
- 2 (10-ounce) packages frozen creamed spinach, thawed
- 1 (10-ounce) package thin Italian cheese-flavored pizza crust
- 3/4 cup (3 ounces) crumbled feta cheese with garlic and herbs

1. Preheat oven to 450°.
2. Coat a large nonstick skillet with cooking spray; place over medium-high heat until hot. Add onion; sauté 4 minutes or until crisp-tender. Reduce heat to medium; sauté 10 minutes or until golden brown, adding water, 1 tablespoon at a time, during last 3 minutes. Remove from heat, and stir in balsamic vinegar.
3. Spread spinach evenly over pizza crust, and top with onion mixture and cheese. Bake pizza at 450° for 10 minutes or until crust is crisp and topping is thoroughly heated.

NOTE: We used Green Giant creamed spinach in this recipe. If it isn't available, use the following substitution: Combine 2 1/4 teaspoons cornstarch and 1/2 cup fat-free nondairy creamer (such as Cremora) in a 2-cup glass measure; stir until blended. Add 1 tablespoon margarine, 1/4 teaspoon butter extract, and 1/8 teaspoon each of onion powder, garlic powder, salt, and sugar; stir well. Microwave at HIGH 1 1/2 minutes or until thick, stirring every 30 seconds. Stir cream sauce into 2 (10-ounce) packages frozen chopped spinach, thawed, drained, and squeezed dry. Spread spinach mixture over cheese-flavored pizza crust as directed.

PER SERVING (1/5 of pizza): Calories 308 (30% from fat); Protein 14g; Fat 10g (sat 5g, mono 0g, poly 0g); Carbohydrate 40g; Fiber 4g; Cholesterol 18mg; Iron 2mg; Sodium 1,002mg; Calcium 274mg

french bread caprese pizza

Prep: *7 minutes* **Cook:** *10 minutes*
Serves 6

Here's a chance to use that bumper crop of basil from your garden. Pungent fresh basil leaves crown a simple base of French bread and tomato sauce.

- 1 (16-ounce) loaf French bread
- 1 1/2 cups tomato-basil pasta sauce
- 2 tablespoons capers
- 6 (1-ounce) slices part-skim mozzarella cheese
- 24 fresh basil leaves

1. Preheat oven to 425°.
2. Cut bread loaf in half horizontally; spread pasta sauce evenly over cut sides of each piece of bread. Sprinkle capers evenly over sauce; top evenly with cheese slices.
3. Place pizza on a baking sheet, and bake at 425° for 10 minutes or until cheese melts. Arrange basil leaves on top of cheese. Cut pizza into 12 equal portions.

PER SERVING (2 pieces): Calories 316 (21% from fat); Protein 15g; Fat 7g (sat 4g, mono 2g, poly 1g); Carbohydrate 47g; Fiber 3g; Cholesterol 17mg; Iron 2mg; Sodium 1,015mg; Calcium 247mg

campanelle with summer vegetables

pictured on page 138

Prep: *20 minutes* **Cook:** *7 minutes*
Serves 4

You'll satisfy your daily requirements for beta-carotene and B-vitamins with this assortment of fresh green veggies.

- 8 ounces uncooked campanelle (bellflower-shaped pasta)
- 4 cups broccoli florets
- 2 cups (1-inch) sliced asparagus (about 1 pound)
- 1 medium zucchini, halved and thinly sliced (about 1 pound)
- 1 cup frozen green peas
- 1 cup (4 ounces) crumbled feta with peppercorns or plain feta
- 1 teaspoon salt
- 1/2 teaspoon dried oregano
- 1 teaspoon grated lemon rind
- 1 tablespoon fresh lemon juice

1. Bring a large saucepan of water to a boil. Cook pasta 3 minutes. Add broccoli and asparagus; cook 2 minutes. Add zucchini and peas; cook 2 minutes. Drain pasta and vegetables using a colander over a bowl, reserving 1/4 cup pasta water.
2. Place feta in a large bowl. Pour 1/4 cup cooking liquid over cheese, and stir until cheese is slightly melted. Add pasta mixture and remaining 4 ingredients; toss well. Serve immediately.

PER SERVING (2 cups): Calories 354 (19% from fat); Protein 18g; Fat 7g (sat 4g, mono 1g, poly 1g); Carbohydrate 55g; Fiber 9g; Cholesterol 25mg; Iron 4mg; Sodium 967mg; Calcium 234mg

sicilian vegetable pasta

Prep: *10 minutes* **Cook:** *20 minutes*
Serves 5

Olive oil-flavored cooking spray
- 3 cups cubed eggplant
- 1 cup sliced fresh mushrooms
- ¾ cup coarsely chopped onion
- 1 zucchini, quartered lengthwise and cut into 1-inch pieces
- 1 small green bell pepper, coarsely chopped
- 1 garlic clove, minced
- 1 (14.5-ounce) can no-salt-added stewed tomatoes, undrained
- 1 (15-ounce) can chickpeas (garbanzo beans), drained
- 2 tablespoons dry red wine
- 2 tablespoons capers
- ½ teaspoon dried rosemary, crushed
- ¼ teaspoon salt
- ¼ teaspoon black pepper
- 4 cups hot cooked penne (about 3 cups uncooked tube-shaped pasta)
- ⅓ cup (1⅓ ounces) finely grated fresh Asiago or Parmesan cheese

1. Coat a Dutch oven with cooking spray; place over medium-high heat until hot. Add eggplant and next 5 ingredients (eggplant through garlic); sauté 7 minutes or until crisp-tender. Stir in tomatoes and next 6 ingredients (tomatoes through pepper). Bring to a boil; cover, reduce heat, and simmer 8 minutes or until vegetables are tender. Spoon vegetable mixture over pasta, and sprinkle with cheese.

PER SERVING (1 cup vegetable mixture, about ¾ cup pasta, and 1 tablespoon cheese): Calories 371 (11% from fat); Protein 17g; Fat 5g (sat 2g, mono 1g, poly 1g); Carbohydrate 68g; Fiber 5g; Cholesterol 5mg; Iron 5mg; Sodium 636mg; Calcium 177mg

roasted butternut squash and swiss chard pasta

pictured on page 138

Prep: *15 minutes* **Cook:** *40 minutes*
Serves 6

Castellane is a conch shell-shaped pasta that holds the squash in its folds. You may substitute orecchiette or shells. If you don't mind a little meat, this dish is great sprinkled with a few crumbles of bacon.

- 4 cups (½-inch) cubed peeled butternut squash
- 2 cups (1-inch) chopped red onion
- 4 tablespoons olive oil, divided
- 1¼ teaspoons salt, divided
- ½ teaspoon freshly ground black pepper, divided
- 1 pound uncooked castellane, orecchiette pasta, or other shell pasta
- 4 cups torn Swiss chard leaves, stems discarded (about 5 ounces)
- 2 teaspoons finely chopped fresh sage
- ¼ cup (1 ounce) shaved fresh Parmesan cheese

1. Preheat oven to 450°.
2. Toss squash and onion in a large bowl with 2 tablespoons oil, ½ teaspoon salt, and ¼ teaspoon pepper. Spread in a single layer on a nonstick baking sheet, and bake at 450° for 25 minutes, turning until tender and browned.
3. Cook pasta according to package directions omitting fat and salt. Place chard in a large bowl. Drain pasta in a sieve over bowl of chard; let stand 1 minute. Drain well; squeeze out excess water. Toss with pasta in a large bowl along with roasted squash and onion, remaining 2 tablespoons oil, remaining salt and pepper, and sage. Top with cheese.

PER SERVING (2 cups): Calories 425 (17% from fat); Protein 14g; Fat 8g (sat 2g, mono 4g, poly 1g); Carbohydrate 76g; Fiber 8g; Cholesterol 4mg; Iron 4mg; Sodium 630mg; Calcium 150mg

shells with salsa cruda

Prep: *25 minutes* **Cook:** *10 minutes*
Serves 4

We love the versatility of this uncooked salsa. It's delicious served with fish as an entrée or with chips as an appetizer.

- 5 cups seeded chopped tomatoes (about 2 pounds)
- ½ cup chopped red onion
- ½ cup thinly sliced fresh basil
- ½ cup chopped fresh parsley
- ¼ cup chopped fresh mint
- 2 tablespoons olive oil
- 2 teaspoons balsamic vinegar
- 1 teaspoon salt
- ¼ teaspoon pepper
- 1 garlic clove, minced
- 8 ounces uncooked shell pasta
- ½ cup (2 ounces) shredded sharp provolone cheese

1. Combine first 10 ingredients (tomatoes through garlic) in a large bowl; let mixture marinate at room temperature.
2. Cook pasta according to package directions, omitting salt and fat. Add cooked pasta to bowl; toss gently to coat. Place on 4 plates. Top with provolone.

PER SERVING (2 cups pasta mixture and 2 tablespoons cheese): Calories 407 (27% from fat); Protein 14g; Fat 13g (sat 4g, mono 6g, poly 1g); Carbohydrate 61g; Fiber 6g; Cholesterol 10mg; Iron 4mg; Sodium 741mg; Calcium 166mg

penne with romesco sauce

Prep: *10 minutes* **Cook:** *20 minutes*
Serves 4

Roasting the red peppers turns a simple vegetable into a smokey, rich sauce for pasta.

1 1/2   pounds red bell peppers
Cooking spray
  1 slice white bread
  1 garlic clove, halved
  1 tablespoon olive oil
 1/2 cup slivered almonds, toasted
  1 tablespoon sherry vinegar
 1/4 teaspoon crushed red pepper
  4 cups hot cooked penne (about 8 ounces uncooked tube-shaped pasta)
  2 tablespoons chopped fresh parsley

1. Preheat broiler.
2. Cut bell peppers in half lengthwise; discard seeds and membranes. Place bell pepper halves, skin sides up, on a baking sheet coated with cooking spray; flatten with hand. Broil 15 minutes or until blackened. Place in a zip-top plastic bag; seal. Let stand until cool. Peel and chop.
3. Rub both sides of bread with garlic halves; brush with oil. Mince garlic; set aside. Heat a small skillet over medium-high heat; add bread. Cook 45 seconds per side or until lightly brown.
4. Combine peppers, bread, garlic, almonds, vinegar, and crushed red pepper in a food processor. Process until smooth. Combine pepper sauce and hot pasta in a large bowl; toss gently to coat. Garnish with parsley.

PER SERVING (1 cup): Calories 396 (30% from fat); Protein 12g; Fat 14g (sat 1g, mono 8g, poly 3g); Carbohydrate 58g; Fiber 7g; Cholesterol 0mg; Iron 4mg; Sodium 48mg; Calcium 80mg

How to Roast Peppers

All bell peppers—green, red, and yellow—can be roasted. There are just a few tricks to remember. Follow the steps below for roasting and peeling peppers with ease.

1. Cut bell peppers in half lengthwise; remove and discard seeds and membrane.

2. Place pepper halves, skin sides up, on a foil-lined baking sheet; gently flatten peppers with hand.

3. Broil peppers 15 minutes or until blackened. Place hot peppers in a zip-top plastic bag; seal and let stand for 15 minutes. (This will loosen the skins and make peeling the peppers much easier.)

4. Remove peppers from bag. Peel and discard skins. Use roasted peppers as directed in recipe or store roasted peppers in an airtight container in the refrigerator.

Spinach and Caramelized Onion Pizza, page 134

Roasted Butternut Squash and
Swiss Chard Pasta, page 135

Campanelle with Summer
Vegetables, page 134

Whole Wheat Pasta Shells with
Spicy Tomato Pesto, page 141

hearty meatless dishes

Linguine with Tomatoes, Spinach, and White Beans, page 143

Spinach-Walnut Manicotti, page 142

Spaghetti Squash and Vegetable Ragoût, page 148

*Couscous-Stuffed
Portobellos, page 146*

whole wheat pasta shells with spicy tomato pesto

pictured on page 138

Prep: *15 minutes* **Cook:** *13 minutes*
Stand: *30 minutes*
Serves 5

    1   cup boiling water
 1/2   cup sun-dried tomatoes,
        packed without oil
 1/4   cup sliced almonds
 1/4   cup (1 ounce) grated Parmesan
        cheese
 1/4   cup chopped fresh basil
    2   garlic cloves, minced
 1/2   teaspoon salt
 1/4   teaspoon crushed red pepper
2 1/2   tablespoons olive oil, divided
    1   cup chopped onion
    3   cups trimmed Swiss chard
 1/4   cup water
 1/4   teaspoon salt
 1/4   teaspoon black pepper
    8   cups hot cooked whole wheat
        pasta shells (about 4 cups
        uncooked)
    4   teaspoons grated fresh
        Parmesan cheese

1. Combine boiling water and tomatoes in a bowl; let stand 30 minutes or until soft. Drain tomatoes, reserving 1/2 cup liquid.
2. Drop tomatoes, almonds, cheese, basil, garlic, salt, and red pepper through food chute with food processor on; process until minced. Slowly pour 1 1/2 tablespoons oil through food chute; process until well blended, scraping sides. Add reserved liquid 1 tablespoon at a time until mixture appears smooth.
3. Heat 1 tablespoon oil in a large nonstick skillet over medium-high heat. Add onion; sauté 10 minutes or until lightly browned. Add Swiss chard; stir-fry 1 minute or until leaves turn bright green.

Add water, salt, and pepper; cover and cook 2 minutes.
4. Combine pesto and pasta in a large bowl. Add greens mixture. Sprinkle with Parmesan.

PER SERVING (2 cups): Calories 355 (30% from fat); Protein 14g; Fat 12g (sat 3g, mono 7g, poly 2g); Carbohydrate 52g; Fiber 7g; Cholesterol 5mg; Iron 3mg; Sodium 608mg; Calcium 147mg

penne alla norma

Prep: *20 minutes* **Cook:** *26 minutes*
Serves 6

    2   tablespoons olive oil
    1   cup chopped onion
    4   garlic cloves, minced
    5   cups cubed peeled eggplant
        (about 1 pound)
1 1/2   teaspoons crushed red pepper
    2   cups chopped spinach
    2   cups chopped seeded tomato
 1/2   cup water
    2   tablespoons chopped fresh
        basil
 1/4   teaspoon salt
    1   (8-ounce) can tomato sauce
    8   cups hot cooked penne (about
        1 pound uncooked)
 1/2   cup (2 ounces) grated fresh
        Parmesan cheese

1. Heat oil in a large saucepan over medium-high heat. Add onion and garlic; sauté 4 minutes. Add eggplant and pepper; sauté 5 minutes or until lightly browned. Add spinach and next 5 ingredients (spinach through tomato sauce); reduce heat, and simmer 15 minutes. Combine eggplant mixture and pasta in a large bowl; toss well. Sprinkle with Parmesan cheese.

PER SERVING (1 1/2 cups): Calories 418 (19% from fat); Fat 9g (sat 2g, mono 4g, poly 1g); Protein 16g; Carbohydrate 70g; Fiber 6g; Cholesterol 6mg; Iron 4mg; Sodium 506mg; Calcium 168mg

double-tomato pasta

Prep: *15 minutes* **Cook:** *10 minutes*
Stand: *10 minutes*
Serves 4

    2   teaspoons olive oil
    1   cup sliced red onion
    2   pounds seeded plum tomatoes,
        coarsely chopped
 1/4   teaspoon salt
 1/2   teaspoon freshly ground black
        pepper
 1/4   teaspoon crushed red pepper
    8   ounces uncooked farfalle (bow-
        tie pasta)
 1/3   cup sun-dried tomatoes,
        packed without oil, sliced
    1   cup (about 4 ounces) grated
        fresh Parmesan cheese, divided
 1/2   cup chopped pitted kalamata
        olives
 1/4   cup chopped fresh parsley

1. Heat oil in a large nonstick skillet over medium-high heat; add onion. Cook 2 minutes, stirring frequently. Add plum tomatoes, salt, black pepper, and red pepper. Reduce heat, and simmer 8 minutes, stirring occasionally.
2. Cook pasta according to package directions, omitting salt and fat. Drain into a sieve over a bowl; add sun-dried tomatoes to reserved pasta water. Let stand 10 minutes; drain. Combine pasta and sun-dried tomatoes.
3. Combine pasta mixture and plum tomato mixture in a large bowl; stir in 3/4 cup cheese, olives, and parsley. Place in 4 bowls. Garnish with cheese.

PER SERVING (1 3/4 cups pasta and 2 tablespoons cheese): Calories 475 (29% from fat); Protein 21g; Fat 15g (sat 6g, mono 7g, poly 2g); Carbohydrate 65g; Fiber 6g; Cholesterol 19mg; Iron 4mg; Sodium 966mg; Calcium 381mg

red wine and rosemary marinara

Prep: *11 minutes* **Cook:** *23 minutes*
Serves 5

- 1 tablespoon olive oil
- 1 cup chopped onion
- 4 garlic cloves, minced
- ³/₄ cup dry red wine
- 2 tablespoons honey
- 2 teaspoons dried basil
- 1 teaspoon dried rosemary
- ¹/₂ teaspoon salt
- ¹/₄ teaspoon crushed red pepper
- 1 (28-ounce) can crushed tomatoes
- 1 (6-ounce) can no-salt-added tomato paste
- 5 cups hot cooked linguine (about 10 ounces uncooked)

1. Heat oil in a large saucepan over medium heat. Add onion and garlic; sauté 3 minutes. Add wine and next 7 ingredients (wine through tomato paste). Bring to a simmer; cook 20 minutes or until thick. Serve over pasta.

PER SERVING (1 cup sauce and 1 cup pasta): Calories 327 (11% from fat); Protein 10g; Fat 4g (sat 1g, mono 2g, poly 1g); Carbohydrate 64g; Fiber 4g; Cholesterol 0mg; Iron 4mg; Sodium 462mg; Calcium 98mg

ravioli casserole

Prep: *5 minutes* **Cook:** *33 minutes*
Serves 6

- 2 (9-ounce) packages fresh reduced-fat cheese ravioli
- 6 cups fresh torn spinach
- 1 (26-ounce) bottle tomato-basil pasta sauce (such as Classico)
- ¹/₂ teaspoon crushed red pepper
- 1 cup (4 ounces) shredded Asiago cheese, divided
- ¹/₄ cup thinly sliced fresh basil

1. Preheat oven to 375°.
2. Cook ravioli in boiling water 3 minutes, omitting salt and fat. Stir in spinach until wilted. Drain.
3. Combine pasta sauce and pepper. Spoon 1½ cups sauce mixture into the bottom of an 11 x 7-inch baking dish. Spoon half of ravioli mixture over sauce. Top with ½ cup cheese. Spoon remaining ravioli mixture over cheese. Top with remaining sauce. Cover with foil; bake at 375° for 25 minutes. Remove foil; sprinkle with ½ cup cheese. Bake, uncovered, an additional 5 minutes or until cheese melts. Garnish with basil.

PER SERVING (¹/₆ of casserole): Calories 350 (25% from fat); Protein 20g; Fat 10g (sat 5g, mono 1g, poly 0g); Carbohydrate 47g; Fiber 4g; Cholesterol 50mg; Iron 1mg; Sodium 848mg; Calcium 302mg

Pasta Myths

You may have heard that pasta can quickly pack on pounds. But truth be told, pasta isn't a fattening food. In fact, pasta contains almost no fat. The key to enjoying pasta while losing weight is learning to control portion sizes. Keep a measuring cup handy when serving up dinner plates; a ¹/₂-cup serving of pasta is around 100 calories and is one carbohydrate exchange. Choose marinaras or broth-based toppings rather than higher-fat Alfredo and cream-based sauces. For more information on carbohydrates and portion control, see Chapter 1.

spinach-walnut manicotti

pictured on page 139

Prep: *14 minutes* **Cook:** *35 minutes*
Serves 6

- ³/₄ cup (3 ounces) preshredded part-skim mozzarella cheese, divided
- 1¹/₄ cups fat-free ricotta cheese
- 1 cup 2% low-fat cottage cheese
- ¹/₂ cup fat-free cream cheese, softened
- ¹/₄ cup chopped walnuts
- ¹/₄ cup (1 ounce) grated fresh Romano cheese
- ¹/₂ teaspoon Italian seasoning
- 1 (10-ounce) package frozen chopped spinach, thawed, drained, and squeezed dry
- 1 large egg
- 1 garlic clove, minced
- 12 uncooked manicotti
- Cooking spray
- 1 (26-ounce) bottle tomato and garlic pasta sauce

1. Preheat oven to 350°.
2. Combine ½ cup mozzarella cheese, ricotta, and next 8 ingredients (cottage cheese through garlic) in a large bowl; stir well.
3. Cook manicotti according to package directions, omitting salt and fat; drain. Rinse under cold water; drain well. Spoon cheese mixture evenly into cooked manicotti, and arrange in a 13 x 9-inch baking dish coated with cooking spray. Pour pasta sauce over stuffed manicotti.
4. Bake, uncovered, at 350° for 25 minutes. Sprinkle with remaining mozzarella; bake 10 minutes or until cheese melts.

PER SERVING (2 manicotti): Calories 392 (23% from fat); Protein 29g; Fat 10g (sat 4g, mono 3g, poly 3g); Carbohydrate 47g; Fiber 5g; Cholesterol 72mg; Iron 4mg; Sodium 806mg; Calcium 433mg

pane cotto

Prep: *15 minutes* **Cook:** *33 minutes*
Stand: *5 minutes*
Serves 6

Traditionally, pane cotto, which is an eggless custard, is sweet and served for dessert. Our savory version makes a great main dish or a complementary side to chicken, pork, or beef.

     6 cups (1-inch) cubed stale Italian bread (about 12 ounces)
$^1/_2$ cup dry white wine, divided
Cooking spray
$1^1/_2$ teaspoons olive oil
     3 cups slivered onion
     2 (10-ounce) packages frozen chopped spinach, unthawed
$^1/_4$ cup chopped pitted kalamata olives
$^1/_4$ teaspoon salt
$^1/_4$ teaspoon crushed red pepper
     6 garlic cloves, minced
     6 (1-ounce) slices provolone cheese

1. Place bread in a large bowl. Drizzle $^1/_4$ cup white wine over bread, tossing well to coat.
2. Coat a large nonstick skillet with cooking spray; add olive oil, and place over medium-high heat until hot. Add onion; sauté 5 minutes. Reduce heat to medium; sauté 15 minutes or until golden brown. Remove onion from pan, and set aside.
3. Pour remaining $^1/_4$ cup wine into pan. Add chopped spinach and next 4 ingredients (spinach through garlic); cover and cook over medium-high heat 8 minutes, stirring occasionally to break up spinach. Reduce heat to medium; add bread and onion. Cook, uncovered, 5 minutes, tossing gently. Top with provolone slices. Remove from heat; cover and let stand 5 minutes or until cheese melts.

PER SERVING (about 1$^1/_3$ cups): Calories 321 (28% from fat); Protein 16g; Fat 10g (sat 5g, mono 2g, poly 1g); Carbohydrate 43g; Fiber 6g; Cholesterol 20mg; Iron 4mg; Sodium 819mg; Calcium 354mg

linguine with tomatoes, spinach, and white beans

pictured on page 139

Prep: *8 minutes* **Cook:** *17 minutes*
Serves 6

This recipe is surprisingly high in calcium, providing about 25% of the amount you need in a day.

     2 teaspoons olive oil
     1 tablespoon minced garlic
     2 (14$^1/_2$-ounce) cans diced Italian-flavored tomatoes
     1 (15-ounce) can cannellini beans or other white beans, drained
     1 (10-ounce) package frozen chopped spinach, thawed, drained, and squeezed dry
     6 cups hot cooked linguine (about 12 ounces uncooked)
     6 tablespoons grated Romano cheese

1. Heat oil in a large nonstick skillet over medium-high heat. Add garlic; sauté 1 minute. Add tomatoes, beans, and spinach; bring to a boil. Reduce heat, and simmer 15 minutes, stirring occasionally. Spoon sauce over pasta; sprinkle with cheese.

PER SERVING (1 cup pasta, 1 cup sauce, and 1 tablespoon cheese): Calories 365 (10% from fat); Protein 16g; Fat 4g (sat 1g, mono 2g, poly 0g); Carbohydrate 67g; Fiber 5g; Cholesterol 5mg; Iron 6mg; Sodium 978mg; Calcium 240mg

white bean-and-tofu-stuffed shells

Prep: *28 minutes* **Cook:** *30 minutes*
Serves 9

     2 (10.5-ounce) packages firm tofu
     2 (15-ounce) cans cannellini beans, rinsed and drained
$1^1/_2$ cups (6 ounces) shredded part-skim mozzarella cheese, divided
     2 tablespoons sun-dried tomatoes, packed without oil, rehydrated and chopped
     1 tablespoon chopped fresh basil
     1 teaspoon Italian seasoning
$^1/_2$ teaspoon crushed red pepper
     2 garlic cloves, minced
     2 cups low-fat pasta sauce
Cooking spray
    18 cooked jumbo macaroni shells
     2 tablespoons grated Parmesan cheese

1. Preheat oven to 375°.
2. Place tofu in a food processor; process until smooth. Spoon tofu onto several layers of heavy-duty paper towels; spread to ½-inch thickness. Cover with additional paper towels; let stand 5 minutes. Scrape back into processor using a rubber spatula; add beans and next 6 ingredients (beans through garlic), and pulse until beans are coarsely chopped.
3. Spread 1 cup pasta sauce on bottom of a 13 x 9-inch baking dish coated with cooking spray. Spoon ¼ cup tofu mixture into each shell. Arrange shells in dish. Spoon remaining pasta sauce over shells; sprinkle with cheese. Bake at 375° for 30 minutes or until cheese is bubbly.

PER SERVING (2 shells): Calories 444 (19% from fat); Protein 24g; Fat 9g (sat 3g, mono 2g, poly 3g); Carbohydrate 66g; Fiber 4g; Cholesterol 12mg; Iron 6mg; Sodium 162mg; Calcium 245mg

barbecued beans 'n' rice

Prep: *9 minutes* **Cook:** *68 minutes*
Serves 8

If you prefer mild food, use only one chile. If chipotle chiles aren't available, substitute 1 to 2 drained canned jalapeños and a few drops of mesquite-flavored barbecue smoke seasoning (such as Mesquite Liquid Smoke).

- 2 teaspoons olive oil
- 1 cup frozen chopped onion
- 1 to 2 drained canned chipotle chiles, minced
- 1 tablespoon bottled minced garlic
- 1 (16-ounce) can pinto beans, drained
- 1 (16-ounce) can kidney beans, drained
- 1 (15-ounce) can black beans, drained
- 1 cup hickory barbecue sauce (such as KC Masterpiece)
- 1 tablespoon Dijon mustard
- 6 cups hot cooked long-grain rice

Chopped fresh chives (optional)

1. Preheat oven to 350°.
2. Heat oil in a nonstick skillet over medium heat. Add onion, chiles, and garlic; sauté 5 minutes. Remove from heat. Stir in beans, barbecue sauce, and mustard. Spoon mixture into a 1½-quart casserole; cover and bake at 350° for 1 hour. Serve over rice; garnish with chives, if desired.

PER SERVING (½ cup beans and ¾ cup rice): Calories 372 (5% from fat); Protein 12g; Fat 2g (sat 0g, mono 1g, poly 1g); Carbohydrate 76g; Fiber 5g; Cholesterol 0mg; Iron 5mg; Sodium 540mg; Calcium 53mg

fall vegetable braise with white beans

Prep: *18 minutes* **Cook:** *59 minutes*
Serves 4

Winter vegetables seasoned with garlic and fresh herbs create a warming one-dish meal.

- 1 tablespoon olive oil
- 3½ cups (1-inch) cubed seeded peeled butternut squash (about 1½ pounds)
- 2 cups (1-inch-thick) sliced parsnip
- 2 cups finely chopped leek
- 4 large garlic cloves, minced
- 2 tablespoons chopped fresh or 2 teaspoons rubbed sage
- 1 teaspoon chopped fresh or ¼ teaspoon dried rosemary, crumbled
- ¼ teaspoon salt
- ¼ teaspoon freshly ground black pepper
- 1 bay leaf
- ¾ cup canned vegetable broth
- ⅓ cup medium sherry
- 1 (19-ounce) can cannellini beans or other white beans, drained
- 2 tablespoons grated fresh Parmesan cheese

1. Preheat oven to 325°.
2. Heat oil in a 4-quart oven-proof Dutch oven until very hot. Add squash and parsnip; sauté 5 minutes or until edges are browned (be careful not to burn vegetables). Remove vegetables from pan; set aside.
3. Reduce heat to medium. Add leek and garlic; sauté 2 minutes or until leek is tender. Stir in sage and next 4 ingredients (sage through bay leaf). Return squash mixture to pan (do not stir). Pour broth and sherry over vegetables; bring to a simmer.
4. Cover pan with a tight-fitting lid; bake at 325° for 40 minutes.

Stir in beans. Cover and bake an additional 10 minutes. Remove and discard bay leaf. Spoon into bowls; sprinkle with cheese.

PER SERVING (about 1½ cups vegetable mixture and 1½ teaspoons cheese): Calories 301 (17% from fat); Protein 10g; Fat 6g (sat 1g, mono 3g, poly 1g); Carbohydrate 49g; Fiber 4g; Cholesterol 3mg; Iron 4mg; Sodium 831mg; Calcium 202mg

four-corn pie

Prep: *15 minutes* **Cook:** *50 minutes*
Serves 4

There's hardly any preparation for this dish—a little chopping and opening a few cans. It's like a quiche but easier because you don't have to make a crust.

Cooking spray
- 1 cup chopped onion
- 2 (8¾-ounce) cans no-salt-added whole-kernel corn, drained
- 1 (8.5-ounce) can no-salt-added cream-style corn
- 1 (15.5-ounce) can white hominy, drained
- 1 (4.5-ounce) can chopped green chiles, drained
- ¼ cup chopped fresh cilantro
- ¾ cup (3 ounces) shredded colby-Jack cheese, divided
- ¾ cup egg substitute
- 1 cup cornflakes, finely crushed
- 4 tablespoons fat-free sour cream

1. Preheat oven to 400°.
2. Place a small nonstick skillet coated with cooking spray over medium heat until hot. Add onion; sauté 5 minutes or until lightly browned. Combine onion, whole-kernel corn, cream-style corn, hominy, chiles, and cilantro in a large bowl; stir in ½ cup cheese and egg substitute. Spoon mixture into a 9-inch pie

plate coated with cooking spray. Combine ¼ cup cheese and cornflakes; toss well. Sprinkle over corn mixture.

3. Bake at 400° for 50 minutes or until top is browned and mixture is set. Serve with 1 tablespoon sour cream.

PER SERVING (¼ of pie): Calories 352 (24% from fat); Protein 16g; Fat 9g (sat 5g, mono 2g, poly 1g); Carbohydrate 51g; Fiber 5g; Cholesterol 20mg; Iron 3mg; Sodium 561mg; Calcium 188mg

black bean enchiladas with tomatillo sauce

Prep: *10 minutes* **Cook:** *30 minutes*
Serves 6

This recipe uses Black Bean Chili (page 222) as part of the bean filling for these enchiladas.

1½ cups picante sauce or salsa
1 (8-ounce) can sodium-free tomato sauce
Cooking spray
12 (6-inch) corn tortillas
4 cups bean mixture reserved from Black Bean Chili (page 222)
1½ cups (6 ounces) low-fat Monterey Jack cheese with jalapeño peppers, shredded
¾ cup chopped peeled tomatillos
2 tablespoons chopped seeded jalapeño pepper
¼ cup chopped onion
¼ cup chopped fresh cilantro
⅛ teaspoon salt
1 garlic clove
½ ripe peeled avocado, seeded and mashed
2 teaspoons fresh lime juice

1. Preheat oven to 350°.
2. Combine picante sauce and tomato sauce in a small bowl. Spread 1 cup picante mixture in the bottom of a 13 x 9-inch baking dish coated with cooking spray. Set aside remaining mixture.
3. Warm tortillas according to package directions. Spoon about ⅓ cup bean mixture down center of each tortilla; roll up. Place each tortilla, seam side down, in baking dish. Top enchiladas with remaining picante mixture; sprinkle with cheese. Cover dish with foil. Bake at 350° for 25 minutes or until thoroughly heated. Remove foil; bake 5 minutes or until cheese melts.
4. Combine tomatillos and next 5 ingredients (tomatillos through garlic) in a blender or food processor; process until coarsely ground. Combine tomatillo mixture, avocado, and lime juice. Serve with enchiladas.

PER SERVING (2 enchiladas and 2½ tablespoons tomatillo sauce): Calories 346 (20% from fat); Protein13g; Fat 8g (sat 2g, mono 3g, poly 2g); Carbohydrate 58g; Fiber 13g; Cholesterol 10mg; Iron 4mg; Sodium 936mg; Calcium 409mg

Meatless Merits

More and more people are discovering the health benefits of meat-free meals. In fact, 24% of American households eat at least one or more meat-free meals each week. Most meatless meals have vegetables, beans, grains, or soy (tofu) as a base. These ingredients give meatless dishes plenty of cancer-preventing antioxidants and fiber. People who follow a meatless diet typically have lower cholesterol levels, lower body weights, and less of a risk of cancer. Aside from the health benefits, many meatless dishes are quick to prepare and economical.

curried chickpeas in coconut-cilantro broth

Prep: *11 minutes* **Cook:** *25 minutes*
Serves 5

Regular coconut milk (rather than light) provides a rich, full flavor to this dish.

1 teaspoon butter or stick margarine
1 cup chopped onion
1 garlic clove, minced
1 (14.5-ounce) can diced tomatoes, undrained
⅔ cup canned coconut milk
1 tablespoon minced seeded jalapeño pepper
1 to 2 teaspoons curry powder
1 (19-ounce) can chickpeas (garbanzo beans), drained
⅓ cup chopped fresh cilantro
5 cups hot cooked basmati rice

1. Heat butter in a large skillet over medium-high heat. Add onion and garlic; sauté 3 minutes or until tender. Stir in tomatoes and next 3 ingredients (tomatoes through curry); reduce heat, and simmer 5 minutes. Add chickpeas; partially cover, and simmer 15 minutes. Remove from heat; stir in cilantro. Serve over rice.

PER SERVING (¾ cup chickpea mixture and 1 cup rice): Calories 485 (19% from fat); Protein 14g; Fat 10g (sat 7g, mono 1g, poly 1g); Carbohydrate 86g; Fiber 10g; Cholesterol 2mg; Iron 7mg; Sodium 442mg; Calcium 81mg

two-cheese enchiladas

Prep: *10 minutes* **Cook:** *20 minutes*
Serves 4

- 1 (15-ounce) can pinto beans, drained
- 1 cup frozen whole-kernel corn, thawed
- 1/2 cup Monterey Jack cheese with jalapeño peppers, shredded
- 1/2 cup chopped fresh cilantro, divided
- 2 (10-ounce) cans red enchilada sauce, divided
- 1/2 cup fresh refrigerated salsa

Cooking spray

- 8 (6-inch) corn tortillas
- 1/2 cup (2 ounces) crumbled queso fresco or queso añejo

1. Preheat oven to 375°.
2. In a medium bowl, partially mash beans with a fork. Add corn, Jack cheese, ⅓ cup cilantro, and ¼ cup enchilada sauce.
3. In another bowl, combine remaining enchilada sauce and salsa.
4. Lightly coat a 13 x 9-inch baking dish with cooking spray. Pour ½ cup of enchilada sauce mixture in bottom of dish.
5. Warm tortillas in microwave according to package directions. Spoon about ⅓ cup bean mixture down center of each tortilla; roll up. Arrange tortillas, seam sides down, in baking dish; top with remaining enchilada sauce mixture and crumbled queso. Bake at 375° for 20 minutes or until thoroughly heated. Sprinkle with remaining cilantro.

PER SERVING (2 enchiladas): Calories 332 (21% from fat); Fat 8g (sat 2g, mono 1g, poly 1g); Protein 11g; Carbohydrate 56g; Fiber 8g; Cholesterol 10mg; Iron 3mg; Sodium 866mg; Calcium 287mg

tomato-green bean risotto with feta cheese

Prep: *16 minutes* **Cook:** *26 minutes*
Serves 4

- 1/2 ounce sun-dried tomatoes, packed without oil (about 8)
- 1 (14½-ounce) can cut green beans, undrained
- 2/3 cup dry white wine
- 3 (10½-ounce) cans fat-free, less-sodium chicken broth
- 2 teaspoons olive oil
- 1 cup chopped onion
- 2 garlic cloves, crushed
- 1½ cups uncooked Arborio or other short-grain rice
- 1 teaspoon dried basil
- 1/8 teaspoon salt
- 3/4 cup (3 ounces) crumbled feta cheese with peppercorns

1. Cut sun-dried tomatoes into thin strips; set aside.
2. Drain beans in a colander over a medium saucepan; set beans aside. Add wine and broth to reserved canned liquid; bring to a simmer (do not boil). Combine ½ cup warm broth mixture and tomatoes in a bowl. Cover; set aside. Keep remaining broth mixture warm over low heat.
3. Heat oil in a large saucepan over medium heat. Add onion and garlic; sauté 3 minutes. Add rice; cook 1 minute, stirring constantly. Add warm broth mixture, 1 cup at a time, stirring constantly until each portion of broth mixture is absorbed (about 20 minutes total). Add tomato mixture, beans, basil, and salt; cook 2 minutes, stirring constantly. Remove from heat; stir in cheese.

PER SERVING (1 cup): Calories 420 (19% from fat); Fat 9g (sat 3g, mono 3g, poly 0g); Protein 12g; Carbohydrate 74g; Fiber 3g; Cholesterol 20mg; Iron 6mg; Sodium 771mg; Calcium 156mg

couscous-stuffed portobellos

pictured on pages 131 and 140

Prep: *10 minutes* **Cook:** *33 minutes*
Stand: *7 minutes*
Serves 4

- 1 (6-ounce) package fat-free couscous with wild mushrooms (such as Marrakesh Express)
- 1½ cups water
- 3/4 cup finely chopped red bell pepper
- 1 cup chopped arugula
- 3/4 cup (3 ounces) preshredded fresh Parmesan cheese, divided
- 1/2 cup (2 ounces) crumbled feta cheese
- 1 tablespoon balsamic vinegar
- 1 teaspoon olive oil
- 1/4 teaspoon black pepper
- 4 large portobello mushroom caps (about 1 pound)

1. Preheat oven to 350°.
2. Combine seasoning packet from couscous and water in a saucepan; bring to a boil. Gradually stir in couscous and bell pepper. Remove from heat; cover and let stand 7 minutes. Fluff with a fork; stir in arugula, ½ cup Parmesan cheese, and feta cheese. Set aside.
3. Combine vinegar, oil, and pepper; brush over mushroom caps. Top each cap with 1 cup couscous mixture, pressing firmly to pack. Place stuffed caps in a shallow roasting pan; add water to pan to depth of ¼ inch. Bake at 350° for 20 minutes. Sprinkle with remaining Parmesan cheese; bake 10 minutes or until cheese melts.

PER SERVING (1 stuffed cap): Calories 310 (30% from fat); Protein 18g; Fat 10g (sat 6g, mono 3 g, poly 1g); Carbohydrate 37g; Fiber 3g; Cholesterol 27mg; Iron 3mg; Sodium 739mg; Calcium 339mg

portobello mushroom fajitas with cilantro sauce

Prep: *26 minutes* **Cook:** *10 minutes*
Serves 6

You may substitute 2 fresh tomatillos for the tomatillo salsa, if desired. Just remove the husks from tomatillos, and cut them into wedges. Then add to the food processor as directed below for salsa.

1½ medium yellow bell peppers
 ½ cup cilantro sprigs
   4 ounces ⅓-less-fat cream cheese (about ½ cup)
 ¼ cup tomatillo salsa
   1 ed bell pepper, cut into strips
   1 medium red onion, thinly sliced
   2 (6-ounce) packages portobello mushroom slices
   2 teaspoons ground cumin
   2 teaspoons chili powder
 ¼ teaspoon adobo seasoning with pepper
   2 teaspoons olive oil
   6 (8-inch) fat-free flour tortillas

1. Place yellow bell pepper half, cilantro, cheese, and salsa in a food processor; process until smooth. Set cilantro sauce aside.
2. Cut remaining yellow bell pepper into strips. Combine yellow and red pepper strips, onion, and mushrooms in a bowl. Sprinkle with cumin, chili powder, and adobo seasoning; toss vegetables gently to coat.
3. Heat oil in a large nonstick skillet over medium-high heat. Add vegetable mixture, and sauté 8 minutes or until crisp-tender. Remove from heat, and set aside.
4. Heat tortillas according to package directions. Spread 2 tablespoons cilantro sauce over each tortilla. Divide vegetable mixture evenly among tortillas; roll up. Spoon 1 tablespoon cilantro sauce over each fajita.

PER SERVING (1 fajita): Calories 225 (27% from fat); Protein 7g; Fat 7g (sat 3g, mono 1g, poly 0g); Carbohydrate 35g; Fiber 4g; Cholesterol 14mg; Iron 4mg; Sodium 594mg; Calcium 41mg

polenta with mushroom-tomato sauce

Prep: *6 minutes* **Cook:** *17 minutes*
Serves 4

Mushroom polenta, instead of pasta, serves as the base for a hearty mushroom sauce.

   1 (16-ounce) tube mushroom polenta, cut into 16 slices
Cooking spray
   3 tablespoons olive oil, divided
   1 (8-ounce) package presliced button mushrooms
   2 garlic cloves, minced
   2 tablespoons minced fresh parsley
   1 (14½-ounce) can diced Italian herb tomatoes
 ¼ teaspoon salt
 ¼ teaspoon pepper

1. Preheat oven to 450°.
2. Place polenta slices on a baking sheet coated with cooking spray. Lightly brush with 1 tablespoon oil. Bake at 450° for 5 minutes or until polenta is slightly browned. Turn polenta over; bake 5 minutes.
3. Sauté mushrooms in 2 tablespoons oil until soft. Add garlic, parsley, tomatoes, salt, and pepper. Simmer 5 minutes or until thick. Spoon over polenta.

PER SERVING (4 polenta slices and ½ cup sauce): Calories 195 (33% from fat); Protein 5g; Fat 7g (sat 1g, mono 5g, poly 1g); Carbohydrate 27g; Fiber 4g; Cholesterol 0mg; Iron 2mg; Sodium 743mg; Calcium 59mg

polenta with roasted red peppers and fontina cheese

Prep: *17 minutes* **Cook:** *42 minutes*
Stand: *15 minutes*
Serves 6

Roasted peppers, tomatoes, polenta, and fontina star in this remake of traditional lasagna.

   3 large red bell peppers
   1 (14.5-ounce) can whole tomatoes, chopped
Cooking spray
   1 (16-ounce) tube polenta, cut crosswise into 12 slices
1¼ cups (5 ounces) shredded fontina cheese

1. Preheat broiler. Cut peppers in half lengthwise; discard seeds and membranes. Place pepper halves, skin sides up, on a foil-lined baking sheet; flatten with hand. Broil 10 minutes or until blackened. Place in a zip-top plastic bag; seal. Let stand 15 minutes. Peel; cut into strips. Set aside.
2. Preheat oven to 350°.
3. Drain tomatoes in a sieve over bowl; reserve liquid. Set aside.
4. Place a large skillet over medium-low heat; add tomatoes. Cook 1 minute. Gradually add tomato liquid; simmer 1 minute. Add pepper strips; simmer 5 minutes. Remove from heat.
5. Spread ¼ cup pepper sauce in bottom of a 13 x 9-inch baking dish coated with cooking spray. Arrange polenta slices over pepper sauce, and spread remaining pepper sauce over polenta. Sprinkle with cheese. Bake at 350° for 25 minutes.

PER SERVING (⅙ of casserole): Calories 187 (38% from fat); Protein 9g; Fat 8g (sat 5g, mono 2g, poly 1g); Carbohydrate 20g; Fiber 3g; Cholesterol 27mg; Iron 2mg; Sodium 622mg; Calcium 151mg

How to Bake Spaghetti Squash

The recipe at right calls for spaghetti squash that's cooked in the microwave. If you prefer to bake the squash rather than microwave it, follow the directions below.

1. Preheat oven to 350°. Cut squash in half lengthwise with a heavy knife, and scrape out seeds.

2. Place cut sides down in baking dish; add water to a depth of 1/2 inch before cooking. Bake 45 minutes or until squash is tender when pierced with a fork.

3. Scrape out strands of squash using a fork.

---

spaghetti squash with vegetable ragoût

pictured on page 139

Prep: *5 minutes* **Cook:** *68 minutes*
Stand: *5 minutes*
Serves 6

A ragoût is a thick, rich, stewlike dish perfect for serving over the tender strands of spaghetti squash.

- 1 cup water
- 2 cups frozen black-eyed peas
- 1 (16-ounce) bag frozen vegetable gumbo mixture (such as McKenzie's)
- 2 (15-ounce) cans chunky garlic and herb tomato sauce
- 1 1/2 teaspoons Creole seasoning
- 1/4 teaspoon ground red pepper
- 1 (2 1/2-pound) spaghetti squash

1. Bring 1 cup water to a boil in a large saucepan; add peas. Cover, reduce heat, and simmer 35 minutes or until tender. Add frozen gumbo mixture and next 3 ingredients (gumbo through red pepper); bring to a boil. Reduce heat, and simmer 10 minutes or until thoroughly heated. Set aside; keep warm.
2. Pierce squash several times with a fork, and place on paper towels in a microwave oven. Microwave at HIGH 15 minutes or until tender, turning squash every 3 minutes. Let squash stand 5 minutes; cut in half lengthwise, and discard seeds. Remove spaghetti-like strands with a fork to yield about 6 cups. Spoon vegetable mixture over squash.

PER SERVING (1 cup squash and about 1 cup vegetable mixture): Calories 220 (13% from fat); Protein 8g; Fat 3g (sat 0g, mono 0g, poly 1g); Carbohydrate 40g; Fiber 7g; Cholesterol 0mg; Iron 3mg; Sodium 780mg; Calcium 178mg

---

broccoli-tofu stir-fry with cashews

Prep: *12 minutes* **Cook:** *4 minutes*
Stand: *15 minutes*
Serves 5

- 3 tablespoons soy sauce
- 2 tablespoons seasoned rice vinegar
- 1 1/2 teaspoons bottled minced garlic
- 2 teaspoons fresh or bottled chopped ginger
- 1 (1-pound) package firm tofu, drained and cut into 1/2-inch cubes
- 1 tablespoon dark sesame oil, divided
- 5 cups fresh broccoli florets
- 1/2 cup chopped green onions
- 2 tablespoons minced seeded jalapeño pepper
- 1/3 cup cashews
- 5 cups hot cooked somen (wheat noodles) or angel hair pasta

1. Combine first 4 ingredients (soy sauce through ginger) in a shallow dish, and stir well. Add tofu cubes, stirring gently to coat. Let stand 15 minutes. Remove tofu from dish, reserving marinade.
2. Heat 2 teaspoons oil in a wok or nonstick skillet over high heat. Add tofu; cook 2 minutes or until browned. Remove tofu; set aside, and keep warm.
3. Add remaining 1 teaspoon oil, broccoli, green onions, and jalapeño pepper to pan; sauté 2 minutes. Stir in reserved marinade, tofu, and cashews; serve over noodles.

PER SERVING (about 1 1/2 cups stir-fry and 1 cup noodles): Calories 358 (29% from fat); Protein 18g; Fat 11g (sat 2g, mono 4g, poly 3g); Carbohydrate 49g; Fiber 6g; Cholesterol 0mg; Iron 8mg; Sodium 567mg; Calcium 145mg

tender, juicy meats

Southwestern Grilled Flank Steak, page 151

almost classic meat loaf

Prep: *9 minutes* **Cook:** *1 hour 15 minutes*
Stand: *5 minutes*
Serves 10

We took mom's traditional meat loaf recipe and spiced it up a bit with Italian-seasoned breadcrumbs, Dijon mustard, and garlic.

- 2 cups refrigerated shredded hash browns (such as Simply Potatoes)
- 1 cup Italian-seasoned breadcrumbs
- 1 cup chopped onion
- 1/2 cup ketchup
- 1/4 cup Dijon mustard
- 2 teaspoons dried oregano
- 1/2 teaspoon salt
- 2 large eggs, lightly beaten
- 2 garlic cloves, minced
- 2 pounds lean ground beef
- Cooking spray
- 1/3 cup ketchup

1. Preheat oven to 375°.
2. Combine first 9 ingredients (hashbrowns through garlic) in a bowl; stir mixture well. Crumble ground beef over potato mixture; stir just until blended. Shape mixture into an 8½ x 4½-inch loaf. Place loaf in an 11 x 7-inch baking dish coated with cooking spray. Spread 1/3 cup ketchup over top of loaf.
3. Bake at 375° for 1 hour and 15 minutes or until an instant-read thermometer registers 160°. Let stand 5 minutes before slicing.

PER SERVING (1/10 of loaf): Calories 246 (31% from fat); Protein 28g; Fat 9g (sat 4g, mono 4g, poly 1g); Carbohydrate 22g; Fiber 1g; Cholesterol 115mg; Iron 4mg; Sodium 912mg; Calcium 41mg

italiano meat loaf

Prep: *10 minutes* **Cook:** *1 hour*
Stand: *5 minutes*
Serves 6

Tiny pasta and a savory meat sauce combine to create a zesty loaf.

- 1 cup chopped onion
- 1 cup chopped green bell pepper
- 3/4 cup Italian-seasoned breadcrumbs
- 1/4 cup grated Parmesan cheese
- 2 teaspoons dried basil
- 1/2 teaspoon salt
- 1/4 teaspoon black pepper
- 1 (8-ounce) can tomato sauce
- 3 large egg whites, lightly beaten
- 2 garlic cloves, minced
- 1 cup cooked orzo (about 1/3 cup uncooked rice-shaped pasta)
- 1 pound lean ground round
- Cooking spray
- 3 cups fresh tomato and basil pasta sauce (such as Five Brothers)
- Basil sprigs (optional)

1. Preheat oven to 375°.
2. Combine first 10 ingredients (onion through garlic) in a large bowl; stir well. Stir in orzo. Crumble beef over orzo mixture, and stir just until blended. Shape mixture into a 9 x 4½-inch loaf. Place loaf in an 11 x 7-inch baking dish coated with cooking spray.
3. Bake at 375° for 1 hour or until an instant-read thermometer registers 160°. Let stand 5 minutes before slicing. Cut into 6 slices; top each slice with ½ cup pasta sauce. Garnish with basil, if desired.

PER SERVING (1/6 of loaf): Calories 351 (34% from fat); Protein 27g; Fat 13g (sat 5g, mono 3g, poly 1g); Carbohydrate 36g; Fiber 5g; Cholesterol 57mg; Iron 4mg; Sodium 1,433mg; Calcium 150mg

chipotle chile pie

Prep: *8 minutes* **Cook:** *29 minutes*
Stand: *5 minutes*
Serves 6

If chipotle chile salsa is not available in your area, stir 1 tablespoon chopped, drained canned chipotle chile and 1/4 teaspoon sugar into 1 cup plus 2 tablespoons of a basic salsa like Old El Paso.

- 1 pound lean ground round
- 1 cup chopped onion
- 1 cup chopped green bell pepper
- 1 (10-ounce) can enchilada sauce
- 1 cup frozen shoepeg white corn, thawed
- 1 cup (4 ounces) shredded reduced-fat sharp Cheddar cheese
- 1 cup chipotle chile salsa
- 2/3 cup white cornmeal (not self-rising cornmeal or cornmeal mix)
- 1 tablespoon all-purpose flour
- 1 teaspoon baking powder
- 1/2 teaspoon salt
- 1/4 cup fat-free milk
- 3 tablespoons chipotle chile salsa
- 1 large egg

1. Preheat oven to 400°.
2. Cook first 3 ingredients (ground round through bell pepper) in a 9-inch cast-iron skillet over medium-high heat until beef is browned, stirring to crumble. Drain well, and return beef mixture to pan. Stir in enchilada sauce and next 3 ingredients (sauce through chile salsa). Remove from heat; set aside.
3. Combine cornmeal and next 3 ingredients (cornmeal through salt) in a bowl; make a well in center of mixture. Combine milk, 3 tablespoons salsa, and egg; stir well. Add milk mixture to dry ingredients, stirring just

until moist. Spoon batter over beef mixture in skillet, spreading batter evenly to edges of pan (batter will be thin). Bake at 400° for 22 minutes or until cornbread is golden. Let stand 5 minutes before serving.

PER SERVING (1/6 of pie): Calories 303 (31% from fat); Protein 22g; Fat 10g (sat 1g, mono 3g, poly 1g); Carbohydrate 31g; Fiber 2g; Cholesterol 83mg; Iron 4mg; Sodium 594mg; Calcium 168mg

fajita pizzas

Prep: *8 minutes* **Cook:** *10 minutes*
Serves 2

- 6 ounces lean flank steak, thinly sliced
- 3/4 cup green bell pepper strips
- 1/8 teaspoon salt
- 4 (10-inch) flour tortillas
- Cooking spray
- 1/2 cup salsa
- 1/2 cup (2 ounces) shredded reduced-fat Mexican cheese blend

1. Preheat oven to 450°.
2. Place a small nonstick skillet over high heat until hot. Add steak, bell pepper, and salt; sauté 2 minutes or until steak is desired degree of doneness.
3. Place 2 tortillas on a baking sheet. Coat both tortillas with cooking spray; top each with another tortilla. Spread salsa over top of each tortilla stack, leaving a ½-inch border. Divide beef mixture evenly between tortillas; sprinkle with cheese. Bake at 450° for 8 minutes or until cheese melts and edges of tortillas are crisp.

PER SERVING (1 pizza): Calories 433 (34% from fat); Protein 33g; Fat 17g (sat 4g, mono 5g, poly 1g); Carbohydrate 38g; Fiber 3g; Cholesterol 65mg; Iron 5mg; Sodium 951mg; Calcium 346mg

italian beef and potato casserole

Prep: *15 minutes* **Cook:** *1 hour 12 minutes*
Stand: *10 minutes*
Serves 8

This hearty dish can satisfy even the hungriest appetite.

- 1 pound ground chuck
- 1 cup chopped onion
- 1 (8-ounce) package presliced fresh mushrooms
- 2 garlic cloves, minced
- 1 (27.5-ounce) jar fat-free chunky mushroom and garlic pasta sauce (such as Ragú Light)
- 1 (10-ounce) package frozen chopped spinach, thawed, drained, and squeezed dry
- 1/4 cup water
- 1/4 teaspoon fennel seeds, crushed
- 1/4 teaspoon salt
- 1/4 teaspoon pepper
- Cooking spray
- 4 medium baking potatoes, peeled and cut into 1/4-inch slices (about 2 pounds)
- 1/2 cup (2 ounces) finely grated fresh Parmesan cheese

1. Preheat oven to 350°.
2. Combine first 4 ingredients (ground chuck through garlic) in a nonstick skillet; cook over medium heat until beef is browned, stirring to crumble. Drain well; return to pan. Add pasta sauce and next 5 ingredients (pasta sauce through pepper); bring to a boil. Reduce heat; simmer 5 minutes.
3. Spread half of beef mixture in a 13 x 9-inch baking dish coated with cooking spray. Arrange half of potato slices over mixture, slightly overlapping slices. Repeat with remaining beef mixture and potato slices, ending with potato slices. Coat with cooking spray. Cover and bake at

350° for 30 minutes. Uncover; bake 20 minutes or until golden. Top with cheese; bake an additional 10 minutes. Let stand 10 minutes before serving.

PER SERVING (1/8 of casserole): Calories 300 (30% from fat); Protein 18g; Fat 10g (sat 4g, mono 3g, poly 0g); Carbohydrate 33g; Fiber 6g; Cholesterol 38mg; Iron 4mg; Sodium 528mg; Calcium 162mg

southwestern grilled flank steak

pictured on pages 149 and 159

Prep: *5 minutes* **Cook:** *8 minutes*
Marinate: *4 hours* **Stand:** *5 minutes*
Serves 6

- 1 (1½-pound) lean flank steak (about 3/4 inch thick)
- 2 tablespoons Hungarian sweet paprika
- 1 tablespoon chili powder
- 2 teaspoons ground cumin
- 1 teaspoon ground cinnamon
- 1/2 teaspoon salt
- Cooking spray

1. Trim excess fat from steak. Combine paprika and next 4 ingredients (paprika through salt); rub over both sides of steak. Place steak in a dish; cover and marinate in refrigerator at least 4 hours.
2. Prepare grill.
3. Place steak on grill rack coated with cooking spray; cover and grill 4 minutes on each side or until desired degree of doneness. Remove steak from grill; let stand 5 minutes before slicing. Cut steak diagonally across the grain into thin slices.

PER SERVING (3 ounces): Calories 189 (43% from fat); Protein 24g; Fat 9g (sat 4g, mono 4g, poly 0g); Carbohydrate 2g; Fiber 1g; Cholesterol 59mg; Iron 3mg; Sodium 280mg; Calcium 19mg

chili-crusted flank steak fajitas

pictured on page 159

Prep: *20 minutes* **Cook:** *28 minutes*
Marinate: *30 minutes* **Stand:** *5 minutes*
Serves 4

1	(¹/₂-pound) lean flank steak
1	medium red bell pepper, quartered and seeded
1	medium green bell pepper, quartered and seeded
1	medium yellow bell pepper, quartered and seeded
4	plum tomatoes, cut in half
2	tablespoons lime juice, divided
2	tablespoons Worcestershire sauce, divided
³/₄	teaspoon salt, divided
3	garlic cloves, minced and divided
1¹/₂	teaspoons chili powder
1	medium red onion, cut into ¹/₄-inch-thick slices
	Cooking spray
8	(6¹/₂-inch) flour tortillas
4	tablespoons fat-free sour cream

1. Trim fat from steak, and set steak aside.
2. Combine bell pepper pieces, tomato halves, 1 tablespoon lime juice, 1 tablespoon Worcestershire sauce, ¼ teaspoon salt, and half of minced garlic in a bowl. Toss gently.
3. Combine remaining lime juice, remaining Worcestershire sauce, ¼ teaspoon salt, remaining garlic, and flank steak in a zip-top plastic bag; seal bag, and marinate in refrigerator at least 30 minutes. Remove steak from bag, reserving marinade. Rub chili powder over steak. Remove bell pepper pieces and tomato halves from bowl, reserving marinade.
4. Prepare grill.
5. Place steak, bell pepper pieces, tomato halves, and onion slices on grill rack coated with cooking spray. Grill tomato halves 3 minutes on each side. Grill steak 5 minutes on each side or until desired degree of doneness, basting occasionally with reserved marinade. Grill bell pepper pieces and onion slices 6 minutes on each side or until tender, basting occasionally with reserved marinade.
6. Remove steak and vegetables from grill. Let steak stand 5 minutes; cut steak diagonally across grain into thin slices. Cut bell pepper pieces into ¼-inch-thick strips; cut onion slices in half. Sprinkle remaining ¼ teaspoon salt evenly over vegetables.
7. Heat flour tortillas according to package directions. Place 2 tortillas on each of 4 plates. Divide steak, bell pepper, and onion evenly among tortillas. Top each fajita with 1 tomato half and 1½ teaspoons fat-free sour cream; roll up tortillas. Serve fajitas warm.

NOTE: To prepare indoors, cut each bell pepper in half lengthwise; discard seeds and membranes. Place halves, skin sides up, on a broiler pan lined with foil. Flatten peppers with hand. Place onion slices on broiler pan, and broil 5 minutes. Turn onions over; add tomatoes, and broil 5 minutes or until onions, peppers, and tomatoes are lightly browned.

While vegetables cook, place a grill pan over medium-high heat until hot; coat with cooking spray. Add steak; cook 3 minutes on each side or until desired degree of doneness.

PER SERVING (2 fajitas): Calories 303 (22% from fat); Protein 18g; Fat 8g (sat 3g, mono 2g, poly 2g); Carbohydrate 47g; Fiber 11g; Cholesterol 28mg; Iron 4mg; Sodium 661mg; Calcium 139mg

peppered flank steak with chive-buttermilk mashers

pictured on page 4 and back cover

Prep: *15 minutes* **Cook:** *25 minutes*
Marinate: *30 minutes*
Serves 4

Here's a meat-and-potatoes meal you can feel good about eating.

¹/₄	cup balsamic vinegar
1	(1-pound) flank steak, trimmed
4¹/₂	cups cubed Yukon gold potatoes (about 1¹/₂ pounds)
¹/₂	cup low-fat buttermilk
1	tablespoon butter
1	tablespoon chopped fresh chives
1	teaspoon salt, divided
³/₄	teaspoon seasoned pepper
	Cooking spray

1. Combine vinegar and steak in a zip-top plastic bag. Seal; marinate in refrigerator 30 minutes.
2. While steak marinates, place potatoes in a saucepan, and cover with water; bring to a boil. Reduce heat; simmer 15 minutes or until tender; drain. Return potatoes to pan. Add buttermilk, butter, chives, and ¾ teaspoon salt; beat with a mixer at medium speed until smooth. Keep warm.
3. Preheat broiler.
4. Remove steak from bag; discard marinade. Sprinkle steak with ¼ teaspoon salt and seasoned pepper. Place steak on broiler pan coated with cooking spray; broil 6 minutes on each side or until desired degree of doneness. Cut steak diagonally across the grain into thin slices. Serve with mashed potatoes.

PER SERVING (3 ounces beef and 1 cup potatoes): Calories 377 (29% from fat); Fat 12g (sat 6g, mono 5g, poly 1g); Protein 28g; Carbohydrate 39g; Fiber 3g; Cholesterol 67mg; Iron 3mg; Sodium 731mg; Calcium 57mg

beef and green beans with black bean sauce

pictured on page 160

Prep: *30 minutes* **Cook:** *13 minutes*
Marinate: *20 minutes*
Serves 6

Fermented black beans are small black soy beans preserved in salt. Find them in Asian markets.

- 1 (12-ounce) flank steak, trimmed
- 1 tablespoon cornstarch
- 6 tablespoons low-sodium soy sauce, divided
- 5 tablespoons minced garlic, divided
- 6 tablespoons sake (rice wine), divided
- 1/4 cup fermented black beans, rinsed and drained
- 3 tablespoons minced peeled fresh ginger
- 1 teaspoon crushed red pepper
- 3/4 cup fat-free, less-sodium chicken broth
- 1 1/2 tablespoons sugar
- 1 1/2 teaspoons cornstarch
- 4 cups (2-inch) cut green beans
- 3 tablespoons vegetable oil, divided
- 2 1/2 cups sliced red onion
- 2 cups red bell pepper strips
- 4 1/2 cups hot cooked long-grain rice

1. Cut steak with the grain into 2-inch-thick slices. Cut slices diagonally into thin strips. Combine steak, cornstarch, 3 tablespoons soy sauce, 2 tablespoons minced garlic, and 3 tablespoons sake in a large bowl; stir to coat. Cover and marinate in refrigerator 20 minutes.
2. Combine black beans, 3 tablespoons garlic, ginger, and crushed red pepper. Set aside.
3. Combine 3 tablespoons soy sauce, 3 tablespoons sake, chicken broth, sugar, and 1 1/2 teaspoons cornstarch in a medium bowl, stirring with a whisk. Set aside.
4. Place green beans in a large saucepan of boiling water; cook 4 minutes. Drain and plunge beans into ice water; drain.
5. Heat 1 tablespoon vegetable oil in a large nonstick skillet or wok over medium-high heat. Drain beef; discard marinade. Add beef to pan; stir-fry 2 minutes. Remove beef from pan. Wipe pan with paper towels. Heat 2 tablespoons vegetable oil in pan. Add bean mixture and onion; stir-fry 1 minute. Add bell pepper; stir-fry 1 1/2 minutes. Add green beans and soy sauce mixture. Bring to a boil; cook 4 minutes or until thick. Add beef. Serve with rice.

PER SERVING (1 1/3 cups beef mixture and 3/4 cup rice): Calories 440 (27% from fat); Protein 21g; Fat 13g (sat 3g, mono 6g, poly 2g); Carbohydrate 55g; Fiber 4g; Cholesterol 29mg; Iron 5mg; Sodium 725mg; Calcium 89mg

grilled mexican pizzas

Prep: *14 minutes* **Cook:** *13 minutes*
Serves 8

With over 240 milligrams of calcium per serving, this recipe is a great way to get more calcium in your diet.

- 2 leeks (about 1 pound)
- 2 fresh poblano chiles
- 1/4 teaspoon adobo seasoning
- 2 (6-ounce) filet mignon steaks
  Cooking spray
- 1/2 cup fire-roasted garlic salsa
- 1/3 cup tomato chutney
- 2 (8-ounce) packages small Italian cheese-flavored pizza crusts (such as Boboli)
- 3/4 cup (3 ounces) shredded reduced-fat Monterey Jack cheese

1. Remove roots, outer leaves, and tops from leeks, leaving 2 inches of dark leaves; set aside. Cut chiles in half lengthwise; discard stems, seeds, and membranes. Set aside.
2. Prepare grill.
3. Sprinkle adobo seasoning evenly over steaks. Place steaks, leeks, and chile halves on grill rack coated with cooking spray; cover and grill 5 minutes. Turn steaks and vegetables; cover and grill an additional 5 minutes or until steaks are desired degree of doneness. Slice steaks and vegetables into thin strips.
4. Combine salsa and chutney; stir well. Spread evenly over 4 pizza crusts. Top each crust evenly with steak and vegetable strips; sprinkle evenly with cheese. Place pizzas on grill rack coated with cooking spray; cover and grill 3 minutes or until cheese melts. Serve immediately.

NOTE: If tomato chutney isn't available in your area, combine 3 tablespoons fire-roasted garlic salsa and 2 tablespoons sun-dried tomato paste. If fire-roasted garlic salsa isn't available, stir 1 teaspoon bottled roasted minced garlic into any basic salsa. Grilling adds a great smokey flavor to these pizzas, but the steak and vegetables may also be broiled. Then bake pizzas at 425° for 5 minutes.

PER SERVING (1/2 pizza): Calories 278 (29% from fat); Protein 19g; Fat 9g (sat 3g, mono 1g, poly 0g); Carbohydrate 29g; Fiber 1g; Cholesterol 34mg; Iron 3mg; Sodium 592mg; Calcium 247mg

dijon pot roast and vegetables

pictured on page 158

Prep: *17 minutes* **Cook:** *8 hours 15 minutes*
Serves 9

Dijon mustard and beef broth add flavor and gently braise the roast and vegetables.

1	(3-pound) boned chuck roast
3	Vidalia or other sweet onions, each cut into 6 wedges
1½	pounds carrots, cut into 2-inch pieces
2	bay leaves
½	cup beef broth
¼	cup Dijon mustard
3	tablespoons red wine vinegar
1	tablespoon Worcestershire sauce
1½	teaspoons dried thyme
1½	teaspoons dried parsley
¾	teaspoon coarsely ground black pepper
½	teaspoon salt
3	garlic cloves, crushed
3½	tablespoons all-purpose flour
3	tablespoons water
1	(12-ounce) package wide egg noodles

1. Trim fat from roast.
2. Place roast in a 5-quart electric slow cooker; add onion, carrot, and bay leaves. Combine broth and next 8 ingredients (broth through garlic); stir well, and pour over roast. Cover with lid; cook on low-heat setting for 8 hours.
3. Place roast, onion, and carrot on a platter; set aside, and keep warm. Discard bay leaves. Reserve cooking liquid in slow cooker (turn cooker to high-heat setting). Combine flour and 3 tablespoons water in a small bowl; stir with a whisk until blended. Add flour mixture to reserved liquid in slow cooker; cook, uncovered, on high-heat setting 15 minutes or until thick, stirring frequently.
4. Cook noodles according to package directions, omitting salt and fat. Drain. Spoon gravy over roast and vegetables. Serve with noodles.

PER SERVING (3 ounces beef, 2 onion wedges, ⅑ of carrots, 1 cup noodles, and ⅓ cup gravy): Calories 411 (21% from fat); Protein 39g; Fat 10g (sat 3g, mono 3g, poly 4g); Carbohydrate 40g; Fiber 4g; Cholesterol 126mg; Iron 7mg; Sodium 538mg; Calcium 54mg

braised beef with prunes and caramelized onions

pictured on page 158

Prep: *15 minutes* **Cook:** *2 hours 50 minutes*
Serves 6

Follow the step-by-step photos on braising on the next page to ensure your roast comes out moist, juicy, and flavorful.

1	cup dry red wine
1	tablespoon Worcestershire sauce
2	teaspoons grated lemon rind
1	(2-pound) beef brisket
½	teaspoon salt
¼	teaspoon pepper
1	tablespoon vegetable oil
1	pound small boiling onions (about 20), peeled
1	cup pitted prunes
¼	cup water
2	tablespoons tomato paste
½	teaspoon paprika
¼	teaspoon ground allspice
1⅓	cups beef broth, divided
1	teaspoon cornstarch
4½	cups hot cooked medium egg noodles (4½ cups uncooked)

1. Preheat oven to 325°.
2. Combine first 3 ingredients (wine through rind) in a small bowl; set aside.
3. Trim fat from brisket. Sprinkle salt and pepper over both sides of brisket.
4. Heat oil in an ovenproof Dutch oven over medium-high heat until very hot. Add brisket; cook 2 minutes on each side or until browned. Remove from pan; set aside. Reduce heat to medium. Add onions, prunes, and water; cook 8 minutes or until onions are golden, stirring frequently. Stir in tomato paste, paprika, and allspice. Return brisket to pan, placing over onion mixture. Pour wine mixture and 1¼ cups broth over brisket; bring to a simmer.
5. Cover pan with a tight-fitting lid; bake at 325° for 2½ hours or until brisket is tender. Remove brisket from pan; keep warm. Combine remaining beef broth and cornstarch; stir well. Place pan over medium-high heat; bring liquid to a boil. Add cornstarch mixture, and cook 1 minute or until thick, scraping pan to loosen browned bits. Return brisket to pan; spoon sauce evenly over brisket. Serve over noodles.

PER SERVING (about 2½ ounces beef, ¾ cup sauce, and ¾ cup noodles): Calories 455 (26% from fat); Protein 29g; Fat 13g (sat 4g, mono 7g, poly 1g); Carbohydrate 56g; Fiber 6g; Cholesterol 102mg; Iron 5mg; Sodium 553mg; Calcium 58mg

How to Braise Meats

Braising is basically a moist heat cooking method which tenderizes food and produces a tasty sauce. Because you use a small amount of liquid, the food is simmered and steamed, maximizing its flavors and tenderizing it. This method is ideal for tougher cuts of meat, such as London broil, top and bottom round, brisket, and flank steak.

1. Heat oil in a large ovenproof Dutch oven over medium-high heat until very hot. Add meat, turning to sear on both sides.

2. Remove meat, leaving browned bits in pan to add flavor and color. Add onions, prunes, water, and seasonings; sauté to blend flavors.

3. Return meat to pan, placing over onion mixture. Pour wine-broth mixture over meat; bring to a simmer. Cover pan with tight-fitting lid, and bake.

4. After braising, meat should be so tender you can tear it apart easily with two forks.

chili meat loaf

Prep: *8 minutes* **Cook:** *45 minutes*
Stand: *5 minutes*
Serves 6

Served with a side of slaw and corn bread, this Tex-Mex main dish is a nice change from barbecued chicken or pork.

- 1 cup chopped onion
- ¾ cup hickory-flavored barbecue sauce (such as KC Masterpiece), divided
- ½ cup dry breadcrumbs
- 1 tablespoon chili powder
- ½ teaspoon hot sauce
- 1 (16-ounce) can kidney beans, drained
- 2 large egg whites, lightly beaten
- ¾ pound lean ground pork
- Cooking spray

1. Preheat oven to 375°.
2. Combine chopped onion, ½ cup barbecue sauce, breadcrumbs, and next 4 ingredients (chili powder through egg whites) in a large bowl; stir well. Crumble pork over bean mixture, and stir just until blended. Shape mixture into a 7½ x 3½-inch loaf. Place in an 11 x 7-inch baking dish coated with cooking spray. Spread remaining ¼ cup barbecue sauce over top of loaf.
3. Bake at 375° for 45 minutes or until an instant-read thermometer registers 160°. Let stand 5 minutes before slicing.

PER SERVING (⅙ of loaf): Calories 297 (29% from fat); Protein 22g; Fat 10g (sat 3g, mono 2g, poly 2g); Carbohydrate 30g; Fiber 3g; Cholesterol 47mg; Iron 3mg; Sodium 569mg; Calcium 72mg

cantonese pork with honey-ginger glaze

Prep: *10 minutes* **Cook:** *30 minutes*
Stand: *15 minutes*
Serves 4

Cantonese cuisine, unique to the southeast region of China, is famous for its roasted meats.

Cooking spray
- 1/4 cup honey
- 2 tablespoons sherry
- 1 tablespoon hoisin sauce
- 1 tablespoon minced peeled fresh ginger
- 2 garlic cloves, minced
- 1/2 teaspoon dry mustard
- 1 (1-pound) pork tenderloin
- 2 cups uncooked instant brown rice
- 1/4 cup chopped scallions

Salt and freshly ground black pepper

1. Preheat oven to 450°.
2. Coat a shallow roasting pan with cooking spray; set aside.
3. In a large shallow dish, whisk together honey, sherry, hoisin sauce, ginger, garlic, and mustard. Add pork, and turn to coat. Transfer pork to prepared pan, and pour any remaining marinade over it. Roast at 450° for 20 minutes, or until an instant-read thermometer inserted deep into the meat reads 160°. Remove from oven, cover pork with foil, and let stand 10 minutes.
4. Meanwhile, in a medium-sized saucepan over high heat, bring 2 cups water to a boil. Add rice, reduce heat to low, cover, and cook 5 minutes. Remove from heat, and let stand 5 minutes. Add scallions, and fluff with a fork. Season to taste with salt and pepper.
5. Transfer pork to a cutting board, and cut crosswise into 1-inch-thick slices.
6. Place pork slices on serving plates, and drizzle remaining marinade from roasting pan over pork. Serve with rice.

PER SERVING (3 ounces pork and 1/4 of rice): Calories 380 (12% from fat); Protein 28g; Fat 5g (sat 1g, mono 2g, poly 0g); Carbohydrate 56g; Fiber 2g; Cholesterol 67mg; Iron 2mg; Sodium 133mg; Calcium 33mg

barbecued pork and broccoli stir-fry

Prep: *20 minutes* **Cook:** *45 minutes*
Marinate: *1 hour* **Stand:** *5 minutes*
Serves 4

Similar to the dish you've probably seen on the menu at Asian restaurants, this version cuts the fat way down and adds an extra serving of vegetables.

- 1/3 cup hoisin sauce
- 3 tablespoons ketchup
- 2 tablespoons sake (rice wine)
- 1 tablespoon low-sodium soy sauce
- 1 tablespoon minced garlic
- 1 pound pork tenderloin, trimmed

Cooking spray
- 3/4 cup fat-free, less-sodium chicken broth
- 3 tablespoons oyster sauce
- 2 tablespoons sake (rice wine)
- 2 teaspoons cornstarch
- 1 1/2 teaspoons sugar
- 1 teaspoon dark sesame oil
- 1 1/2 tablespoons vegetable oil
- 1/4 cup minced green onions
- 2 tablespoons minced garlic
- 1 1/2 tablespoons minced peeled fresh ginger
- 4 cups small broccoli florets
- 3 cups hot cooked basmati rice

1. Preheat oven to 375°.
2. Combine first 5 ingredients (hoisin through garlic) in a large zip-top plastic bag. Add pork; seal and marinate in refrigerator 1 hour, turning bag occasionally. Remove pork from bag, reserving 1/4 cup marinade. Discard remaining marinade.
3. Place pork on a broiler pan coated with cooking spray; insert meat thermometer into thickest portion of pork. Bake at 375° for 35 minutes or until thermometer registers 160°. Let stand 5 minutes. Cut pork in half lengthwise. Cut each half crosswise into 1/4-inch-thick slices; keep warm.
4. Combine chicken broth and next 5 ingredients (chicken broth through sesame oil) in a bowl. Set aside.
5. Heat vegetable oil in a wok or large Dutch oven over high heat. Add onions, garlic, and ginger; stir-fry 10 seconds. Add reserved marinade, oyster sauce mixture, and broccoli; bring to a boil over high heat. Cook 1 1/2 minutes or until slightly thickened, stirring constantly. Stir in pork; cook 1 minute or until thoroughly heated. Serve over rice.

PER SERVING (1 cup pork mixture and 3/4 cup rice): Calories 460 (19% from fat); Protein 32g; Fat 9g (sat 3g, mono 4g, poly 2g); Carbohydrate 59g; Fiber 3g; Cholesterol 75mg; Iron 5mg; Sodium 974mg; Calcium 62mg

Maple-Mustard Pork Roast, page 162

Braised Beef with Prunes and Caramelized Onions
page 154

Dijon Pot Roast and Vegetables, page 154

Southwestern Grilled Flank Steak, page 151 and Marinated Tomato Salad, page 191

Spinach and Bacon Spaghettini, page 165

Chili-Crusted Flank Steak Fajitas, page 152

Asian Barbecued Pork, page 161

*Beef and Green Beans
with Black Bean Sauce,
page 153*

asian barbecued pork

pictured on page 159

Prep: *5 minutes* **Cook:** *23 minutes*
Stand: *5 minutes*
Serves 4

Plan ahead, and you'll have two dinners ready: 1.) this recipe, and 2.) the recipe at right, Asian Pork Stir-Fry.

Cooking spray
1   (1¹/₂-pound) pork tenderloin, trimmed
¹/₈   teaspoon salt
2   tablespoons hoisin sauce
2   tablespoons ketchup
2   tablespoons low-sodium soy sauce
1   teaspoon chili garlic sauce (such as Lee Kum Kee)
2   garlic cloves, crushed
1¹/₂   teaspoons minced peeled fresh ginger
Chopped fresh cilantro (optional)

1. Preheat oven to 425°.
2. Heat a large ovenproof skillet coated with cooking spray over medium-high heat. Sprinkle pork with salt. Add pork to pan; cook 2 minutes on all sides or until browned. Remove pork from heat.
3. Combine hoisin sauce and next 5 ingredients (hoisin through ginger) in a small bowl. Spread hoisin mixture over tenderloin. Insert meat thermometer into thickest portion of tenderloin. Bake at 425° for 15 minutes or until thermometer registers 160°. Place pork on a platter; let stand 5 minutes. Reserve 8 ounces (about ⅓) of tenderloin for Asian Pork Stir-Fry. Cut remaining tenderloin into ¼-inch-thick slices. Garnish with cilantro, if desired.

NOTE: Hoisin sauce and chili garlic sauce may be found in the Asian-food section of most large supermarkets.

PER SERVING (about 3 ounces pork): Calories 175 (30% from fat); Protein 26g; Fat 6g (sat 2g, mono 2g, poly 1g); Carbohydrate 3g; Fiber 0g; Cholesterol 80mg; Iron 1mg; Sodium 362mg; Calcium 8mg

asian pork stir-fry

Prep: *25 minutes* **Cook:** *10 minutes*
Serves 5

This recipe uses leftover tenderloin from Asian Barbecued Pork. You can substitute 8 ounces of cooked teriyaki-marinated pork tenderloin.

8   ounces green beans
2   tablespoons peanut oil, divided
2   cups sliced onion
1¹/₂   tablespoons chopped peeled fresh ginger
4   garlic cloves, minced
1   cup red bell pepper, cut into thin strips
¹/₃   cup cream sherry
1   tablespoon cornstarch
8   ounces Asian Barbecued Pork (recipe at left), sliced into thin strips
¹/₂   cup fat-free, less-sodium chicken broth
3   tablespoons low-sodium soy sauce
1   teaspoon hoisin sauce
¹/₄   teaspoon crushed red pepper
2²/₃   cups hot cooked rice

1. Trim green bean ends; remove strings. Place beans into a large saucepan of boiling water; cook 3 minutes. Drain and plunge beans into ice water; drain. Set aside.
2. Heat 1 tablespoon oil in a nonstick skillet over medium-high heat. Add onion, ginger, and garlic; cook 3 minutes or until onions are crisp-tender, stirring frequently. Remove mixture from pan; set aside.
3. Heat remaining 1 tablespoon oil in pan over medium-high heat. Add bell pepper strips; cook 3 minutes or until crisp-tender, stirring frequently.
4. Combine sherry and cornstarch in a small bowl.
5. Add green beans, onion mixture, pepper strips, cornstarch mixture, Asian Barbecued Pork, and next 4 ingredients (broth through red pepper) to pan. Bring to a boil, stirring constantly. Cook 1 minute or until sauce thickens. Serve with rice.

PER SERVING (1 cup stir-fry and ²/₃ cup rice): Calories 467 (24% from fat); Protein 31g; Fat 12g (sat 3g, mono 5g, poly 3g); Carbohydrate 53g; Fiber 5g; Cholesterol 75mg; Iron 4mg; Sodium 879mg; Calcium 62mg

The Light and Lean of Pork

Today's pork offers more nutrient value for fewer calories than before. Packed with essential vitamins and minerals, pork is a smart choice in a healthful eating plan and is considered a lean meat. An average 3-ounce serving of lean pork contains 200 calories or less and has only 80 milligrams of cholesterol. And less than one-third of the fat in pork is saturated.

In fact, most trimmed cuts of pork, with the exception of ribs, are lean and some may even be extra lean. Good cuts to try are the tenderloin, loin roast, and sirloin or loin chops. If you're in a hurry, check out the premarinated pork tenderloins and loin roasts.

carolina-style barbecued pork sandwiches

Prep: *17 minutes* **Cook:** *22 minutes*
Stand: *5 minutes*
Serves 4

For a taste of the South, serve these sandwiches with Piccalilli-Flavored Salsa, page 63.

  1 (1-pound) pork tenderloin
 1/4 cup dark brown sugar, divided
 1/4 cup cider vinegar
  2 tablespoons ketchup
 1/2 teaspoon salt, divided
 1/4 teaspoon ground red pepper, divided
  1 teaspoon paprika
  1 teaspoon ground cumin
 1/2 teaspoon dry mustard
 1/4 teaspoon garlic powder
Cooking spray
  4 (2-ounce) sesame seed sandwich rolls, split
 12 dill pickle slices

1. Trim fat from pork, and set pork aside.
2. Combine 2 teaspoons brown sugar, vinegar, ketchup, 1/4 teaspoon salt, and 1/8 teaspoon ground red pepper; stir well. Set sauce aside.
3. Combine remaining brown sugar, remaining salt, remaining red pepper, paprika, and next 3 ingredients (cumin through garlic powder); stir well. Rub mixture over pork.
4. Prepare grill.
5. Place pork on grill rack coated with cooking spray; cover and grill 22 minutes or until thermometer registers 160° (slightly pink), turning pork occasionally.
6. Remove pork from grill; let stand 5 minutes. Cut pork into 1/4-inch-thick slices. Spoon 1 tablespoon sauce onto bottom half of each roll; top with sliced pork and remaining sauce. Top each sandwich with 3 pickle slices and top half of roll.

NOTE: To prepare indoors, place a grill pan over medium heat until hot; coat with cooking spray. Add pork, and cook 24 minutes or until thermometer registers 160° (slightly pink), turning occasionally.

PER SERVING (1 sandwich): Calories 330 (20% from fat); Protein 32g; Fat 7g (sat 2g, mono 2g, poly 2g); Carbohydrate 35g; Fiber 1g; Cholesterol 84mg; Iron 4mg; Sodium 1,005mg; Calcium 84mg

maple-mustard pork roast

pictured on page 157

Prep: *14 minutes* **Cook:** *2 hours*
Stand: *10 minutes*
Serves 10

Maple-flavored light syrup adds a touch of sweetness and helps the breadcrumb coating stick to the meat.

  1 (2 1/2-pound) lean, boneless pork loin roast
 1 1/2 tablespoons Dijon mustard
  2 teaspoons light maple-flavored syrup
 1 1/4 cups fresh whole wheat breadcrumbs
  1 tablespoon dried parsley
  2 teaspoons cracked pepper
 1/2 teaspoon dried marjoram
 1/4 teaspoon salt
 1/8 teaspoon garlic powder
Cooking spray
Parsley sprigs (optional)
Maple-Mustard Sauce

1. Preheat oven to 325°.
2. Trim fat from pork loin roast. Combine mustard and syrup, and spread evenly over roast. Combine breadcrumbs and next 5 ingredients (breadcrumbs through garlic powder); press into mustard mixture, coating roast with crumb mixture.
3. Place roast on a broiler pan coated with cooking spray, and insert meat thermometer into thickest portion of roast.
4. Bake at 325° for 1 1/2 hours. Cover loosely with foil to prevent crumb mixture from burning; bake an additional 30 minutes or until meat thermometer registers 160° (slightly pink).
5. Remove from oven; uncover and let stand 10 minutes before slicing. Garnish with parsley sprigs, if desired. Serve with Maple-Mustard Sauce.

maple-mustard sauce:

 1 1/2 tablespoons all-purpose flour
 3/4 cup evaporated fat-free milk
 1/2 cup fat-free chicken broth
  2 tablespoons Dijon mustard
  1 tablespoon light maple-flavored syrup
 1/4 teaspoon salt
 1/4 teaspoon pepper

1. Place flour in a medium saucepan. Gradually add milk and chicken broth, stirring with a whisk until blended. Stir in mustard and remaining ingredients. Place over medium heat; cook 10 minutes or until thick and bubbly, stirring constantly. Yield: 1 1/4 cups.

PER SERVING (3 ounces pork and 2 tablespoons sauce): Calories 222 (35% from fat); Protein 27g; Fat 9g (sat 3g, mono 4g, poly 1g); Carbohydrate 7g; Fiber 0g; Cholesterol 72mg; Iron 1mg; Sodium 398mg; Calcium 69mg

margarita pork with black bean salsa

Prep: *23 minutes* **Cook:** *30 minutes*
Marinate: *2 hours* **Stand:** *10 minutes*
Serves 6

- 1/3 cup fresh lime juice
- 1/3 cup tequila
-   2 tablespoons brown sugar
-   2 teaspoons bottled minced roasted garlic
-   2 teaspoons low-sodium soy sauce
-   1 dried New Mexican chile
-   1 (1-pound) pork tenderloin
-   1 (10-ounce) package saffron rice mix (such as Mahatma)
- Cooking spray
-   1 cup chopped red bell pepper
-   1 cup chopped tomato
-   1 (15-ounce) can black beans, drained

1. Combine first 5 ingredients (lime juice through soy sauce); stir well, and set aside. Remove and discard stem and seeds from chile, keeping chile intact.
2. Place a small skillet over medium-high heat until hot. Add chile, and cook 1 minute on each side or until chile is blackened. Add lime juice mixture, and remove from heat. Cover and let cool. Place chile mixture in a food processor, and process until smooth.
3. Trim fat from pork tenderloin. Combine pork and chile mixture in a large zip-top plastic bag; seal bag. Marinate in refrigerator 2 hours, turning bag occasionally.
4. Prepare rice mix according to package directions, omitting fat. Set aside, and keep warm.
5. Prepare grill.
6. Remove pork from bag, reserving marinade. Place pork on grill rack coated with cooking spray; cover and grill 20 minutes or until instant-read thermometer registers 160° (slightly pink), turning pork occasionally. Let stand 10 minutes, and cut into 1/4-inch-thick slices.
7. Combine reserved marinade and bell pepper in a large skillet; bring to a boil. Reduce heat, and simmer 5 minutes. Stir in tomato and black beans; cook until thoroughly heated. Spoon rice onto plates, and top with pork slices. Spoon bean mixture over pork and rice.

PER SERVING (3 ounces pork, 2/3 cup rice, and 1/2 cup bean mixture): Calories 355 (9% from fat); Protein 25g; Fat 3g (sat 1g, mono 1g, poly 0g); Carbohydrate 56g; Fiber 4g; Cholesterol 53mg; Iron 4mg; Sodium 1,036mg; Calcium 63mg

smoked spicy pork roast

Prep: *24 minutes* **Cook:** *4 hours*
Marinate: *8 hours* **Stand:** *10 minutes*
Serves 12

If you need help preparing this recipe, refer to the step-by-step photos on smoking chicken (page 176). Serve with hamburger buns or barbecue bread and barbecue sauce.

-   1 tablespoon cumin seeds
-   1 tablespoon coriander seeds
- 1 1/2 teaspoons black peppercorns
- 1 1/2 teaspoons mustard seeds
-   1 tablespoon dark brown sugar
- 2 1/4 teaspoons chili powder
- 1 1/2 teaspoons paprika
- 1/2 teaspoon salt
- 1/4 teaspoon ground red pepper
- 1/4 teaspoon ground cinnamon
-   1 (3-pound) lean, boneless pork loin roast
-   4 (3-inch) chunks mesquite wood
-   6 (12-ounce) cans beer or 9 cups hot water

1. Place a small skillet over medium heat until hot. Add first 4 ingredients (cumin seeds through mustard seeds); sauté 2 minutes or until fragrant. Remove from heat; let cool completely. Place spice mixture in a spice grinder, mini food processor, or blender; process until ground.
2. Combine freshly ground spices, brown sugar, and next 5 ingredients (chili powder through cinnamon); set aside. Trim fat from roast; rub spice mixture evenly over roast. Place roast in a large heavy-duty zip-top plastic bag; seal bag, and marinate in refrigerator 8 hours, turning bag occasionally.
3. Soak mesquite chunks in water 30 minutes to 1 hour. Drain well.
4. Prepare charcoal fire in meat smoker; let burn 15 to 20 minutes or until center coals are covered with gray ash. Place soaked mesquite wood chunks on top of coals. Place water pan in smoker, and add beer or hot water to pan to within 1 inch of rim.
5. Place roast on rack in smoker; insert meat thermometer into thickest portion of roast. Cover with smoker lid; cook 4 hours or until thermometer registers 160° (slightly pink). Refill water pan with water, and add charcoal to fire as needed.
6. Remove roast from smoker; let stand 10 minutes before slicing.

PER SERVING (3 ounces pork): Calories 211 (51% from fat); Protein 23g; Fat 12g (sat 4g, mono 4g, poly 1g); Carbohydrate 1g; Fiber 0g; Cholesterol 77mg; Iron 1mg; Sodium 162mg; Calcium 14mg

florentine ham and potato casserole

Prep: *20 minutes* **Cook:** *1 hour 38 minutes*
Serves 6

2	pounds Yukon gold or red potatoes
	Cooking spray
2	cups sliced mushrooms
1/2	cup chopped onion
1	garlic clove, minced
1/4	cup fat-free, less-sodium chicken broth
1	(10-ounce) package frozen chopped spinach, thawed, drained, and squeezed dry
1	teaspoon salt, divided
1/2	teaspoon pepper, divided
3/4	cup chopped reduced-fat ham
2 1/2	cups 1% low-fat milk
2	tablespoons all-purpose flour
4	large eggs, lightly beaten
1/2	cup (2 ounces) shredded fontina cheese
2	tablespoons grated Parmesan cheese

1. Place potatoes in a stockpot; cover with water (to 2 inches above potatoes); bring to a boil. Cook 40 minutes or until tender. Drain. Cool; peel and cut into 1/4-inch-thick slices.
2. Heat a large nonstick skillet coated with cooking spray over medium-high heat. Add mushrooms; sauté 5 minutes. Add onion and garlic; sauté 3 minutes. Add broth; cook until evaporated. Stir in spinach, 1/2 teaspoon salt, and 1/4 teaspoon pepper.
3. Preheat oven to 350°.
4. Place half the potatoes in a single layer on the bottom of an 11 x 7-inch baking dish. Spoon mushroom mixture over potatoes; sprinkle with ham. Layer remaining potatoes over top.
5. Combine 1/2 teaspoon salt, 1/4 teaspoon pepper, milk, flour, and eggs. Pour over potatoes (dish will be full). Bake at 350° for 30 minutes. Sprinkle with cheeses; bake an additional 20 minutes.

PER SERVING (1/6 of casserole): Calories 328 (25% from fat); Protein 20g; Fat 9g (sat 4g, mono 3g, poly 1g); Carbohydrate 43g; Fiber 2g; Cholesterol 166mg; Iron 4mg; Sodium 909mg; Calcium 294mg

smokey ham and bean corn bread pizzas

Prep: *13 minutes* **Cook:** *9 minutes*
Serves 8

1	(10-ounce) package frozen chopped broccoli, thawed and drained
1 2/3	cups diced lean smoked ham (about 1/2 pound)
1	(15-ounce) can navy beans, rinsed and drained
1/4	teaspoon pepper
1	(11.5-ounce) can refrigerated corn bread twists dough
	Cooking spray
1	cup (4 ounces) shredded reduced-fat sharp Cheddar cheese

1. Preheat oven to 425°.
2. Pat broccoli dry with paper towels. Combine broccoli, ham, beans, and pepper. Stir well.
3. Separate dough into 8 slices. Place 1 slice on a baking sheet coated with cooking spray, and roll into a 5 1/2-inch circle. Repeat with remaining slices. Place 1/2 cup ham mixture onto each crust; sprinkle evenly with cheese. Bake at 425° for 9 minutes or until crusts are golden.

PER SERVING (1 pizza): Calories 266 (35% from fat); Protein 17g; Fat 11g (sat 4g, mono 1g, poly 0g); Carbohydrate 28g; Fiber 3g; Cholesterol 25mg; Iron 3mg; Sodium 940mg; Calcium 164mg

bourbon-glazed ham steaks

Prep: *7 minutes* **Cook:** *11 minutes*
Serves 4

To make this dish a little more kid-friendly, substitute the same amount of apple juice for the bourbon.

1/4	cup bourbon
3	tablespoons brown sugar
3	tablespoons apple juice concentrate, undiluted
1/2	teaspoon stone-ground mustard
	Cooking spray
4	(3-ounce) slices lean boneless ham (such as Hormel Cure 81)

1. Combine bourbon, brown sugar, apple juice concentrate, and mustard; stir well, and set aside.
2. Coat a large nonstick skillet with cooking spray, and place over medium-high heat until hot. Add ham slices, and cook 2 minutes on each side or until lightly browned. Reduce heat to medium-low, and add bourbon mixture. Cook 7 minutes or until bourbon mixture is slightly thick, stirring mixture and turning ham occasionally. Cut each slice in half, if desired. Place slices on individual plates; top evenly with bourbon mixture.

PER SERVING (1 ham slice): Calories 149 (28% from fat); Protein 15g; Fat 5g (sat 2g, mono 0g, poly 0g); Carbohydrate 12g; Fiber 0g; Cholesterol 45mg; Iron 1mg; Sodium 876mg; Calcium 9mg

microwave risotto with ham and corn

Prep: *10 minutes* **Cook:** *32 minutes*
Serves 6

Put your microwave to work while you relax. This hands-free, one-pot meal is going to become your new favorite comfort food.

  2 cups chopped onion
1½ cups uncooked Arborio rice
  3 tablespoons olive oil
 ½ cup white wine
  1 (14-ounce) can fat-free,
     less-sodium chicken broth
  2 cups hot water
1½ cups cubed ham
  1 cup coarsely chopped red bell
     pepper
 ¾ cup frozen corn kernels
 ¼ cup shredded provolone
     cheese
 ¼ cup grated fresh Parmesan
     cheese
 ½ teaspoon salt
 ¼ teaspoon freshly ground black
     pepper
 ¼ cup chopped fresh flat-leaf
     parsley

1. Combine first 3 ingredients (onion through oil) in a 2-quart casserole dish; microwave at HIGH 5 minutes. Stir in wine and broth; microwave at HIGH 12 minutes.
2. Stir in water and ham; microwave at HIGH 12 minutes. Stir in bell pepper and next 5 ingredients (bell pepper through black pepper); microwave at HIGH 3 minutes. Stir in parsley. Serve immediately.

PER SERVING (1 cup): Calories 415 (26% from fat); Fat 12g (sat 3g, mono 6g, poly 1g); Protein 17g; Carbohydrate 57g; Fiber 3g; Cholesterol 19mg; Iron 1mg; Sodium 943mg; Calcium 129mg

spinach and bacon spaghettini

pictured on page 159

Prep: *20 minutes* **Cook:** *10 minutes*
Serves 4

Just a little bit of bacon adds ample richness to this simple dish.

 12 ounces uncooked spaghettini
     or thin spaghetti noodles
  4 slices bacon
 ¼ to ½ teaspoon crushed red
     pepper
  3 garlic cloves, minced
  1 (6-ounce) package fresh baby
     spinach
 ¾ cup (3 ounces) grated fresh
     Pecorino Romano cheese
 ½ teaspoon salt

1. Cook noodles according to package directions, omitting fat and salt. Drain pasta over a small bowl, reserving ½ cup cooking liquid.
2. Cook bacon in a large non-stick skillet over medium heat until crisp. Remove bacon; reserve 1 tablespoon drippings in pan. Crumble bacon; set aside. Add red pepper and garlic to pan; cook 30 seconds. Add spinach; cook 1 minute or until slightly wilted. Remove from heat. Add pasta, reserved cooking liquid, cheese, and salt. Toss gently. Sprinkle with bacon.

PER SERVING (1½ cups): Calories 481 (24% from fat); Protein 21g; Fat 13g (sat 6g, mono 4g; poly 1g); Carbohydrate 70g; Fiber 5g; Cholesterol 33mg; Iron 5mg; Sodium 685mg; Calcium 264mg

moroccan lamb meat loaf

Prep: *10 minutes* **Cook:** *45 minutes*
Stand: *5 minutes*
Serves 4

If you can't find lean ground lamb at the meat counter, ask your butcher to grind a lean boneless leg of lamb or shoulder.

  1 cup finely chopped onion
 ⅓ cup golden raisins
 ¼ cup uncooked bulgur or
     cracked wheat
 ¼ cup chopped fresh mint
 ¼ cup coarsely chopped
     pimiento-stuffed olives
  2 tablespoons lemon juice
  1 teaspoon ground cumin
 ½ teaspoon salt
 ½ teaspoon ground coriander
 ¼ teaspoon ground red pepper
  2 large egg whites, lightly beaten
  1 pound lean ground lamb
Cooking spray

1. Preheat oven to 375°.
2. Combine first 11 ingredients (onion through egg whites) in a bowl; stir well. Crumble lamb over onion mixture; stir just until blended. Shape mixture into an 8 x 4-inch loaf. Place loaf in 11 x 7-inch baking dish coated with cooking spray.
3. Bake at 375° for 45 minutes or until an instant-read thermometer registers 145° (medium-rare) to 160° (medium). Let stand 5 minutes before slicing.

PER SERVING (¼ of loaf): Calories 318 (30% from fat); Protein 32g; Fat 11g (sat 4g, mono 3g, poly 4g); Carbohydrate 24g; Fiber 4g; Cholesterol 91mg; Iron 4mg; Sodium 515mg; Calcium 55mg

rosemary-mustard lamb chops

Prep: *4 minutes* **Cook:** *16 minutes*
Marinate: *30 minutes*
Serves 4

A savory marinade infuses lamb chops with fabulous flavor, and grilling seals in the moistness.

>   2 tablespoons Dijon mustard
>   2 tablespoons chopped fresh
>   rosemary
> ¹/₄ teaspoon salt
> ¹/₄ teaspoon pepper
>   2 garlic cloves, minced
>   8 (4-ounce) lean lamb loin chops
>   (about 1¹/₄ inches thick)
> Cooking spray

1. Combine first 5 ingredients (mustard through garlic) in a small bowl; stir well. Rub mixture evenly over both sides of lamb chops. Place chops on a baking sheet or platter; cover and marinate in refrigerator at least 30 minutes.
2. Prepare grill.
3. Place lamb loin chops on grill rack coated with cooking spray; grill 8 minutes on each side or until lamb is desired degree of doneness.

NOTE: To prepare indoors, place a grill pan over high heat until hot; coat with cooking spray. Add lamb, and cook 8 minutes on each side or until desired degree of doneness.

PER SERVING (2 lamb chops): Calories 203 (39% from fat); Protein 27g; Fat 9g (sat 3g, mono 4g, poly 1g); Carbohydrate 2g; Fiber 1g; Cholesterol 86mg; Iron 3mg; Sodium 459mg; Calcium 40mg

A Quick Cooking Tip for Lamb

Lamb is a lean, healthy meat. While this is good news for your health, it can be bad news for your dinner plan if you don't watch the cooking time. Most meat thermometers recommend an internal temperature of 180° to 185°, but because most of lamb's fat is on the outside, not the inside, the meat will usually be tough and dry if it's well done. For the best flavor and tenderness, cook lamb only until it's pink: medium-rare (145°) or medium (160°).

wine-braised lamb shanks with white beans

Prep: *30 minutes* **Cook:** *1 hour 15 minutes*
Serves 4

The step-by-step photos on braising (page 155) may come in handy when you're preparing this recipe.

>   3 tablespoons all-purpose flour
> ³/₄ teaspoon freshly ground black
>   pepper
>   4 (10-ounce) lamb shanks,
>   trimmed
>   1 tablespoon olive oil
>   1 medium onion, chopped
>   4 garlic cloves, minced
>   1 cup fat-free beef broth
>   1 cup dry red wine, such as
>   merlot
> 1¹/₂ teaspoons dried rosemary,
>   crushed
>   1 pound baby carrots
>   1 (19-ounce) can cannellini
>   beans, rinsed and drained
> Rosemary sprigs (optional)

1. Preheat oven to 350°.
2. Combine flour and pepper in a plastic. Add lamb shanks (in batches if necessary); shake to coat well. Reserve any remaining flour in bag.
3. Heat a 5-quart Dutch oven or ovenproof covered casserole over medium heat. Add oil; when it's hot, add lamb shanks (in batches if necessary). Brown shanks on all sides, about 10 minutes. Transfer shanks to a plate; set aside.
4. Pour off all but 1 teaspoon drippings from Dutch oven. Add onion and garlic; cook 4 minutes, stirring occasionally. Sprinkle reserved flour mixture over vegetables; cook and stir 1 minute. Add broth, wine, and dried rosemary; bring to a boil, scraping up any browned bits from bottom of Dutch oven. Return lamb shanks to Dutch oven. Cover; cook at 350° for 45 minutes. Stir in carrots; cover and continue to braise 30 minutes or until lamb is fork tender.
5. Remove from oven, and transfer lamb shanks and carrots to a serving platter. Tent with foil; keep warm. Spoon off and discard fat from pan juices. Boil pan juices in Dutch oven over high heat until thickened, about 3 minutes; stir in beans, and heat thoroughly. Spoon bean mixture over shanks and carrots; garnish with rosemary sprigs, if desired.

PER SERVING (4 ounces lamb and ¹/₄ of bean mixture): Calories 339 (27% from fat); Protein 28g; Fat 10g (sat 2g, mono 5g, poly 1g); Carbohydrate 34g; Fiber 7g; Cholesterol 66mg; Iron 5mg; Sodium 434mg; Calcium 89mg

succulent poultry

Smoked Chicken,
page 176

barbecue chicken and corn pizza

pictured on page 178

Prep: *10 minutes* **Cook:** *10 minutes*
Serves 6

We liked this pizza best made with Bull's Eye original barbecue sauce.

1 (1-pound) package Italian cheese-flavored pizza crust (such as Boboli)
1/2 cup barbecue sauce, divided
1 (4.69-ounce) package ready-to-eat roasted skinless, boneless chicken breast, chopped (such as Tyson)
1/2 cup fresh corn kernels (1 ear)
1 1/4 cups (5 ounces) shredded Monterey Jack cheese

1. Preheat oven to 450°.
2. Place crust on a baking sheet; spread 1/4 cup sauce over crust. Combine remaining 1/4 cup barbecue sauce and chicken in a bowl; stir well. Spoon chicken mixture over crust; top evenly with corn and cheese. Bake at 450° for 10 minutes or until cheese melts.

PER SERVING (1/6 of pizza): Calories 366 (31% from fat); Protein 223g; Fat 13g (sat 6g, mono 3g, poly 1g); Carbohydrate 39g; Fiber 2g; Cholesterol 44mg; Iron 3mg; Sodium 862mg; Calcium 263mg

roasted pepper, chicken, and goat cheese pizza

Prep: *13 minutes* **Cook:** *24 minutes*
Serves 6

Goat cheese and roasted red peppers make savory toppings on crusty French bread slices. This pizza can also be cut into small bites and served as an appetizer.

1 (12-ounce) bottle roasted red bell peppers, undrained
Cooking spray
1 cup thinly sliced shallots
1 (16-ounce) loaf French bread
2 (6-ounce) packages Italian-flavored ready-to-eat skinless, boneless chicken breast strips (such as Louis Rich)
1 (3.5-ounce) package goat cheese, crumbled

1. Preheat oven to 425°.
2. Drain bell peppers, reserving liquid. Chop bell peppers; set aside.
3. Coat a medium nonstick skillet with cooking spray; place over medium-high heat until hot. Add shallots; sauté 5 minutes or until lightly browned. Reduce heat to medium; add bell peppers and reserved liquid. Cook 5 minutes or until most of liquid evaporates.
4. Cut bread loaf in half horizontally; place on a baking sheet. Spread shallot mixture evenly over cut sides of each piece of bread; top with chicken strips and goat cheese. Bake at 425° for 10 minutes.

PER SERVING (1/6 of pizza): Calories 388 (23% from fat); Protein 25g; Fat 10g (sat 5g, mono 2g, poly 1g); Carbohydrate 49g; Fiber 4g; Cholesterol 50mg; Iron 4mg; Sodium 1,101mg; Calcium 122mg

curried chicken and vegetable couscous

Prep: *10 minutes* **Cook:** *14 minutes*
Stand: *5 minutes*
Serves 8

2 teaspoons olive oil
1 cup frozen chopped onion
4 cups fat-free, less-sodium chicken broth, divided
1 (16-ounce) package frozen mixed vegetables
1 (15-ounce) can chickpeas (garbanzo beans), drained
1 (10-ounce) can chunk white chicken in water, drained
1/2 cup golden raisins
1/4 cup hot mango chutney
1 tablespoon lemon juice
2 1/2 teaspoons curry powder
2 garlic cloves, minced
1/4 teaspoon ground red pepper
2 tablespoons water
1 (10-ounce) package couscous
1/4 cup chopped unsalted, dry-roasted peanuts

1. Heat oil in a nonstick skillet over medium-high heat. Add onion; sauté 3 minutes. Add 2 cups broth, vegetables, and next 8 ingredients (vegetables through pepper); bring to a boil. Cover, reduce heat, and simmer 6 minutes or until vegetables are tender.
2. Bring remaining 2 cups broth and 2 tablespoons water to a boil in a saucepan. Add couscous; stir well. Remove from heat; cover. Let stand 5 minutes. Fluff couscous with a fork.
3. Spoon couscous into individual bowls; top with vegetable mixture. Sprinkle with peanuts.

PER SERVING (about 2/3 cup couscous, 3/4 cup vegetable mixture, and 1 1/2 teaspoons peanuts): Calories 414 (14% from fat); Protein 21g; Fat 6g (sat 1g, mono 2g, poly 1g); Carbohydrate 70g; Fiber 6g; Cholesterol 0mg; Iron 3mg; Sodium 560mg; Calcium 36mg

peanut noodles with chicken

Prep: *15 minutes* **Cook:** *10 minutes*
Stand: *5 minutes*
Serves 6

Fettuccine and chicken take on an Asian accent in this flavorful dish.

- 8 ounces uncooked fettuccine
- 2 cups chopped roasted skinless, boneless chicken breast
- 2 cups thinly sliced red bell pepper
- 1 teaspoon dark sesame oil
- 2 garlic cloves, minced
- 1 tablespoon minced peeled fresh ginger
- $2/3$ cup water
- $1/3$ cup natural-style peanut butter, well-stirred
- $1/3$ cup hoisin sauce
- 1 tablespoon seasoned rice wine vinegar
- $1/2$ teaspoon Asian chile sauce
- $1/2$ cup chopped green onions
- $1/2$ cup chopped fresh cilantro

1. Cook pasta according to package directions, omitting salt and fat. Combine chicken and bell pepper in a colander. Drain pasta over chicken mixture; let stand 5 minutes.
2. Heat oil in a small saucepan over medium-high heat; add garlic and ginger. Cook 1 minute, stirring frequently; add water and next 4 ingredients (water through chile sauce). Cook 1 minute or until thoroughly heated, stirring with a whisk. Combine pasta mixture and sauce in a large bowl; toss to coat. Stir in onions and cilantro.

PER SERVING ($1^{1}/3$ cups): Calories 334 (28% from fat); Protein 21g; Fat 11g (sat 2g, mono 5g, poly 3g); Carbohydrate 41g; Fiber 3g; Cholesterol 33mg; Iron 2mg; Sodium 317mg; Calcium 39mg

saucy chicken lo mein

pictured on page 177

Prep: *15 minutes* **Cook:** *13 minutes*
Serves 6

This saucy stir-fry delivers a healthy serving of fresh vegetables.

- 8 ounces uncooked linguine
- $1/3$ cup low-sodium soy sauce
- 2 tablespoons sake (rice wine)
- $1^{1}/2$ teaspoons dark sesame oil
- 1 tablespoon cornstarch
- $1/2$ teaspoon sugar
- $1/4$ teaspoon freshly ground black pepper
- 2 tablespoons vegetable oil
- $3^{1}/2$ cups fresh bean sprouts
- 3 cups (1-inch) sliced green onions
- 2 cups shredded carrot
- 2 tablespoons minced peeled fresh ginger
- $1^{1}/2$ cups shredded cooked chicken breast (about 8 ounces)

1. Cook pasta according to package directions, omitting salt and fat; drain and keep warm.
2. While pasta is cooking, combine soy sauce and next 5 ingredients (soy sauce through pepper) in a bowl, stirring with a whisk; set aside.
3. Heat vegetable oil in a wok over medium-high heat. Add sprouts, onions, carrot, and ginger; stir-fry 3 minutes or until tender. Add chicken; stir-fry 1 minute or until thoroughly heated. Stir in soy sauce mixture and pasta; cook 4 minutes until pasta is coated, stirring well.

PER SERVING ($1^{1}/3$ cups): Calories 333 (24% from fat); Protein 19g; Fat 9g (sat 2g, mono 3g, poly 4g); Carbohydrate 44g; Fiber 5g; Cholesterol 31mg; Iron 4mg; Sodium 527mg; Calcium 69mg

jerk-spiced chicken couscous

pictured on page 54

Prep: *11 minutes* **Cook:** *8 minutes*
Stand: *5 minutes*
Serves 6

- 1 pound chicken breast tenders, cut into 1-inch cubes
- 1 tablespoon Jamaican jerk seasoning
- 1 teaspoon vegetable oil
- 1 (15.75-ounce) can fat-free, less-sodium chicken broth
- 1 (10-ounce) box plain, uncooked couscous
- $1/3$ cup golden raisins
- $1/3$ cup dried sweet cherries
- $1/4$ cup orange juice
- $1/4$ cup red wine vinegar
- 2 tablespoons olive oil
- $1/2$ teaspoon salt
- $1/2$ teaspoon pepper
- $1/8$ teaspoon ground nutmeg
- $1/2$ cup sliced green onions
- $1/4$ cup minced fresh cilantro
- 2 tablespoons sliced almonds

1. Combine chicken and jerk seasoning in a zip-top plastic bag; seal and shake well. Heat oil in a large nonstick skillet over medium-high heat. Add chicken, and cook 3 minutes. Add broth; bring to a boil. Add couscous, raisins, and cherries; stir well. Remove from heat; cover and let stand 5 minutes. Fluff with a fork.
2. Combine orange juice and next 5 ingredients (orange juice through nutmeg) in a bowl; stir with a whisk. Pour over chicken mixture. Top with onions, cilantro, and almonds.

PER SERVING (1 cup): Calories 386 (18% from fat); Protein 25g; Fat 8g (sat 1g, mono 5g, poly 1g); Carbohydrate 52g; Fiber 4g; Cholesterol 44mg; Iron 1mg; Sodium 570mg; Calcium 37mg

milanese chicken breasts

Prep: *10 minutes* **Cook:** *18 minutes*
Serves 4

Dishes prepared Milanese style are typically dipped in breadcrumbs and cheese, and then fried in butter. We omitted the butter to keep the fat low, and added a mustard-chutney sauce to boost the flavor.

- 2 garlic cloves, minced
- 2 tablespoons Dijon or hot Dijon mustard, divided
- 1/4 teaspoon pepper
- 4 (4-ounce) skinless, boneless chicken breast halves
- 3/4 cup toasted breadcrumbs
- 1/2 cup grated Parmesan or Romano cheese
- 1/4 cup mango or cranberry chutney

1. Preheat oven to 450°.
2. In a bowl, combine garlic, 1 tablespoon mustard, and pepper; mix well. Spread mixture over 1 side of each chicken breast half.
3. In a shallow plate or pie plate, combine breadcrumbs and cheese; mix well. Press each piece of chicken, mustard side down, into crumbs; transfer, crumb side up, to a baking sheet. Sprinkle any remaining crumb mixture over chicken. Bake at 450° until chicken is cooked through and coating is a deep golden brown (about 18 minutes).
4. In a small bowl, combine remaining 1 tablespoon mustard and chutney. Serve sauce with chicken.

PER SERVING (1 chicken breast half and 1 tablespoon sauce): Calories 242 (23% from fat); Fat 6g (sat 3g, mono 2g, poly 1g); Protein 33g; Carbohydrate 13g; Fiber 1g; Cholesterol 76mg; Iron 2mg; Sodium 542mg; Calcium 210mg

chicken sauté with peaches and basil

Prep: *10 minutes* **Cook:** *15 minutes*
Serves 4

If you use fresh peaches in this recipe, blanch them in boiling water for 1 minute. Peel, pit, and cut into 1/2-inch-thick wedges to measure 2 cups.

- 1/2 teaspoon salt
- 1/4 teaspoon freshly ground black pepper
- 4 (4-ounce) skinless, boneless chicken breast halves
- 2 tablespoons butter
- 2 cups fresh or frozen sliced peaches
- 3/4 cup fat-free, less-sodium chicken broth
- 1/4 cup chopped shallots
- 1/4 teaspoon finely grated lemon zest
- 3 large fresh basil leaves, torn

1. Combine salt, pepper, and chicken in a zip-top plastic bag. Seal and shake well. Melt butter in a large nonstick skillet over medium-high heat until bubbly. Add chicken, and cook 5 minutes per side until cooked through. Transfer to a plate, and cover with foil; keep warm.
2. Combine peaches, broth, shallots, and lemon zest in skillet with drippings. Bring to a simmer, and cook 3 minutes or until heated through.
3. Remove from heat, and stir in basil. Spoon sauce and peaches over chicken.

PER SERVING (1 chicken breast half and 1/2 cup peach mixture): Calories 224 (28% from fat); Protein 28g; Fat 7g (sat 4g, mono 2g, poly 1g); Carbohydrate 12g; Fiber 2g; Cholesterol 81mg; Iron 1mg; Sodium 511mg; Calcium 26mg

dijon chicken-mushroom stroganoff

pictured on page 179

Prep: *15 minutes* **Cook:** *28 minutes*
Serves 4

- 1 cup fat-free chicken broth
- 1 cup water
- 1/2 cup chopped onion
- 2 tablespoons Dijon mustard
- 1 teaspoon dried thyme
- 1/4 teaspoon salt
- Dash of white pepper
- 1 garlic clove, minced
- 1 (8-ounce) package fresh mushrooms
- 4 (4-ounce) skinless, boneless chicken breast halves
- 1/2 cup low-fat sour cream
- 2 cups hot cooked egg noodles (about 4 ounces uncooked)
- Thyme sprigs (optional)

1. Combine first 9 ingredients (broth through mushrooms) in a skillet. Bring to a boil. Cover, reduce heat, and simmer 5 minutes (poaching liquid will appear curdled). Arrange chicken in a single layer in pan; cover and simmer 15 minutes (do not boil). Remove from pan with a slotted spoon; keep warm.
2. Bring poaching liquid to a boil. Cook, uncovered, 8 minutes or until reduced to 1/2 cup. Remove from heat; let cool slightly. Stir in sour cream. Return chicken and juices to pan, turning chicken to coat.
3. Serve chicken and sauce over noodles. Garnish with thyme sprigs, if desired.

PER SERVING (1/2 cup cooked noodles, 1 chicken breast half, and about 1/3 cup sauce): Calories 307 (21% from fat); Protein 33g; Fat 7g (sat 3g, mono 1g, poly 1g); Carbohydrate 26g; Fiber 3g; Cholesterol 103mg; Iron 3mg; Sodium 583mg; Calcium 67mg

chicken roulade with mushroom-tarragon cream sauce

pictured on page 179

Prep: *29 minutes* **Cook:** *52 minutes*
Stand: *10 minutes*
Serves 6

A mixture of finely chopped mushrooms, onions, and shallots is cooked in butter and then used as a filling in this chicken roll.

- 1 tablespoon light butter , divided
- 1 (8-ounce) package fresh cremini or button mushrooms, sliced
- 1 tablespoon chopped shallots (about 1 small)
- 2 garlic cloves, chopped
- 1/2 cup dry white wine
- 3/4 pound skinless, boneless chicken breast halves
- 10 sheets frozen phyllo dough, thawed
- Cooking spray
- 1/2 cup fresh spinach leaves
- 3/4 cup (3 ounces) crumbled feta cheese
- 2 tablespoons all-purpose flour
- 1 cup 1% low-fat milk
- 1/2 cup 1/3-less-salt chicken broth
- 2 teaspoons chopped fresh or 1/2 teaspoon dried tarragon
- 1/2 teaspoon sea salt or salt
- 1/2 teaspoon freshly ground black pepper
- Additional freshly ground black pepper (optional)

1. Preheat oven to 375°.
2. Melt 2 teaspoons butter in a large nonstick skillet over medium-high heat. Add mushrooms, shallot, and garlic; sauté 3 minutes or until mushrooms are tender. Add wine; bring to a boil. Reduce heat, and simmer, uncovered, 5 minutes or until most of liquid evaporates. Remove from heat; let cool.

3. Place each chicken breast half between 2 sheets of heavy-duty plastic wrap; flatten to 1/4-inch thickness, using a meat mallet or rolling pin. Set aside.
4. Place 1 phyllo sheet on a large baking sheet coated with cooking spray (cover remaining dough to keep from drying); lightly coat phyllo with cooking spray. Repeat procedure with remaining phyllo and cooking spray, forming a stack of phyllo.
5. Place chicken breasts along 1 long edge of phyllo stack, leaving a 1-inch border around edges. Place spinach leaves over chicken; top with mushroom mixture and feta cheese. Fold over short edges of phyllo to cover 1 inch of chicken mixture on each end. Fold over long edge of phyllo to cover 1 inch of chicken mixture, and roll up jelly-roll fashion. Lightly coat top of roulade with cooking spray.
6. Bake at 375° for 30 minutes or until an instant-read thermometer inserted in center registers 160°. Let stand 10 minutes.
7. Place flour in a saucepan. Gradually add milk and chicken broth, stirring with a whisk until blended. Stir in remaining 1 teaspoon butter, tarragon, salt, and pepper. Place over medium heat, and cook 8 minutes or until sauce is thick and coats the back of a spoon.
8. Cut roulade into 6 slices. Spoon 3 1/2 tablespoons sauce on each of 6 plates; place roulade slices on sauce. Sprinkle with additional pepper, if desired. Serve immediately.

PER SERVING: Calories 270 (30% from fat); Protein 21g; Fat 9g (sat 5g, mono 2g, poly 1g); Carbohydrate 25g; Fiber 1g; Cholesterol 58mg; Iron 3mg; Sodium 687mg; Calcium 163mg

chicken with lemon-caper sauce

pictured on page 178

Prep: *5 minutes* **Cook:** *15 minutes*
Serves 4

Splashes of tart lemon juice and bites of tangy capers transform the plain chicken breast into a mouth-watering dish.

- 1/4 teaspoon salt, divided
- 1/4 teaspoon pepper, divided
- 4 (4-ounce) skinless, boneless chicken breast halves
- 1 tablespoon olive oil
- Cooking spray
- 1/3 cup extra-dry vermouth
- 3 tablespoons fresh lemon juice
- 1 1/2 tablespoons capers
- 1 tablespoon chopped fresh parsley

1. Sprinkle 1/8 teaspoon salt and 1/8 teaspoon pepper over chicken. Heat oil in a large nonstick skillet coated with cooking spray over medium-high heat. Add chicken; cook 6 minutes on each side or until done. Remove from pan. Set aside; keep warm.
2. Add 1/8 teaspoon salt, 1/8 teaspoon pepper, vermouth, lemon juice, and capers to pan, scraping pan to loosen browned bits. Cook until reduced to 1/4 cup (about 2 minutes). Stir in parsley. Spoon sauce over chicken.

PER SERVING (1 chicken breast half and 1 tablespoon sauce): Calories 163 (27% from fat); Protein 27g; Fat 5g (sat 1g, mono 3g, poly 1g); Carbohydrate 2g; Fiber 0g; Cholesterol 66mg; Iron 1mg; Sodium 474mg; Calcium 17mg

spicy korean chicken

Prep: *10 minutes* **Cook:** *35 minutes*
Serves 4

Red pepper flakes heat up this dish; decrease the amount or omit them if you don't care for so much heat.

Cooking spray
- ¹/₄ cup all-purpose flour
- 4 (6-ounce) skinless chicken breast halves (bone-in)
- 2 tablespoons reduced-sodium soy sauce
- 2 tablespoons mirin or rice wine
- 2 tablespoons honey
- 2 teaspoons hot chili-sesame oil (or regular dark sesame oil)
- ¹/₂ teaspoon garlic powder
- ¹/₂ teaspoon crushed red pepper flakes
- 1 cup uncooked jasmine rice
- 1 green bell pepper, seeded and finely chopped
- ¹/₄ teaspoon salt
- ¹/₈ teaspoon freshly ground black pepper

1. Preheat oven to 400°.
2. Coat a baking sheet with cooking spray; set aside.
3. Place flour in a shallow dish, add chicken, and turn to lightly coat both sides. Shake off excess flour; set aside.
4. In a shallow dish, whisk together soy sauce, mirin, honey, chili-sesame oil, garlic powder, and red pepper flakes. Add chicken, and turn to coat.
5. Arrange chicken on prepared baking sheet, and pour any remaining honey mixture over it. Roast at 400° for 35 minutes, or until chicken is cooked through.
6. Meanwhile, in a medium-sized saucepan over medium-high heat, bring 2 cups water to a boil. Add jasmine rice, reduce heat to low, cover, and cook 15 minutes, or until rice is tender and liquid is absorbed. Add green pepper, and fluff with a fork. Sprinkle with salt and pepper. Serve chicken with rice.

PER SERVING (1 chicken breast half and about 1 cup rice): Calories 412 (12% from fat), Fat 5g (sat 1g, mono 1g, poly 1g); Protein 32g; Carbohydrate 59g; Fiber 2g; Cholesterol 72mg; Iron 2mg; Sodium 343mg; Calcium 20mg

coq au vin

Prep: *15 minutes* **Cook:** *40 minutes*
Serves 4

Coq au vin, a classic French dish, combines chicken and vegetables in a rich wine-flavored broth.

- ¹/₄ cup all-purpose flour
- 2 teaspoons paprika
- 2 teaspoons dried thyme
- ¹/₂ teaspoon salt
- ¹/₂ teaspoon freshly ground black pepper
- 4 (6-ounce) chicken breast halves (bone-in)
- 1 tablespoon olive or vegetable oil
- 12 cipollini onions, medium shallots, or large pearl onions, peeled
- 1 pound button mushrooms, halved if large
- 1 pound baby carrots
- 1 cup white wine
- 1 cup fat-free, less-sodium chicken broth
- 2 tablespoons chopped fresh thyme (optional)

1. Preheat oven to 350°.
2. Combine flour, paprika, thyme, salt, and pepper in a plastic or paper bag. Rinse chicken in cold water; shake off excess water. Add chicken to flour mixture 1 or 2 pieces at a time, shaking to coat. Reserve flour mixture remaining in bag.
3. Heat a 5-quart Dutch oven or oven-proof covered casserole over medium heat until hot. Add oil; when it's hot, add chicken, meaty side down, and cook 4 minutes or until golden brown. Turn; continue to cook 3 minutes. Transfer chicken to a plate; set aside.
4. Add onions, mushrooms, and carrots to Dutch oven; cook 1 minute, stirring often. Add reserved flour mixture; mix well. Add wine and broth; bring to a boil. Set reserved chicken over vegetables and cover; cook at 350° for about 40 minutes or until chicken is cooked through.
5. With a slotted spoon, transfer chicken and vegetables to a serving platter; tent with foil, and keep warm. Boil pan juices in Dutch oven over high heat until reduced to 1¹/₂ cups (about 8 minutes). Serve chicken and vegetables with pan juices. Garnish with chopped fresh thyme, if desired.

PER SERVING (about 3 ounces chicken and ¹/₄ vegetable mixture): Calories: 401 (29% from fat); Fat 13g (sat 3g, mono 3g, poly 1g); Protein 35g; Carbohydrate 27g; Fiber 4g; Cholesterol 82mg; Iron 5mg; Sodium 510mg; Calcium 73mg

lemon-garlic grilled chicken

Prep: *24 minutes* **Cook:** *30 minutes*
Serves 6

To intensify the lemon-garlic flavor, rub the herb mixture under the chicken skin, and chill the chicken until ready to cook. Be sure to remove the skin before serving.

- 3 (6-ounce) chicken breast halves (bone-in)
- 3 (5-ounce) chicken thighs
- 4 garlic cloves, peeled
- 1 cup fresh parsley sprigs
- 1 teaspoon grated lemon rind
- 3 tablespoons fresh lemon juice
- $1/2$ teaspoon salt
- $1/4$ teaspoon pepper
- Garlic-flavored cooking spray

1. Rinse chicken under cold water; pat dry. Loosen skin from chicken by inserting fingers under skin and gently pushing fingers between skin and meat.
2. Drop garlic through food chute with food processor on; process until minced. Add parsley and next 4 ingredients (parsley through pepper); process until finely minced. Rub parsley mixture over chicken under loosened skin. Coat chicken with cooking spray.
3. Prepare grill.
4. Place chicken on grill rack; cover and grill 30 minutes or until chicken is done, turning occasionally. Remove skin before serving.

PER SERVING (1 chicken breast half or 1 thigh): Calories 188 (35% from fat); Protein 27g; Fat 7g (sat 2g, mono 3g, poly 2g); Carbohydrate 2g; Fiber 1g; Cholesterol 85mg; Iron 2mg; Sodium 286mg; Calcium 31mg

jerk chicken thighs

Prep: *15 minutes* **Cook:** *30 minutes*
Marinate: *4 hours* **Stand:** *5 minutes*
Serves 4

- 2 teaspoons dried thyme
- 1 teaspoon ground allspice
- 1 onion, peeled and quartered (about $1/2$ pound)
- 8 garlic cloves, peeled
- 2 serrano chiles, seeded
- 2 tablespoons fresh lime juice
- 8 chicken thighs, skinned (about 3 pounds)
- Cooking spray
- 2 teaspoons olive oil
- $3/4$ cup uncooked jasmine rice
- 1 (15.75-ounce) can fat-free, less-sodium chicken broth
- $2 1/2$ cups ($1/2$-inch) cubed peeled sweet potato
- 1 (15-ounce) can black beans, rinsed and drained
- $1/4$ cup Pickapeppa sauce (optional)

1. Combine first 5 ingredients (thyme through chiles) in a food processor; process until finely chopped. Remove $1/4$ cup chile mixture, and set aside. Add lime juice to food processor; process until smooth.
2. Arrange chicken in a large shallow dish. Spread lime juice mixture over chicken. Cover and marinate in refrigerator 4 hours.
3. Preheat broiler.
4. Place chicken on a broiler pan coated with cooking spray; broil 15 minutes on each side or until done. Keep warm.
5. Heat oil in a large saucepan over medium-high heat. Add reserved $1/4$ cup chile mixture; sauté 2 minutes. Stir in rice. Add broth; bring to a boil. Cover, reduce heat, and simmer 5 minutes. Stir in sweet potato; cook 10 minutes. Stir in beans; cook 3 minutes or until liquid is absorbed. Remove from heat; let stand, covered, 5 minutes. Drizzle with Pickapeppa sauce, if desired.

PER SERVING (2 chicken thighs, $1 1/3$ cups rice mixture, and 1 tablespoon sauce): Calories 468 (15% from fat); Protein 37g; Fat 8g (sat 2g, mono 3g, poly 2g); Carbohydrate 63g; Fiber 8g; Cholesterol 121mg; Iron 4mg; Sodium 731mg; Calcium 96mg

moroccan chicken thighs

Prep: *9 minutes* **Cook:** *12 minutes*
Stand: *10 minutes*
Serves 4

- 4 (4-ounce) skinless, boneless chicken thighs
- $1 1/2$ teaspoons ground cumin
- 2 teaspoons grated lemon rind
- $1/2$ teaspoon ground ginger
- $1/2$ teaspoon salt
- $1/4$ teaspoon ground cinnamon
- 2 garlic cloves, minced
- 2 teaspoons olive oil
- Cooking spray
- Pita bread (optional)

1. Trim fat from chicken thighs, and set aside.
2. Combine cumin and next 5 ingredients (cumin through garlic) in a large bowl. Brush olive oil evenly over chicken. Add chicken to bowl, and toss well to coat chicken with spice mixture. Let chicken stand 10 minutes.
3. Prepare grill.
4. Place chicken on grill rack coated with cooking spray. Cover; grill 6 minutes on each side or until done. Serve with pita bread, if desired.

PER SERVING (1 thigh): Calories 161 (39% from fat); Protein 23g; Fat 7g (sat 2g, mono 3g, poly 1g); Carbohydrate 1g; Fiber 0g; Cholesterol 94mg; Iron 2mg; Sodium 392mg; Calcium 25mg

braised chicken thighs with artichokes and greek olives

Prep: *15 minutes* **Cook:** *41 minutes*
Serves 8

Braising the chicken in wine and broth makes it extra tender and juicy. For more information on how to braise, see page 155.

  2 tablespoons olive oil
  8 skinless, boneless chicken thighs (about 2 pounds)
  ³/₄ pound cremini mushrooms, quartered
  2 cups chopped onion
  4 garlic cloves, crushed
  ³/₄ cup fat-free, less-sodium chicken broth, divided
  ³/₄ cup red wine, divided
  3 tablespoons balsamic vinegar
  2 tablespoons tomato paste
  2 cups small red potatoes, halved
  ¹/₂ cup kalamata olives, pitted
  ¹/₂ teaspoon salt
  1 teaspoon dried thyme
  ¹/₄ teaspoon freshly ground black pepper
  1 (14-ounce) can water-packed artichoke hearts, drained and quartered
  ¹/₃ cup chopped fresh flat-leaf parsley

1. Heat oil in a large skillet over medium-high heat. Add chicken; cook 3 minutes on each side or until browned. Remove chicken from pan; set aside. Add mushrooms, onion, and garlic; sauté 5 minutes or until tender. Remove from pan. Add ¼ cup broth and ¼ cup wine to pan; stir to loosen browned bits. Stir in vinegar and tomato paste.
2. Return chicken and onion mixture to pan; add ½ cup broth, ½ cup wine, potatoes, and next 5 ingredients (olives through artichokes), stirring gently. Bring to a boil; cover, reduce heat, and simmer 30 minutes or until chicken is done. Sprinkle with parsley.

PER SERVING (1 thigh and about ¹/₂ cup artichoke mixture): Calories 303 (28% from fat); Protein 27g; Fat 9g (sat 2g, mono 4g, poly 1g); Carbohydrate 25g; Fiber 3g; Cholesterol 94mg; Iron 3mg; Sodium 709mg; Calcium 31mg

chicken thighs with wild mushroom sauce and noodles

Prep: *10 minutes* **Cook:** *30 minutes*
Stand: *20 minutes*
Serves 4

Porcini mushrooms are a little pricier than others, but the rich, hearty flavor they impart is well worth the extra cost.

  1¹/₂ cups fat-free, less-sodium chicken broth
  1 cup dried porcini mushrooms (about 1 ounce)
Cooking spray
  1 (8-ounce) package presliced button mushrooms
  8 skinless, boneless chicken thighs (about 2 pounds)
  ¹/₂ teaspoon salt
  ¹/₄ teaspoon freshly ground black pepper
  1 tablespoon chopped fresh or 1 teaspoon dried thyme
  4 cups hot cooked medium egg noodles (about 8 ounces uncooked)

1. Place broth in a microwave-safe bowl. Microwave at HIGH 1½ minutes or until broth comes to a boil; add porcini mushrooms. Cover and let stand 20 minutes or until tender. Strain broth mixture through a sieve into a bowl, reserving liquid. Chop porcini mushrooms.
2. Heat a large skillet coated with cooking spray over medium heat. Add button mushrooms; sauté 5 minutes. Remove from pan.
3. Sprinkle chicken with salt and pepper. Heat pan coated with cooking spray over medium-high heat. Add chicken; cook 4 minutes on each side or until browned. Cover, reduce heat to medium, and cook 10 minutes or until chicken is done. Remove chicken from pan. Stir in reserved liquid, scraping pan to loosen browned bits; cook 1 minute. Add chicken and porcini and button mushrooms to pan; cook 1 minute or until thoroughly heated. Sprinkle with thyme, and serve over hot noodles.

PER SERVING (2 thighs, 6 tablespoons mushroom mixture, and 1 cup noodles): Calories 466 (18% from fat); Protein 48g; Fat 9g (sat 2g, mono 3g, poly 2g); Carbohydrate 46g; Fiber 4g; Cholesterol 194mg; Iron 7mg; Sodium 517mg; Calcium 53mg

Porcini Primer

Porcini mushrooms are one of the more tasty delicacies in the mushroom family. Their earthy, nutty flavor makes them especially good in meat and poultry dishes. Sold both fresh and dried, they're most often found dried in markets in the United States. To rehydrate dried porcinis, simply let the mushrooms soak in hot water for 20 minutes before using.

roast provençal chicken

Prep: *10 minutes* **Cook:** *1 hour 3 minutes*
Serves 6

Vermouth is a dry white wine flavored with aromatic herbs. You may, however, use fat-free, less-sodium chicken broth in its place.

    3 tablespoons hot Dijon mustard
 3¹/₂ teaspoons chopped fresh
       thyme, divided
  ¹/₂ teaspoon black pepper
    1 garlic clove, minced
    1 (3¹/₂-pound) roasting chicken
    1 tablespoon olive oil
 2¹/₂ cups fat-free, less-sodium
       chicken broth, divided
    2 tablespoons all-purpose flour
  ¹/₂ cup dry vermouth
  ¹/₂ teaspoon salt

1. Preheat oven to 400°.
2. Combine mustard, 3 teaspoons thyme, pepper, and garlic in a small bowl.
3. Rinse chicken with cold water; pat dry. Trim excess fat. Starting at neck cavity, loosen skin from breast by inserting fingers between skin and meat. Rub mustard mixture under skin. Lift wing tips up and over back, and tuck under chicken. Brush oil over chicken skin.
4. Place chicken in a large oven-proof skillet. Pour 1½ cups broth around chicken; bake at 400° for 1 hour or until juices run clear.
5. Remove chicken from skillet. Remove and reserve broth mixture. Skim fat from surface of broth; discard fat. Combine reserved broth mixture, 1 cup broth, and flour, stirring with a whisk until blended. Heat skillet over medium-high heat; add vermouth, and cook 2 minutes. Add broth mixture, and bring to a boil; cook 1 minute or until slightly thick, stirring constantly. Stir in ½ teaspoon thyme and salt. Serve chicken with gravy.

PER SERVING (3 ounces chicken and about ¹/₄ cup gravy): Calories 291 (26% from fat); Protein 44g; Fat 8g (sat 2g, mono 3g, poly 2g); Carbohydrate 4g; Fiber 0g; Cholesterol 135mg; Iron 3mg; Sodium 791mg; Calcium 26mg

rosemary-roasted chicken with mushroom-shallot gravy

Prep: *32 minutes* **Cook:** *1 hour 18 minutes*
Serves 4

Roasting the vegetables with the chicken adds a sweet, caramelized flavor to the gravy. For easy cleanup, line the broiler pan with foil before adding the rack.

    1 tablespoon chopped fresh
       rosemary
    1 teaspoon olive oil
  ¹/₂ teaspoon salt
  ¹/₄ teaspoon coarsely ground
       pepper
    1 (3-pound) chicken
       Cooking spray
    2 shallots, halved
    2 unpeeled garlic cloves
    1 (8-ounce) package fresh
       mushrooms
 1¹/₂ tablespoons all-purpose flour
  ³/₄ cup ¹/₃-less-salt chicken broth
  ¹/₃ cup 2% reduced-fat milk
    1 tablespoon dry sherry
       Rosemary sprigs (optional)

1. Preheat oven to 375°.
2. Combine 1 tablespoon rosemary, oil, salt, and pepper in a small bowl; stir well.
3. Remove and discard giblets and neck from chicken. Rinse chicken under cold water, and pat dry. Trim excess fat. Starting at neck cavity, loosen skin from breast and drumsticks by inserting fingers, gently pushing between skin and meat. Rub rosemary mixture under loosened skin over breast and drumsticks. Lift wing tips up and over back, and tuck under chicken.
4. Place chicken, breast side up, on a broiler pan coated with cooking spray. Insert meat thermometer into meaty part of thigh, making sure not to touch bone. Coat shallots and garlic cloves with cooking spray, and arrange around chicken. Bake at 375° for 40 minutes. Coat mushrooms with cooking spray, and arrange around chicken. Bake an additional 30 minutes or until thermometer registers 180°.
5. Remove chicken from broiler pan, reserving pan drippings. Place chicken on a platter; cover loosely with foil. Set aside. Remove vegetables from broiler pan, and slice shallots and mushrooms. Squeeze garlic cloves to extract pulp; place pulp in a medium saucepan. Add flour to pan; gradually add chicken broth and milk, stirring with a whisk until blended. Set aside.
6. Skim fat from reserved drippings. Add skimmed drippings to broth mixture; cook over medium heat 5 minutes or until mixture is thick, stirring constantly with a whisk. Stir in shallots, mushrooms, and sherry; cook until thoroughly heated. Set aside, and keep warm.
7. Remove and discard skin from chicken. Serve chicken with gravy.

PER SERVING (3 ounces chicken and 7 tablespoons gravy): Calories 220 (32% from fat); Protein 25g; Fat 8g (sat 2g, mono 2g, poly 1g); Carbohydrate 11g; Fiber 1g; Cholesterol 71mg; Iron 2mg; Sodium 488mg; Calcium 53mg

How to Smoke Chicken

This cooking method can be addictive, but it's a good habit to pick up. Get started with this recipes and the step-by-step photographs below.

1. Fill charcoal pan with 8 to 10 pounds of briquettes. Carefully light charcoal. Allow to burn 15 to 20 minutes or until coals are covered with gray ash. Place soaked wood chunks on top of coals, using long tongs.

2. Place water pan in smoker. Carefully fill pan with hot water or other liquid as specified in recipe to within 1 inch below the rim of the water pan. Work quickly so smoke and heat do not escape.

3. Coat grill racks with cooking spray for easy cleanup; place racks in the smoker. Arrange food on racks. Cover with smoker lid, and cook food according to recipe directions.

4. Use the access door to add liquid or charcoal. A long heavy-duty metal funnel or watering can with a long spout works best for refilling water pan and long tongs can be used for adding charcoal.

smoked chicken

pictured on pages 167 and 178

Prep: *25 minutes* **Cook:** *3 hours*
Marinate: *2 hours* **Stand:** *10 minutes*
Serves 8

The red-hot habanero is the hottest of all chile peppers. If habanero pepper sauce isn't available, substitute any red hot sauce.

- 2   medium-sized limes
- 1   medium-sized orange
- 2/3   cup sliced green onions
- 1/4   cup habanero pepper sauce
- 1 1/2   tablespoons dried thyme
- 1 1/2   teaspoons ground allspice
- 1   teaspoon freshly ground pepper
- 1/2   teaspoon salt
- 1/4   teaspoon ground cloves
- 3   garlic cloves, peeled
- 2   (3-pound) chickens
- 4   (3-inch) chunks hickory wood

1. Squeeze juice from limes and orange; set citrus rinds aside. Combine citrus juice, onions, and next 7 ingredients (pepper sauce through garlic) in a blender or food processor; process until well blended.

2. Remove and discard giblets and neck from chickens. Rinse chickens under cold water; pat dry. Trim excess fat from chickens. Starting at neck cavities, loosen skin from breasts and drumsticks by gently pushing fingers between skin and meat. Place citrus rinds in body cavities. Tie legs together with string, and lift wings up and over backs; tuck under chickens.

3. Place chickens in a large zip-top plastic bag. Pour juice mixture under loosened skin of chickens. Seal bag, and marinate in refrigerator at least 2 hours, turning bag occasionally.

4. Soak hickory chunks in water 30 minutes to 1 hour. Drain well.

5. Prepare charcoal fire in meat smoker; let burn 15 to 20 minutes or until center coals are covered with gray ash. Place soaked hickory chunks on top of coals. Remove chickens from bag, reserving marinade. Place water pan in smoker; add reserved marinade and hot water to pan to within 1 inch of rim.

6. Place chickens, breast side up, on rack in smoker, allowing enough room between chickens for air to circulate. Insert meat thermometer into thickest portion of thigh, making sure not to touch bone. Cover with lid; cook 3 hours or until thermometer registers 185°. Refill water pan, and add charcoal as needed.

7. Remove chickens from smoker; let stand 10 minutes. Discard skin before serving.

PER SERVING (3 ounces chicken): Calories 158 (31% from fat); Protein 23g; Fat 6g (sat 2g, mono 1g, poly 1g); Carbohydrate 3g; Fiber 1g; Cholesterol 68mg; Iron 2mg; Sodium 258mg; Calcium 38mg

Saucy Chicken Lo Mein,
page 169

Smoked Chicken,
page 176

Barbecue Chicken and Corn
Pizza, page 168

Chicken with Lemon-Caper
Sauce, page 171

*Dijon Chicken-Mushroom
Stroganoff, page 170*

*Chicken Roulade with Mushroom-
Tarragon Cream Sauce,
page 171*

*Turkey Enchiladas Suizas,
page 184*

*Garlic-Rubbed Hen with
Sun-Dried Tomato Sauce
and Polenta, page 181*

cornish hens with port wine sauce

Prep: *20 minutes* **Cook:** *1 hour 36 minutes*
Stand: *10 minutes*
Serves 4

  2 (1¹/₂-pound) Cornish hens
¹/₂ teaspoon sea salt or salt,
       divided
¹/₂ teaspoon freshly ground black
       pepper, divided
Cooking spray
  1 tablespoon butter
¹/₄ cup minced shallots
  2 garlic cloves, minced
³/₄ cup chicken broth
¹/₂ cup port or other sweet red
       wine
¹/₃ cup dried tart cherries
¹/₄ cup black cherry juice (such as
       R.W. Knudsen Family)
  1 teaspoon chopped fresh thyme

1. Preheat oven to 350°.
2. Remove and discard giblets
and necks from hens. Rinse
hens under cold water; pat dry.
Trim excess fat. Starting at neck
cavities, loosen skin from
breasts and drumsticks by gently
pushing fingers between skin
and meat.
3. Rub ¼ teaspoon salt and ¼
teaspoon pepper over breasts
and drumsticks under loosened
skin of hens. Place hens, breast
side up, on a broiler pan coated
with cooking spray. Bake at
350° for 55 minutes or until
juices run clear. Cover hens
loosely with foil; let stand 10
minutes. Discard skin. Split hens
in half lengthwise; set aside, and
keep warm.
4. Melt butter in a medium
saucepan over medium-high
heat. Add shallots and garlic;
sauté 3 minutes. Add remaining
¼ teaspoon salt, ¼ teaspoon
pepper, broth, and next 4 ingredients (port through thyme);

bring to a boil. Reduce heat,
and simmer, uncovered, 30 minutes or until sauce is reduced to
½ cup. Spoon sauce over hens.

PER SERVING (1 hen half and 2 tablespoons sauce):
Calories 221 (30% from fat); Protein 22g; Fat 7g (sat 3g,
mono 2g, poly 1g); Carbohydrate 17g; Fiber 1g;
Cholesterol 101mg; Iron 2mg; Sodium 571mg;
Calcium 39mg

garlic-rubbed hen with sun-dried tomato sauce and polenta

pictured on page 180

Prep: *33 minutes* **Cook:** *2 hours 22 minutes*
Stand: *25 minutes*
Serves 8

  1 (5-pound) hen
  4 garlic cloves, minced
³/₄ teaspoon sea salt or salt,
       divided
Cooking spray
  2 tablespoons olive oil, divided
  1 cup chopped green onions
3¹/₂ cups ¹/₃-less-salt chicken broth,
       divided
¹/₄ cup sun-dried tomato sprinkles
  1 (14¹/₂-ounce) can stewed
       tomatoes with basil, garlic, and
       oregano, chopped
  1 cup water, divided
  1 (0.35-ounce) package dried
       porcini mushrooms
  1 cup yellow cornmeal
¹/₄ cup (1 ounce) shredded fresh
       Parmesan cheese

1. Preheat oven to 350°.
2. Remove and discard giblets
and neck from hen. Rinse hen
under cold water; pat dry. Trim
excess fat. Starting at neck cavity, loosen skin from breast and
drumsticks by gently pushing
fingers between skin and meat.
3. Combine garlic and ½

teaspoon salt. Rub garlic mixture under loosened skin over
breast and drumsticks and into
body cavity. Lift wing tips up
and over back; tuck under hen.
4. Place hen, breast side up, on
a broiler pan coated with cooking spray. Insert meat thermometer into meaty part of
thigh, making sure not to touch
bone. Bake at 350° for 1 hour
and 30 minutes or until thermometer registers 180°. Cover
hen loosely with foil; let stand
10 minutes. Discard skin;
remove meat from bones.
5. Heat 1 tablespoon oil in a large
nonstick skillet over medium-high
heat. Add green onions; sauté 2
minutes. Add ½ cup chicken
broth, sun-dried tomatoes, and
stewed tomatoes; bring to a boil.
Reduce heat, and simmer,
uncovered, 10 minutes or until
slightly thick.
6. Bring ½ cup water to a boil in
a medium saucepan; stir in
mushrooms. Remove from heat;
let stand 15 minutes. Remove
mushrooms from saucepan with
a slotted spoon, and coarsely
chop. Return mushrooms to
water in pan. Add remaining ½
cup water, 3 cups broth, and ¼
teaspoon salt; bring to a boil.
Gradually add cornmeal,
stirring constantly with a whisk.
Reduce heat to medium, and
cook 15 minutes or until thick,
stirring frequently. Remove
from heat; stir in remaining 1
tablespoon oil and cheese.
7. Spoon polenta onto plates;
top with sliced hen. Spoon
tomato sauce over hen and
polenta.

PER SERVING (¹/₂ cup polenta, about 3 ounces hen,
and ¹/₄ cup tomato sauce): Calories 270 (30% from fat);
Protein 31g; Fat 9g (sat 2g, mono 4g, poly 2g);
Carbohydrate 19g; Fiber 3g; Cholesterol 84mg;
Iron 3mg; Sodium 898mg; Calcium 70mg

baked quail with mushrooms and wild rice

Prep: *16 minutes* **Cook:** *1 hour 45 minutes*
Serves 4

Impress your guests with this game winner. It's bound to win raves.

- 1 (6-ounce) package wild rice (about 1 cup uncooked)
- Cooking spray
- 1/2 cup all-purpose flour
- 1/2 teaspoon sea salt or salt
- 1/2 teaspoon freshly ground black pepper
- 8 (4-ounce) semiboned quail, skinned, or 2 (16-ounce) packages frozen semiboned quail, thawed and skinned
- 2 tablespoons olive oil, divided
- 1/2 cup chopped red onion
- 1 (8-ounce) package sliced fresh mushrooms
- 3 cups 1/3-less-salt chicken broth
- 3/4 cup dry sherry
- 2/3 cup seedless red grapes, halved

1. Sprinkle rice in a 13- x 9-inch baking dish coated with cooking spray; set aside.
2. Combine flour, salt, and pepper in a pie plate or shallow dish; stir well. Dredge quail in flour mixture, reserving remaining flour mixture. Heat 1½ tablespoons oil in a large skillet over medium heat. Add quail; cook 2 minutes on each side or until browned. Place quail on top of rice; set aside.
3. Heat ½ teaspoon oil in skillet over medium-high heat. Add onion and mushrooms; sauté 3 minutes or until tender. Spoon over quail.
4. Preheat oven to 350°.
5. Place remaining 1 teaspoon oil in skillet; add reserved flour mixture, stirring with a whisk. Place skillet over medium heat, and cook 1 minute, stirring constantly. Gradually add chicken broth and sherry, stirring with a whisk until well blended. Bring to a boil, stirring constantly. Reduce heat, and simmer 10 minutes or until slightly thick, stirring occasionally. Pour gravy over quail mixture; top with grapes. Cover and bake at 350° for 1 hour and 15 minutes or until rice is tender.

PER SERVING (2 quail and about 3/4 cup rice mixture): Calories 462 (25% from fat); Protein 35g; Fat 13g (sat 3g, mono 6g, poly 2g); Carbohydrate 53g; Fiber 4g; Cholesterol 0mg; Iron 7mg; Sodium 822mg; Calcium 36mg

plum-glazed turkey and vegetables

Prep: *25 minutes* **Cook:** *2 hours 33 minutes*
Serves 12

The red plum jam coats the turkey and sweet potatoes with a sweet, tart glaze.

- 2/3 cup red plum jam
- 1/2 cup apple cider
- 1 tablespoon cornstarch
- 2 teaspoons grated lemon rind
- 2 tablespoons fresh lemon juice
- 3/4 teaspoon dry mustard
- 1/2 teaspoon salt
- 1 cup sliced plums
- 1 (5-pound) whole turkey breast
- Cooking spray
- 4 medium sweet potatoes (about 2 pounds), peeled and each cut into 8 pieces
- 6 large shallots, peeled and quartered

1. Preheat oven to 350°.
2. Combine first 7 ingredients (plum jam through salt) in a medium saucepan; stir well. Bring to a boil; cook 1 minute or until thick and bubbly, stir-ring constantly. Remove from heat; stir in plums. Reserve ½ cup plum mixture in a bowl to brush over cooked turkey.
3. Starting at neck cavity, loosen skin from breast, gently pushing fingers between skin and meat. Spread ½ cup plum mixture over breast meat under skin. Place on a broiler pan coated with cooking spray. Insert meat thermometer into turkey breast, making sure not to touch bone. Bake at 350° for 45 minutes.
4. Combine 2/3 cup plum mixture, sweet potatoes, and shallots in a bowl; toss well to coat. Arrange sweet potato mixture around turkey on broiler pan. Bake at 350° an additional 1 hour and 45 minutes or until thermometer registers 170° and vegetables are tender (cover turkey loosely with foil to prevent overbrowning, if necessary).
5. Place turkey on a serving platter; spoon sweet potato mixture around turkey. Brush reserved ½ cup plum mixture over turkey and sweet potato mixture. Discard skin before serving turkey.

PER SERVING (3 ounces turkey and 1/2 cup sweet potato mixture): Calories 294 (4% from fat); Protein 28g; Fat 1g (sat 0g, mono 0g, poly 0g); Carbohydrate 43g; Fiber 4g; Cholesterol 72mg; Iron 2mg; Sodium 185mg; Calcium 42mg

molasses-glazed turkey breast

Prep: *13 minutes* **Cook:** *1 hour 35 minutes*
Serves 8

- 1 (2-pound) skinless, boneless smoked turkey breast (such as Sara Lee)
- 1 cup molasses
- 1/2 cup brewed coffee
- 2 tablespoons tomato paste
- 2 tablespoons cider vinegar
- 1/4 teaspoon salt
- 1/4 teaspoon freshly ground pepper
- 1 drained canned chipotle chile in adobo sauce
- 1 garlic clove, peeled

1. Preheat oven to 325°.
2. Place turkey in a shallow baking pan; add 1/2 cup water. Cover with foil. Bake at 325° for 45 minutes.
3. Place molasses and remaining 7 ingredients (molasses through garlic) in a blender, and process until smooth. Strain mixture through a sieve into a medium saucepan; discard solids. Bring mixture to a boil over medium-high heat. Reduce heat to medium, and simmer 25 minutes or until mixture is reduced to 1 cup, stirring occasionally.
4. Drain turkey, and return to baking pan. Brush 1/4 cup molasses glaze over turkey. Bake, uncovered, an additional 20 minutes, basting turkey occasionally with pan drippings. Thinly slice turkey, and serve with remaining molasses glaze.

PER SERVING (3 ounces turkey and 1 1/2 tablespoons glaze): Calories 268 (3% from fat); Protein 34g; Fat 1g (sat 0g, mono 0g, poly 0g); Carbohydrate 30g; Fiber 0g; Cholesterol 94mg; Iron 4mg; Sodium 175mg; Calcium 101mg

turkey breast with apple-sage sauce

Prep: *15 minutes* **Cook:** *28 minutes*
Serves 4

- 2 tablespoons all-purpose flour
- 1 tablespoon water
- 1/4 cup reduced-fat sour cream
- 1 teaspoon vegetable oil
- 1 cup quartered fresh mushrooms
- 1 cup coarsely chopped Golden Delicious apple
- 1/2 cup finely chopped onion
- 1 teaspoon sugar
- 1 cup apple juice
- 1 cup fat-free, less-sodium chicken broth
- 1 teaspoon finely chopped fresh sage
- 1/2 teaspoon salt
- 3/4 pound sliced cooked turkey breast
- 4 cups hot cooked long-grain rice

1. Combine flour and water in a bowl; stir with a whisk until blended. Stir in sour cream.
2. Heat oil in a nonstick skillet over medium-high heat. Add mushrooms; sauté 2 minutes. Add apple, onion, and sugar; sauté 4 minutes or until onion is lightly browned. Add apple juice and next 3 ingredients (apple juice through salt); bring to a boil. Reduce heat; simmer 15 minutes or until reduced to 1 1/2 cups. Reduce heat to medium-low. Stir in sour cream mixture; cook 1 minute or until thick, stirring constantly.
3. Add turkey to sauce; cook 2 minutes or until heated. Serve turkey and sauce over rice.

PER SERVING (3 ounces turkey, 1/2 cup sauce, and 1 cup rice): Calories 431 (9% from fat); Protein 32g; Fat 4g (sat 2g, mono 1g, poly 1g); Carbohydrate 63g; Fiber 2g; Cholesterol 78mg; Iron 4mg; Sodium 507mg; Calcium 60mg

turkey with gremolata

Prep: *12 minutes* **Cook:** *1 hour 5 minutes*
Serves 4

Gremolata is a sprightly mixture of lemon zest, parsley, and garlic that adds zing to leftover turkey.

- 2 tablespoons grated lemon rind
- 2 tablespoons minced parsley
- 5 garlic cloves, minced and divided
- Cooking spray
- 2 cups chopped red bell pepper
- 1 cup coarsely chopped onion
- 2 (14-ounce) cans fat-free, less-sodium chicken broth
- 5 thyme sprigs
- 3 cups chopped cooked dark turkey
- 1/4 teaspoon salt
- 1 tablespoon all-purpose flour
- 2 tablespoons water
- 4 cups hot cooked basmati rice

1. Combine lemon rind, parsley, and 2 garlic cloves; stir well.
2. Coat a large nonstick skillet with cooking spray, and place over medium-high heat until hot. Add remaining garlic, pepper, and onion; sauté 5 minutes. Add broth and thyme; bring to a boil. Stir in turkey and salt. Cover, reduce heat to medium-low, and simmer 30 minutes. Increase heat to medium-high; cook, uncovered, 15 minutes.
3. Reduce heat to medium-low. Combine flour and water, stirring until blended. Add to turkey mixture; simmer 5 minutes or until thick, stirring occasionally. Spoon over rice; sprinkle with gremolata.

PER SERVING (3/4 cup turkey mixture and 1 cup rice): Calories 423 (15% from fat); Protein 33g; Fat 7g (sat 2g, mono 1g, poly 2g); Carbohydrate 54g; Fiber 2g; Cholesterol 74mg; Iron 5mg; Sodium 841mg; Calcium 69mg

turkey enchiladas suizas

pictured on page 179

Prep: *22 minutes* **Cook:** *41 minutes*
Serves 6

- ³/₄ cup 33%-less-fat sour cream
- ¹/₄ cup fat-free milk
- 1 tablespoon finely chopped fresh cilantro
- 1 to 2 tablespoons seeded minced jalapeño pepper
- 1 tablespoon fresh lime juice
- 3 garlic cloves, minced and divided
- ¹/₂ teaspoon salt, divided
- Cooking spray
- 1 cup chopped onion
- 1 (14-ounce) can fat-free, less-sodium chicken broth
- 2 cups chopped cooked white and dark turkey
- 2 teaspoons ground cumin
- 12 (6-inch) corn tortillas
- 1 (16-ounce) jar tomatillo salsa
- Cilantro sprigs (optional)

1. Preheat oven to 350°.
2. Combine first 5 ingredients (sour cream through lime juice) in a small bowl. Add 1 garlic clove and ¼ teaspoon salt; stir well, and set aside.
3. Coat a large nonstick skillet with cooking spray; place over medium-high heat until hot. Add onion; sauté 5 minutes or until golden. Add remaining 2 garlic cloves; sauté 1 minute. Add remaining ¼ teaspoon salt, chicken broth, turkey, and cumin. Reduce heat, and simmer, uncovered, 12 minutes or until most of liquid evaporates.
4. Heat tortillas according to package directions. Spread about 2 tablespoons turkey mixture down center of each tortilla; roll up. Place enchiladas, seam side down, in a 13 x 9-inch bak-ing dish. Spread salsa over enchiladas. Cover and bake at 350° for 20 minutes. Drizzle sour cream mixture over enchiladas before serving. Garnish with cilantro sprigs, if desired.

PER SERVING (2 enchiladas): Calories 280 (21% from fat); Protein 21g; Fat 7g (sat 3g, mono 2g, poly 2g); Carbohydrate 33g; Fiber 4g; Cholesterol 47mg; Iron 2mg; Sodium 949mg; Calcium 201mg

tex-mex turkey meat loaf

Prep: *8 minutes* **Cook:** *55 minutes*
Stand: *5 minutes*
Serves 5

- 2 cups (8 ounces) shredded reduced-fat sharp Cheddar cheese
- 1 cup chunky salsa
- ¹/₄ cup canned chopped green chiles
- 1 (15-ounce) can black beans, rinsed and drained
- 1 pound ground turkey breast
- Cooking spray
- Additional chunky salsa (optional)
- Sliced green onions (optional)

1. Preheat oven to 375°.
2. Combine first 4 ingredients (cheese through beans) in a large bowl; stir well. Crumble turkey over bean mixture, and stir just until blended. Shape mixture into a 6½ x 4½-inch loaf. Place loaf in an 11 x 7-inch baking dish coated with cooking spray.
3. Bake at 375° for 55 minutes or until an instant-read thermometer registers 160°. Let stand 5 minutes before slicing. Serve with additional salsa, and garnish with green onions, if desired.

PER SERVING (¹/₅ of loaf): Calories 306 (29% from fat); Protein 38g; Fat 10g (sat 6g, mono 0g, poly 0g); Carbohydrate 17g; Fiber 3g; Cholesterol 78mg; Iron 2mg; Sodium 925mg; Calcium 431mg

turkey hash with poached eggs

Prep: *12 minutes* **Cook:** *30 minutes*
Serves 5

- 2 cups diced peeled baking potato (about 1 pound)
- 1 teaspoon butter
- Cooking spray
- 1 cup chopped onion
- 1 cup chopped celery
- 2 garlic cloves, minced
- 2 cups chopped cooked white and dark turkey
- 2 teaspoons poultry seasoning
- ¹/₄ cup 2% reduced-fat milk
- 2 tablespoons chopped fresh chives
- 1¹/₂ teaspoons chopped fresh thyme
- ¹/₂ teaspoon salt
- ¹/₂ teaspoon pepper
- 5 large eggs, poached
- Cracked black pepper (optional)

1. Place potato in a large saucepan, and cover with water. Bring to a boil, and cook 7 minutes or just until tender. Drain; set aside.
2. Melt butter in a large nonstick skillet coated with cooking spray over medium-high heat. Add onion, celery, and garlic; sauté 10 minutes or until tender and golden. Add potato, turkey, and poultry seasoning; sauté 5 minutes. Reduce heat to medium; stir in milk and next 4 ingredients (milk through pepper). Cook 2 minutes or until thoroughly heated, stirring frequently.
3. Spoon hash onto plates; top with poached eggs. Sprinkle with cracked pepper, if desired.

PER SERVING (1 cup hash and 1 egg): Calories 272 (30% from fat); Protein 25g; Fat 9g (sat 3g, mono 4g, poly 2g); Carbohydrate 21g; Fiber 2g; Cholesterol 259mg; Iron 3mg; Sodium 379mg; Calcium 85mg

fresh, crisp salads

*Chicken-Blue Cheese Salad
with Warm Bacon
Vinaigrette, page 201*

roasted summer fruit salad

Prep: *12 minutes* **Cook:** *13 minutes*
Serves 6

Baking helps to bring out the fruits' natural sugars. Serve this flavorful salad for brunch or as a side dish with pork or ham.

1¹/₂ cups sliced peeled papaya
1¹/₂ cups sliced peeled peaches or
       nectarines
 ³/₄ cup cubed peeled ripe mango
  1 tablespoon fresh lime juice
  1 tablespoon butter, melted
  1 teaspoon sugar
 ¹/₄ cup plus 2 tablespoons
       balsamic vinegar

1. Preheat oven to 475°.
2. Place fruit in an 11 x 7-inch baking dish. Combine lime juice and butter. Drizzle over fruit; sprinkle with sugar. Bake at 475° for 10 minutes.
3. Bring vinegar to a boil in a small saucepan; cook 3 minutes or until vinegar is reduced to 1¹/₂ tablespoons. Drizzle vinegar reduction over roasted fruit, and toss gently.

PER SERVING (¹/₂ cup): Calories 66 (27% from fat); Protein 1g; Fat 2g (sat 0g, mono 1g, poly 1g); Carbohydrate 13g; Fiber 2g; Cholesterol 0mg; Iron 0mg; Sodium 24mg; Calcium 14mg

asian-style slaw

Prep: *9 minutes*
Serves 4

To shred the cabbage, remove any wilted outer leaves; then cut the cabbage in half, remove the core, and thinly slice.

 ¹/₂ cup rice vinegar (unseasoned)
 ¹/₄ cup sugar
  1 tablespoon minced peeled
       fresh ginger
 ¹/₂ teaspoon dark sesame oil
 ¹/₂ teaspoon salt
 ¹/₂ teaspoon crushed red pepper
  5 cups shredded Savoy cabbage
  1 cup matchstick-cut carrots
  1 scallion, cut into 1¹/₂-inch
       julienne pieces
  1 tablespoon thinly sliced fresh
       basil leaves
  1 tablespoon thinly sliced fresh
       mint leaves
  3 tablespoons dry-roasted
       peanuts, chopped

1. Whisk together first 6 ingredients (rice vinegar through red pepper) until sugar is dissolved.
2. In a large bowl, combine cabbage, carrots, scallions, basil, and mint. Add rice vinegar mixture, and toss well to coat. Sprinkle with peanuts.

PER SERVING (about 1 cup slaw and 2 teaspoons peanuts): Calories 116 (23% from fat); Protein 3g; Fat 3g (sat 0g, mono 1g, poly 1g); Carbohydrate 19g; Fiber 4g; Cholesterol 0mg; Iron 1mg; Sodium 361mg; Calcium 49mg

creamy apple-cabbage slaw

Prep: *12 minutes*
Serves 4

Fresh diced apple adds crunch, a splash of color, and a bit of sweetness to the slaw.

  4 cups very thinly sliced cabbage
  2 cups diced Fuji or Red Delicious
       apple (about 1 pound)
 ¹/₂ cup chopped green onions
 ¹/₄ cup chopped fresh parsley
 ¹/₂ cup low-fat sour cream
 ¹/₄ cup plain fat-free yogurt
  2 tablespoons cider vinegar
  2 tablespoons brown sugar
 ¹/₄ teaspoon salt
 ¹/₈ teaspoon pepper
  8 thin slices Fuji apple
 ¹/₄ cup lemon juice

1. Combine first 4 ingredients (cabbage through parsley) in a bowl; toss well. Combine sour cream and next 5 ingredients (sour cream through pepper); add to cabbage mixture, stirring to coat.
2. Toss apple slices with lemon juice; drain apple slices. Serve cabbage mixture with apple slices.

PER SERVING (1 cup cabbage mixture and 2 apple slices): Calories 144 (25% from fat); Protein 3g; Fat 4g (sat 2g, mono 1g, poly 0g); Carbohydrate 27g; Fiber 4g; Cholesterol 12mg; Iron 1mg; Sodium 189mg; Calcium 119mg

confetti slaw with poppy seed dressing

pictured on page 199

Prep: *10 minutes*
Serves 4

  2 tablespoons cider vinegar
1¹/₂ teaspoons honey
1¹/₂ teaspoons Dijon mustard
1¹/₂ teaspoons chopped fresh dill
  1 teaspoon poppy seeds
  1 teaspoon olive oil
¹/₄ teaspoon salt
¹/₄ teaspoon pepper
  1 cup thinly sliced green cabbage
  1 cup thinly sliced red cabbage
¹/₂ cup matchstick-cut carrots

1. Combine first 8 ingredients (vinegar through pepper) in a bowl. Add cabbage and carrots; toss to coat.

PER SERVING (²/₃ cup): Calories 40 (34% from fat); Protein 1g; Fat 2g (sat 0g, mono 1g, poly 0g); Carbohydrate 6g; Fiber 1g; Cholesterol 0mg; Iron 1mg; Sodium 205mg; Calcium 36mg

marinated broccoli-corn salad

pictured on page 198

Prep: *7 minutes* **Cook:** *6 minutes*
Chill: *3 hours*
Serves 6

3¹/₂ cups small fresh broccoli florets
¹/₄ cup rice vinegar
  1 tablespoon Dijon mustard
  1 tablespoon honey
¹/₄ teaspoon salt
¹/₄ teaspoon black pepper
  1 (16-ounce) package frozen baby white corn, thawed
¹/₂ cup chopped red bell pepper
¹/₂ cup finely chopped red onion

1. Steam broccoli florets, covered, 6 minutes or until crisp-tender. Drain. Rinse under cold water; drain well.
2. Combine vinegar and next 4 ingredients (vinegar through pepper) in a medium bowl; stir well. Add broccoli, corn, bell pepper, and onion; stir well. Cover and chill at least 3 hours, stirring occasionally.

PER SERVING (1 cup): Calories 105 (9% from fat); Protein 4g; Fat 1g (sat 0g, mono 0g, poly 0g); Carbohydrate 23g; Fiber 4g; Cholesterol 0mg; Iron 1mg; Sodium 190mg; Calcium 32mg

fennel and orange salad

Prep: *12 minutes* **Chill:** *3 hours*
Serves 6

This traditional Italian salad is crunchy and slightly sweet.

  4 cups chopped fennel bulb (about 2 [1-pound] bulbs)
¹/₂ cup fresh orange juice
  3 large navel oranges, peeled and coarsely chopped
  2 tablespoons chopped fresh mint
  2 tablespoons sherry vinegar
  1 tablespoon extra-virgin olive oil
¹/₂ teaspoon salt
¹/₂ teaspoon freshly ground black pepper

1. Combine all ingredients in a large bowl; toss well. Cover and chill 3 hours.

PER SERVING (1 cup): Calories 81 (29% from fat); Protein 3g; Fat 3g (sat 0g, mono 2g, poly 0g); Carbohydrate 14g; Fiber 4g; Cholesterol 0mg; Iron 2mg; Sodium 202mg; Calcium 93mg

mixed greens with citrus vinaigrette and sugared pecans

Prep: *15 minutes* **Cook:** *4 minutes*
Serves 6

As the sugar melts, it forms a caramelized sugary coating on the pecans. The red pepper adds an unexpected spicy flavor contrast.

  2 teaspoons olive oil
¹/₄ cup chopped pecans
  2 teaspoons sugar
¹/₈ teaspoon ground red pepper
¹/₂ cup fresh orange juice
  2 tablespoons fresh lemon juice
  2 tablespoons olive oil
  1 tablespoon low-sodium soy sauce
  1 tablespoon Dijon mustard
  1 tablespoon honey
  2 teaspoons minced peeled fresh ginger
  9 cups mixed salad greens
  2 cups fresh orange sections

1. Heat oil in a nonstick skillet over medium heat; add pecans. Sprinkle with sugar and red pepper; sauté 2 minutes or until sugar begins to brown. Remove from heat.
2. Place orange juice and next 6 ingredients (orange juice through ginger) in a blender; process until smooth.
3. Combine greens and citrus vinaigrette in a large bowl; toss gently. Place salad on individual plates; top with pecans and oranges.

PER SERVING (1¹/₂ cups salad, 2 teaspoons pecans, and ¹/₃ cup oranges): Calories 127 (53% from fat); Protein 3g; Fat 8g (sat 1g, mono 5g, poly 1g); Carbohydrate 14g; Fiber 4g; Cholesterol 0mg; Iron 1mg; Sodium 85mg; Calcium 58mg

caesar potato salad

Prep: *15 minutes* **Cook:** *18 minutes*
Stand: *30 minutes*
Serves 6

1¹/₂ tablespoons olive oil
2 garlic cloves, minced
2 (1-inch) slices French bread
1¹/₂ pounds small red potatoes
3 tablespoons dry vermouth
2 tablespoons balsamic vinegar
1 tablespoon lemon juice
2 teaspoons Dijon mustard
2 teaspoons anchovy paste
¹/₄ teaspoon salt
¹/₈ teaspoon pepper
¹/₄ cup chopped green onions
3 tablespoons finely chopped
   fresh flat-leaf parsley
2 romaine lettuce leaves, cut
   crosswise into ¹/₄-inch-wide
   strips
¹/₄ cup grated fresh Parmesan
   cheese

1. Combine oil and garlic; let stand 30 minutes.
2. Preheat oven to 350°.
3. Brush 1¹/₂ teaspoons oil mixture over bread; cut into cubes. Place cubes in a single layer on a jelly-roll pan. Bake at 350° for 9 minutes or until toasted.
4. Arrange potatoes in a steamer basket over boiling water. Cover and steam 18 minutes or until tender. Let cool; cut into ¹/₄-inch-thick slices. Combine potato slices and vermouth; toss gently to coat.
5. Combine remaining oil mixture, vinegar, and next 7 ingredients (lemon juice through parsley) in a bowl. Pour over potato slices; toss gently to coat. Cover and chill.
6. Stir in lettuce. Sprinkle with croutons and cheese.

PER SERVING (²/₃ cup): Calories 176 (27% from fat);
Protein 6g; Fat 5g (sat 1g, mono 3g, poly 1g);
Carbohydrate 25g; Fiber 3g; Cholesterol 3mg; Iron 2mg;
Sodium 497mg; Calcium 97mg

two-potato salad with mustard-chive dressing

pictured on page 198

Prep: *15 minutes* **Cook:** *20 minutes*
Serves 4

We varied from the traditional peeled, baked white potato in this recipe. We substituted red and sweet potatoes, then roasted them until crusty and browned on the outside.

¹/₂ pound small red-skinned
   potatoes, quartered
¹/₂ pound (¹/₂-inch) peeled cubed
   sweet potato
¹/₂ tablespoon olive oil
Cooking spray
3 tablespoons buttermilk
1 tablespoon mayonnaise
¹/₂ tablespoon finely chopped
   shallots
¹/₂ tablespoon chopped fresh
   chives
¹/₂ tablespoon Dijon mustard
¹/₄ teaspoon pepper
¹/₄ teaspoon salt
¹/₄ cup chopped celery

1. Preheat oven to 425°.
2. Combine red and sweet potatoes with oil on a baking sheet coated with cooking spray; toss to coat. Bake at 425° for 20 minutes or until potatoes are tender.
3. Combine buttermilk and next 6 ingredients (buttermilk through salt) in a large bowl; mix well. Add potatoes and celery, and toss well. Serve immediately.

PER SERVING (³/₄ cup): Calories 154 (29% from fat);
Protein 3g; Fat 5g (sat 1g, mono 1g, poly 0g);
Carbohydrate 25g; Fiber 2g; Cholesterol 3mg; Iron 1mg;
Sodium 435mg; Calcium 38mg

sweet potato salad

Prep: *10 minutes* **Cook:** *20 minutes*
Serves 4

Chutney and cider vinegar create the base for a sweet, tangy dressing for this colorful vegetable.

¹/₄ cup chopped scallions
¹/₄ cup mango chutney (such as
   Major Grey)
1¹/₂ tablespoons vegetable oil
1 tablespoon cider vinegar
¹/₂ teaspoon salt
¹/₈ teaspoon freshly ground black
   pepper
3¹/₂ cups (³/₄-inch) peeled, cubed
   sweet potato (about 1¹/₂
   pounds potatoes)
¹/₄ pound green beans, trimmed
   and halved (about 1 cup)
2 tablespoons chopped fresh
   cilantro

1. Whisk together first 6 ingredients (scallions through pepper).
2. Place potato in a saucepan, cover with water, and bring to a boil. Reduce heat, and simmer 13 minutes or until just tender; drain.
3. Cook beans in boiling salted water 4 minutes until crisp-tender. Drain and rinse beneath cold running water.
4. Combine potato, beans, and cilantro in a medium bowl. Add chutney dressing; toss to coat.

PER SERVING (1 cup): Calories 212 (21% from fat);
Protein 3g; Fat 5g (sat 1g, mono 2g, poly 1g);
Carbohydrate 39g; Fiber 5g; Cholesterol 0mg; Iron 1mg;
Sodium 548mg; Calcium 43mg

white bean and arugula salad

Prep: *9 minutes* **Stand:** *15 minutes*
Serves 5

This bean salad makes a perfect side to serve with Rosemary-Mustard Lamb Chops, page 166.

1 (15-ounce) can cannellini beans or other white beans, rinsed and drained
4 cups chopped arugula
2 1/3 cups chopped tomato (about 1 pound)
1 tablespoon extra-virgin olive oil
1/2 teaspoon crushed red pepper
2 1/2 teaspoons white wine vinegar
1/4 teaspoon salt

1. Combine all ingredients in a bowl, and stir well. Let stand 15 minutes, stirring occasionally. Serve at room temperature.

PER SERVING (1 cup): Calories 113 (27% from fat); Protein 6g; Fat 3g (sat 0g, mono 2g, poly 1g); Carbohydrate 17g; Fiber 3g; Cholesterol 0mg; Iron 2mg; Sodium 277mg; Calcium 90mg

cherry tomato salad

Prep: *10 minutes*
Serves 8

3 pounds cherry tomatoes (about 4 pints), divided
2 tablespoons water
1 tablespoon white wine vinegar
2 teaspoons extra-virgin olive oil
1/2 teaspoon salt
1/4 teaspoon freshly ground black pepper
1 garlic clove, peeled
1/4 cup chopped fresh mint
Freshly ground black pepper (optional)

1. Place 1/2 pound tomatoes (about 3/4 pint), water, and next 5 ingredients (vinegar through garlic) in a blender; process until smooth.
2. Cut remaining tomatoes in half; place in a large bowl. Add puréed tomato mixture and mint; toss gently to coat. Sprinkle with ground pepper, if desired.

PER SERVING (1 cup): Calories 47 (33% from fat); Protein 2g; Fat 2g (sat 0g, mono 1g, poly 0g); Carbohydrate 8g; Fiber 2g; Cholesterol 0mg; Iron 1mg; Sodium 162mg; Calcium 10mg

sweet onion, tomato, and corn salad with basil

Prep: *10 minutes*
Serves 4

You can use dark balsamic vinegar in place of the white, though the salad won't look as pretty.

1 tablespoon chopped fresh basil
2 tablespoons white balsamic vinegar
2 teaspoons extra-virgin olive oil
1 teaspoon Dijon mustard
1/2 cup basil leaves
2 large tomatoes, thinly sliced
1/2 cup thinly sliced Vidalia or other sweet onion
1 cup fresh white corn kernels (about 2 ears)

1. Combine first 4 ingredients (basil through mustard) in a bowl; stir well, and set aside.
2. Combine basil leaves and remaining 3 ingredients; toss well. Drizzle vinegar mixture over salad, and toss gently.

PER SERVING (about 2/3 cup): Calories 89 (32% from fat); Protein 2g; Fat 3g (sat 0g, mono 2g, poly 1g); Carbohydrate 16g; Fiber 3g; Cholesterol 0mg; Iron 1mg; Sodium 52mg; Calcium 17mg

black-eyed pea and basil salad

Prep: *8 minutes* **Cook:** *38 minutes*
Serves 3

Eating this salad is a great way to start the New Year. It's full of fiber and good luck and practically fat free.

1 (10-ounce) package frozen black-eyed peas (about 2 cups)
1 1/4 cups chopped plum tomato (about 3/4 pound)
1/3 cup fat-free Caesar Italian dressing (such as Kraft)
1/4 cup finely chopped fresh parsley
2 teaspoons dried basil
1/4 teaspoon salt

1. Combine 1 1/2 cups water and black-eyed peas in a medium saucepan; bring to a boil. Cover, reduce heat, and simmer 30 minutes or until peas are just tender (do not overcook). Drain; let cool.
2. Combine black-eyed peas, chopped tomato, and remaining ingredients in a medium bowl; toss well. Serve salad chilled or at room temperature.

NOTE: Compared to regular tomatoes, plum tomatoes have more flavor during the winter season and considerably fewer seeds to water down the salad. If you use regular tomatoes, be sure to seed them before chopping.

PER SERVING (1 cup): Calories 159 (5% from fat); Protein 9g; Fat 0g; Carbohydrate 30g; Fiber 3g; Cholesterol 0mg; Iron 3mg; Sodium 468mg; Calcium 51mg

How to Peel and Seed Tomatoes

Make good use of juicy, vine-ripened tomatoes using these step-by-step tips on how to peel and seed them with ease.

1. Cut a shallow "X" at the opposite end from the stem on each tomato, using a small, sharp paring knife.

2. Add tomatoes to a large pot of boiling water; begin timing immediately for 30 seconds or until the skin begins to split at the "X."

3. Remove tomatoes from water, using a slotted spoon; transfer to a bowl of ice water immediately to halt the cooking process. Drain tomatoes when cool to the touch.

4. Using your fingers or a paring knife, peel the skin off in strips, much like peeling a banana. The skin should peel easily, but shouldn't remove much flesh with it.

5. Using a sharp chef's knife, cut each tomato in half crosswise. Then, using your finger or the handle of a small spoon, scoop out the seeds.

blt pasta salad

Prep: *13 minutes* **Cook:** *10 minutes*
Serves 10

Make this salad with ripe summer tomatoes for the best flavor.

$3^2/_3$ cups cooked large elbow macaroni (about 8 ounces uncooked), cooked without salt or fat
4 cups coarsely chopped seeded peeled tomato (about $2^1/_2$ pounds)
4 hickory-smoked bacon slices, cooked and crumbled
3 cups prepackaged very thinly sliced iceberg lettuce (such as Fresh Express "Shreds")
$^1/_2$ cup fat-free mayonnaise
$^1/_3$ cup low-fat sour cream
1 tablespoon Dijon mustard
1 teaspoon sugar
2 teaspoons cider vinegar
$^1/_2$ teaspoon salt
$^1/_2$ teaspoon pepper

1. Combine first 4 ingredients (macaroni through lettuce) in a large bowl; toss gently. Combine mayonnaise and next 6 ingredients (mayonnaise through pepper); stir well. Add dressing to salad, and toss gently. Serve immediately.

PER SERVING (1 cup): Calories 149 (18% from fat); Protein 5g; Fat 3g (sat 1g, mono 1g, poly 0g); Carbohydrate 26g; Fiber 1g; Cholesterol 5mg; Iron 1mg; Sodium 367mg; Calcium 18mg

marinated tomato salad

Prep: *10 minutes* **Marinate:** *1 hour*
Serves 7

- 5 medium tomatoes (about 2 pounds), cut into ³/₄-inch-thick wedges
- 12 large kalamata olives, pitted and chopped
- 1 tablespoon capers
- 2 teaspoons minced fresh oregano
- ¹/₄ teaspoon salt
- ¹/₄ teaspoon pepper
- 2 tablespoons red wine vinegar
- 2 teaspoons extra-virgin olive oil

1. Combine first 6 ingredients (tomato wedges through pepper) in a large bowl. Drizzle vinegar and olive oil over salad; toss gently to coat. Cover and marinate at room temperature 1 hour. Toss gently before serving.

PER SERVING (1 cup): Calories 63 (43% from fat); Protein 2g; Fat 3g (sat 1g, mono 2g, poly 1g); Carbohydrate 9g; Fiber 2g; Cholesterol 0mg; Iron 1mg; Sodium 299mg; Calcium 25mg

wild rice salad with peas

pictured on page 199

Prep: *7 minutes* **Cook:** *10 minutes*
Serves 6

- 1 (6.2-ounce) package fast-cooking long-grain-and-wild rice mix (such as Uncle Ben's)
- 1 (10-ounce) package frozen green peas, thawed
- ²/₃ cup chopped red bell pepper
- ¹/₂ cup sliced almonds, toasted
- ¹/₃ cup teriyaki sauce

1. Cook rice mix according to package directions, omitting seasoning packet and fat. Reserve seasoning packet for another use.
2. Combine rice mix, peas, bell pepper, almonds, and teriyaki sauce in a large bowl. Stir well, and let cool. Serve at room temperature.

PER SERVING (1 cup): Calories 203 (20% from fat); Protein 7g; Fat 5g (sat 1g, mono 3g, poly 1g); Carbohydrate 34g; Fiber 4g; Cholesterol 0mg; Iron 2mg; Sodium 616mg; Calcium 43mg

corn and wild rice salad

Prep: *10 minutes* **Cook:** *15 minutes*
Serves 8

- 1¹/₂ cups uncooked wild rice blend (such as Lundberg Farms)
- 2 cups fresh corn kernels (about 4 ears)
- 1 cup finely chopped celery
- ³/₄ cup shredded carrot
- ³/₄ cup dried cranberries (about 3 ounces)
- ²/₃ cup sunflower seeds or pumpkinseed kernels, toasted
- ¹/₂ cup finely chopped red onion
- ¹/₄ cup raspberry vinegar
- 1 tablespoon olive oil
- 1 tablespoon low-sodium soy sauce
- 1 teaspoon grated orange peel
- ¹/₂ teaspoon pepper

1. Cook rice according to package directions, omitting salt and fat. Set aside; cool.
2. Combine rice, corn, and remaining ingredients in a bowl; stir well. Cover and chill.

PER SERVING (1 cup): Calories 270 (26% from fat); Protein 9g; Fat 8g (sat 1g, mono 3g, poly 3g); Carbohydrate 45g; Fiber 5g; Cholesterol 0mg; Iron 3mg; Sodium 78mg; Calcium 31mg

fruit and bulgur salad

Prep: *11 minutes* **Cook:** *30 minutes*
Stand: *30 minutes*
Serves 5

Full of complex carbohydrates, fruits, and heart-healthy nuts, this salad is great served warm for breakfast or as a side with ham or pork.

- 3 cups water
- ¹/₂ cup yellow split peas
- ³/₄ cup uncooked bulgur or cracked wheat
- ³/₄ cup boiling water
- 1 cup chopped Red Delicious apple
- ¹/₄ cup dried cranberries
- ¹/₄ cup chopped pitted dates
- ¹/₄ cup plain low-fat yogurt
- 2 tablespoons lemon juice
- ¹/₄ teaspoon salt
- ¹/₄ teaspoon curry powder
- 1 (11-ounce) can mandarin oranges in light syrup, drained
- ¹/₄ cup plus 1 tablespoon chopped almonds, toasted

1. Bring 3 cups water and split peas to a boil in a saucepan. Reduce heat; cook, uncovered, 30 minutes or just until split peas are tender. Drain well.
2. Combine bulgur and ³/₄ cup boiling water in a large bowl. Cover and let stand 30 minutes. Add peas, apple, cranberries, and dates; stir well.
3. Combine yogurt and next 3 ingredients (yogurt through curry); add to bulgur mixture, stirring well. Gently stir in oranges. Top salad with toasted almonds.

PER SERVING (1 cup salad and 1 tablespoon almonds): Calories 275 (13% from fat); Protein 11g; Fat 4g (sat 1g, mono 2g, poly 1g); Carbohydrate 53g; Fiber 8g; Cholesterol 1mg; Iron 3mg; Sodium 140mg; Calcium 84mg

black bean and barley salsa salad

Prep: *12 minutes* **Cook:** *14 minutes*
Stand: *5 minutes*
Serves 4

This salad makes a hearty main dish or a zesty side to grilled chicken, pork, or fish.

- 2 cups water
- 1 cup uncooked quick-cooking barley
- 1 cup fresh or frozen whole-kernel corn
- 1 cup chopped tomato
- 1/2 cup minced fresh cilantro
- 1/3 cup chopped red bell pepper
- 1/4 cup finely chopped red onion
- 1/4 cup minced green onions
- 1 (15-ounce) can no-salt-added black beans, rinsed and drained
- 1/4 cup fresh lemon juice
- 1 teaspoon jalapeño hot sauce
- 1 teaspoon olive oil
- 1/4 teaspoon salt
- 1/4 teaspoon ground cumin
- 1/4 teaspoon black pepper

1. Bring 2 cups water to a boil in a medium saucepan. Add barley; cover, reduce heat, and simmer 8 minutes. Add corn (do not stir), and cover. Cook 6 minutes or until barley is tender. Remove barley mixture from heat, and let stand, covered, 5 minutes.
2. Combine barley mixture, tomato, and next 5 ingredients (cilantro through beans) in a large bowl. Combine lemon juice and remaining 5 ingredients (lemon juice through black pepper). Pour lemon dressing over salad; toss gently to coat.

PER SERVING (1 1/2 cups): Calories 330 (7% from fat); Protein 13g; Fat 3g (sat 0g, mono 1g, poly 1g); Carbohydrate 69g; Fiber 13g; Cholesterol 0mg; Iron 4mg; Sodium 176mg; Calcium 62mg

grilled vegetable salad with lentils

Prep: *25 minutes* **Cook:** *35 minutes*
Serves 4

Aside from contributing a healthy dose of fiber, lentils are also a good source of protein and iron.

- 1 1/3 cups dried lentils
- 4 cups water
- 1 bay leaf
- 1/2 cup finely chopped red onion
- 2 tablespoons coarsely chopped walnuts
- 1 1/2 tablespoons extra-virgin olive oil
- 1 1/2 tablespoons red wine vinegar
- 1 teaspoon dried herbes de Provence
- 1/2 teaspoon salt
- 1/4 teaspoon black pepper
- 1 garlic clove, minced
- 24 asparagus spears, trimmed (about 12 ounces)
- 2 zucchini, cut diagonally into 1-inch-thick slices
- 1 small yellow bell pepper, quartered
- 1 small orange bell pepper, quartered
- 1 small red bell pepper, quartered
- 1 (12-ounce) eggplant, cut crosswise into 1/2-inch-thick slices
- 1 1/2 tablespoons olive oil
- 2 teaspoons red wine vinegar
- 1 teaspoon chopped fresh or 1/4 teaspoon dried thyme
- 1 teaspoon dried herbes de Provence
- 1/2 teaspoon salt
- 1/4 teaspoon black pepper

1. Prepare grill.
2. Rinse and drain lentils. Place water, lentils, and bay leaf in a medium saucepan; bring to a boil. Reduce heat, and simmer 20 minutes. Drain; discard bay leaf. Combine lentils, red onion,

and next 7 ingredients (walnuts through garlic) in a large bowl.
3. Combine asparagus and next 6 ingredients (asparagus through oil) in a large bowl; toss well to coat. Grill zucchini, peppers, and eggplant 15 minutes, turning once. Grill asparagus 6 minutes, turning once. Place vegetables in a bowl; drizzle with 2 teaspoons vinegar. Sprinkle with thyme and remaining ingredients; toss well. Serve with lentils.

PER SERVING (1 cup lentils, 3 quarters bell pepper, half a zucchini, and about 3 slices eggplant): Calories 404 (29% from fat); Protein 20g; Fat 14g (sat 2g, mono 8g, poly 3g); Carbohydrate 55g; Fiber 21g; Cholesterol 0mg; Iron 8mg; Sodium 599mg; Calcium 110mg

rotini-vegetable salad with pesto dressing

Prep: *13 minutes* **Cook:** *10 minutes*
Serves 4

- 1 large garlic clove, peeled
- 1 cup packed basil leaves
- 2 tablespoons grated fresh Parmesan cheese
- 1/4 teaspoon salt
- 1/4 teaspoon pepper
- 2 tablespoons water
- 2 tablespoons olive oil
- 3 cups cooked rotini (about 2 cups uncooked corkscrew pasta)
- 1 1/2 cups diced zucchini
- 1 1/2 cups halved cherry tomatoes
- 1 (15-ounce) can cannellini beans or other white beans, rinsed and drained
Basil sprigs (optional)

1. Drop garlic through food chute with food processor on, and process until minced. Add basil leaves, cheese, salt, and pepper; process until finely minced. With food processor

on, slowly pour water and oil through food chute; process until mixture is well blended.
2. Combine rotini and next 3 ingredients (rotini through beans) in a large bowl; toss well. Add pesto mixture, tossing gently to coat. Garnish with basil sprigs, if desired.

PER SERVING (1³/₄ cups): Calories 365 (26% from fat); Protein 15g; Fat 11g (sat 2g, mono 6g, poly 2g); Carbohydrate 55g; Fiber 6g; Cholesterol 2mg; Iron 5mg; Sodium 359mg; Calcium 134mg

tabbouleh cobb salad

pictured on page 3

Prep: *15 minutes* **Stand:** *30 minutes*
Serves 4

Middle Eastern tabbouleh gets tossed with America's classic Cobb salad. The result is a hearty main-dish salad, thanks to the bulgur and turkey.

¹/₂ cup boiling water
¹/₂ cup uncooked bulgur
¹/₄ cup chopped fresh parsley
1 tablespoon fresh lemon juice
1 tablespoon olive oil
¹/₄ teaspoon black pepper
8 cups torn romaine lettuce
2 cups cubed smoked turkey breast (about 12 ounces)
2 cups grape or cherry tomatoes, halved
1 cup peeled chopped seeded cucumber
1 cup thinly sliced green onions
1 (15-ounce) can chickpeas (garbanzo beans), drained
³/₄ cup Roasted Red Pepper Dressing

1. Combine boiling water and bulgur; let stand 30 minutes.

2. Combine bulgur mixture, parsley, lemon juice, oil, and pepper.
3. Place 2 cups lettuce in each of 4 shallow bowls. Place ¹/₄ cup tabbouleh, ¹/₂ cup each turkey and tomatoes, ¹/₄ cup each cucumber and onions, and about ¹/₃ cup chickpeas evenly in rows over lettuce, beginning with tabbouleh. Drizzle with 3 tablespoons dressing.

PER SERVING (1 salad): Calories 336 (26% from fat); Protein 26g; Fat 11g (sat 3g, mono 4g, poly 2g); Carbohydrate 42g; Fiber 12g; Cholesterol 46mg; Iron 5mg; Sodium 1,092mg; Calcium 115mg

roasted red pepper dressing:

1¹/₂ tablespoons vegetable broth
1 tablespoon red wine vinegar
1¹/₂ teaspoons olive oil
¹/₂ teaspoon salt
¹/₂ teaspoon Dijon mustard
¹/₄ teaspoon dried thyme
¹/₄ teaspoon black pepper
2 (7-ounce) bottles roasted red bell peppers, drained

1. Place all ingredients in a blender, and process until smooth. Refrigerate in an airtight container up to 1 week. Yield: ³/₄ cup.

PER SERVING (3 tablespoons): Calories 49 (43% from fat); Protein 1g; Fat 2g (sat 0g, mono 1g, poly 1g); Carbohydrate 6g; Fiber 1g; Cholesterol 0mg; Iron 1mg; Sodium 692mg; Calcium 13mg

mediterranean basmati salad

pictured on page 197

Prep: *10 minutes* **Soak:** *30 minutes*
Cook: *15 minutes* **Stand:** *20 minutes*
Serves 4

2 sun-dried tomatoes, packed without oil
¹/₄ cup hot water
1¹/₄ cups uncooked basmati rice
2 cups water
¹/₂ teaspoon salt
²/₃ cup (2.5 ounces) feta cheese, crumbled
2 tablespoons dried currants
2 tablespoons chopped fresh mint
1 tablespoon olive oil
¹/₄ teaspoon pepper
2 tablespoons pine nuts, toasted
Mint sprigs, (optional)

1. Combine tomatoes and water in a small bowl; let stand 10 minutes. Drain and chop; set aside.
2. Place rice in a large bowl; cover with water to 2 inches above rice. Soak 30 minutes; stirring occasionally. Drain and rinse.
3. Combine rice and 2 cups water in a small saucepan; stir in salt. Bring to a boil over medium-high heat, stirring frequently. Boil 5 minutes or until water level falls just below rice. Cover, reduce heat to low, and cook 10 minutes. Remove from heat; let stand, covered, 10 minutes.
4. Spoon rice into a bowl; cool completely, and fluff with a fork. Stir in tomatoes, feta, and next 4 ingredients (currants through pepper); toss well to combine. Sprinkle with pine nuts. Garnish with mint sprigs, if desired.

PER SERVING (1¹/₂ cups): Calories 358 (29% from fat); Protein 10g; Fat 12g (sat 5g, mono 5g, poly 2g); Carbohydrate 57g; Fiber 1g; Cholesterol 22mg; Iron 1mg; Sodium 609mg; Calcium 142mg

california pasta salad

Prep: *14 minutes* **Cook:** *18 minutes*
Serves 10

Ideal for a brown bag lunch, this salad can be stored in the refrigerator up to a week.

- 1 (16-ounce) package frozen baby lima beans
- 3 cups cooked orecchiette (about 1³/₄ cups uncooked pasta)
- 1¹/₂ cups chopped red bell pepper
- 1 cup finely chopped onion
- 1 cup chopped peeled tomatillos (about 4 large)
- 1 cup fresh corn kernels (about 3 ears)
- ¹/₃ cup minced fresh cilantro
- 2 tablespoons white wine vinegar
- 2 tablespoons extra-virgin olive oil
- ³/₄ teaspoon salt
- 1 (4.5-ounce) can chopped green chiles

1. Cook beans in boiling water 18 minutes or until tender. Drain well.
2. Combine beans, pasta, and remaining ingredients in a bowl. Serve salad at room temperature or chilled.

PER SERVING (1 cup): Calories 159 (20% from fat); Protein 6g; Fat 4g (sat 1g, mono 2g, poly 1g); Carbohydrate 27g; Fiber 3g; Cholesterol 0mg; Iron 2mg; Sodium 248mg; Calcium 30mg

panzanella with tuna

Prep: *14 minutes* **Stand:** *10 minutes*
Serves 8

Though it may seem like a large amount of basil, it's essential for bringing out the fresh flavors of the tomatoes and onions. For extra protein, we added albacore tuna to this traditional Italian bread salad.

- ¹/₄ cup extra-virgin olive oil
- 3 tablespoons red wine vinegar
- ¹/₂ teaspoon salt
- ¹/₄ teaspoon pepper
- 12 cups (³/₄-inch) cubed stale French bread (about 12 ounces)
- 5 cups coarsely chopped tomato (about 2 pounds)
- 1¹/₄ cups thinly sliced red onion, separated into rings
- 1 cup chopped fresh basil
- ¹/₃ cup chopped fresh mint
- 3 (6-ounce) cans albacore tuna in water, drained and flaked

Freshly ground black pepper (optional)

1. Combine first 4 ingredients (oil through pepper) in a small bowl; stir well with a whisk.
2. Combine bread and next 4 ingredients (bread through mint) in a large bowl; toss gently. Add vinaigrette and tuna; toss gently. Cover and let stand at least 10 minutes. Sprinkle each serving with freshly ground pepper, if desired.

PER SERVING (2 cups): Calories 290 (31% from fat); Protein 20g; Fat 10g (sat 2g, mono 6g, poly 1g); Carbohydrate 31g; Fiber 3g; Cholesterol 22mg; Iron 2mg; Sodium 647mg; Calcium 46mg

tuna and artichoke pasta salad

Prep: *9 minutes* **Cook:** *10 minutes*
Chill: *1 hour*
Serves 8

Tuna salad gets a Greek makeover when olive oil, garlic, and artichokes are added.

- 2 teaspoons grated lemon rind
- 3 tablespoons fresh lemon juice
- 3 tablespoons extra-virgin olive oil
- 1 tablespoon minced peeled fresh ginger
- 2 garlic cloves, minced
- 4 cups cooked elbow macaroni (about 8 ounces uncooked)
- 1 cup cherry tomatoes, halved
- ¹/₂ cup chopped green onions
- ¹/₃ cup chopped fresh flat-leaf parsley
- 1 (6-ounce) can albacore tuna in water, drained and flaked
- 1 (14-ounce) can quartered artichoke hearts, drained

1. Combine first 5 ingredients (lemon rind through garlic) in a large bowl. Add pasta and remaining ingredients; toss gently to coat. Cover and chill at least 1 hour.

PER SERVING (1 cup): Calories 185 (29% from fat); Protein 9g; Fat 6g (sat 1g, mono 4g, poly 1g); Carbohydrate 25g; Fiber 2g; Cholesterol 6mg; Iron 2mg; Sodium 91mg; Calcium 30mg

curry-crusted oyster salad

Prep: *23 minutes* **Cook:** *9 minutes*
Serves 4

These oysters are so crunchy and tasty you'll want to serve them solo, too.

Remoulade Dressing
- 6 tablespoons yellow cornmeal
- 1 tablespoon curry powder
- 1 teaspoon dried oregano
- 1/2 teaspoon salt
- 1/4 teaspoon ground red pepper
- 1/3 cup all-purpose flour
- 2 large egg whites
- 2 (8-ounce) containers standard oysters, drained

Cooking spray
- 12 cups mixed baby salad greens
- 1/2 cup thinly sliced red onion, separated into rings
- 2 tomatoes, cut into 24 wedges

1. Prepare Remoulade Dressing; cover and chill.
2. Preheat oven to 475°.
3. Combine cornmeal and next 4 ingredients (cornmeal through red pepper) in a shallow dish; stir well. Place flour in a shallow dish. Place egg whites in a bowl; stir well with a whisk. Dredge oysters, 1 at a time, in flour. Dip each oyster in egg whites; dredge in cornmeal mixture. Place breaded oysters on a baking sheet coated with cooking spray. Lightly coat oysters with cooking spray. Bake at 475° for 5 minutes. Turn oysters over; bake an additional 4 minutes or until golden.
4. Combine salad greens and onion; toss. Spoon 3 cups salad into each of 4 bowls; top each with 6 tomato wedges. Divide oysters evenly over salads.
5. Drizzle 2½ tablespoons Remoulade Dressing over each salad. Serve immediately.

PER SERVING (1 salad): Calories 234 (23% from fat); Protein 14g; Fat 6g (sat 1g, mono 1g, poly 1g); Carbohydrate 32g; Fiber 6g; Cholesterol 50mg; Iron 9mg; Sodium 727mg; Calcium 152mg

remoulade dressing:

- 1/4 cup plain fat-free yogurt
- 2 tablespoons minced onion
- 2½ tablespoons capers
- 2½ tablespoons light mayonnaise
- 1 tablespoon lemon juice
- 1 teaspoon Worcestershire sauce

1. Combine all ingredients in a bowl; stir well. Yield: ⅔ cups.

grilled shrimp salad with smokey tomato vinaigrette

Prep: *22 minutes* **Cook:** *40 minutes*
Serves 6

- 4 (1-inch-thick) slices day-old French bread or other white bread, cut into 1-inch cubes
- 1 large tomato, sliced
- 1 tablespoon plus 1 teaspoon olive oil, divided
- 1/2 teaspoon salt, divided
- 1/2 teaspoon pepper, divided
- 3 tablespoons chopped fresh parsley
- 2 tablespoons fresh lemon juice
- 1 tablespoon canned chipotle chile in adobo sauce
- 1 tablespoon water
- 2 teaspoons ground coriander
- 1 garlic clove, chopped
- 48 large shrimp, peeled and deveined (about 2 pounds)
Cooking spray
- 9½ cups torn romaine lettuce
- 3/4 cup diced peeled avocado
- 1/2 cup sliced red onion

1. Preheat oven to 350°.
2. Place bread cubes in a single layer on a baking sheet. Bake at 350° for 12 minutes or until bread is toasted. Set aside.
3. Brush tomato slices with 1 teaspoon olive oil; sprinkle with 1/4 teaspoon salt and 1/4 teaspoon pepper. Place tomato slices on an aluminum foil-lined baking sheet. Broil 10 minutes on each side or until tomato is blackened. Combine tomato, 1 tablespoon olive oil, 1/4 teaspoon salt, 1/4 teaspoon pepper, parsley, and next 5 ingredients (lemon juice through garlic) in a food processor; process until blended. Divide vinaigrette in half. Set aside.
4. Thread shrimp onto 6 (12-inch) skewers, and brush with half of vinaigrette.
5. Prepare grill.
6. Place kebabs on grill rack coated with cooking spray, and grill 4 minutes on each side or until shrimp are done. Remove shrimp from skewers. Combine remaining vinaigrette, bread cubes, shrimp, lettuce, avocado, and onion in a large bowl; toss gently.

PER SERVING (2½ cups): Calories 257 (30% from fat); Fat 9g (sat 1g, mono 5g, poly 2g); Protein 27g; Carbohydrate 17g; Fiber 3g; Cholesterol 173mg; Iron 5mg; Sodium 495mg; Calcium 112mg

italian bread salad with shrimp

Prep: *20 minutes* **Cook:** *10 minutes*
Serves 6

     6 cups (¹/₂-inch) cubed day-old
        country-style wheat bread
 1¹/₂ tablespoons fresh lemon juice
     3 tablespoons olive oil, divided
     1 teaspoon finely chopped fresh
        rosemary
  ¹/₂ teaspoon salt, divided
  ¹/₄ teaspoon freshly ground black
        pepper
     2 garlic cloves, minced and
        divided
     8 cups chopped plum tomato
        (about 16)
     6 pitted kalamata olives, chopped
 1¹/₂ pounds large shrimp, peeled
        and deveined
     1 cup torn fresh basil leaves

1. Preheat oven to 425°.
2. Arrange bread cubes on a baking sheet; bake at 425° for 5 minutes or until lightly toasted and dry. Cool completely; set aside.
3. Combine lemon juice and 2½ tablespoons oil in a large bowl; stir with a whisk. Stir in rosemary, ¼ teaspoon salt, pepper, and 1 garlic clove. Add tomato and olives; mix well.
4. Heat 1½ teaspoons oil in a large nonstick skillet; add shrimp and ¼ teaspoon salt. Cook 3 minutes, stirring occasionally; add 1 garlic clove. Cook 2 minutes or until shrimp are cooked through. Remove from heat.
5. Add bread cubes and shrimp to tomato mixture; toss. Add basil; toss to combine. Serve immediately.

PER SERVING (2 cups): Calories 498 (28% from fat); Protein 33g; Fat 16g (sat 2g, mono 8g, poly 5g); Carbohydrate 59g; Fiber 8g; Cholesterol 172mg; Iron 7mg; Sodium 767mg; Calcium 125mg

grilled chicken and wheat berry salad

pictured on cover and page 198

Prep: *4 minutes* **Cook:** *2 hours 15 minutes*
Grill: *10 minutes*
Serves 4

Although wheat berries require little tending, they do require a long cooking time. You may want to cook them on the weekend or the night before you make the salad.

     4 cups water
     1 cup hard winter wheat berries,
        rinsed and drained
     1 bay leaf
     2 cups baby spinach leaves,
        divided
     1 cup green apple, peeled and
        cubed
  ¹/₂ cup chopped red bell pepper
     3 tablespoons Cucumber-Yogurt
        Dressing
     2 teaspoons Dijon mustard
     4 (4-ounce) skinless, boneless
        chicken breasts
  ¹/₄ teaspoon salt
  ¹/₄ teaspoon black pepper
  Cooking spray
  ¹/₄ cup chopped green onions
  Green apple slices (optional)

1. Combine first 3 ingredients (water through bay leaf) in a saucepan over medium-high heat. Bring mixture to a simmer; cover and cook 2 hours and 15 minutes or until wheat berries are almost tender. Drain and place in a bowl; discard bay leaf.
2. Coarsely chop 1 cup spinach leaves. Add chopped spinach, apple, chopped bell pepper, dressing, and mustard to wheat berries, and toss well.
3. Prepare grill.
4. Sprinkle chicken with salt and pepper. Place chicken on a grill rack coated with cooking spray; grill 5 minutes on each side or until done. Thinly slice chicken.
5. Divide remaining spinach evenly among 4 plates. Place ½ cup wheat-berry mixture on spinach. Arrange chicken evenly over berry mixture; sprinkle with green onions. Garnish with apple slices, if desired.

PER SERVING (1 salad): Calories 332 (31% from fat); Protein 29g; Fat 12g (sat 2g, mono 7g, poly 1g); Carbohydrate 30g; Fiber 3g; Cholesterol 63mg; Iron 4mg; Sodium 792mg; Calcium 113mg

cucumber-yogurt dressing:

     1 cup chopped seeded peeled
        cucumber
     3 tablespoons plain low-fat
        yogurt
     2 tablespoons olive oil
     1 teaspoon balsamic vinegar
  ¹/₄ teaspoon salt
  ¹/₄ teaspoon black pepper
  ¹/₈ teaspoon dried dill

1. Place all ingredients in a blender; process until smooth. Refrigerate in an airtight container up to 1 week. Yield: 1 cup.

PER SERVING (1 tablespoon): Calories 18 (86% from fat); Protein 0.g; Fat 2g (sat 0g, mono 1g, poly 0g); Carbohydrate 1g; Fiber 0g; Cholesterol 0mg; Iron 0mg; Sodium 39mg; Calcium 7mg

Mediterranean Basmati Salad, page 193

Marinated Broccoli-Corn Salad, page 187

Two-Potato Salad with Mustard-Chive Dressing, page 188

Grilled Chicken and Wheat Berry Salad, page 196

Wild Rice Salad with Peas, page 191

Confetti Slaw with Poppy Seed Dressing, page 187

Asian Noodle and Turkey Salad, page 202

*Chicken-Blue Cheese Salad with
Warm Bacon Vinaigrette, page 201*

saigon chicken salad with figs, melon, and won ton chips

Prep: *25 minutes* **Cook:** *10 minutes*
Serves 4

Find fresh won ton wrappers in Asian markets or in the produce section of major grocery stores.

Olive oil-flavored cooking spray
16 (3-inch) fresh won ton wrappers
$1/2$ teaspoon ground coriander
$1/2$ teaspoon salt
2 cups water
1 pound skinless, boneless chicken breast
3 tablespoons honey
3 tablespoons sherry vinegar
1 teaspoon grated lime zest
2 cups cubed cantaloupe
1 cucumber, seeded and chopped
1 cup sliced dried mission figs
$1/4$ cup chopped fresh mint
4 butter-lettuce leaves
$1/4$ cup coarsely chopped dry-roasted peanuts

1. Preheat oven to 350°.
2. Coat a large baking sheet with cooking spray. Fold each won ton wrapper in half, forming a triangle. Arrange wrappers on baking sheet without overlapping, and coat with cooking spray.
3. In a small bowl, mix together coriander and salt, and sprinkle over wrappers. Bake at 350° for 8 minutes, until just golden. Set aside.
4. Meanwhile, in a medium-sized saucepan, bring 2 cups water to a boil. Add chicken, and reduce heat to medium; cook 10 minutes, or until chicken is cooked through. Drain and cut chicken into 1-inch cubes.
5. In a large bowl, whisk together honey, vinegar, and lime zest. Add chicken; toss to coat. Add cantaloupe, cucumber, figs, and mint; toss to combine.
6. Place 1 lettuce leaf on each serving plate. Spoon chicken mixture evenly onto leaves. Top evenly with peanuts. Serve with won ton chips.

PER SERVING (1 salad and 4 chips): Calories 499 (15% from fat), Protein 34g; Fat 9g (sat 2g, mono 3g, poly 2g); Carbohydrate 72g; Fiber 7g; Cholesterol 75mg; Iron 4mg; Sodium 627mg; Calcium 132mg

chicken-blue cheese salad with warm bacon vinaigrette

pictured on pages 185 and 200

Prep: *12 minutes* **Cook:** *25 minutes*
Serves 6

Assemble the salad before you make the vinaigrette, and then pour the warm vinaigrette over the salad just before serving.

1 cup dry white wine
1 ($14^{1}/4$-ounce) can fat-free chicken broth
1 pound skinless, boneless chicken breast
12 cups mixed baby salad greens
1 medium-sized red Bartlett pear, cored and cut into $1/2$-inch-thick slices
1 medium-sized green Bartlett pear, cored and cut into $1/2$-inch-thick slices
Warm Bacon Vinaigrette
$3/4$ cup (3 ounces) crumbled blue cheese

1. Bring wine and broth to a boil in a large skillet. Add chicken breasts; cover, reduce heat, and simmer 15 minutes or until done. Remove chicken with a slotted spoon; discard wine mixture. Cut chicken diagonally into thin slices.
2. Combine chicken, salad greens, and pear slices in a large bowl. Drizzle Warm Bacon Vinaigrette over salad, and toss gently. Sprinkle with blue cheese.

PER SERVING (2 cups salad greens, about 3 ounces chicken, 4 pear slices, $1/2$ ounce blue cheese, and about $2^{1}/2$ tablespoons vinaigrette): Calories 237 (33% from fat); Protein 24g; Fat 9g (sat 4g, mono 3g, poly 1g); Carbohydrate 16g; Fiber 4g; Cholesterol 67mg; Iron 2mg; Sodium 572mg; Calcium 137mg

warm bacon vinaigrette:

Cooking spray
$1/3$ cup chopped red onion
3 turkey-bacon slices, chopped
$1/2$ cup fat-free chicken broth
$1/3$ cup cider vinegar
2 tablespoons brown sugar
$1/2$ teaspoon salt
$1/4$ teaspoon dry mustard
$1/4$ teaspoon celery seeds
$1/4$ teaspoon pepper

1. Coat a nonstick skillet with cooking spray, and place over medium-high heat until hot. Add chopped onion and bacon, and sauté 10 minutes or until onion is tender and bacon is browned. Remove pan from heat; add chicken broth and remaining ingredients, stirring until sugar dissolves. Yield: 1 cup.

chicken fajita salad

Prep: *20 minutes* **Cook:** *10 minutes*
Serves 4

- $^{1}/_{2}$ teaspoon salt, divided
- 1 teaspoon chili powder
- $^{1}/_{2}$ teaspoon ground cumin
- 4 (6-inch) corn tortillas, cut into $^{1}/_{2}$-inch strips
- Cooking spray
- 1 pound chicken breast tenders, cut in half lengthwise
- $1^{1}/_{2}$ cups sliced green bell pepper
- 1 cup sliced red bell pepper
- $^{1}/_{2}$ cup thinly sliced onion
- $^{1}/_{4}$ cup fresh lime juice
- $2^{1}/_{2}$ tablespoons olive oil
- 7 cups torn romaine lettuce
- 2 cups halved cherry tomatoes

1. Preheat oven to 425°.
2. Combine ¼ teaspoon salt, chili powder, and cumin in a bowl. Place tortilla strips on a baking sheet coated with cooking spray; sprinkle with half of cumin mixture. Bake at 425° for 15 minutes or until tortillas are crisp and lightly browned.
3. Combine remaining cumin mixture and chicken in a zip-top plastic bag; shake to coat. Heat a large nonstick skillet coated with cooking spray over medium-high heat. Add chicken; cook 3 minutes on each side. Add bell peppers and onion; cook 4 minutes or until vegetables are tender, stirring frequently.
4. Combine lime juice, oil, and ¼ teaspoon salt in a large bowl; pour mixture over lettuce; toss well. Place lettuce on plates; top each with chicken mixture, tomatoes, and baked tortilla strips.

PER SERVING ($1^{3}/_{4}$ cups lettuce, $^{3}/_{4}$ cup chicken mixture , $^{1}/_{2}$ cup tomatoes, and 12 tortilla strips): Calories 332 (30% from fat); Protein 31g; Fat 11g (sat 2g, mono 7g, poly 3g); Carbohydrate 29g; Fiber 6g; Cholesterol 66mg; Iron 4mg; Sodium 394mg; Calcium 87mg

asian noodle and turkey salad

pictured on page 199

Prep: *16 minutes* **Cook:** *1 minute*
Serves 8

Make this dish ahead of time, and pack it to go for a quick and healthy lunch.

- 3 cups coarsely chopped bok choy
- 1 cup preshredded carrot
- 1 cup fresh snow peas
- $^{1}/_{2}$ cup hoisin sauce
- $^{1}/_{4}$ cup rice vinegar
- $^{1}/_{4}$ cup low-sodium soy sauce
- 1 tablespoon minced garlic
- 1 tablespoon minced peeled fresh ginger
- 1 tablespoon dark sesame oil
- 4 cups hot cooked angel hair pasta (about 8 ounces uncooked pasta)
- 2 cups chopped cooked white and dark turkey
- 1 cup diagonally sliced green onions
- 4 teaspoons sesame seeds, toasted

1. Cook first 3 ingredients (bok choy through peas) in boiling water 1 minute. Drain; rinse under cold water. Drain well, and let cool.
2. Combine hoisin sauce and next 5 ingredients (hoisin through oil) in a large bowl; stir well. Add bok choy mixture, pasta, turkey, and green onions; toss well. Spoon mixture onto 8 plates; sprinkle with sesame seeds. Serve at room temperature or chilled.

PER SERVING (1 cup salad and $^{1}/_{2}$ teaspoon sesame seeds): Calories 256 (19% from fat); Protein 16g; Fat 5g (sat 1g, mono 1g, poly 2g); Carbohydrate 34g; Fiber 3g; Cholesterol 28mg; Iron 3mg; Sodium 496mg; Calcium 66mg

warm pork tenderloin salad with ginger-lime dressing

Prep: *8 minutes* **Cook:** *20 minutes*
Serves 4

- 1 (1-pound) pork tenderloin, trimmed and halved lengthwise
- $^{1}/_{4}$ teaspoon salt
- $^{1}/_{4}$ teaspoon black pepper
- Cooking spray
- 2 tablespoons chopped seeded jalapeño pepper (about 1 large)
- 2 tablespoons water
- 2 tablespoons fresh lime juice
- 1 tablespoon grated peeled fresh ginger
- 4 teaspoons olive oil
- $^{1}/_{4}$ teaspoon salt
- $^{1}/_{4}$ teaspoon black pepper
- $2^{1}/_{2}$ cups chopped peeled mango
- $1^{1}/_{2}$ cups chopped plum tomato (about $^{3}/_{4}$ pound)
- $^{1}/_{4}$ cup thinly sliced green onions
- 1 (10-ounce) package romaine salad

1. Preheat oven to 425°.
2. Sprinkle pork with ¼ teaspoon salt and ¼ teaspoon black pepper. Place pork in a foil-lined, shallow roasting pan coated with cooking spray. Bake at 425° for 20 minutes or until thermometer registers 160° (slightly pink). Cut pork diagonally across grain into thin slices; keep warm.
3. Combine jalapeño and next 6 ingredients (jalapeño through black pepper); stir well with a whisk.
4. Combine pork, dressing, mango, and remaining ingredients; toss gently to coat.

PER SERVING ($2^{1}/_{4}$ cups): Calories 281 (30% from fat); Protein 27g; Fat 9g (sat 2g, mono 5g, poly 1g); Carbohydrate 24g; Fiber 4g; Cholesterol 79mg; Iron 3mg; Sodium 365mg; Calcium 54mg

delectable side dishes

Oven-Roasted Sweet Potato
Fries, page 210

asian marinated asparagus

Prep: *9 minutes* **Cook:** *2 minutes*
Marinate: *2 hours*
Serves 4

Avoid the heat of the kitchen by making these cool marinated asparagus spears ahead.

- 1 pound asparagus spears
- 2 tablespoons water
- 1/4 cup seasoned rice vinegar
- 2 tablespoons soy sauce
- 2 teaspoons chopped peeled fresh ginger
- 1 teaspoon dark sesame oil

1. Snap off tough ends of asparagus, and remove scales with a knife or vegetable peeler, if desired. Place asparagus spears and water in a shallow microwave-safe dish. Cover dish, and microwave at HIGH 2 to 4 minutes or until asparagus is crisp-tender; drain. Return asparagus to dish.
2. Combine vinegar and next 3 ingredients (vinegar through oil) in a small bowl; stir with a whisk until mixture is blended. Pour vinegar mixture over asparagus, turning asparagus to coat. Cover and marinate in refrigerator at least 2 hours, turning asparagus occasionally.

PER SERVING (1/4 of asparagus): Calories 38 (31% from fat); Protein 3g; Fat 1g (sat 0g, mono 0g, poly 1g); Carbohydrate 5g; Fiber 2g; Cholesterol 0mg; Iron 1mg; Sodium 518mg; Calcium 20mg

broccoli with sharp cheddar cheese sauce

pictured on page 218

Prep: *4 minutes* **Cook:** *9 minutes*
Serves 4

This green veggie becomes much more appealing when topped with a velvety, rich cheese sauce.

- 1 pound fresh broccoli florets
- 2 tablespoons all-purpose flour
- 1/2 teaspoon dry mustard
- 1/4 teaspoon salt
- Dash of ground red pepper
- 3/4 cup 1% low-fat milk
- 3/4 cup (3 ounces) shredded sharp Cheddar cheese

1. Arrange broccoli in a vegetable steamer over boiling water. Cover and steam 5 minutes or until crisp-tender.
2. Combine flour and next 3 ingredients (flour through red pepper) in a saucepan; stir well. Gradually add milk, stirring well with a whisk until blended. Place over medium heat; cook 4 minutes or until thick, stirring constantly. Remove from heat; add cheese, stirring until cheese melts. Spoon cheese sauce over cooked broccoli.

PER SERVING (1/4 of broccoli and 1/4 cup sauce): Calories 151 (48% from fat); Protein 11g; Fat 8g (sat 4g, mono 0g, poly 0g); Carbohydrate 11g; Fiber 4g; Cholesterol 25mg; Iron 1mg; Sodium 336mg; Calcium 264mg

brussels sprouts gratin

Prep: *13 minutes* **Cook:** *43 minutes*
Serves 4

If fresh Brussels sprouts aren't available, substitute 1 (16-ounce) package of frozen Brussels sprouts. Let them thaw, cut them in half, cook according to package directions, and then proceed to Step 3.

- 1 pound fresh Brussels sprouts
- Cooking spray
- 2/3 cup evaporated fat-free milk
- 1/2 teaspoon grated lemon rind
- 2 tablespoons fresh lemon juice
- 1/4 teaspoon salt
- 1/4 teaspoon pepper
- 1 large egg
- 1/2 cup (2 ounces) shredded fresh Parmesan cheese

1. Preheat oven to 375°.
2. Cut each Brussels sprout in half lengthwise. Place in a medium saucepan, and cover with water; bring to a boil. Reduce heat, and simmer 5 minutes or just until tender; drain sprouts well.
3. Arrange Brussels sprouts in a 9-inch quiche dish coated with cooking spray. Combine milk and next 5 ingredients (milk through egg) in a bowl; stir with a whisk until well blended. Pour milk mixture over Brussels sprouts; sprinkle with cheese.
4. Bake at 375° for 35 minutes or until lightly browned. Serve immediately.

PER SERVING (1/4 of gratin): Calories 146 (27% from fat); Protein 13g; Fat 4g (sat 2g, mono 2g, poly 0g); Carbohydrate 17g; Fiber 5g; Cholesterol 64mg; Iron 2mg; Sodium 401mg; Calcium 299mg

sweet-and-sour cabbage and apples

Prep: *10 minutes* **Cook:** *13 minutes*
Serves 6

Hickory-smoked bacon and Granny Smith apples make steamed cabbage a hearty dish.

2 hickory-smoked bacon slices
2 medium Granny Smith apples, each cut into 12 wedges
4 cups thinly sliced red cabbage
$^1/_4$ cup balsamic vinegar
2 tablespoons sugar
$^1/_4$ teaspoon salt
$^1/_4$ teaspoon pepper

1. Cook bacon in a large nonstick skillet over medium-high heat until crisp. Remove bacon from pan, reserving 1 tablespoon bacon fat in pan; crumble bacon, and set aside.
2. Arrange apple wedges, cut sides down, in pan; cook over medium-high heat 3 minutes (do not turn apples or they will overcook). Reduce heat to medium. Add cabbage; cover and cook 5 minutes.
3. Add vinegar and next 3 ingredients (vinegar through pepper); bring to a boil. Reduce heat, and simmer, uncovered, 5 minutes or until liquid almost evaporates, stirring occasionally. Sprinkle with crumbled bacon.

PER SERVING ($^2/_3$ cup): Calories 104 (31% from fat); Protein 2g; Fat 4g (sat 1g, mono 2g, poly 1g); Carbohydrate 18g; Fiber 3g; Cholesterol 4mg; Iron 1mg; Sodium 143mg; Calcium 31mg

roasted baby carrots with fresh thyme

Prep: *5 minutes* **Cook:** *30 minutes*
Serves 4

Fresh thyme offers a minty, lemony flavor to carrots.

1 pound baby carrots
2 teaspoons olive oil
1 tablespoon chopped fresh thyme
$^1/_2$ teaspoon salt
1 teaspoon grated lemon rind
$^1/_8$ teaspoon pepper
1 finely chopped green onion

1. Preheat oven to 450°.
2. In a large bowl, combine carrots and next 3 ingredients (carrots through salt); toss well.
3. Spread carrots in a single layer on a baking sheet. Bake at 450° for 30 minutes or until tender and lightly browned, stirring every 10 minutes. Remove from oven. Transfer to a serving bowl. Sprinkle with lemon rind, pepper, and green onion; toss well. Serve immediately.

PER SERVING (about $^2/_3$ cup): Calories 65 (37% from fat); Protein 1g; Fat 3g (sat 0g, mono 2g, poly 1g); Carbohydrate 10g; Fiber 2g; Cholesterol 0mg; Iron 1mg; Sodium 334mg; Calcium 30mg

honey-mustard carrots

Prep: *4 minutes* **Cook:** *14 minutes*
Serves 4

You'll love eating your vegetables once you've tasted these baby carrots in their sweet, tangy glaze.

1 pound baby carrots
1 tablespoon brown sugar
1 tablespoon butter
1 tablespoon honey mustard
1 tablespoon frozen orange juice concentrate
$^1/_4$ teaspoon salt
$^1/_8$ teaspoon pepper

1. Place carrots in a small saucepan, and cover with water; bring to a boil. Reduce heat, and simmer 8 minutes or just until carrots are tender. Drain carrots well.
2. Return hot carrots to pan. Add sugar and remaining ingredients; stir well. Cook over medium-low heat until butter melts and carrots are coated, stirring constantly.

PER SERVING ($^3/_4$ cup): Calories 98 (28% from fat); Protein 1g; Fat 4g (sat 2g, mono 1g, poly 1g); Carbohydrate 17g; Fiber 4g; Cholesterol 8mg; Iron 1mg; Sodium 223mg; Calcium 42mg

lemony spring vegetables

pictured on page 219

Prep: *16 minutes* **Cook:** *13 minutes*
Serves 10

These fresh vegetables are an easy side dish to prepare for a crowd.

2³/₄ cups diagonally sliced carrot
5¹/₂ cups (1-inch) sliced asparagus (about 2 pounds)
4¹/₄ cups sugar snap peas, trimmed
 ¹/₄ cup light butter
 3 cups thinly sliced leek (about 3 medium)
 2 teaspoons grated lemon rind
 2 tablespoons fresh lemon juice
 2 tablespoons chopped fresh thyme
 ¹/₂ teaspoon salt

1. Arrange carrot in a vegetable steamer in a Dutch oven; cover and steam 4 minutes. Add asparagus, and steam 2 minutes. Add peas; steam 3 minutes. Remove vegetables and steamer from Dutch oven. Set aside. Discard water from Dutch oven.
2. Melt butter in Dutch oven over medium-high heat. Add leek, and sauté 2 minutes. Add vegetables, lemon rind, and remaining ingredients; cook 2 minutes, stirring frequently.

PER SERVING (1 cup): Calories 88 (28% from fat); Protein 4g; Fat 3g (sat 2g, mono 0g, poly 0g); Carbohydrate 13g; Fiber 4g; Cholesterol 8mg; Iron 2mg; Sodium 165mg; Calcium 53mg

corn bread, cherry, and bacon stuffing

Prep: *45 minutes* **Cook:** *20 minutes*
Serves 12

 ²/₃ cup fat-free milk
 2 large eggs
 2 (8¹/₂-ounce) packages corn muffin mix
Cooking spray
 6 bacon slices
 2 cups chopped onion
 2 cups chopped carrot
 2 cups chopped celery
 ¹/₂ cup dried tart cherries
 1 (14.5-ounce) can fat-free, less-sodium chicken broth
 1 cup chopped fresh parsley
 1 teaspoon dried thyme
 ¹/₂ teaspoon salt
 ¹/₄ teaspoon black pepper

1. Preheat oven to 400°.
2. Combine milk and eggs in a bowl; stir well with a whisk. Stir in muffin mix; let stand 2 minutes. Pour corn bread mixture in a 13 x 9-inch baking dish coated with cooking spray. Bake at 400° for 20 minutes or until a wooden pick inserted in center comes out clean. Cool and cut into ¹/₂-inch cubes. Place cubes on a baking sheet; bake at 400° for 10 minutes or until golden brown.
3. Cook bacon in a large nonstick skillet over medium heat until crisp. Remove bacon from pan, reserving 1 teaspoon drippings in pan. Crumble bacon; set aside. Add onion, carrot, and celery to pan; sauté 5 minutes over medium-high heat. Stir in cherries and broth; cook 5 minutes.
4. Combine corn bread cubes, bacon, onion mixture, parsley, thyme, salt, and pepper in a large bowl; stirring until well blended. Spoon corn bread mixture into a 13 x 9-inch baking dish coated with cooking spray. Bake at 400° for 20 minutes or until thoroughly heated, stirring after 10 minutes.

PER SERVING (³/₄ cup): Calories 248 (28% from fat); Protein 6g; Fat 8g (sat 2g, mono 3g, poly 2g); Carbohydrate 39g; Fiber 3g; Cholesterol 41mg; Iron 2mg; Sodium 524mg; Calcium 113mg

double corn polenta

Prep: *5 minutes* **Cook:** *15 minutes*
Serves 4

This side gets a double punch of corn from the cornmeal and the fresh corn kernels. If fresh corn is unavailable at your supermarket, you can substitute frozen corn.

 ³/₄ cup stone-ground cornmeal
 ³/₄ cup fresh corn kernels (about 2 ears)
2¹/₂ cups fat-free, less-sodium chicken broth
 1 teaspoon finely chopped fresh oregano
 ¹/₂ teaspoon salt
 ¹/₂ teaspoon pepper

1. Place cornmeal and corn kernels in a large saucepan. Gradually add chicken broth, stirring constantly with a whisk. Bring mixture to a boil; reduce heat to medium, and cook 12 minutes, stirring frequently. Stir in oregano, salt, and pepper. Serve immediately.

PER SERVING (¹/₂ cup): Calories 128 (14% from fat); Protein 5g; Fat 2g (sat 1g, mono 0g, poly 1g); Carbohydrate 24g; Fiber 2g; Cholesterol 2mg; Iron 1mg; Sodium 373mg; Calcium 14mg

creamy corn and rice casserole

Prep: *8 minutes* **Cook:** *51 minutes*
Stand: *5 minutes*
Serves 8

　1　tablespoon butter
Cooking spray
　1　(8-ounce) package presliced
　　　fresh mushrooms
　1/2　cup chopped onion
1 1/3　cups chicken broth
　1/2　cup uncooked converted rice
　1　(10 3/4-ounce) can reduced-fat,
　　　reduced-sodium cream of
　　　mushroom soup, undiluted
　2　(11-ounce) cans vacuum-
　　　packed corn with red and
　　　green peppers (such as
　　　Mexicorn), undrained
　1/2　cup (2 ounces) shredded
　　　reduced-fat sharp Cheddar
　　　cheese
Red bell pepper strips (optional)

1. Preheat oven to 350°.
2. Melt butter in a saucepan coated with cooking spray over medium-high heat. Add mushrooms and onion; sauté 6 minutes. Add broth; bring to a boil. Add rice; cover, reduce heat, and simmer 20 minutes. Remove from heat; let stand, covered, 5 minutes. Stir in soup and corn. Spoon mixture into an 8-inch square baking dish coated with cooking spray. Bake at 350° for 15 minutes. Top with cheese; bake 5 minutes or until cheese melts. Garnish with red bell pepper strips, if desired.

PER SERVING (2/3 cup): Calories 176 (21% from fat); Protein 7g; Fat 4g (sat 2g, mono 1g, poly 0g); Carbohydrate 29g; Fiber 2g; Cholesterol 8mg; Iron 1mg; Sodium 780mg; Calcium 109mg

garlicky green bean casserole

Prep: *8 minutes* **Cook:** *45 minutes*
Stand: *5 minutes*
Serves 4

　2/3　cup water
　4　garlic cloves, minced
　1　(16-ounce) package frozen cut
　　　green beans
　1　(10 3/4-ounce) can condensed
　　　reduced-fat, reduced-sodium
　　　cream of mushroom soup,
　　　undiluted
　1　cup coarsely crushed onion
　　　Melba toast (about 10
　　　rectangular crackers), divided
　1/4　teaspoon salt
　1/4　teaspoon pepper
Butter-flavored cooking spray

1. Preheat oven to 350°.
2. Combine water and garlic in a saucepan; bring to a boil, and cook 2 minutes. Add green beans, and return to a boil. Cover, reduce heat, and simmer 8 minutes or until crisp-tender. Drain beans, reserving cooking liquid. Set beans aside.
3. Return cooking liquid to pan; bring to a boil, and cook 2 minutes or until reduced to 2 tablespoons. Add soup, stirring until smooth. Add green beans, 1/2 cup Melba toast, salt, and pepper. Spoon mixture into a 1-quart casserole dish coated with cooking spray. Sprinkle remaining 1/2 cup Melba toast evenly over casserole; coat generously with cooking spray.
4. Bake, uncovered, at 350° for 25 minutes; let stand 5 minutes before serving.

PER SERVING (about 1 cup): Calories 104 (14% from fat); Protein 4g; Fat 2g (sat 1g, mono 0g, poly 0g); Carbohydrate 18g; Fiber 3g; Cholesterol 3mg; Iron 2mg; Sodium 544mg; Calcium 58mg

buttery herbed green beans

pictured on page 219

Prep: *2 minutes* **Cook:** *12 minutes*
Serves 3

Substitute other dried herbs such as oregano, basil, or thyme for the tarragon, if desired.

　2　(9-ounce) packages frozen
　　　whole green beans (about 5
　　　cups)
　2　teaspoons butter
　2　tablespoons finely chopped
　　　fresh parsley
　2　teaspoons cider or balsamic
　　　vinegar
　1/2　teaspoon salt
　1/2　teaspoon dried tarragon
Parsley sprigs (optional)

1. Bring 1/2 cup water to a boil over high heat in a large nonstick skillet; add green beans. Cover and cook 8 minutes or until beans are crisp-tender; drain.
2. Combine beans and butter in skillet; cook over low heat until butter melts. Add chopped parsley, vinegar, salt, and tarragon; toss well. Garnish with parsley, if desired.

PER SERVING (1 cup): Calories 80 (32% from fat); Protein 3g; Fat 3g (sat 1g, mono 1g, poly 0g); Carbohydrate 13g; Fiber 5g; Cholesterol 0mg; Iron 2mg; Sodium 231mg; Calcium 78mg

parmesan-breaded portobellos

Prep: *10 minutes* **Cook:** *14 minutes*
Serves 4

Parmesan cheese rather than breadcrumbs provides the tasty crust for these mushrooms.

- 2 tablespoons grated fresh Parmesan cheese
- 1 tablespoon minced fresh or 1 teaspoon dried basil
- 1 large egg, lightly beaten
- 1 large egg white, lightly beaten
- 4 (4-inch) portobello mushroom caps
- 2 tablespoons all-purpose flour
- 1 tablespoon olive oil
- 2 tablespoons lemon juice

1. Preheat oven to 400°.
2. Combine first 4 ingredients (cheese through egg white) in a small bowl. Place mushrooms and flour in a plastic bag; seal and shake gently to coat.
3. Heat oil in a large nonstick skillet over medium heat. Dip mushrooms in egg mixture. Place mushrooms, cap sides down, in pan; sauté 2 minutes per side or until golden brown. Sprinkle lemon juice evenly over mushrooms. Remove mushrooms from pan, and place on a baking sheet. Bake at 400° for 10 minutes or until mushrooms are tender.

PER SERVING (1 mushroom): Calories 94 (55% from fat); Protein 5g; Fat 6g (sat 2g, mono 3g, poly 1g); Carbohydrate 6g; Fiber 1g; Cholesterol 58mg; Iron 1mg; Sodium 88mg; Calcium 53mg

portobello mushrooms with thyme and shallots

Prep: *20 minutes* **Cook:** *20 minutes*
Serves 4

- 4 large portobello mushrooms (about 1 pound)
- Cooking spray
- 1 teaspoon olive oil
- 1/2 cup finely chopped red bell pepper
- 1/4 cup finely chopped shallots
- 1/2 teaspoon salt
- 1/4 teaspoon freshly ground black pepper
- 2 teaspoons chopped fresh or 1/2 teaspoon dried thyme
- 1 cup toasted breadcrumbs
- 1/4 cup (1 ounce) shredded Asiago or Romano cheese

1. Preheat oven to 375°.
2. Clean mushrooms; remove stems. Finely chop stems. Using a paring knife, scrape out and discard gills from caps. Coat both sides of caps with cooking spray. Arrange caps, rounded sides down, on a jelly-roll pan or baking sheet.
3. Heat oil in a large nonstick skillet over medium heat. Add chopped mushroom stems, bell pepper, shallots, salt, and black pepper; cook 5 minutes, stirring occasionally. Stir in thyme; spoon mixture into mushroom caps. Combine breadcrumbs and cheese; sprinkle evenly over mushrooms. Coat crumb mixture with cooking spray. Bake at 375° for 12 to 14 minutes or until crumbs are golden brown and mushrooms are tender.

PER SERVING (1 mushroom): Calories 101 (29% from fat); Protein 6g; Fat 4g (sat 1g, mono 2g, poly 0g); Carbohydrate 13g; Fiber 0g; Cholesterol 7mg; Iron 1mg; Sodium 373mg; Calcium 104mg

sweet onions with pistachios

pictured on page 218

Prep: *23 minutes* **Cook:** *25 minutes*
Serves 4

Pistachios add a subtle nutty flavor and nice crunch to sweet onions. Plus, they're a good source of iron and vitamin A. Store leftover pistachios in an airtight container in the freezer.

- 2 Vidalia or other sweet onions
- 1/4 cup brown sugar, divided
- 1 teaspoon ground cinnamon, divided
- 1/2 teaspoon freshly ground black pepper, divided
- 1/4 teaspoon salt, divided
- 1 tablespoon balsamic vinegar
- 1 tablespoon minced pistachios

1. Peel onions; cut a 1/4-inch slice from each end so onions sit flat. Cut onions in half crosswise. Place in a large saucepan; add just enough water to cover. Bring to a boil; cover, reduce heat, and simmer 10 minutes or until slightly tender. Drain; let cool completely.
2. Prepare grill.
3. Place a 10-inch cast-iron skillet on grill rack over hot coals; let skillet heat at least 10 minutes or until very hot.
4. Combine 2 tablespoons brown sugar, 1/2 teaspoon cinnamon, 1/4 teaspoon pepper, and 1/8 teaspoon salt in a shallow dish; stir well. Press widest cut side of each onion half in sugar mixture to coat.
5. Place onions, sugar sides down, in heated skillet; cook 6 minutes or until caramelized. Turn onions over; cook an additional 6 minutes. Place onions on a serving plate.

6. Combine vinegar, remaining brown sugar, cinnamon, pepper, and salt. Stir well; drizzle over onions. Sprinkle with pistachios.

PER SERVING (1/2 onion): Calories 97 (14% from fat); Protein 2g; Fat 2g (sat 0g, mono 0g, poly 0g); Carbohydrate 21g; Fiber 2g; Cholesterol 0mg; Iron 1mg; Sodium 154mg; Calcium 38mg

potato, corn, and red pepper hash

Prep: *23 minutes* **Cook:** *50 minutes*
Serves 8

Be sure to use the shelled, green kernel of the pumpkinseed, not the whole seed. If pumpkinseed kernels aren't available, substitute roasted sunflower seed kernels or toasted pine nuts.

    1   pound Yukon gold or red
        potatoes
1 1/2   teaspoons olive oil, divided
    1   cup chopped onion
    1   cup fresh corn kernels or frozen
        whole-kernel corn
    1   (7-ounce) jar roasted red bell
        peppers, drained and chopped
    1   teaspoon ground cumin
Dash of ground red pepper
    2   tablespoons chopped, unsalted
        pumpkinseed kernels, toasted
    3   tablespoons chopped fresh
        parsley
  1/2   teaspoon salt
  1/4   teaspoon black pepper

1. Place potatoes in a large Dutch oven, and cover with water; bring to a boil. Reduce heat, and simmer 30 minutes or until tender; drain. Let cool; peel potatoes, and cut into 1/2-inch cubes.
2. Heat 1/2 teaspoon oil in a large nonstick skillet over medium-high heat. Add onion; sauté 5 minutes. Add corn; sauté 3 min-

utes. Stir in roasted peppers, cumin, and ground red pepper. Spoon mixture into a bowl; set aside.
3. Heat 1/2 teaspoon olive oil in skillet over medium-high heat. Add half of potato cubes, and cook 5 minutes or until lightly browned, stirring once (frequent stirring prevents browning). Add potatoes to corn mixture, and set aside. Repeat procedure with remaining 1/2 teaspoon olive oil and potatoes.
4. Return potato-corn mixture to skillet; cook over medium-high heat 1 minute or until warm. Remove from heat; stir in pumpkinseed kernels, parsley, salt, and black pepper.

PER SERVING (1/2 cup): Calories 89 (22% from fat); Protein 3g; Fat 2g (sat 0g, mono 1g, poly 1g); Carbohydrate 16g; Fiber 2g; Cholesterol 0mg; Iron 2mg; Sodium 517mg; Calcium 28mg

golden garlic mashed potatoes

Prep: *8 minutes* **Cook:** *22 minutes*
Serves 4

Nothing beats the creamy flavor and fluffy texture of fresh mashed potatoes. For easy cleanup, mash the potatoes right in the pan. Use a potato masher if you like a chunky texture. For creamy potatoes, use a handheld mixer.

4 1/2   cups cubed peeled Yukon gold
        or baking potato
  3/4   cup 2% reduced-fat milk
    1   tablespoon butter
  3/4   teaspoon salt
  1/8   to 1/4 teaspoon pepper
    2   garlic cloves, minced

1. Place potato cubes in a medium saucepan, and cover with water; bring to a boil. Reduce

heat. Simmer 15 minutes or until potatoes are tender; drain. Mash potatoes; add milk, butter, salt, pepper, and minced garlic, stirring well.

PER SERVING (1 cup): Calories 214 (17% from fat); Protein 5g; Fat 4g (sat 2g, mono 1g, poly 0g); Carbohydrate 41g; Fiber 3g; Cholesterol 11mg; Iron 1mg; Sodium 506mg; Calcium 72mg

loaded mashed potatoes

Prep: *6 minutes* **Cook:** *14 minutes*
Serves 6

Though this recipe uses frozen mashed potatoes, we were pleasantly surprised at the end result. The spuds only take minutes to make and are sure to be a hit at dinnertime.

2 1/4   cups 1% low-fat milk
    1   (22-ounce) bag frozen mashed
        potatoes
  1/2   cup light cream cheese,
        softened
  1/3   cup thinly sliced green onions
  1/4   cup (1 ounce) shredded
        reduced-fat sharp Cheddar
        cheese
  1/2   teaspoon salt
  1/4   teaspoon pepper

1. Heat milk over medium-high heat in a large heavy saucepan to 180° or until tiny bubbles form around edge of pan (do not boil). Add potatoes, and cook 9 minutes, stirring constantly. Remove from heat; add cream cheese, stirring until smooth. Stir in onions and remaining ingredients.

PER SERVING (1 cup): Calories 230 (34% from fat); Protein 9g; Fat 9g (sat 5g, mono 0g, poly 0g); Carbohydrate 28g; Fiber 2g; Cholesterol 24mg; Iron 0mg; Sodium 616mg; Calcium 225mg

cranberry-sweet potato skillet

Prep: *14 minutes* **Cook:** *14 minutes*
Serves 5

We captured some favorite flavors of Thanksgiving in this easy side.

- 4 cups chopped peeled sweet potato (about 2 large)
- 2 teaspoons butter
- 1 cup chopped plum (about 2 medium)
- 1 (12-ounce) container cranberry-orange crushed fruit (such as Ocean Spray)
- 1/4 teaspoon salt
- 1/4 teaspoon ground red pepper
- 2 tablespoons chopped pecans, toasted

1. Place sweet potato in a large nonstick skillet, and cover with water; bring to a boil. Reduce heat, and simmer 7 minutes or until tender; drain well in a colander. Set aside.
2. Melt butter in skillet over medium heat. Add plum; cook 2 minutes. Stir in sweet potato, crushed fruit, salt, and pepper; cook 5 minutes or until thoroughly heated, stirring occasionally. Sprinkle with pecans.

PER SERVING (1 cup): Calories 291 (14% from fat); Protein 2g; Fat 4g (sat 1g, mono 2g, poly 1g); Carbohydrate 61g; Fiber 5g; Cholesterol 4mg; Iron 1mg; Sodium 183mg; Calcium 27mg

stuffed sweet potatoes

Prep: *17 minutes* **Cook:** *1 hour*
Serves 6

Sweet potatoes are a terrific source of fiber and cancer-fighting antioxidants. For more information on antioxidants, see page 19.

- 6 small sweet potatoes (about 2 1/2 pounds)
- 1 (15-ounce) can pear halves in juice, undrained
- 1/4 cup firmly packed brown sugar
- 1/4 teaspoon salt
- 1/4 cup sweetened dried cranberries (such as Craisins) or raisins
- 1/3 cup chopped pecans, toasted and divided

1. Preheat oven to 375°.
2. Wrap potatoes in foil; bake at 375° for 50 minutes or until done. Let cool slightly. Cut a slit in top of each potato; carefully scoop out pulp, leaving a 1/4-inch-thick shell.
3. Drain pears, reserving 1/4 cup juice. Place pear halves and reserved juice in a food processor; process until smooth. Add potato pulp, sugar, and salt; process until blended. Stir in cranberries and 4 tablespoons pecans.
4. Stuff shells with pulp mixture; sprinkle with remaining pecans. Place potatoes on a baking sheet; bake at 375° for 10 minutes or until thoroughly heated.

PER SERVING (1 potato): Calories 324 (14% from fat); Protein 4g; Fat 5g (sat 1g, mono 3g, poly 0g); Carbohydrate 68g; Fiber 7g; Cholesterol 0mg; Iron 1mg; Sodium 131mg; Calcium 52mg

oven-roasted sweet potato fries

pictured on pages 203 and 219

Prep: *5 minutes* **Cook:** *30 minutes*
Serves 4

To create a brown, crispy crust for these sweet potato wedges, first preheat the pan in the oven so the potatoes sizzle when added to the pan. They'll be crispier if you stir them a few times as they bake.

- 3 small sweet potatoes, each peeled and cut lengthwise into 8 wedges (about 2 pounds)
- 1 1/2 tablespoons olive oil
- 1/2 teaspoon dry mustard
- 2 teaspoons minced fresh rosemary
- 1/2 teaspoon salt

1. Preheat oven to 450°.
2. In a large bowl, combine sweet potato wedges and remaining ingredients; toss well to coat.
3. Arrange potatoes in a single layer on a baking sheet. Bake at 450° for 30 minutes or until crisp and lightly browned, stirring occasionally.

PER SERVING (6 wedges): Calories 189 (25% from fat); Protein 3g; Fat 5g (sat 1g, mono 4g, poly 1g); Carbohydrate 34g; Fiber 4g; Cholesterol 0mg; Iron 1mg; Sodium 307mg; Calcium 41mg

creamed spiced rutabaga

Prep: *16 minutes* **Cook:** *36 minutes*
Serves 8

Rutabaga tastes similar to cabbage and turnips. Select those that are smooth, firm, and heavy for their size. For a savory alternative to this slightly sweet side dish, omit sugar, allspice, and nutmeg. Substitute ½ teaspoon dried marjoram and ½ teaspoon black pepper.

- 6 cups cubed peeled rutabaga (about 1½ pounds)
- 4 cups cubed peeled Yukon gold or baking potato (about 1 pound)
- ¼ cup fat-free milk
- 2 tablespoons butter
- 1½ tablespoons brown sugar
- ½ teaspoon salt
- ¼ teaspoon ground allspice
- ¼ teaspoon ground nutmeg

Additional ground nutmeg (optional)

1. Place rutabaga in a large Dutch oven, and cover with water; bring to a boil. Reduce heat, and simmer 15 minutes. Add cubed potato, and bring to a boil. Reduce heat, and simmer an additional 15 minutes or until rutabaga and potato are tender.
2. Drain and return rutabaga-potato mixture to pan. Add milk and next 5 ingredients (milk through ¼ teaspoon nutmeg); beat with a mixer at medium speed until smooth. Spoon into a serving bowl; sprinkle with additional nutmeg, if desired.

PER SERVING (1 cup): Calories 136 (21% from fat); Protein 3g; Fat 3g (sat 1g, mono 1g, poly 0g); Carbohydrate 25g; Fiber 2g; Cholesterol 0mg; Iron 1mg; Sodium 215mg; Calcium 81mg

hoisin snow peas and peppers

Prep: *12 minutes* **Cook:** *9 minutes*
Serves 4

Look for prewashed and trimmed snow peas at your supermarket; they're usually near the packaged lettuces.

- 1 cup fat-free, less-sodium chicken broth
- 2 tablespoons hoisin sauce
- 1½ tablespoons dry sherry
- 2 teaspoons cornstarch

Cooking spray
- 1 teaspoon peanut or vegetable oil
- 3 cups fresh snow peas, trimmed
- 1 cup red bell pepper strips
- 2 teaspoons finely chopped unsalted, dry-roasted peanuts

1. Combine first 4 ingredients (broth through cornstarch) in a small bowl; stir well, and set aside.
2. Coat a large nonstick skillet with cooking spray; add peanut oil, and place over medium-high heat until hot. Add snow peas and bell pepper; sauté 3 minutes or until vegetables are crisp-tender. Add broth mixture, and cook 2 minutes or until mixture is thick, stirring constantly. Sprinkle with peanuts.

PER SERVING (1 cup vegetables and ½ teaspoon peanuts): Calories 95 (26% from fat); Protein 5g; Fat 3g (sat 1g, mono 1g, poly 1g); Carbohydrate 13g; Fiber 3g; Cholesterol 6mg; Iron 2mg; Sodium 116mg; Calcium 37mg

cheesy spinach and mushrooms

Prep: *3 minutes* **Cook:** *16 minutes*
Serves 4

As the cheese melts, it forms a rich, creamy sauce for the spinach and mushrooms.

- 2 (10-ounce) packages frozen chopped spinach

Cooking spray
- 1 cup chopped onion
- 1 (8-ounce) package presliced fresh mushrooms
- 6 tablespoons spreadable cheese with garlic and herbs (such as Alouette), softened
- 2 tablespoons grated Parmesan cheese

1. Cook spinach according to microwave directions on package, and drain (do not squeeze out excess moisture). Set spinach aside.
2. Coat a large nonstick skillet with cooking spray; place over medium-high heat until hot. Add onion and mushrooms, and sauté 5 minutes or until tender.
3. Stir in spinach. Drop spreadable cheese by heaping teaspoonfuls over hot spinach mixture, stirring gently until cheese melts. Sprinkle with Parmesan cheese.

PER SERVING (¾ cup): Calories 123 (49% from fat); Protein 7g; Fat 7g (sat 4g, mono 0g, poly 0g); Carbohydrate 12g; Fiber 6g; Cholesterol 25mg; Iron 4mg; Sodium 256mg; Calcium 215mg

summer squash croquettes

pictured on page 218

Prep: *22 minutes* **Cook:** *24 minutes*
Chill: *3 hours*
Serves 6

A croquette, like a fritter, is deep-fried and usually contains a mixture of vegetables or meat. We steamed summer squash and onions together, shaped the mixture into patties, and then pan-fried them. The result is a delicious side dish with half the fat.

1¼   pounds yellow squash, coarsely chopped
½   cup chopped onion
1   cup crushed saltine crackers (about 33 crackers)
¾   teaspoon salt
½   teaspoon sugar
2   large eggs
¼   cup yellow cornmeal
Cooking spray
1   tablespoon vegetable oil, divided
Parsley sprigs (optional)

1. Steam squash and onion, covered, 15 minutes or until vegetables are tender; drain well. Mash squash mixture with a potato masher or fork, and stir in crushed crackers and next 3 ingredients (crackers through eggs). Cover and chill mixture at least 3 hours.
2. Place ¼ cup yellow cornmeal in a large shallow dish. Divide squash mixture into 12 equal portions. Working quickly, dredge squash mixture, one portion at a time, in cornmeal, shaping into 3-inch patties, and coat each patty with cooking spray.
3. Coat a large nonstick skillet with cooking spray, and add 1 teaspoon vegetable oil. Place pan over medium-high heat until hot.

Add 4 patties, and cook 1½ minutes on each side or until golden. Remove patties from pan; set aside, and keep warm. Repeat procedure with remaining vegetable oil and patties. Garnish with parsley sprigs, if desired. Serve immediately.

PER SERVING (2 croquettes): Calories 161 (35% from fat); Protein 5g; Fat 6g (sat 1g, mono 3g, poly 1g); Carbohydrate 21g; Fiber 3g; Cholesterol 71mg; Iron 2mg; Sodium 556mg; Calcium 57mg

garlicky acorn squash and wild rice stuffing

Prep: *14 minutes* **Cook:** *1 hour 20 minutes*
Stand: *5 minutes*
Serves 7

1   medium acorn squash (about 1¼ pounds)
1   teaspoon butter
½   cup chopped onion
3   garlic cloves, minced
1   (14½-ounce) can chicken broth
¾   cup dried sweetened cranberries
½   cup orange juice
1   teaspoon minced fresh rosemary
⅛   teaspoon salt
¼   teaspoon pepper
1   (6-ounce) package long-grain-and-wild rice mix
3   tablespoons chopped walnuts, toasted

1. Preheat oven to 350°.
2. Cut squash in half lengthwise; discard seeds and membrane. Place squash, cut sides down, in a baking dish. Bake at 350° for 45 minutes or until tender. Use a spoon to scoop 1¾ cups squash pulp from halves in 1-inch chunks; set aside. Reserve remaining squash for another use.
3. Melt butter in a saucepan over medium-high heat. Add onion and garlic. Reduce heat to medium; sauté 3 minutes or until tender. Add broth and next 5 ingredients (broth through pepper); bring to a boil. Stir in rice mix and 1 tablespoon of contents from seasoning packet. Bring to a boil; cover, reduce heat, and simmer 25 minutes or until liquid is absorbed. Remove from heat; stir in 1¾ cups squash and walnuts. Cover; let stand 5 minutes.

PER SERVING (about ¾ cup): Calories 193 (14% from fat); Protein 5g; Fat 4g (sat 1g, mono 1g, poly 2g); Carbohydrate 38g; Fiber 3g; Cholesterol 0mg; Iron 2mg; Sodium 184mg; Calcium 46mg

Making Sense of Squash

Squash are members of the gourd family and vary widely in size, shape, and color. Although they're now available year-round, squash are generally divided into two categories: summer squash and winter squash.

Summer Squash—Yellow (crookneck), patty pan, and zucchini are three common types of summer squash identified by thin, edible skins and soft seeds. Summer squash requires a short cooking time and is often steamed, baked, sautéed, or deep-fried. It's a good source of vitamins A, C, and niacin.

Winter Squash—Butternut and acorn are the most common varieties. Unlike their summer cousins, these squash have firm, orange-colored flesh protected by a thick skin. Thanks to this tough outer layer, the vegetable can be stored in a cool, dark place at room temperature for a month or more. Winter squash is an excellent source of vitamins A and C, iron, and riboflavin.

The Easy Way to Handle Tough Squash

Despite the virtues of a long shelf life, delicious taste, and nutritional value, winter squash are often passed over for vegetables that appear simpler to prepare. But, with a sharp knife and a meat mallet (even a hammer will do), you can tap into what might become a favorite vegetable.

The technique photos show you how to prepare a butternut squash. Handle acorn squash the same way.

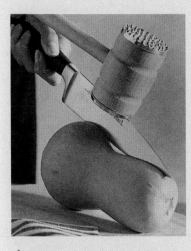

1. Place squash on a cutting board. Using a mallet, gently tap the sharp end of a large knife into the squash. Cut squash in half.

2. Scrape seeds from squash. Bake squash in a baking dish, cut sides down, at 350° for 45 minutes or until tender. Or, microwave at HIGH about 10 minutes.

3. Use a spoon to scoop squash pulp from each half. Use pulp as directed in recipe.

butternut squash crunch

Prep: *18 minutes* **Cook:** *37 minutes*
Serves 7

- ¹/₃ cup granulated sugar
- ¹/₄ cup fat-free milk
- 1 teaspoon ground cinnamon
- 1 teaspoon vanilla extract
- ¹/₄ teaspoon salt
- ¹/₄ teaspoon ground nutmeg
- 1 large egg
- 1 large egg white
- 1 (3¹/₂-pound) butternut squash
- ¹/₄ cup water
- Cooking spray
- 1 cup miniature marshmallows
- ¹/₂ cup firmly packed brown sugar
- 2 tablespoons all-purpose flour
- 1 tablespoon butter, melted

1. Preheat oven to 350°.
2. Combine first 8 ingredients (sugar through egg white) in a large bowl; stir well, and set aside.
3. Cut squash in half lengthwise, and discard seeds and membrane. Place squash halves, cut sides down, in a shallow baking dish, and add water. Cover with heavy-duty plastic wrap, and vent. Microwave at HIGH 10 minutes or until very tender, rotating dish a half-turn after 5 minutes. Remove squash halves from dish, and discard water. Let squash cool slightly.
4. Scoop out squash pulp, and mash to desired consistency, reserving 4½ cups. Add 4½ cups mashed squash to egg mixture, stirring well. Spoon into a

1½-quart baking dish coated with cooking spray, and top with marshmallows.
5. Combine brown sugar, flour, and butter in a small bowl; stir well, and sprinkle over marshmallows. Bake at 350° for 25 minutes or until filling is bubbly and marshmallows are lightly browned.

PER SERVING (³/₄ cup): Calories 212 (11% from fat); Protein 3g; Fat 3g (sat 1g, mono 1g, poly 0g); Carbohydrate 47g; Fiber 2g; Cholesterol 32mg; Iron 2mg; Sodium 139mg; Calcium 88mg

NOTE: You can substitute 3 (10-ounce) packages frozen butternut squash, thawed, for the fresh, if desired.

marinated tomatoes and pasta

Prep: *8 minutes* **Cook:** *12 minutes*
Chill: *4 hours*
Serves 4

Briefly boiling the tomatoes makes the skins split and slip off easily. If the skins don't split, they can be carefully slit with a paring knife, and then removed. See page 190 for more tips on how to peel tomatoes with ease.

    8 cups water
    1 pint cherry tomatoes
    1 cup uncooked gemelli or fusilli (twisted or spiraled pasta)
    1 medium cucumber, peeled, halved lengthwise, seeded, and sliced (about 1¹/₃ cups)
  ¹/₂ cup fat-free Italian dressing
    2 tablespoons chopped fresh parsley
  ¹/₄ teaspoon salt
  ¹/₄ teaspoon pepper

1. Bring water to a boil in a large saucepan. Add cherry tomatoes, and cook 45 seconds (do not overcook). Remove tomatoes from boiling water with a slotted spoon, and set aside. Add gemelli to boiling water, and cook 12 minutes or until tender. Drain well, and set aside.
2. Remove and discard tomato skins. Combine tomatoes, pasta, cucumber slices, and remaining ingredients in a large bowl; toss gently. Cover and chill at least 4 hours.

PER SERVING (1 cup): Calories 142 (4% from fat); Protein 4g; Fat 1g (sat 0g, mono 0g, poly 0g); Carbohydrate 31g; Fiber 1g; Cholesterol 0mg; Iron 1mg; Sodium 594mg; Calcium 14mg

grilled rosemary plum tomatoes

Prep: *5 minutes* **Cook:** *3 minutes*
Serves 4

    1 tablespoon minced shallots
  1¹/₂ teaspoons olive oil
    1 teaspoon chopped fresh rosemary
  ¹/₂ teaspoon grated lemon rind
  ¹/₂ teaspoon freshly ground black pepper
  ¹/₄ teaspoon salt
    8 plum tomatoes, halved lengthwise
       Cooking spray

1. Prepare grill.
2. Combine first 6 ingredients (shallots through salt) in a small bowl. Add tomatoes; toss to coat. Place tomatoes, cut sides up, on grill rack coated with cooking spray. Cook 3 minutes or until thoroughly heated.

PER SERVING (4 halves): Calories 44 (39% from fat); Protein 1g; Fat 2g (sat 0g, mono 1g, poly 0g); Carbohydrate 6g; Fiber 2g; Cholesterol 0mg; Iron 1mg; Sodium 158mg; Calcium 9mg

zucchini-tomato sauté with feta cheese

Prep: *9 minutes* **Cook:** *10 minutes*
Serves 4

  ¹/₂ teaspoon olive oil
    1 cup coarsely chopped onion
    4 cups (about 1 pound) sliced zucchini
  ¹/₂ teaspoon salt
  ¹/₈ teaspoon freshly ground black pepper
    2 cups cherry tomatoes
  ¹/₄ cup (1 ounce) crumbled feta cheese
    2 teaspoons chopped fresh dill

1. Heat oil in a large nonstick skillet over medium-high heat. Add onion, and sauté 3 minutes. Add zucchini, salt, and pepper; sauté 3 minutes. Add tomatoes, and sauté 4 minutes. Remove from heat. Stir in cheese and chopped dill.

PER SERVING (¹/₄ of sauté): Calories 77 (30% from fat); Fat 3g (sat 1g, mono 1g, poly 0g); Protein 4g; Carbohydrate 12g; Fiber 2g; Cholesterol 6mg; Iron 1mg; Sodium 385mg; Calcium 71mg

white bean and tomato gratin

Prep: *8 minutes* **Cook:** *16 minutes*
Serves 4

If your skillet is not ovenproof, wrap the handle with a double thickness of aluminum foil.

    3 teaspoons olive oil, divided
  ¹/₃ cup sliced shallots or sweet onion, such as Vidalia or walla walla
    3 garlic cloves, minced
    1 (19-ounce) can cannellini beans, drained
    1 (14¹/₂-ounce) can Italian-style stewed tomatoes
    1 tablespoon chopped fresh rosemary or 1 teaspoon dried rosemary, crushed
  ¹/₄ teaspoon freshly ground black pepper
  ³/₄ cup toasted breadcrumbs

1. Preheat oven to 425°.
2. Heat 1 teaspoon oil in an ovenproof 10-inch nonstick skillet over medium heat. Add shallots; cook 3 minutes, stirring occasionally. Add garlic; cook 3 minutes. Remove from heat; stir in beans, tomatoes, rosemary, and pepper. Sprinkle bread-crumbs over bean mixture.

Drizzle remaining 2 teaspoons olive oil over mixture. Transfer to oven; bake at 425° for 10 minutes or until crumbs are golden brown and mixture is bubbly.

PER SERVING (¼ of gratin): Calories 195 (20% from fat); Protein 7g; Fat 4g (sat 1g, mono 2g, poly 1g); Carbohydrate 32g; Fiber 6g; Cholesterol 0mg; Iron 1mg; Sodium 452mg; Calcium 52mg

southwestern macaroni and cheese

Prep: *3 minutes* **Cook:** *12 minutes*
Serves 8

Spicy taco seasoning and chunky salsa put a Mexican twist on a creamy family favorite.

- 1 (8-ounce) package uncooked large elbow macaroni
- 5 ounces light processed cheese, cubed (such as Velveeta Light)
- 1 teaspoon taco seasoning
- ½ cup salsa
- ⅓ cup thinly sliced green onions (optional)

1. Cook macaroni in boiling water 9 minutes, omitting salt and fat. Drain and return macaroni to pan. Add cheese and taco seasoning, stirring until cheese melts. Stir in salsa. Sprinkle with green onions, if desired.

PER SERVING (about ⅔ cup): Calories 150 (14% from fat); Protein 7g; Fat 2g (sat 1g, mono 0g, poly 0g); Carbohydrate 25g; Fiber 1g; Cholesterol 9mg; Iron 1mg; Sodium 355mg; Calcium 109mg

lemon-parsley orzo

Prep: *10 minutes* **Cook:** *7 minutes*
Stand: *5 minutes*
Serves 4

Tired of rice with every meal? Give this rice-shaped pasta a try.

- 1 (14-ounce) can fat-free, less-sodium chicken broth
- 1 cup uncooked orzo (rice-shaped pasta)
- 2 teaspoons olive oil
- ¾ cup finely chopped seeded plum tomato (about 2)
- 1 garlic clove, minced
- ¼ teaspoon salt
- ¼ teaspoon pepper
- 2 tablespoons chopped fresh parsley
- 1½ teaspoons grated lemon rind

1. Bring broth and orzo to a boil in a medium saucepan; cover, reduce heat, and simmer 7 minutes or until tender. Remove from heat; let stand 5 minutes.
2. While orzo cooks, heat oil in a small nonstick skillet over medium heat. Add tomato, garlic, salt, and pepper; sauté 2 minutes. Combine with orzo and remaining ingredients.

PER SERVING (½ cup): Calories 214 (16% from fat); Protein 8g; Fat 4g (sat 1g, mono 2g, poly 1g); Carbohydrate 37g; Fiber 2g; Cholesterol 2mg; Iron 2mg; Sodium 199mg; Calcium 22mg

edamame couscous

pictured on page 217

Prep: *10 minutes* **Cook:** *11 minutes*
Stand: *5 minutes*
Serves 4

Edamame are fresh soybeans picked before fully grown so they can be eaten while they're still young and tender. You'll find that they have a mild, slightly nutty flavor similar to a lima or fava bean.

- 1 cup water
- ½ teaspoon salt
- 1 cup frozen shelled edamame, thawed
- ¾ cup uncooked couscous
- 1½ tablespoons minced fresh parsley
- ½ teaspoon grated lemon rind
- 1 tablespoon fresh lemon juice
- ⅛ teaspoon freshly ground black pepper

1. Bring 1 cup water and salt to a boil in a medium saucepan. Add edamame, and cook 30 seconds. Stir in couscous and remaining ingredients. Remove from heat, cover, and let stand 5 minutes. Fluff with a fork just before serving.

PER SERVING (¾ cup): Calories 218 (21% from fat); Protein 13g; Fat 5g (sat 1g, mono 1g, poly 2g); Carbohydrate 30g; Fiber 4g; Cholesterol 0mg; Iron 3mg; Sodium 306mg; Calcium 138mg

cheddar, chive, and canadian bacon soufflé

Prep: *30 minutes* **Cook:** *1 hour 3 minutes*
Serves 6

This soufflé doesn't puff up like a traditional soufflé, but we like the texture and taste all the same.

    1 (8-ounce) loaf French bread
    1 teaspoon butter
    2 tablespoons minced shallot
  1/2 teaspoon salt
    2 cups 1% low-fat milk
  1/2 cup (2 ounces) shredded
       reduced-fat Cheddar cheese
  1/3 cup chopped Canadian bacon
  1/4 teaspoon dry mustard
  1/4 cup chopped fresh chives
    3 large egg yolks
Cooking spray
    4 large egg whites
  1/4 teaspoon cream of tartar

1. Preheat oven to 375°.
2. Place bread in a food processor; pulse 10 times or until the coarse crumbs measure 4 cups. Set aside. Melt butter in a small skillet over medium heat; add shallot. Sauté 3 minutes or until soft (do not brown); stir in salt. Combine shallot mixture, milk, and next 5 ingredients (cheese through egg yolks) in a large bowl; stir well. Add 3½ cups breadcrumbs; stir until well blended.
3. Coat a 1½-quart soufflé dish with cooking spray; sprinkle remaining ½ cup breadcrumbs over bottom and sides.
4. Place egg whites and cream of tartar in a large bowl; beat with a mixer at high speed until stiff peaks form. Gently stir ¼ egg-white mixture into breadcrumb mixture; gently fold in remaining egg-white mixture. Spoon into prepared soufflé dish. Bake at 375° for 1 hour or until soufflé is set. Serve immediately.

PER SERVING (1/6 of soufflé): Calories 238 (29% from fat); Protein 16g; Fat 8g (sat 3g, mono 3g, poly 1g); Carbohydrate 25g; Fiber 1g; Cholesterol 121mg; Iron 2mg; Sodium 736mg; Calcium 233mg

creamy polenta with artichoke ragoût

pictured on page 220

Prep: *30 minutes* **Cook:** *1 hour*
Stand: *30 minutes*
Serves 4

    5 cups water
    1 tablespoon butter
  1/4 teaspoon salt
    1 cup stone-ground yellow
       cornmeal
    1 cup frozen whole-kernel corn,
       thawed
  1/2 cup (2 ounces) shredded fresh
       Parmesan cheese
    3 tablespoons fat-free sour cream
    1 tablespoon chopped fresh basil
    1 cup boiling water
  1/2 cup sun-dried tomatoes,
       packed without oil
    2 tablespoons olive oil
    3 cups thinly sliced onion
    2 cups chopped red bell pepper
    4 garlic cloves, minced
    1 teaspoon Hungarian sweet
       paprika
  1/4 teaspoon crushed red pepper
  1/2 cup dry white wine
  1/2 cup water
    1 (14-ounce) can artichoke
       hearts, drained and chopped
    2 tablespoons sliced ripe olives
Chopped fresh basil (optional)

1. Bring water to a boil in a large saucepan; stir in butter and salt. Gradually add cornmeal, stirring well with a whisk. Cook 5 minutes, stirring constantly. Reduce heat to medium; cook 15 minutes, stirring frequently. Stir in corn; cook 1 minute. Remove from heat; stir in cheese, sour cream, and basil. Cover; set aside.
2. Combine boiling water and sun-dried tomatoes in a bowl; let stand 30 minutes or until soft. Drain and slice.
3. Heat oil in a large nonstick skillet over medium-high heat. Add onion; cook 15 minutes or until lightly browned, stirring frequently. Add bell pepper and garlic; cook 15 minutes or until golden brown, stirring frequently. Stir in paprika and crushed red pepper. Add tomatoes, wine, water, and artichokes; stir well. Cover, reduce heat to low; simmer 10 minutes.
4. Stir in olives. Serve over polenta. Garnish with chopped basil, if desired.

PER SERVING (1/2 cup polenta and 1/3 cup ragoût): Calories 183 (29% from fat); Fat 6g (sat 3g, mono 2g, poly 1g); Protein 7g; Carbohydrate 26g; Fiber 4g; Cholesterol 9mg; Iron 1mg; Sodium 492mg; Calcium 108mg

NOTE: This side dish also makes a filling vegetarian main dish. To serve as a main dish, double the serving size above. Remember, the nutritional analysis will double, too.

Edamame Couscous, page 215

*Summer Squash Croquettes,
page 212*

*Broccoli with Sharp Cheddar
Cheese Sauce, page 204*

*Sweet Onions with
Pistachios, page 208*

delectable side dishes

Lemony Spring Vegetables, page 206

Oven-Roasted Sweet Potato Fries, page 210

Buttery Herbed Green Beans, page 207

Creamy Polenta with Artichoke Ragoût, page 216

comforting soups & sandwiches

Black-Eyed Pea and Chutney Chili, page 224

black bean chili

pictured on page 237

Prep: *15 minutes* **Cook:** *45 minutes*
Serves 4

*Set aside leftover chili to use in
Black Bean Enchiladas with
Tomatillo Sauce on page 145.*

  1   tablespoon vegetable oil
  6   cups chopped onion
 1/2 teaspoon salt
  1   large red bell pepper, chopped
  6   garlic cloves, minced
  1   (7-ounce) can chipotle chiles in
      adobo sauce
  1   tablespoon ground cumin
 1 1/2 teaspoons dried oregano
  4   (15-ounce) cans black beans,
      drained
  1   (14 1/2-ounce) can 99%-fat-free
      vegetable broth
  1   (14 1/2-ounce) can Italian-style
      stewed tomatoes, chopped
 1/2 cup chopped fresh cilantro
 1/4 cup fresh lime juice (about
      1 large)

1. Heat oil in a large stockpot or
Dutch oven over medium-high
heat. Add onion and salt; cook
10 minutes or until onion is soft.
Add bell pepper and garlic; cook
5 minutes, stirring frequently.
2. Remove 1 chile from can and
mince; repeat as needed to
equal 1 tablespoon. Reserve
remaining chiles and sauce for
another use.
3. Add minced chile, cumin, and
next 4 ingredients (oregano
through tomatoes). Reduce heat
to low; simmer 30 minutes,
stirring occasionally. Stir in
cilantro and lime juice.

PER SERVING (1 1/2 cups): Calories 242 (15% from fat);
Protein 12g; Fat 4g (sat 0g, mono 1g, poly 2g);
Carbohydrate 40g; Fiber 13g; Cholesterol 0mg;
Iron 5mg; Sodium 946mg; Calcium 117mg

meatless white chili

Prep: *11 minutes* **Cook:** *26 minutes*
Stand: *15 minutes*
Serves 5

*A sprinkle of feta cheese will bring
out the flavors of the spices and chiles
in this bean soup.*

  2   fresh poblano chiles
  2   (16-ounce) cans cannellini
      beans, drained and divided
  4   ounces (about 3/4 cup) 1/3-less-
      fat cream cheese, softened
  2   teaspoons olive oil
  1   cup chopped onion
  1   cup chopped red bell pepper
  1   (14 1/2-ounce) can vegetable
      broth
  2   teaspoons ground cumin
  1   teaspoon ground coriander
 1/3 cup chopped plum tomato

1. Preheat broiler.
2. Place chiles on a foil-lined baking sheet; broil 10 minutes or
until blackened, turning occasionally. Place chiles in a zip-top
plastic bag; seal and let stand 15
minutes. Peel chiles; cut in half
lengthwise. Discard stems, seeds,
and membranes.
3. In a processor, process chiles,
half of beans, and cheese until
smooth.
4. Heat oil in a nonstick skillet
over medium-high heat. Add
onion and bell pepper; sauté 5
minutes or until tender. Add
broth, cumin, and coriander;
bring to a boil. Reduce heat;
simmer 5 minutes. Add bean
mixture and remaining beans;
cook until thoroughly heated.
Sprinkle with tomato.

PER SERVING (1 cup): Calories 256 (28% from fat);
Protein 13g; Fat 8g (sat 4g, mono 3g, poly 1g);
Carbohydrate 34g; Fiber 7g; Cholesterol 17mg;
Iron 4mg; Sodium 969mg; Calcium 94mg

mexican green chili

Prep: *7 minutes* **Cook:** *8 hours*
Serves 9

*Cooking this chili in a slow cooker
gives the steak, salsa, and spices
hours to marinate and simmer.
Plus, it gives you a work-free dinner.*

 1 1/2 pounds lean top round steak,
      cut into 1-inch pieces
  1   (16-ounce) jar tomatillo salsa
      (such as Jardine's)
  1   (14 1/2-ounce) can Mexican-style
      stewed tomatoes with garlic,
      cumin, and jalapeños,
      undrained and chopped
  1   (14 1/4-ounce) can fat-free beef
      broth
  2   (4.5-ounce) cans chopped
      green chiles, undrained
  1   cup chopped onion
  2   teaspoons ground cumin
  1   teaspoon freshly ground black
      pepper
  2   garlic cloves, minced
  2   teaspoons chili oil

1. Place all ingredients in a
5-quart electric slow cooker; stir
well. Cover; cook on low-heat
setting 8 hours.

PER SERVING (1 cup): Calories 156 (24% from fat);
Protein 19g; Fat 4g (sat 1g, mono 2g, poly 0g);
Carbohydrate 9g; Fiber 1g; Cholesterol 43mg; Iron 2mg;
Sodium 675mg; Calcium 52mg

Tomatillos

Tomatillos are Mexican green tomatoes encased in a papery outer cov-
ering. They impart a lemony, herbal
flavor and are popular in Mexican
and Tex-Mex dishes. They're used
raw in guacamole and salsas (salsa
verde), or can be roasted or
poached for sauces. Don't let the
green color of the salsa scare you
away! Tomatillo salsa is just as flavorful as traditional red salsas.

red chipotle chili with lamb

Prep: *14 minutes* **Cook:** *8 hours*
Serves 8

Chipotle chiles are actually jalapeño peppers that have been dried and smoked—two processes which intensify the peppers' flavor and heat.

1 1/2 pounds lean boneless leg of lamb
2 teaspoons olive oil
2 (14 1/2-ounce) cans Mexican-style stewed tomatoes, undrained
1/4 cup all-purpose flour
1 (15-ounce) can kidney beans, drained
1 (12-ounce) bottle Mexican dark beer (such as Dos Equis)
1 teaspoon dried thyme
1 teaspoon black pepper
2 teaspoons bottled minced garlic
2 to 4 chipotle chiles in adobo sauce, chopped
4 cups hot cooked couscous

1. Trim fat from leg of lamb, and cut lamb into bite-sized pieces. Heat olive oil in a large nonstick skillet over medium-high heat. Add lamb pieces, browning on all sides. Drain well, and set aside.
2. Drain tomatoes, reserving juice. Place flour in a bowl; slowly add reserved tomato juice, stirring with a whisk until blended.
3. Place lamb, tomatoes, flour mixture, beans, and next 5 ingredients (beer through chipotle chiles) in a 5-quart electric slow cooker; stir well. Cover and cook on low-heat setting 8 hours. Serve over couscous.

PER SERVING (1 cup chili and 1/2 cup couscous): Calories 307 (17% from fat); Protein 23g; Fat 6g (sat 2g, mono 2g, poly 1g); Carbohydrate 42g; Fiber 4g; Cholesterol 46mg; Iron 3mg; Sodium 500mg; Calcium 39mg

pork and black bean chili

Prep: *9 minutes* **Cook:** *8 hours*
Serves 4

Toss eight ingredients into a slow cooker in the morning, and come home to a simmering pot of chili.

1 pound lean boneless pork loin roast
1 (16-ounce) jar thick-and-chunky salsa
2 (15-ounce) cans no-salt-added black beans, undrained
1 cup chopped red bell pepper
3/4 cup chopped onion
1 teaspoon ground cumin
1 teaspoon chili powder
1 teaspoon dried oregano
1/4 cup fat-free sour cream

1. Trim fat from pork; cut pork into 1-inch pieces. Place pork and next 7 ingredients (pork through oregano) in a 4-quart electric slow cooker; stir well. Cover and cook on low-heat setting 8 hours or until pork is tender. Ladle chili into bowls; top with sour cream.

PER SERVING (2 cups chili and 1 tablespoon sour cream): Calories 379 (22% from fat); Protein 37g; Fat 9g (sat 3g, mono 3g, poly 1g); Carbohydrate 45g; Fiber 14g; Cholesterol 62mg; Iron 6mg; Sodium 405mg; Calcium 136mg

caribbean chicken chili

Prep: *11 minutes* **Cook:** *24 minutes*
Serves 9

Allspice and orange juice give this chicken and black bean chili a Jamaican flair.

2 teaspoons olive oil, divided
1 pound skinless, boneless chicken breast halves, cut into 1/2-inch pieces
1/4 cup sliced shallots
2 tablespoons seeded minced jalapeño pepper
1 tablespoon bottled chopped ginger
2 teaspoons bottled minced garlic
1 cup fresh orange juice
3/4 teaspoon dried thyme
1/2 teaspoon ground allspice
3 (14.5-ounce) cans diced tomatoes, undrained
1 (15-ounce) can black beans, rinsed and drained
1 (11-ounce) can vacuum-packed whole-kernel corn, drained

1. Heat 1 teaspoon oil in a large Dutch oven over medium-high heat. Add chicken; sauté 6 minutes or until browned. Remove chicken from pan, and set aside.
2. Heat remaining oil in pan over medium heat. Add shallots and next 3 ingredients (shallots through garlic); sauté 3 minutes. Add orange juice and next 3 ingredients (orange juice through tomatoes); bring to a boil. Reduce heat; simmer, uncovered, 8 minutes. Stir in chicken, beans, and corn; cook until thoroughly heated.

PER SERVING (1 cup): Calories 194 (14% from fat); Protein 17g; Fat 3g (sat 1g, mono 1g, poly 0g); Carbohydrate 28g; Fiber 3g; Cholesterol 32mg; Iron 2mg; Sodium 685mg; Calcium 41mg

chipotle chili con carne

Prep: *15 minutes* **Cook:** *50 minutes*
Stand: *5 minutes*
Serves 6

Find cans of chipotle chiles in the ethnic section of the supermarket. Purée the chiles in a blender or a food processor. Refrigerate unused purée up to 1 week or freeze up to 3 months.

- 1 pound lean boneless pork shoulder or beef chuck roast, cut into $1/2$-inch cubes
- $1^1/2$ tablespoons chili powder
- $1^1/2$ tablespoons ground cumin
- $1/4$ teaspoon salt
- 2 teaspoons vegetable oil
- 1 large onion, chopped
- 4 garlic cloves, minced
- 1 (10-ounce) can tomatoes with green chiles, undrained
- 1 cup beer (not dark)
- 1 to 2 tablespoons puréed chipotle chiles in adobo sauce
- 2 teaspoons dried oregano, preferably Mexican
- 1 (16-ounce) can pinto or black beans, rinsed and drained
- 1 (15-ounce) can 50%-less-salt black beans (such as S & W brand), rinsed and drained
- $1/2$ cup coarsely chopped fresh cilantro

1. Preheat oven to 350°.
2. Toss meat with chili powder, cumin, and salt; set aside. Heat a 4- to 5-quart Dutch oven over medium heat. Add oil; when it's hot, add onion and garlic, and cook 5 minutes, stirring occasionally. Add seasoned meat; continue to cook 5 minutes, stirring occasionally.
3. Stir in tomatoes, beer, chipotle chiles, and oregano; bring to a boil. Cover; cook in oven 50 minutes or until meat is fork tender. Stir in beans and cilantro; cover and let stand 5 minutes. Ladle into bowls.

PER SERVING (about $1^1/4$ cups): Calories 282 (26% from fat); Protein 23g; Fat 8g (sat 2g; mono 4g; poly 1g); Carbohydrate 28g; Fiber 9g; Cholesterol 51mg; Iron 2mg; Sodium 682mg; Calcium 82mg

black-eyed pea and chutney chili

pictured on pages 221 and 238

Prep: *12 minutes* **Cook:** *25 minutes*
Serves 6

- 1 pound lean ground pork
- $1^1/4$ cups chopped red onion
- $1^1/4$ cups chopped green bell pepper
- $1/2$ cup hot mango chutney
- $1/4$ cup low-sodium soy sauce
- $1/2$ teaspoon ground allspice
- 2 ($14^1/2$-ounce) cans diced tomatoes with garlic and onion, undrained
- 1 (15.8-ounce) can black-eyed peas, rinsed and drained
- 3 cups hot cooked instant brown rice

1. Cook pork in skillet over medium-high heat until browned, stirring to crumble. Drain in a colander.
2. Add onion and next 4 ingredients (onion through allspice) to skillet; cook over medium heat 7 minutes, stirring occasionally. Add tomatoes; bring to a boil. Cover, reduce heat, and simmer 5 minutes. Add pork and peas; cover and cook until thoroughly heated. Serve over rice.

PER SERVING (1 cup chili and $1/2$ cup rice): Calories 445 (21% from fat); Protein 23g; Fat 10g (sat 3g, mono 3g, poly 1g); Carbohydrate 63g; Fiber 6g; Cholesterol 54mg; Iron 2mg; Sodium 1,339mg; Calcium 42mg

thai shrimp soup

Prep: *8 minutes* **Cook:** *16 minutes*
Serves 7

- 1 (14-ounce) can light coconut milk
- $1^1/2$ tablespoons bottled chopped ginger
- 1 tablespoon chili paste with garlic
- 2 pounds fresh shrimp, peeled
- 2 tablespoons all-purpose flour
- 3 tablespoons low-sodium soy sauce
- 1 (14.5-ounce) can diced tomatoes, undrained
- $1/2$ cup sliced green onions
- 2 tablespoons fresh lime juice
- $1/2$ teaspoon brown sugar
- $1^1/2$ cups sliced fresh shiitake or oyster mushroom caps
- 7 teaspoons chopped fresh cilantro

1. Combine first 3 ingredients (coconut milk through chili paste) in a saucepan, and bring mixture to a boil. Add shrimp; reduce heat, and simmer 3 minutes or until done. Remove shrimp with a slotted spoon.
2. Combine flour and soy sauce in a small bowl, and stir with a whisk; add to coconut milk mixture. Add tomatoes and next 3 ingredients (tomatoes through sugar); bring to a boil, stirring constantly. Reduce heat; simmer 5 minutes or until mixture is slightly thick, stirring occasionally. Stir in mushrooms; cook 2 minutes. Return shrimp to pan, and cook until thoroughly heated. Ladle into bowls, and sprinkle with cilantro.

PER SERVING (1 cup chili and 1 teaspoon cilantro): Calories 168 (26% from fat); Protein 21g; Fat 5g (sat 2g, mono 0g, poly 1g); Carbohydrate 9g; Fiber 1g; Cholesterol 148mg; Iron 3mg; Sodium 573mg; Calcium 78mg

springtime asparagus soup

Prep: *10 minutes* **Cook:** *22 minutes*
Serves 4

 2 pounds asparagus spears
 2 (14.25-ounce) cans fat-free chicken broth
 1 medium baking potato, peeled and sliced
 1 tablespoon chopped fresh or 1 teaspoon dried thyme
 1/4 cup evaporated fat-free milk or fat-free half-and-half
 1/2 teaspoon salt
Dash of pepper
Lemon slices and thyme sprigs (optional)

1. Snap off tough ends of asparagus spears; remove scales with a knife or vegetable peeler, if desired. Cut asparagus spears into 1-inch pieces.
2. Combine chicken broth, potato, and chopped thyme in a large saucepan; bring mixture to a boil. Cover, reduce heat, and simmer 5 minutes. Add asparagus; bring to a boil. Cover, reduce heat, and simmer 15 minutes or until vegetables are tender. Remove from heat, and let cool slightly.
3. Drain vegetable mixture through a sieve over a large bowl, reserving 1½ cups cooking liquid. Place vegetable mixture in a food processor, and process until mixture is smooth. Strain puréed vegetable mixture through a sieve into saucepan. Stir in reserved cooking liquid, milk, salt, and pepper. Serve warm or chilled. Garnish with lemon slices and thyme sprigs, if desired.

PER SERVING (1 cup): Calories 128 (4% from fat); Protein 7g; Fat 1g (sat 0g, mono 0g, poly 0g); Carbohydrate 24g; Fiber 5g; Cholesterol 1mg; Iron 2mg; Sodium 322mg; Calcium 95mg

creamy pumpkin soup

Prep: *16 minutes* **Cook:** *32 minutes*
Serves 5

If desired, sprinkle with toasted croutons for a little added crunch to this silky soup.

 2 teaspoons butter
 1 cup chopped onion
 3/4 teaspoon dried rubbed sage
 1/2 teaspoon curry powder
 1/4 teaspoon ground nutmeg
 3 tablespoons all-purpose flour
 3 (10½-ounce) cans low-sodium chicken broth
 1 tablespoon tomato paste
 1/4 teaspoon salt
 3 cups cubed peeled cooking pumpkin (about 1 pound)
 1 cup peeled chopped McIntosh or other sweet cooking apple
 1/2 cup evaporated fat-free milk
Sage sprigs (optional)

1. Melt butter in a Dutch oven over medium heat. Add onion; sauté 3 minutes. Add rubbed sage, curry powder, and nutmeg; cook 30 seconds. Stir in flour, and cook 30 seconds. Add broth, tomato paste, and salt, stirring well with a whisk. Stir in pumpkin and apple; bring to a boil. Cover, reduce heat, and simmer 25 minutes or until pumpkin is tender, stirring occasionally. Remove from heat; cool slightly.
2. Place mixture in a blender or food processor; cover and process until smooth. Return mixture to Dutch oven; add milk. Cook until thoroughly heated. Garnish with sage sprigs, if desired.

PER SERVING (1 cup): Calories 122 (23% from fat); Protein 6g; Fat 3g (sat 1g, mono 1g, poly 1g); Carbohydrate 20g; Fiber 2g; Cholesterol 1mg; Iron 2mg; Sodium 228mg; Calcium 102mg

What's the Difference?

Chowder, bisque, chili, stew—these various dishes all warm you up on a cold day, are served in a soup bowl, and are eaten with a spoon. But what's the real difference between them? To point out the differences, here are the definitions:

Bisque—a thick, rich soup made of puréed food and cream or milk. It may contain vegetables, seafood, or poultry.

Chowder—a thick, rich, chunky soup made with seafood or vegetables.

Chili—a blend of diced or ground beef, tomatoes, chiles, chili powder, and often beans. Vegetarian and chicken chilis are also options.

Gumbo—a thick, stewlike dish that begins with a dark roux, which lends a rich flavor. Vegetables found in gumbo include tomatoes, onions, and okra, which serves as a thickener. Gumbo also includes a variety of meats or shellfish, such as chicken, sausage, and shrimp.

Soup—a combination of vegetables and meat cooked in a broth; it may be served hot or cold.

Stew—a combination of meat, vegetables, and a thick broth created from the stewing liquid and the natural juices of the food being cooked.

How to Caramelize Onions

1. Slice the onion in half vertically. Place cut side down on cutting board, and slice into thin slivers.

2. Cook onion in oil over medium heat. After about 10 minutes, the onions will begin to soften and release their liquid. Keep stirring.

3. After 15 to 20 minutes, the onions begin to take on a golden color, but they're not quite done yet. After 10 more minutes of cooking the onions are deep golden brown and done.

caramelized onion and roasted garlic bisque

Prep: *12 minutes* **Cook:** *2 hours 38 minutes*
Cool: *10 minutes*
Serves 6

   1 large whole garlic head
1¹/₂ tablespoons olive oil, divided
   9 cups thinly sliced Vidalia or other sweet onion (about 4 large)
2¹/₂ cups sliced leek (about 2 medium)
   1 teaspoon salt, divided
   1 teaspoon dried thyme
   2 tablespoons all-purpose flour
 ¹/₃ cup dry white wine
   3 (10¹/₂-ounce) cans low-sodium chicken broth
   2 cups 2% low-fat milk
 ¹/₄ cup plus 2 tablespoons fat-free sour cream

1. Preheat oven to 350°.
2. Remove white papery skin from garlic head (do not peel or separate cloves). Rub 1¹/₂ teaspoons oil over garlic head; wrap in aluminum foil. Bake at 350° for 1 hour; let cool 10 minutes. Separate cloves; squeeze to extract pulp. Discard skins. Set pulp aside.
3. Heat remaining 1 tablespoon oil in a Dutch oven over medium heat. Add onion and leek; cook 30 minutes, stirring often. Add ¹/₂ teaspoon salt and thyme. Cook 30 minutes or until onion is golden, stirring occasionally. Stir in flour. Add wine and broth; bring mixture to a boil. Reduce heat, and simmer 30 minutes. Add garlic pulp, remaining ¹/₂ teaspoon salt, and milk; simmer 8 minutes or until thoroughly heated.
4. Place half of onion mixture in a blender. Process until smooth; pour mixture into a bowl. Repeat procedure with remaining onion mixture. Ladle into individual bowls. Top with sour cream.

PER SERVING (1 cup soup and 1 tablespoon sour cream): Calories 249 (24% from fat); Protein 10g; Fat 7g (sat 2g, mono 3g, poly 1g); Carbohydrate 40g; Fiber 6g; Cholesterol 7mg; Iron 3mg; Sodium 510mg; Calcium 200mg

santa fe ravioli soup

pictured on page 238

Prep: *5 minutes* **Cook:** *10 minutes*
Serves 4

Keep these ingredients on hand for when you need a quick meal. From start to finish it takes 15 minutes.

   2 (15.75-ounce) cans fat-free, less-sodium chicken broth
   1 (9-ounce) package fresh light cheese ravioli (such as Buitoni)
   1 cup refrigerated salsa (such as Melissa's)
   1 (15-ounce) can black beans, rinsed and drained
 ¹/₄ cup reduced-fat sour cream
 ¹/₄ cup chopped fresh cilantro

1. Bring broth to a boil in a large saucepan. Reduce heat to low; add ravioli, and simmer 5 minutes or until almost tender. Add salsa and beans; cook 5 minutes or until thoroughly heated. Remove from heat. Top with sour cream, and sprinkle with cilantro.

PER SERVING (1¹/₄ cups soup, 1 tablespoon sour cream, and 1 tablespoon cilantro): Calories 247 (14% from fat); Protein 14g; Fat 4g (sat 2g, mono 0g, poly 0g); Carbohydrate 41g; Fiber 5g; Cholesterol 30mg; Iron 2mg; Sodium 856mg; Calcium 119mg

potato-mushroom soup

Prep: *10 minutes* **Cook:** *38 minutes*
Serves 4

Yukon gold potatoes are prized for their golden flesh and sweet, buttery flavor. These spuds are ideal in thick soups because of their natural creaminess when mashed.

- 2 bacon slices
- 4 cups chopped cremini mushrooms
- 1/2 cup chopped shallots
- 3 1/2 cups cubed Yukon Gold or baking potato
- 1 (14 1/2-ounce) can fat-free chicken broth
- 2 cups 1% low-fat milk
- 2 tablespoons sherry
- 1/2 teaspoon salt
- 1/4 teaspoon pepper

1. Cook bacon in a Dutch oven over medium heat until crisp. Remove bacon from Dutch oven; crumble and set aside. Add mushrooms and shallots to bacon drippings in Dutch oven; sauté 5 minutes or until mushrooms are soft. Remove from Dutch oven; set aside.
2. Add potato and broth to Dutch oven; bring to a boil. Cover, reduce heat, and simmer 12 minutes or until potato is very tender. Transfer potato mixture to a food processor; process until smooth. Return to Dutch oven. Add mushroom mixture, milk, and remaining 3 ingredients; cook over low heat 10 minutes or until thoroughly heated. Ladle soup into bowls; top evenly with bacon.

PER SERVING (1 1/2 cups): Calories 236 (13% from fat); Protein 13g; Fat 4g (sat 2g, mono 1g, poly 0g); Carbohydrate 39g; Fiber 3g; Cholesterol 9mg; Iron 2mg; Sodium 521mg; Calcium 172mg

roasted tomato and red pepper soup

Prep: *8 minutes* **Cook:** *25 minutes*
Stand: *10 minutes*
Serves 5

- 1 1/2 pounds red bell peppers
- 2 pounds tomatoes, halved and seeded
- 2 tablespoons olive oil
- 1 cup chopped onion
- 4 garlic cloves, minced
- 1 1/2 cups tomato juice
- 1 tablespoon chopped fresh marjoram
- 1/2 teaspoon salt
- 1/4 teaspoon black pepper

1. Preheat broiler.
2. Cut bell peppers in half lengthwise; discard seeds and membranes. Place peppers and tomatoes, skin sides up, on an aluminum foil-lined baking sheet; flatten peppers with hand. Broil 15 minutes or until vegetables are blackened. Place pepper in a zip-top plastic bag; seal and let stand 10 minutes. Peel peppers and tomatoes; chop. Place half of chopped pepper and half of chopped tomato in a blender; process until smooth. Set aside.
3. Heat olive oil in a saucepan over medium-low heat. Add onion and garlic; cover and cook 5 minutes. Add puréed vegetables, chopped pepper and tomato, tomato juice, and remaining 3 ingredients; cook mixture over medium heat until thoroughly heated.

PER SERVING (1 cup): Calories 126 (25% from fat); Protein 4g; Fat 4g (sat 1g, mono 2g, poly 0g); Carbohydrate 23g; Fiber 6g; Cholesterol 0mg; Iron 3mg; Sodium 521mg; Calcium 42mg

vegetable-pasta soup

Prep: *5 minutes* **Cook:** *16 minutes*
Serves 10

With only 120 calories per serving, this soup makes a great light lunch for days when you want to save calories so you can splurge at dinner.

- 3 cups reduced-sodium vegetable juice
- 2 cups water
- 1 (14 1/2-ounce) can diced tomatoes with basil, garlic, and oregano
- 1 (1-pound) package frozen pasta, broccoli, corn, and carrots in garlic-seasoned sauce (such as Green Giant Pasta Accents)
- 1 (16-ounce) package frozen zucchini, cauliflower, and carrot blend
- 1/3 cup (1 1/3 ounces) grated fresh Parmesan cheese
- Freshly ground black pepper (optional)

1. Combine first 3 ingredients (juice through tomatoes) in a Dutch oven; bring to a boil. Stir in frozen pasta and vegetables; return to a boil. Reduce heat. Simmer, uncovered, 10 minutes. Ladle soup into bowls; sprinkle with cheese. Serve with pepper, if desired.

PER SERVING (1 cup soup and about 1 1/2 teaspoons cheese): Calories 120 (28% from fat); Protein 4g; Fat 4g (sat 2g, mono 0g, poly 0g); Carbohydrate 17g; Fiber 2g; Cholesterol 6mg; Iron 1mg; Sodium 559mg; Calcium 73mg

tortellini, white bean, and spinach soup

Prep: *13 minutes* **Cook:** *12 minutes*
Serves 6

Full of Mediterranean veggies like tomatoes and artichokes, this broth-based soup is a good source of iron and fiber.

- 1 teaspoon olive oil
- 2 cups chopped onion
- 1/2 cup chopped red bell pepper
- 1 teaspoon dried Italian seasoning
- 3 garlic cloves, minced
- 2 cups coarsely chopped spinach
- 2/3 cup water
- 1 (16-ounce) can navy beans, drained
- 1 (14 1/2-ounce) can vegetable broth
- 1 (14.5-ounce) can no-salt-added whole tomatoes, undrained and chopped
- 1 (14-ounce) can quartered artichoke hearts, drained
- 1 (9-ounce) package uncooked fresh cheese tortellini
- 1/4 cup (1 ounce) grated fresh Parmesan cheese

1. Heat oil in a large Dutch oven over medium-high heat. Add onion and next 3 ingredients (onion through garlic); sauté 5 minutes or until tender. Add spinach and next 5 ingredients (spinach through artichokes); bring to a boil. Reduce heat; simmer 2 minutes. Add tortellini; cook until thoroughly heated. Ladle soup into individual bowls. Sprinkle with cheese.

PER SERVING (1 1/2 cups soup and 2 teaspoons cheese): Calories 281 (18% from fat); Fat 6g (sat 2g, mono 2g, poly 1g); Protein 15g; Carbohydrate 44g; Fiber 4g; Cholesterol 23mg; Iron 3mg; Sodium 562mg; Calcium 158mg

salmon chowder

Prep: *10 minutes* **Cook:** *15 minutes*
Serves 4

Similar to a classic New England clam chowder, this soup features fresh salmon instead of clams and uses fat-free half-and-half to keep the fat down.

- 2 teaspoons olive oil
- 2 leeks, rinsed well, ends trimmed and chopped
- 2 garlic cloves, minced
- 2 bay leaves
- 1 teaspoon dried tarragon
- 1/2 teaspoon salt
- 1/4 teaspoon black pepper
- 6 small red potatoes (about 1/2 pound total), cut into 1-inch cubes
- 2 1/2 cups fat-free, less-sodium chicken broth
- 1 pound salmon fillet, skinned and cut into 1-inch cubes
- 1/2 cup fat-free half-and-half
- 4 teaspoons minced fresh chives (optional)

1. Heat oil in a large stockpot over medium-high heat. Add leeks and garlic, and sauté 3 minutes, stirring until tender. Add bay leaves, tarragon, salt, and pepper; stir to coat. Add potatoes and chicken broth, and bring mixture to a boil. Reduce heat to medium-low, and simmer 8 minutes. Add salmon, and simmer 2 minutes or until fish is cooked through and potatoes are fork-tender.
2. Remove from heat, discard bay leaves, and stir in half-and-half. Ladle chowder into bowls, and top with chives, if desired.

PER SERVING (about 1 1/2 cups): Calories 304 (29% from fat); Protein 26g; Fat 10g (sat 1g, mono 5g, poly 2g); Carbohydrate 27g; Fiber 3g; Cholesterol 61mg; Iron 3mg; Sodium 666mg; Calcium 62mg

minestrone

Prep: *15 minutes* **Cook:** *35 minutes*
Stand: *5 minutes*
Serves 6

- 1 ounce pancetta or 2 bacon slices, chopped
- 1 cup thinly sliced leeks (white and light green parts only)
- 1 cup thinly sliced carrots
- 5 garlic cloves, coarsely chopped
- 1 (28-ounce) can Italian-seasoned diced tomatoes or Italian plum tomatoes, coarsely chopped, juice reserved
- 1 (14-ounce) can fat-free beef broth
- 1 cup water
- 2 ounces (1/2 cup) uncooked ditalini or small shell pasta
- 2 teaspoons dried basil
- 1 teaspoon dried oregano
- 1/4 teaspoon red chili pepper flakes (optional)
- 1 (16-ounce) can cannellini or Great Northern beans, rinsed and drained
- 1 cup frozen baby peas, thawed
- 1/4 cup (1 ounce) grated Parmigiano-Reggiano cheese
- 1 tablespoon olive oil
- 2 tablespoons chopped fresh basil or fresh flat-leaf parsley

1. Preheat oven to 350°.
2. In a 5-quart Dutch oven or ovenproof covered casserole, cook pancetta over medium heat until it starts to brown, about 3 minutes. Add leeks, carrots, and garlic; cook 3 minutes, stirring occasionally.
3. Stir in tomatoes and juice, broth, water, pasta, dried basil and oregano, and pepper flakes; bring to a full boil. Cover; cook at 350° for 35 minutes or until vegetables are tender. Stir in beans and peas; cover and let stand 5 minutes. Ladle into bowls; top with cheese. Drizzle

½ teaspoon oil over each serving; garnish with fresh basil.

PER SERVING (about 1⅓ cups soup and 2 teaspoons cheese): Calories 261 (30% from fat); Protein 11g; Fat 9g (sat 3g, mono 4g, poly 1g); Carbohydrate 33g; Fiber 7g; Cholesterol 8mg; Iron 3mg; Sodium 564mg; Calcium 132mg

roasted corn and chicken soup

Prep: *55 minutes* **Cook:** *18 minutes*
Chill: *8 hours*
Serves 7

This is a standard in Pennsylvania Dutch cooking. In our version, cheese-filled tortellini are used in place of traditional egg noodles.

- 6 cups water
- ¼ cup chopped fresh parsley or 1 tablespoon dried parsley flakes
- ½ teaspoon black peppercorns
- 3 pounds chicken pieces
- 5 (10½-ounce) cans low-sodium chicken broth
- 3 medium carrots, quartered
- 3 medium parsnips, quartered
- 2 celery stalks, quartered
- 1 medium onion, quartered
- 4 whole cloves
- 3 garlic cloves
- 2 bay leaves
- 2 cups frozen whole-kernel corn, thawed
- Cooking spray
- ½ cup finely chopped celery
- ⅓ cup minced fresh parsley or 1 tablespoon dried parsley flakes
- ¾ teaspoon salt
- ½ teaspoon poultry seasoning
- ½ teaspoon pepper
- 1 (9-ounce) package uncooked fresh cheese tortellini

1. Combine first 12 ingredients (water through bay leaves) in a stockpot; bring to a boil. Reduce heat; simmer, uncovered, 40 minutes. Remove from heat. Remove chicken from stock; cool. Remove skin from chicken; remove chicken from bones. Discard skin and bones. Shred chicken into bite-sized pieces; cover and chill.
2. Return stock to a boil. Reduce heat; simmer, uncovered, 1 hour. Strain stock through a sieve into a large bowl; discard solids. Cover and chill stock 8 hours. Skim solidified fat from surface; discard.
3. Preheat broiler.
4. Place corn on a jelly-roll pan coated with cooking spray; broil 8 minutes or until corn is light brown. Combine stock and chicken in stockpot; bring to a boil. Stir in corn, ½ cup celery, and remaining ingredients; bring to a boil. Reduce heat, and simmer, uncovered, 10 minutes.

PER SERVING (2 cups): Calories 278 (20% from fat); Protein 26g; Fat 6g (sat 3g, mono 2g, poly 1g); Carbohydrate 29g; Fiber 2g; Cholesterol 70mg; Iron 2mg; Sodium 525mg; Calcium 19mg

turkey-orzo soup with black-eyed peas

pictured on page 240

Prep: *17 minutes* **Cook:** *36 minutes*
Serves 6

Serve this soup immediately; left standing, the orzo absorbs liquid and the soup gets very thick.

- 2 teaspoons olive oil
- 1 cup sliced leeks
- ¾ cup chopped peeled turnip
- ½ cup chopped celery
- 2 garlic cloves, minced
- 2 (14-ounce) cans fat-free, less-sodium chicken broth
- 1 (15.8-ounce) can black-eyed peas, rinsed and drained
- 1 (14.5-ounce) can stewed tomatoes with basil, garlic, and oregano, chopped
- 1 cup chopped cooked white and dark turkey
- ½ cup uncooked orzo (rice-shaped pasta)
- ¾ teaspoon dried marjoram
- ¼ teaspoon freshly ground black pepper
- ¼ cup (1 ounce) shredded fresh Parmesan cheese

1. Heat oil in a saucepan over medium-high heat. Add leek and next 3 ingredients (leek through garlic); sauté 12 minutes. Add broth, peas, and tomatoes; bring to a boil. Reduce heat, and simmer 10 minutes. Add turkey and next 3 ingredients (turkey through pepper); simmer 10 minutes. Ladle into bowls; sprinkle with cheese.

PER SERVING (1⅓ cups soup): Calories 226 (18% from fat); Protein 17g; Fat 5g (sat 1g, mono 2g, poly 1g); Carbohydrate 29g; Fiber 2g; Cholesterol 23mg; Iron 3mg; Sodium 816mg; Calcium 96mg

tortilla chicken soup

pictured on page 154

Prep: *15 minutes* **Cook:** *57 minutes*
Serves 5

Ground cumin, which has a pungent, sharp, and slightly bitter flavor, combines with the tomatoes and chiles to give this soup its Mexican flavor.

      4 teaspoons peanut oil, divided
      4 (4-ounce) skinless, boneless chicken thighs
      1 (4-ounce) skinless, boneless chicken breast
 7^1/$_2$ cups sliced onion
   ^{1}/$_2$ cup chopped celery
      3 garlic cloves, chopped
      2 cups water
      2 (14-ounce) cans fat-free, less-sodium chicken broth
      1 cup frozen whole-kernel corn
      2 tablespoons chili powder
      1 tablespoon ground cumin
      1 (28-ounce) can tomatoes, drained and chopped
      2 (5.25-ounce) cans chopped green chiles
      1 finely chopped pickled, seeded jalapeño pepper
      4 (6-inch) corn tortillas, cut into triangles
      5 tablespoons low-fat sour cream
Cilantro sprigs (optional)

1. Heat 1 tablespoon oil in a large Dutch oven over medium-high heat. Add chicken; cook 2½ minutes on each side or until browned. Remove from pan. Cool slightly; coarsely chop. Add 1 teaspoon oil, onion, and celery to pan; sauté 5 minutes or until tender. Add garlic; sauté 2 minutes. Stir in water and broth, scraping pan to loosen browned bits. Stir in chicken, corn, and next 5 ingredients (chili powder through jalapeño pepper). Bring to a boil; reduce heat, and simmer 45 minutes.

2. Stir in tortilla triangles. Ladle into bowls. Top with sour cream. Garnish with cilantro sprigs, if desired.

PER SERVING (1½ cups soup and 1 tablespoon sour cream): Calories 394 (24% from fat); Protein 32g; Fat 11g (sat 3g, mono 3g, poly 3g); Carbohydrate 44g; Fiber 9g; Cholesterol 93mg; Iron 4mg; Sodium 973mg; Calcium 173mg

italian vegetable stew

Prep: *12 minutes* **Cook:** *45 minutes*
Serves 6

Canned beans make this stew an easy, nutritious, meatless main dish. Serve with store-bought bread-sticks and a tossed green salad.

      1 tablespoon olive oil
      1 cup chopped onion
      1 cup chopped green bell pepper
      4 garlic cloves, minced
      1 cup thinly sliced zucchini
      1 teaspoon dried Italian seasoning
   ^{1}/$_4$ to ^{1}/$_2$ teaspoon dried crushed red pepper
      1 (14.5-ounce) can diced tomatoes, undrained
      1 (10½-ounce) can low-sodium chicken broth
      1 (8-ounce) package presliced mushrooms
      1 (8-ounce) can no-salt-added tomato sauce
      1 (16-ounce) can kidney beans, drained
      1 (14.5-ounce) can cut Italian green beans, drained
   ^{1}/$_4$ cup chopped fresh parsley
   ^{3}/$_4$ cup (3 ounces) preshredded part-skim mozzarella cheese

1. Heat oil in a large Dutch oven over medium-high heat. Add onion, bell pepper, and garlic; sauté 5 minutes or until tender. Add zucchini and next 6 ingredients (zucchini through tomato sauce); bring to a boil. Cover, reduce heat, and simmer 30 minutes. Add kidney beans, green beans, and parsley; simmer, uncovered, 5 minutes or until thoroughly heated. Ladle into bowls; sprinkle with cheese.

PER SERVING (1½ cups stew and 2 tablespoons cheese): Calories 169 (30% from fat); Protein 10g; Fat 6g (sat 2g, mono 2g, poly 1g); Carbohydrate 23g; Fiber 5g; Cholesterol 8mg; Iron 3mg; Sodium 437mg; Calcium 162mg

north african lentil stew

Prep: *5 minutes* **Cook:** *45 minutes*
Serves 4

This warming vegetable stew provides a powerful punch of fiber from the lentils and vegetables.

      1 tablespoon olive or vegetable oil
      1 cup chopped onion
      2 teaspoons ground cumin
      2 teaspoons curry powder
   ^{1}/$_2$ teaspoon salt
   ^{1}/$_8$ teaspoon cayenne pepper
      1 (28-ounce) can crushed tomatoes
      2 (14½-ounce) cans reduced-sodium vegetable broth
      2 tablespoons honey
 1^1/$_4$ cups lentils, rinsed and picked over to remove debris
      4 small red potatoes (about ^{1}/$_2$ pound), cut into 1-inch chunks
      2 carrots, peeled and chopped
      1 cup frozen green peas, thawed
   ^{1}/$_4$ cup chopped fresh parsley

1. Heat oil in a large saucepan over medium-high heat. Add onion, and sauté 2 minutes or until translucent. Add cumin, curry, salt, and cayenne, and stir to coat. Add tomatoes, broth, and honey, and mix well.

2. Add lentils, potatoes, and carrots, and bring mixture to a boil. Reduce heat to low, cover, and simmer 30 to 40 minutes, until lentils are tender, stirring occasionally. Stir in peas, and simmer 1 minute. Remove from heat, and spoon into serving bowls; garnish evenly with parsley.

PER SERVING (about 2 cups): Calories 471 (9% from fat); Protein 24g; Fat 5g (sat 1g, mono 3g, poly 1g); Carbohydrate 84g; Fiber 27g; Cholesterol 0mg; Iron 10mg; Sodium 935mg; Calcium 144mg

lamb-sweet potato-curry stew

Prep: *15 minutes* **Cook:** *1 hour 15 minutes*
Serves 8

Hot couscous soaks up the savory juices of this lamb stew and makes it a hearty one-dish meal.

- 1   tablespoon peanut oil
- 2   pounds lean lamb stew meat, trimmed
- 3¹/₄ cups coarsely chopped onion
- 1   cup (¹/₂-inch-thick) sliced carrot
- 1   cup chopped green bell pepper
- 2   tablespoons ground cumin
- 1   teaspoon curry powder
- ¹/₂ teaspoon ground turmeric
- 4   cups chopped tomato
- 2   cups cubed peeled sweet potato
- 1   (15¹/₂-ounce) can chickpeas, drained
- 1   (14-ounce) can fat-free, less-sodium chicken broth
- 1   teaspoon salt
- ¹/₄ teaspoon black pepper
- 1   (10-ounce) box couscous

1. Heat oil in a Dutch oven over medium-high heat. Add lamb; cook 5 minutes or until browned, stirring frequently. Stir in onion and next 5 ingredients (onion through turmeric); cook 5 minutes. Stir in tomato and next 5 ingredients (tomato through pepper). Bring to a boil; cover, reduce heat, and simmer 35 minutes. Uncover, and simmer 30 minutes.

2. Prepare couscous according to package directions, omitting salt and fat.

3. Serve stew over hot couscous.

PER SERVING (1¹/₄ cups stew and ¹/₂ cup couscous): Calories 449 (20% from fat); Protein 30g; Fat 10g (sat 3g, mono 4g, poly 2g); Carbohydrate 60g; Fiber 8g; Cholesterol 65mg; Iron 4mg; Sodium 608mg; Calcium 77mg

cannellini, sausage, and sage stew

Prep: *10 minutes* **Cook:** *10 minutes*
Serves 4

One cup of this winter stew provides a healthy dose of fiber and iron. If fresh sage isn't available, substitute ¹/₄ to ¹/₂ teaspoon of dried sage.

- 2   (3¹/₂-ounce) links turkey Italian sausage
- 2   garlic cloves, minced
- 2   cups chopped seeded plum tomato
- 1   to 2 tablespoons chopped fresh sage
- 1   teaspoon dried thyme
- 1   teaspoon fennel seeds, crushed
- ¹/₂ teaspoon pepper
- 1   (16-ounce) can cannellini beans, rinsed and drained
- 1   (15.75-ounce) can fat-free, less-sodium chicken broth

1. Remove casings from sausage. Cook sausage and garlic in a large nonstick skillet over medium-high heat until browned, stirring to crumble. Stir in tomato and remaining ingredients. Bring to a boil; lower heat, cover, and simmer 5 minutes.

PER SERVING (1 cup): Calories 147 (28% from fat); Protein 12g; Fat 5g (sat 1g, mono 1g, poly 2g); Carbohydrate 15g; Fiber 4g; Cholesterol 25mg; Iron 3mg; Sodium 428mg; Calcium 51mg

white bean-pesto pitas

Prep: *12 minutes*
Serves 4

If you prepare this sandwich the night before you plan to eat it, simply wrap the sandwich in plastic wrap, and chill. Lining the pita with a dry lettuce leaf helps protect the bread from moisture.

- 1   (19-ounce) can cannellini beans or other white beans, undrained
- 1   tablespoon prepared pesto
- ¹/₂ cup seeded chopped tomato
- 2   (7-inch) pita bread rounds, cut in half
- 4   curly leaf lettuce leaves

1. Drain cannellini beans, reserving 2¹/₂ tablespoons bean liquid. Place beans, reserved liquid, and prepared pesto in a food processor. Process until bean mixture is smooth. Combine puréed mixture and chopped tomato in a small bowl, and stir well.

2. Line each pita half with a lettuce leaf; fill each with ¹/₂ cup bean mixture.

PER SERVING (1 pita half): Calories 235 (6% from fat); Protein 13g; Fat 2g (sat 0g, mono 0g, poly 0g); Carbohydrate 45g; Fiber 4g; Cholesterol 0mg; Iron 3mg; Sodium 389mg; Calcium 92mg

hummus pitas with feta-olive salsa

Prep: *15 minutes*
Serves 4

- 1 (15-ounce) can no-salt-added chickpeas (garbanzo beans)
- 1 tablespoon tahini (sesame seed paste)
- 1 garlic clove, peeled

Dash of crushed red pepper

- 3 tablespoons fresh lemon juice
- 1 cup chopped tomato
- 3/4 cup chopped seeded English cucumber
- 1/4 cup chopped green onions
- 1/4 cup chopped pitted kalamata olives
- 1/4 cup (1 ounce) crumbled feta cheese
- 2 tablespoons minced fresh cilantro
- 1 tablespoon minced fresh mint
- 4 (6-inch) pita bread rounds, halved

1. Drain chickpeas in a colander over a bowl, reserving 1 tablespoon liquid. Combine chickpeas, tahini, garlic, and red pepper in a food processor, and process until smooth, scraping sides of processor bowl once. Add lemon juice and reserved chickpea liquid; process until smooth. Spoon mixture into a bowl; set aside.
2. Combine tomato and next 6 ingredients (tomato through mint) in a bowl. Spoon 1/4 cup hummus mixture into each pita half; top with 1/4 cup feta-olive salsa.

PER SERVING (2 stuffed pita halves): Calories 299 (22% from fat); Protein 13g; Fat 7g (sat 2g, mono 2g, poly 2g); Carbohydrate 48g; Fiber 5g; Cholesterol 8mg; Iron 4mg; Sodium 337mg; Calcium 135mg

fresh tomato chutney sandwiches

pictured on page 239

Prep: *11 minutes* **Cook:** *39 minutes*
Serves 4

Fresh mozzarella may be labeled "Italian style." It's softer than regular mozzarella and has a sweet, delicate flavor. Look for fresh mozzarella in Italian markets, cheese shops, and some supermarkets.

- 1 cup chopped red bell pepper
- 1/2 cup water
- 1/4 cup firmly packed brown sugar
- 1/4 cup cider vinegar
- 2 tablespoons chopped onion
- 1 teaspoon mustard seeds
- 1/8 teaspoon salt
- 1/8 teaspoon ground red pepper
- 2 cups peeled, seeded, chopped tomato
- 4 (6-inch) pita bread rounds, cut in half
- 4 (1-ounce) slices fresh mozzarella cheese, cut in half
- 2 cups trimmed arugula or torn curly leaf lettuce

1. Combine first 8 ingredients (bell pepper through ground red pepper) in a medium saucepan; bring to a boil. Reduce heat, and simmer, uncovered, 35 minutes or until thick, stirring occasionally. Remove from heat, and stir in tomato. Let mixture cool to room temperature.
2. Fill each pita half with 1/2 ounce cheese and 1/4 cup arugula. Spoon 1/4 cup tomato chutney into each pita half, using a slotted spoon.

PER SERVING (2 stuffed pita halves): Calories 331 (21% from fat); Protein 13g; Fat 8g (sat 4g, mono 2g, poly 1g); Carbohydrate 55g; Fiber 3g; Cholesterol 22mg; Iron 3mg; Sodium 502mg; Calcium 238mg

portobello "steak" burgers with caramelized onions

Prep: *17 minutes* **Cook:** *15 minutes*
Chill: *24 hours*
Serves 6

Marinating the mushrooms for 24 hours gives them time to fully soak up all of the flavors in the balsamic-olive oil mixture, ensuring a well-seasoned "steak."

- 1 cup balsamic vinegar
- 2 tablespoons olive oil
- 1 teaspoon dried basil
- 1/4 teaspoon kosher salt
- 1/4 teaspoon ground white pepper
- 2 garlic cloves, minced
- 6 portobello mushroom caps (about 1 1/2 pounds)

Cooking spray

- 1 tablespoon olive oil
- 1 1/2 cups sliced onion
- 1/4 cup low-fat mayonnaise
- 1 teaspoon bottled minced roasted garlic
- 6 (2-ounce) whole-wheat Kaiser rolls or hamburger buns
- 6 curly leaf lettuce leaves
- 6 large (1/4-inch-thick) slices tomato

1. Combine first 6 ingredients (vinegar through minced garlic) in a large zip-top plastic bag. Add mushroom caps; seal and marinate in refrigerator 24 hours.
2. Prepare grill or broiler.
3. Remove mushroom caps from bag, discarding marinade. Place caps on grill rack or broiler pan coated with cooking spray; cook 5 minutes or until tender.
4. Heat oil in a medium nonstick skillet over medium-high heat. Add onion; cover and cook 10 minutes or until golden brown, stirring frequently.
5. Combine mayonnaise and roasted garlic in a small bowl.

Spread ½ tablespoon mayonnaise mixture evenly over the top halves of buns; top each bottom half of bun evenly with lettuce, tomato, mushrooms, and caramelized onion, and top half of bun.

PER SERVING (1 sandwich): Calories 274 (30% from fat); Protein 9g; Fat 9g (sat 1g, mono 4g, poly 3g); Carbohydrate 40g; Fiber 4g; Cholesterol 3mg; Iron 4mg; Sodium 420mg; Calcium 74mg

grilled vegetable sandwich

Prep: *16 minutes* **Cook:** *13 minutes*
Stand: *10 minutes*
Serves 4

- 1 (1-pound) eggplant, cut crosswise into ½-inch slices
- 2 yellow squash, sliced
- 1 red bell pepper, quartered
- ½ small red onion, sliced
- ⅔ cup fat-free balsamic vinaigrette, divided
- Cooking spray
- 2 tablespoons light mayonnaise
- 1 tablespoon minced fresh basil
- 1 (8-ounce) loaf French bread, cut in half lengthwise
- 4 (¾-ounce) slices provolone cheese, each cut in half

1. Place first 4 ingredients (eggplant through onion) in a large dish; brush half of vinaigrette over vegetables. Let stand 10 minutes. Set remaining vinaigrette aside.
2. Prepare grill.
3. Place eggplant and squash on grill rack coated with cooking spray; cover and grill 6 minutes. Add bell pepper; cover and grill 3 minutes. Add onion; cover and grill 2 minutes, turning vegetables and basting occasionally with remaining vinaigrette.

4. Combine mayonnaise and basil; spread over top half of bread. Arrange half of cheese slices on bottom half of bread; top with vegetables, remaining cheese slices, and top half of bread.
5. Place sandwich on grill rack coated with cooking spray; grill 2 minutes or until cheese melts and bread is toasted.

PER SERVING (¼ of sandwich): Calories 318 (29% from fat); Protein 13g; Fat 10g (sat 4g, mono 1g, poly 1g); Carbohydrate 45g; Fiber 6g; Cholesterol 18mg; Iron 3mg; Sodium 773mg; Calcium 230mg

grilled eggplant-tomato sandwiches with sun-dried tomato pesto

Prep: *13 minutes* **Cook:** *16 minutes*
Serves 4

You'll have leftover pesto, which is great as a topping for pasta or as a dip. Store it in the refrigerator in an airtight container.

- ½ teaspoon dried basil
- ¼ teaspoon dried oregano
- ¼ teaspoon salt
- ⅛ teaspoon pepper
- 8 (¼-inch-thick) slices eggplant (about 1½ pounds)
- 4 (½-inch-thick) slices yellow tomato (about 10 ounces)
- 4 (½-inch-thick) slices tomato
- Cooking spray
- 8 (1½-ounce) slices French bread
- ½ cup Sun-Dried Tomato Pesto
- 2 (1½-ounce) slices provolone cheese, each cut in half
- 1 cup gourmet salad greens

1. Prepare grill or broiler.
2. Combine first 4 ingredients (basil through pepper) in a small bowl. Sprinkle evenly over eggplant and tomato slices.

3. Place eggplant on a grill rack or broiler pan coated with cooking spray; cook 5 minutes on each side or until eggplant is tender and browned. Place tomato on grill rack or broiler pan coated with cooking spray, and cook 2 minutes on each side or until tomato is done. Place bread on grill rack or broiler pan coated with cooking spray; cook 1 minute on each side or until bread is lightly toasted.
4. Spread 1 tablespoon Sun-Dried Tomato Pesto on each bread slice, and place ½ slice cheese on each of 4 bread slices. Arrange greens, eggplant, and tomato evenly over cheese, and top with 4 bread slices.

PER SERVING (1 sandwich): Calories 442 (27% from fat); Protein 18g; Fat 13g (sat 5g, mono 5g, poly 2g); Carbohydrate 67g; Fiber 10g; Cholesterol 15mg; Iron 4mg; Sodium 986mg; Calcium 267mg

Sun-Dried Tomato Pesto:

- ½ cup sun-dried tomatoes, packed without oil
- ¾ cup boiling water
- 1 cup chopped seeded plum tomato
- ½ cup basil leaves
- 2 tablespoons pine nuts
- 1 tablespoon olive oil
- ⅛ teaspoon pepper
- 4 garlic cloves

1. Combine sun-dried tomatoes and boiling water in a bowl; let stand 4 minutes. Drain and chop.
2. Combine tomatoes, plum tomato, and remaining ingredients in a blender or food processor, and process 20 seconds or until a paste forms. Yield: 1 cup.

PER SERVING (2 tablespoons): Calories 28 (64% from fat); Protein 1g; Fat 2g (sat 0g, mono 1g, poly 1g); Carbohydrate 3g; Fiber 1g; Cholesterol 0mg; Iron 0mg; Sodium 58mg; Calcium 7mg

lentil burgers with tzatziki

Prep: *37 minutes* **Cook:** *44 minutes*
Serves 8

In addition to providing protein and fiber, lentils are a significant source of folic acid. Even more folic acid comes from the wheat germ used to bind the burgers, and from the whole wheat buns. Tzatziki, which is a Greek garlicky yogurt sauce, makes a healthful and tasty alternative to mayonnaise.

- 2 teaspoons olive oil
- 1 cup chopped onion
- 3/4 teaspoon dried oregano
- 1/8 teaspoon crushed red pepper
- 2 garlic cloves, minced
- 1 1/2 cups fat-free, less-sodium chicken broth
- 2/3 cup dried lentils
- 1/4 cup sun-dried tomato sprinkles
- 2/3 cup (2 1/2 ounces) crumbled feta cheese
- 1/2 cup grated carrot
- 1/3 cup Italian-seasoned breadcrumbs
- 1/3 cup toasted wheat germ
- 3 tablespoons chopped pitted kalamata olives
- 1/4 cup chopped fresh flat-leaf parsley
- 1/4 teaspoon freshly ground black pepper
- Cooking spray
- Tzatziki
- 8 (1 1/2-ounce) whole wheat hamburger buns, toasted
- 12 arugula leaves
- 2 tomatoes, cut into 1/4-inch-thick slices (about 3/4 pound)

1. Heat 2 teaspoons oil in a medium saucepan over medium-high heat. Add onion; sauté 2 minutes or until tender. Stir in oregano, red pepper, and garlic; cook for 30 seconds, stirring constantly. Stir in broth, lentils, and sun-dried tomatoes; bring to a boil. Cover, reduce heat, and simmer 35 minutes or until lentils are tender; drain. Cool.
3. Place lentil mixture, cheese, and next 6 ingredients (carrot through black pepper) in a food processor; pulse until coarsely ground. Divide lentil mixture into 8 equal portions, shaping each into a 1/2-inch-thick patty.
4. Heat a large nonstick skillet coated with cooking spray over medium-high heat. Add patties, and cook 3 minutes. Turn patties over, and cook over medium heat 3 minutes. Spread 1 tablespoon Tzatziki evenly on each bun top and bottom. Arrange arugula, patties, and tomato slices over bottom halves of buns; top with remaining bun halves.

NOTE: You can freeze any uncooked lentil patties up to 1 month: Separate the patties with wax paper, place in a heavy-duty zip-top plastic bag, remove excess air, seal, and freeze. Thaw in refrigerator before cooking.

PER SERVING (1 burger): Calories 328 (27% from fat); Protein 16g; Fat 10g (sat 3g, mono 5g, poly 1g); Carbohydrate 47g; Fiber 9g; Cholesterol 11mg; Iron 5mg; Sodium 891mg; Calcium 250mg

Tzatziki:

- 1 cup grated peeled English cucumber
- 1 1/2 cups plain low-fat yogurt
- 1/2 teaspoon salt
- 2 garlic cloves, crushed
- 1/4 cup chopped green onions
- 1 teaspoon extra-virgin olive oil

1. Place cucumber on paper towels, and squeeze until barely moist. Place in a medium bowl. Spoon yogurt onto several layers of heavy-duty paper towels; spread to 1/2-inch thickness. Cover with additional paper towels, and let stand 5 minutes. Scrape into bowl using a rubber spatula. Add salt, crushed garlic, green onions, and extra-virgin olive oil; stir well. Cover and chill until serving.

roast chicken and cranberry sandwiches

pictured on page 240

Prep: *12 minutes*
Serves 4

Chutney adds a pleasing sweetness to this new twist on the chicken sandwich. We prefer cranberry chutney, but any variety will do.

- 1/4 cup (2 ounces) 1/3-less-fat cream cheese
- 1/4 cup bottled cranberry chutney (such as Crosse & Blackwell)
- 8 (1-ounce) slices multigrain bread
- 1/2 cup thinly sliced radishes
- 1/2 cup trimmed arugula or spinach
- 2 cups chopped roasted skinless, boneless chicken breast

1. Combine cream cheese and cranberry chutney in a small bowl. Spread 1 tablespoon cream cheese mixture over each bread slice. Arrange 1/4 of radishes, arugula, and chicken on each of 4 bread slices. Top with remaining bread slices.

PER SERVING (1 sandwich): Calories 361 (23% from fat); Protein 30g; Fat 9g (sat 4g, mono 3g, poly 1g); Carbohydrate 40g; Fiber 3g; Cholesterol 76mg; Iron 3mg; Sodium 459mg; Calcium 63mg

chicken blt on red-onion focaccia

Prep: *25 minutes* **Cook:** *37 minutes*
Rise: *1 hour*
Serves 6

The focaccia for this sandwich is made from frozen bread dough. For a shortcut, use prepared focaccia or another type of sandwich bread.

- 1 (1-pound) loaf frozen white bread dough
- 3 1/2 teaspoons olive oil, divided
- 1/2 cup thinly sliced red onion
- 1/2 teaspoon dried oregano
- 2 tablespoons yellow cornmeal
- 1/4 cup all-purpose flour, divided
- 1/4 teaspoon kosher salt
- 1/2 tablespoon dried basil
- 1/8 teaspoon salt
- 1/8 teaspoon black pepper
- 6 (4-ounce) skinless, boneless chicken breast halves
- 1/2 teaspoon olive oil
- 1 (7-ounce) bottle roasted red bell peppers, drained
- 3 tablespoons light mayonnaise
- 1 teaspoon balsamic vinegar
- 1/2 teaspoon chili-garlic sauce
- 1 garlic clove, chopped
- 6 romaine lettuce leaves
- 2 large ripe tomatoes, thinly sliced (about 1 pound)
- 12 bacon slices, fried crisp and halved lengthwise

1. Thaw dough in refrigerator 12 hours.
2. Heat 2 teaspoons oil in a small nonstick skillet over medium heat; add onions. Sauté 5 minutes or until soft, stirring often. Stir in oregano; set aside, and cool to room temperature.
3. Combine cornmeal and 2 tablespoons flour; sprinkle cornmeal mixture over clean work surface. Turn dough out onto coated surface. Knead in 2 tablespoons onion mixture and cornmeal mixture for 6 minutes (hard kneading is necessary to soften the elastic in frozen dough); cover with a clean towel, and let rest 5 minutes. Roll dough into a 9 x 13-inch rectangle; use remaining flour as needed to keep dough from sticking to work surface. Coat bottom of a 9 x 13-inch baking pan with 1/2 teaspoon oil; place dough in pan, stretching sides to cover bottom. Sprinkle remaining 1 teaspoon oil, remaining onion mixture, and kosher salt evenly over dough. Cover; let rise in a warm place (85°) 1 hour, or until doubled in size.
4. Preheat oven to 400°.
5. Bake at 400° for 20 minutes or until underside of bread sounds hollow when tapped. Cool on a rack. Cut focaccia in half lengthwise; cut each half into three equal pieces. Cut each piece in half horizontally.
6. To prepare chicken, combine basil, 1/8 teaspoon salt, and pepper; sprinkle evenly over chicken. Heat 1/2 teaspoon oil in a large nonstick skillet over medium-high heat; add chicken. Cook 4 to 6 minutes on each side or until thoroughly cooked; cool completely. Cut chicken into thin diagonal strips.
7. To prepare mayonnaise, combine roasted peppers and next 4 ingredients (peppers through garlic) in a blender; blend until smooth.
8. To prepare sandwich, spread 1 tablespoon mayonnaise on bottom half of each focaccia piece. Divide lettuce leaves, tomato slices, chicken, and bacon evenly among sandwich bottoms. Cover with top half of focaccia.

PER SERVING (1/6 of sandwich): Calories 519 (30% from fat); Protein 40g; Fat 17g (sat 3g, mono 6g, poly 2g); Carbohydrate 52g; Fiber 4g; Cholesterol 79mg; Iron 5mg; Sodium 954mg; Calcium 60mg

chipotle chicken melts

Prep: *20 minutes* **Cook:** *10 minutes*
Serves 4

A quick chile mayonnaise adds a spicy zip to the plain chicken sandwich.

- 1 (7-ounce) can chipotle chiles in adobo sauce
- 3 tablespoons light mayonnaise
- 1 1/2 teaspoons water
- 4 (3-ounce) submarine or hoagie rolls, split lengthwise
- 4 (4-ounce) skinless, boneless chicken breast halves
- 1/4 teaspoon salt
- 1/4 teaspoon pepper
- Cooking spray
- 4 (1/2-ounce) slices Havarti or Monterey Jack cheese
- 2 cups packaged coleslaw mix

1. Remove 1 chile from can; reserve remaining chiles for another use. Finely chop chile. Combine chile, mayonnaise, and water in a bowl. Spread about 1 tablespoon chile mixture evenly over top half of rolls.
2. Place each chicken breast half between 2 sheets of heavy-duty plastic wrap; pound to 1/2-inch thickness using a meat mallet or rolling pin. Sprinkle each evenly with salt and pepper.
3. Heat a large nonstick skillet coated with cooking spray over medium-high heat. Add chicken; sauté 3 minutes on each side or until done. Remove chicken from pan; top each with a slice of cheese. Arrange coleslaw mix over bottom half of rolls; top with chicken and remaining half. Serve immediately.

PER SERVING (1 sandwich): Calories 476 (29% from fat); Protein 37g; Fat 15g (sat 6g, mono 3g, poly 1g); Carbohydrate 46g; Fiber 3g; Cholesterol 87mg; Iron 4mg; Sodium 926mg; Calcium 225mg

turkey-boursin wraps

pictured on page 238

Prep: *10 minutes*
Serves 6

This wrap makes a great lunch for when you're on the go. Make it the night before or that morning, and pack it to go along with a piece of fresh fruit.

2	cups shredded cabbage and carrot coleslaw mix
3	ounces arugula leaves, stems discarded
$^3/_4$	cup alfalfa sprouts
1	tablespoon extra-virgin olive oil
$^1/_4$	teaspoon salt
$^1/_8$	teaspoon pepper
6	tablespoons light Boursin cheese, about $^2/_3$ package
6	(8-inch) spinach, tomato-basil, or plain flour tortillas
36	($^1/_8$-inch-thick) slices cucumber, about half a large cucumber
18	($^1/_8$-inch-thick) slices plum tomatoes, about 3 tomatoes
12	ounces thinly sliced cooked smoked turkey breast

1. Combine first 6 ingredients (coleslaw mix through pepper) in a large bowl, tossing to coat.
2. Spread 1 tablespoon Boursin cheese over each tortilla. Top each tortilla with 6 slices cucumber, 3 slices tomato, and approximately 2 ounces turkey. Divide slaw mixture evenly among tortillas; spread on each, and roll up. Cut each rolled wrap in half diagonally. Wrap each tortilla in plastic wrap.

PER SERVING (1 wrap): Calories 276 (28% from fat); Protein 17g; Fat 9g (sat 3g, mono 3g, poly 1g); Carbohydrate 33g; Fiber 1g; Cholesterol 34mg; Iron 2mg; Sodium 998mg; Calcium 190mg

turkey burgers with sweet red onion relish

pictured on page 238

Prep: *13 minutes* **Cook:** *24 minutes*
Serves 6

1	tablespoon extra-virgin olive oil
$2^1/_2$	cups finely chopped red onion
3	tablespoons balsamic vinegar, divided
1	teaspoon chopped fresh thyme
$1^1/_2$	pounds ground turkey breast
$^1/_4$	cup chili sauce
2	tablespoons grape jelly
$^1/_2$	teaspoon salt
$^1/_4$	teaspoon pepper
	Cooking spray
6	curly leaf lettuce leaves
6	($1^1/_2$-ounce) sesame hamburger buns, split

1. Heat oil in a nonstick skillet over medium-high heat. Add onion; sauté 10 minutes or until lightly browned, stirring occasionally. Add 2 tablespoons vinegar and thyme; sauté 30 seconds or just until liquid evaporates. Remove from heat; keep warm.
2. Combine remaining 1 tablespoon vinegar, turkey, and next 4 ingredients (chile sauce through pepper) in a bowl; stir until blended. Divide mixture into 6 equal portions, shaping into $^1/_2$-inch-thick patties.
3. Prepare grill.
4. Place patties on grill rack coated with cooking spray; grill 5 minutes on each side or until done.
5. Place 1 lettuce leaf on bottom half of each bun; top each with 1 patty, 3 tablespoons onion relish, and top half of bun.

PER SERVING (1 sandwich): Calories 304 (19% from fat); Protein 31g; Fat 6g (sat 2g, mono 2g, poly 1g); Carbohydrate 33g; Fiber 2g; Cholesterol 60mg; Iron 2mg; Sodium 791mg; Calcium 53mg

italian sausage sandwiches

Prep: *5 minutes* **Cook:** *15 minutes*
Serves 4

2	teaspoons vegetable oil
$2^1/_2$	cups thinly sliced onion
1	cup sliced green bell pepper
1	cup sliced red bell pepper
2	garlic cloves, minced
$^1/_8$	teaspoon salt
4	(3.5-ounce) links sweet Italian turkey sausage, cut in half lengthwise
1	(8-ounce) loaf French bread, cut in quarters diagonally
4	ounces reduced-fat Jarlsberg or Swiss cheese, thinly sliced
2	tablespoons country-style Dijon mustard

1. Heat oil in a large nonstick skillet over medium heat. Add onion, bell peppers, and garlic; sauté 10 minutes or until onion is golden brown. Remove from heat. Sprinkle with salt.
2. Preheat oven to 450°.
3. Cook sausage according to package directions.
4. Slice each bread quarter in half horizontally, cutting almost through to the other side. Arrange bread on a baking sheet, cut sides up. Top half of each portion with 1 ounce cheese. Bake at 450° for 3 minutes or until cheese melts and bread is lightly toasted. Remove from oven.
5. Spread mustard evenly over bread. Top with 2 sausage halves and $^1/_2$ cup onion mixture.

PER SERVING (1 sandwich): Calories 455 (30% from fat); Protein 34g; Fat 15g (sat 4g, mono 6g, poly 5g); Carbohydrate 47g; Fiber 5g; Cholesterol 72mg; Iron 5mg; Sodium 725mg; Calcium 332mg

Black Bean Chili, page 222

Turkey Burgers with Sweet Red Onion Relish, page 236

Santa Fe Ravioli Soup, page 226

Black-Eyed Pea and Chutney Chili, page 224

Turkey-Boursin Wraps, page 236

Fresh Tomato Chutney
Sandwiches, page 232

*Roast Chicken and Cranberry
Sandwiches, page 234*

*Turkey-Orzo Soup with
Black-Eyed Peas, page 229*

a month of healthy meals

Putting together healthy meals is easy with these handy menu plans. We've created four weeks of menus offering breakfast, lunch, dinner, and snack suggestions for each day. But we've gone one step further. We've planned at least one meal a day (sometimes more) around a recipe from this cookbook. These recipes with page numbers are in bold type for easy reference. We've included the other menu items which require little or no preparation or cooking—fresh fruits, vegetables, breads, and grains—to round out the meals. And we've included the recommended serving size.

Each day's menu gives you suggestions that will equal between 1500 and 1800 calories. In addition, each daily menu is guaranteed to give you at least five servings of fruits and vegetables and two servings of a milk product.

Our suggested menu plan is not meant to be an exact prescription, but an example. Everyone's preferences and needs differ, so don't hesitate to tailor the menus to meet your needs. Start with these menu plans for ideas, and then create your own menu plans using other recipes in the book.

One day's menu provides at least two servings of milk and at least five servings of fruits and/or vegetables, and contains 1500 to 1800 calories.

	MONDAY	TUESDAY	WEDNESDAY	THURSDAY
BREAKFAST	**Four-Grain Flapjacks, page 85,** 1 serving strawberries, 1 cup fat-free milk, 1 cup	bran flakes, 1 cup banana, 1 medium fat-free milk, 1 cup grapefruit juice, 1 cup	Banana-Peanut Butter Smoothie: Combine 1 cup fat-free milk, 1 tablespoon peanut butter, and 1 peeled banana in a blender; process until smooth.	**South-of-the-Border Breakfast Wrap, page 132,** 1 serving orange wedges, 1 medium
LUNCH	**Barbecue Chicken and Corn Pizza, page 168,** 1 serving orange wedges, 1 medium fat-free milk, 1 cup	Hummus-Veggie Pita: Spread ¼ cup prepared hummus on 1 (8-inch) flour tortilla; top with ⅓ cup *each of* sliced red bell pepper, zucchini, and yellow squash. Sprinkle with 3 tablespoons crumbled feta cheese. low-fat fruit yogurt, 1 (8-ounce) container seedless grapes, 1 cup	Chicken-Veggie Wrap: Top 1 (8-inch) flour tortilla with 3 ounces chopped chicken and ¼ cup *each of* sliced bell pepper, spinach, yellow squash, chopped tomato, and shredded carrot. Sprinkle with 3 tablespoons crumbled feta cheese; roll up. fat-free milk, 1 cup seedless grapes, 1 cup	bean burrito, 1 fast food carrot sticks, 1 cup fat-free milk, 1 cup
DINNER	**Baked Catfish with Tomato-Kalamata Salsa, page 114,** 1 serving steamed rice, 1 cup low-fat coleslaw, ½ cup	**Dijon Chicken-Mushroom Stroganoff, page 170,** 1 serving steamed carrots, 1 cup	**Peppered Flank Steak with Chive-Buttermilk Mashers, page 152,** 1 serving steamed broccoli, 1 cup whole grain dinner roll, 1	**Spinach-Steamed Mussels with Thin Spaghetti, page 127,** 1 serving mixed salad greens, 2 cups low-fat dressing, 2 tablespoons French bread, 2 ounces
SNACK	chocolate low-fat frozen yogurt, 1 cup	whole wheat crackers, 6 peanut butter, 2 tablespoons	pita bread, 1 (6-inch) round hummus, ¼ cup	low-fat fruit yogurt, 1 (8-ounce) container strawberries, 1 cup
TOTAL	approximately 1705 calories	approximately 1697 calories	approximately 1543 calories	approximately 1737 calories

	FRIDAY	SATURDAY	SUNDAY
BREAKFAST	bran flakes, 1 cup strawberries, 1 cup fat-free milk, 1 cup low-fat fruit yogurt, 1 (8-ounce) container	**Caramel Upside-Down Pull-Apart Loaf, page 83,** 1 serving fat-free milk, 1 cup grapefruit juice, 1 cup	Bacon, Mushroom, and Cheese Omelet: Combine 1 egg, 1 egg white, 2 tablespoons water, and a dash *each of* salt and pepper; pour into a small nonstick skillet, and cook over medium heat 1 minute or until almost set. Top with ¼ cup diced lean Canadian bacon, ¼ cup sliced mushrooms, and ¼ cup shredded reduced-fat Cheddar cheese; fold in half. strawberries, 1 cup
LUNCH	tomato soup, 1¼ cups Spinach Salad: Combine 1 cup torn fresh spinach, ½ cup red bell pepper strips, ½ cup shredded carrot, and 2 tablespoons reduced-fat Catalina dressing; toss well. whole wheat crackers, 6	**Microwave Risotto with Ham and Corn, page 165,** 1 serving carrot sticks, 1 cup low-fat fruit yogurt, 1 (8-ounce) container	hamburger, 1 fast food side salad, 1 fast food reduced-fat dressing, 2 tablespoons fat-free milk, 1 cup
DINNER	**Barbecued Pork and Broccoli Stir-Fry, page 156,** 1 serving fat-free milk, 1 cup	**Mediterranean Garlic Pizza, page 133,** 1 serving mixed salad greens, 2 cups reduced-fat dressing, 2 tablespoons	**Honey-Glazed Salmon, page 116,** 1 serving couscous, ½ cup steamed asparagus, 14 spears
SNACK	chocolate low-fat frozen yogurt, 1 cup	**Mocha Mudslide, page 72,** 1 serving	Peanut Butter Toast: Spread 2 tablespoons peanut butter evenly over 2 slices whole wheat toast. fat-free milk, 1 cup
TOTAL	approximately 1555 calories	approximately 1605 calories	approximately 1715 calories

One day's menu provides at least two servings of milk and at least five servings of fruits and/or vegetables, and contains 1500 to 1800 calories.

	MONDAY	TUESDAY	WEDNESDAY	THURSDAY
BREAKFAST	low-fat granola, ⅔ cup fat-free milk, 1 cup blueberries, 1 cup	oatmeal, 1 cup orange juice, 1 cup cantaloupe, 1 wedge	scrambled eggs, 1 egg and 3 egg whites whole wheat toast, 2 slices fat-free milk, 1 cup blueberries, 1 cup	low-fat granola, ⅔ cup fat-free milk, 1 cup dried plums, 5
LUNCH	**Rainbow Fried Rice, page 130,** 1 serving peach, 1 fat-free milk, 1 cup	turkey sandwich on wheat bread, 1 (6-inch) sub (without mayonnaise and cheese) baked chips, 1 ounce fat-free milk, 1 cup	vegetable soup, 1½ cups whole wheat crackers, 6 peach, 1	**Pesto-Bean Pizza with Fresh Tomatoes, page 133,** 1 serving cantaloupe, 1 wedge orange juice, 1 cup
DINNER	**Maple-Mustard Pork Roast, page 162,** 1 serving baked sweet potato, 1 medium sautéed squash and zucchini, 1 cup	**Orange-Teriyaki Grouper Kebabs, page 114,** 1 serving steamed brown rice, 1 cup roasted asparagus, 14 spears	**Turkey Enchiladas Suizas, page 184,** 1 serving mixed salad greens, 2 cups reduced-fat dressing, 2 tablespoons	**Italian Beef and Potato Casserole, page 151,** 1 serving steamed green beans, 1 cup French bread, 2 ounces
SNACK	**Peanut Butter-Granola Trail Mix, page 70,** 1 serving dried plums, 5	dried plums, 5 low-fat fruit yogurt, 1 (8-ounce) container	**Peanut Butter-Granola Trail Mix, page 70,** 1 serving fat-free milk, 1 cup	Berry-Yogurt Parfait: Place ½ cup blueberries in bottom of a tall glass; top with half of an 8-ounce carton of raspberry low-fat yogurt. Add another ½ cup blueberries and remaining yogurt. Sprinkle with 2 tablespoons low-fat granola.
TOTAL	approximately 1662 calories	approximately 1772 calories	approximately 1635 calories	approximately 1575 calories

	FRIDAY	SATURDAY	SUNDAY
BREAKFAST	**Sticky Caramel-Pecan Rolls, page 82,** 1 serving fat-free milk, 1 cup peach, 1	Cheese Toast: Place ½ cup shredded reduced-fat Cheddar cheese on 1 slice whole wheat bread. Broil until bubbly. orange juice, 1 cup dried plums, 5	**Western Egg Casserole, page 132,** 1 serving orange juice, 1 cup low-fat fruit yogurt, 1 (8-ounce) container
LUNCH	Tuna Salad Pita: Combine ½ cup canned tuna packaged in water, drained; 4 teaspoons light mayonnaise, and ⅛ teaspoon *each of* dried dill and pepper; mix well. Cut 1 (2-ounce) pita in half; line each half with 2 lettuce leaves and 2 tomato slices. Stuff halves evenly with tuna mixture. baked chips, 1 ounce orange juice, 1 cup	Spinach-Stuffed Potato: Split a medium baked potato, and stuff with ½ cup fresh chopped spinach, ¼ cup shredded Cheddar cheese, and 1 table-spoon reduced-fat sour cream. Add a dash *each of* salt and pepper. Bake at 350° for 10 minutes. fat-free milk, 1 cup	grilled chicken sandwich, 1 fast food (without mayonnaise) blueberries, 1 cup
DINNER	**Chicken Thighs with Wild Mushroom Sauce and Noodles, page 174,** 1 serving sautéed spinach, 1 cup	**Kung Pao Scallops with Snap Peas, page 127,** 1 serving	**Grilled Mexican Pizzas, page 153,** 1 serving mixed salad greens, 2 cups reduced-fat dressing, 2 tablespoons
SNACK	low-fat fruit yogurt, 1 (8-ounce) container cantaloupe, 1 wedge	Blueberry-Peach Parfait: In a tall glass, layer ½ cup *each of* peach low-fat yogurt and blueberries and ¼ cup low-fat granola. Repeat layers once.	whole wheat crackers, 6 sliced sharp Cheddar cheese, 1 ounce fat-free milk, 1 cup
TOTAL	approximately 1663 calories	approximately 1515 calories	approximately 1746 calories

One day's menu provides at least two servings of milk and at least five servings of fruits and/or vegetables and contains 1500 to 1800 calories.

	MONDAY	TUESDAY	WEDNESDAY	THURSDAY
BREAKFAST	whole wheat bagel, 1 small peanut butter, 2 tablespoons fat-free milk, 1 cup banana, 1 medium	cooked oatmeal, 1 cup raisins, 2 tablespoons brown sugar, 1 tablespoon fat-free milk, 1 cup	**Nutty Sweet Potato Biscuits, page 87,** 1 serving butter, 1 teaspoon low-fat fruit yogurt, 1 (8-ounce) container	whole wheat bagel, 1 small honey-nut cream cheese, 2 tablespoons blueberries, 1 cup fat-free milk, 1 cup
LUNCH	**BLT Pasta Salad, page 190,** 1 serving whole wheat crackers, 6 apple, 1 medium	Ham Sandwich: 2 slices whole grain bread, 3 ounces lean ham, lettuce, tomato slices, and 3 teaspoons reduced-fat mayonnaise. blueberries, 1 cup celery sticks, 1 cup	Tomato-Avocado Bagel Sandwich: Top bottom half of a bagel with 2 tablespoons mashed avocado; ¼ cup shredded reduced-fat sharp Cheddar cheese; 1 small tomato, sliced; ⅛ teaspoon *each of* salt and pepper; and other half of bagel. apple, 1 medium	**French Bread Caprese Pizza, page 134,** 1 serving celery sticks, 1 cup fat-free milk, 1 cup
DINNER	**Lemon-Garlic Grilled Chicken, page 173,** 1 serving mashed potatoes, 1 cup steamed snow peas, 1 cup	**Thai Crab Cakes with Cilantro-Peanut Sauce, page 125,** 1 serving mixed salad greens, 2 cups reduced-fat salad dressing, 2 tablespoons	**Southwestern Grilled Flank Steak, page 151,** 1 serving saffron rice, 1 cup steamed broccoli, 1 cup	**Curried Chicken and Vegetable Couscous, page 168,** 1 serving steamed asparagus, 14 spears
SNACK	mozzarella cheese stick, 1 watermelon chunks, 1½ cups	**Trail Blazin' Mix, page 71,** 1 serving low-fat fruit yogurt, 1 (8-ounce) container	**Trail Blazin' Mix, page 71,** 1 serving fat-free milk, 1 cup	low-fat popcorn, 1 microwave bag apple, 1 medium
TOTAL	approximately 1637 calories	approximately 1665 calories	approximately 1512 calories	approximately 1660 calories

	FRIDAY	SATURDAY	SUNDAY
BREAKFAST	cooked oatmeal, 1 cup chopped walnuts, 2 tablespoons honey, 1 tablespoon fat-free milk, 1 cup	**Dried Cherry Scones, page 86,** 1 serving fat-free milk, 1 cup banana, 1 medium	whole wheat bagel, 1 small peanut butter, 2 tablespoons fat-free milk, 1 cup blueberries, 1 cup
LUNCH	Ham and Egg Bagel Sandwich: Cook 2 egg whites or ¼ cup egg substitute in a nonstick skillet coated with cooking spray until firm, stirring constantly. Spread 2 teaspoons light mayonnaise over bottom half of 1(2-ounce) bagel; top with egg, 1 ounce sliced lean ham, and other half of bagel. watermelon chunks, 1½ cups low-fat fruit yogurt, 1 (8-ounce) container	White Bean and Tomato Salad: Combine 1 cup canned navy or white beans and ½ cup chopped tomato. Add 2 table-spoons *each of* light balsamic vinaigrette and crumbled feta cheese; mix well. Sprinkle with pepper; serve over lettuce. mozzarella cheese stick, 1	Broccoli-and-Cheese-Stuffed Potato: Split a large cooked baking potato, and stuff with ¾ cup steamed broccoli flo-rets, ¼ cup shredded reduced-fat sharp Cheddar cheese, and 1 tablespoon *each of* reduced-fat sour cream and chopped green onions. fat-free milk, 1 cup
DINNER	**Sicilian Tuna with Fettuccine, page 124,** 1 serving sautéed spinach, 1 cup French bread, 1 ounce	**Carolina-Style Barbecued Pork Sandwiches, page 162,** 1 serving baked steak fries, 8 low-fat coleslaw, ½ cup	**Spinach and Caramelized Onion Pizza, page 134,** 1 serving mixed salad greens, 2 cups reduced-fat dressing, 2 tablespoons
SNACK	**Dried Cherry Scones, page 86,** 1 serving fat-free milk, 1 cup	low-fat fruit yogurt, 1 (8-ounce) container blueberries, 1 cup	watermelon chunks, 1½ cups
TOTAL	approximately 1727 calories	approximately 1710 calories	approximately 1598 calories

One day's menu provides at least two servings of milk and at least five servings of fruits and/or vegetables, and contains 1500 to 1800 calories.

	MONDAY	TUESDAY	WEDNESDAY	THURSDAY
BREAKFAST	oatmeal, 1 cup dried cranberries, 2 tablespoons brown sugar, 1 tablespoon fat-free milk, 1 cup	**Lemon-Glazed Cranberry Rolls, page 83,** 1 serving low-fat fruit yogurt, 1 (8-ounce) container strawberries, 1 cup	whole wheat toast, 2 slices scrambled eggs, 1 egg and 3 egg whites butter, 1 teaspoon apple juice, 1 cup	**Banana-Nut Energy Bars, page 70,** 1 serving low-fat fruit yogurt, 1 (8-ounce) container strawberries, 1 cup apple juice, 1 cup
LUNCH	**Fajita Pizzas, page 151,** 1 serving mixed salad greens, 2 cups low-fat dressing, 2 tablespoons orange wedges, 1 medium	Bow-Tie Pasta Pepper Toss: Combine 1 cup cooked bow-tie pasta, ½ cup *each of* drained canned chickpeas (garbanzo beans), chopped red bell pepper, and chopped green bell pepper, ¼ cup chopped tomato, 3 tablespoons crumbled feta cheese, and 2 tablespoons reduced-fat Caesar dressing; toss to coat. fat-free milk, 1 cup	**Vegetable and Cheddar Frittata, page 132,** 1 serving raspberries, 1 cup fat-free milk, 1 cup	**Roasted Pepper, Chicken, and Goat Cheese Pizza, page 168,** 1 serving seedless grapes, 1 cup fat-free milk, 1 cup
DINNER	**Florentine Ham and Potato Casserole, page 164,** 1 serving steamed green beans, 1 cup	**Chicken and Shellfish Paella, page 130,** 1 serving mixed salad greens, 2 cups reduced-fat dressing, 2 tablespoons	**Dijon Pot Roast and Vegetables, page 154,** 1 serving sautéed spinach, 1 cup	**Roasted Tomato and Red Pepper Soup, page 227,** 1 serving **Spinach-Feta Bread, page 85,** 1 serving fat-free milk, 1 cup
SNACK	whole grain toast, 1 slice peanut butter, 2 tablespoons	mozzarella cheese stick, 1 low-fat popcorn, 1 microwave bag	**Banana-Nut Energy Bars, page 70,** 1 serving fat-free milk, 1 cup	vanilla low-fat ice cream, 1 cup
TOTAL	approximately 1701 calories	approximately 1706 calories	approximately 1524 calories	approximately 1610 calories

	FRIDAY	SATURDAY	SUNDAY
BREAKFAST	oatmeal, 1 cup raisins, 2 tablespoons brown sugar, 2 tablespoons fat-free milk, 1 cup	**Orange-Banana Shake, page 72,** 1 serving whole wheat toast, 2 slices butter, 1 teaspoon	**Quick Cornmeal Cakes, page 85,** 1 serving maple syrup, 2 tablespoons raspberries, 1 cup fat-free milk, 1 cup
LUNCH	Chicken Caesar Salad: Combine 2 cups sliced romaine lettuce, 1 chopped plum tomato, 2 ounces thinly sliced roasted chicken breast, and 2 tablespoons reduced-fat Caesar dressing; toss well. Sprinkle with 3 tablespoons shredded part-skim mozzarella cheese. French bread, 1 ounce low-fat fruit yogurt, 1 (8-ounce) container	grilled chicken sandwich, 1 fast food (without mayonnaise) fat-free milk, 1 cup	**Pesto Pizza with Shrimp, Asparagus, and Prosciutto, page 128,** 1 serving seedless grapes, 1 cup
DINNER	**Orange-Ginger Salmon with Sautéed Greens, page 116,** 1 serving curried couscous, ½ cup steamed asparagus, 14 spears	**Margarita Pork with Black Bean Salsa, page 163,** 1 serving saffron rice, ½ cup steamed green beans, 1 cup	**Peanut Noodles with Chicken, page 169,** 1 serving steamed sugar snap peas, 1 cup fat-free milk, 1 cup
SNACK	**Peanut Butter-Chocolate Shake, page 72,** 1 serving	mozzarella cheese stick, 1 apple juice, 1 cup	vanilla low-fat ice cream, 1 cup strawberries, 1 cup
TOTAL	approximately 1612 calories	approximately 1560 calories	approximately 1605 calories

recipe index